D1282888

The International Distribution of News

Based on newly available and extensive archival evidence, this book traces the history of international news agencies and associations around the world from 1848 to 1947. Jonathan Silberstein-Loeb argues that newspaper publishers formed news associations and patronized news agencies to cut the costs of news collection and exclude competitors from gaining access to the news. In this way, cooperation facilitated the distribution of news. The extent to which state regulation permitted cooperation, or prohibited exclusivity, determined the benefit newspaper publishers derived from these organizations. This book revises our understanding of the operation and organization of the Associated Press, the BBC, the Press Association, Reuters, and the United Press. It also sheds light on the history of competition policy respecting the press, intellectual property, and the regulation of telecommunications.

Jonathan Silberstein-Loeb received his PhD from the University of Cambridge in 2009. He is Senior Lecturer in History at Keble College, University of Oxford.

CAMBRIDGE STUDIES IN THE EMERGENCE OF GLOBAL ENTERPRISE

The world economy has experienced a series of globalizations in the past two centuries, and each has been shaped by business enterprises, by their national political contexts, and by new sets of international institutions. Cambridge Studies in the Emergence of Global Enterprise focuses on those business firms that have given the global economy many of its most salient characteristics, particularly regarding how they have fostered new technology, new corporate cultures, new networks of communication, and new strategies and structures designed to meet global competition. All the while, they have accommodated to changes in national and international regulations, environmental standards, and cultural norms. This is a history that needs to be understood because we all have a stake in the performance and problems of global enterprise.

Editors

Louis Galambos, The Johns Hopkins University
Geoffrey Jones, Harvard Business School

Other Books in the Series:

Teresa da Silva Lopes, *Global Brands: The Evolution of Multinationals in Alcoholic Beverages*

Christof Dejung and Niels P. Petersson, *The Foundations of Worldwide Economic Integration: Power, Institutions, and Global Markets, 1850–1930*

William J. Hausman, *Global Electrification: Multinational Enterprise and International Finance in the History of Light and Power, 1878–2007*

Christopher Kobrak, *Banking on Global Markets: Deutsche Bank and the United States, 1870 to the Present*

Christopher Kobrak, *National Cultures and International Competition: The Experience of Schering AC, 1851–1950*

Christopher D. McKenna, *The World's Newest Profession: Management Consulting in the Twentieth Century*

Johann Peter Murmann, *Knowledge and Competitive Advantage: The Coevolution of Firms, Technology, and National Institutions*

Neil Rollings, *British Business in the Formative Years of European Integration, 1945–1973*

Andrew L. Russell, *Open Standards and the Digital Age: History, Ideology, and Networks*

The International Distribution of News

The Associated Press, Press Association, and Reuters, 1848–1947

JONATHAN SILBERSTEIN-LOEB

University of Oxford

CAMBRIDGE
UNIVERSITY PRESS

32 Avenue of the Americas, New York NY 10013-2473, USA

Cambridge University Press is part of the University of Cambridge.

It furthers the University's mission by disseminating knowledge in the pursuit of education, learning, and research at the highest international levels of excellence.

www.cambridge.org
Information on this title: www.cambridge.org/9781107657830

First published 2014

Printed in the United States of America

A catalog record for this publication is available from the British Library.

Library of Congress Cataloging in Publication data
Silberstein-Loeb, Jonathan, 1981–
The international distribution of news : the Associated Press, Press Association, and Reuters, 1848–1947 / Jonathan Silberstein-Loeb.
    pages   cm. – (Cambridge studies in the emergence of global enterprise)
Includes bibliographical references and index.
ISBN 978-1-107-03364-1 (hardback)
 1. News agencies – United States – History.   2. News agencies – Great Britain – History.
3. Associated Press – History.   4. Press Association (Great Britain) – History.   5. Reuters
Limited – History.   6. Foreign news – United States – History.   7. Foreign news – Great
Britain – History.   8. Press law – United States.   9. Press law – Great Britain.   I. Title.
PN4841.A1S55   2014
070.4'350941–dc23   2013042666

ISBN 978-1-107-03364-1 Hardback
ISBN 978-1-107-65783-0 Paperback

For my parents

Contents

Tables

Acknowledgments

I owe Martin Daunton a great deal of gratitude for his criticism, insight, and patience. I am particularly grateful to Richard John, who has provided inspiration and advice and shared with me his extensive knowledge of the subject. Michael Stamm and Heidi Tworek graciously read the entire manuscript and offered numerous helpful suggestions. David Hochfelder also offered criticisms and useful materials from repositories I did not have time to visit. Louis Galambos and Geoffrey Jones offered helpful feedback as the book progressed. I am thankful for the insightful comments and advice of Atif Ansar, Lionel Bently, Jos Betts, Alexis Broderick Neumann, Pernille Røge, Joseph Sandham, Jesko Schmoller, and Alex Stein. Jim Bamberg was gracious with his time and advice when I was writing my doctorate, and Leslie Hannah and Adam Tooze offered valuable criticism as my examiners.

I am thankful for the support I received at the numerous archives I visited. John Entwisle permitted me open access to the Reuters Archives and shared with me his extensive knowledge of that company's history, and Valerie Komor allowed me to use the Associated Press Corporate Archives while her team was still cataloging materials there. Francesca Pitaro and Sam Markham provided valuable assistance as I slowly made my way through the large quantity of material held at the AP. Daniel DiLandro at the Butler Library generously sent large quantities of documents to me at no expense.

An Alfred Chandler traveling fellowship from Harvard Business School defrayed the costs of visits to Baker Library at Harvard, and I am grateful to Walter Friedman for this opportunity. A fellowship at the Newberry Library, Chicago, permitted me to consult the Victor Lawson and Melville Stone papers. A fellowship at the Lilly Library and at the Roy Howard Archives, both at the University of Indiana, Bloomington, afforded me an opportunity to read the papers of Kent Cooper and Roy Howard. I am also grateful for funding from the Cambridge Overseas Trust; the managers of the Ellen McArthur, Sarah Norton, and Prince Consort funds; and the DAAD.

The Warden and Fellows of Keble College, and especially Ian Archer, Michael Hawcroft, Jenny Tudge, and Simon Whalley have kindly offered me all the benefits of collegiate life and an opportunity to keep my teaching, if not my studies, firmly rooted in history. Christopher McKenna, Rupert Younger, and the staff and research Fellows of the Oxford University Centre for Corporate Reputation provided me with the wonderful opportunity of a research fellowship in a congenial and stimulating environment. Frederique Bendjelloul, Nicholas Barr, and John O'Connor offered me a fun place to work and occasionally relax. My parents, to whom this book is dedicated, have unfailingly and unflinchingly provided love and support.

I

Introduction

For centuries the supply of news has been protected from market forces. Various institutional arrangements have provided protection by subsidizing the provision of news. Direct government grants or subventions have been relatively rare. Although at various times during the nineteenth century political patronage of the press was commonplace in Britain and the United States, rarely was it sustained. Instead, subsidies were largely indirect. A classic example, about which much has been written, is postal subsidies for the distribution of newspapers. Postal subsidies have a long history stretching back to seventeenth-century England. A group of post office officials called the Clerks of the Road could frank newspapers for domestic and foreign distribution, which were then free from postage. For this service they charged newspapers a small fee, which they pocketed personally.[1] In the American colonies and later in the United States, the Post Office also subsidized the distribution of newspapers.[2] With successive developments in telecommunications, such as telegraphy and radio broadcasting, new institutional arrangements were devised that protected the supply of news. The twin subsidies of cooperation and exclusivity and the way in which state action and business activities shaped these subsidies are the focus of this book. Looking closely at the processes by which newspapers obtained news provides a clearer sense of how the supply of news was funded.

---

[1] K. Ellis, *The Post Office in the Eighteenth Century: A Study in Administrative History* (London: Oxford University Press, 1958), p. 48; J. Greenwood, *Newspapers and the Post Office, 1635–1834* (Reigate: Postal History Society, 1971); H. Robinson, *The British Post Office: A History* (Princeton, NJ: Princeton University Press, 1948), p. 117; S.E. Whyman, "Postal Censorship in England 1635–1844," p. 9. www.psc.gov.uk (retrieved January 6, 2013).

[2] R. John, *Spreading the News: The American Postal System from Franklin to Morse* (Cambridge, MA: Harvard University Press, 1998); R. Kielbowicz, *News in the Mail: The Press, Post Office, and Public Information, 1700–1860s* (New York: Greenwood, 1989).

Cooperation subsidized the supply of news in two ways. First, by cooperating, newspaper publishers could share with each other the costs of gathering news. During the 1850s and 1860s, the promise of reduced telegraphy costs encouraged newspapers around the world to form associations to collect news. These associations occupied the top of the news pyramid. They supplied reports of breaking news to newspapers and other news outlets such as newsrooms and later radio stations. In turn, these reports either formed the basis for further reporting or were reproduced verbatim. The British Press Association (PA), established in 1868, is the oldest surviving news association. The American Associated Press (AP), incorporated in 1892, grew out of several regional news associations that emerged across the United States during the 1840s, 1850s, and 1860s. In these associations the cost of collecting the news was apportioned among the members of the association according to their respective use of the news reports. The assessments levied on the newspapers were in turn used to meet the costs of supplying the news.

The second way in which cooperation subsidized the supply of news was by facilitating exclusion. Joining together to form an association was like forming a country club. The members of the association owned the organization. They produced, or paid for, its product, namely the news reports, and they restricted access to it. The most important assets of an association were not its offices or technology, but its members.[3] The newspaper publishers who controlled these associations could either privilege themselves or disadvantage their rivals by granting them lesser status in the association, charging them more, or excluding them entirely. Cooperation among news outlets to form news associations was by definition an exercise in exclusion. No matter how inclusive associations were, certain newspapers were permitted to join and other news outlets were barred. Even those associations that admitted all daily newspapers typically disadvantaged or excluded other types of publication, such as biweekly or triweekly newspapers. Some associations were only for newspapers and refused to admit other news outlets; others admitted alternative outlets, such as radio stations, but granted newspapers preferential treatment.

Just as cooperation produced exclusivity, the benefits of exclusivity reinforced cooperation. Exclusive access to news made it valuable. The value gained from exclusive possession of news made cooperation not only economical but profitable. In this way the subsidy of exclusivity was a double-edged sword. On the one hand, exclusive possession of news increased its value, which encouraged its collection and sale. On the other hand, if news was controlled exclusively, access to it could be constrained and the benefit of it to the public could be curtailed. Further, or alternatively, exclusive possession of the news could lead to monopoly, which threatened to make news unverifiable and potentially

---

[3] On the connection between country clubs and firms, see A.A. Alchian and S. Woodward, "The Firm Is Dead; Long Live the Firm: A Review of Oliver Williamson's *The Economic Institutions of Capitalism*," *Journal of Economic Literature*, 26 (1988), 77.

subject to manipulation. Today, the dilemma between exclusion and access is particularly apparent in arguments over intellectual property. In the nineteenth and the first half of the twentieth century, so-called property rights in news were also divisive. But property rights in news were only a part, albeit a large one, of a more general debate respecting the various ways in which business practice either facilitated or impinged on the collection of news. Much of the concern centered around the interplay between the twin subsidies of cooperation and exclusivity. Those newspapers or other news outlets that were excluded from cooperation argued that exclusivity restricted trade or freedom of the press, while publishers privy to cooperation claimed that exclusivity was a necessary incentive to encourage the collection of news.

Any balance struck between exclusivity and cooperation in the market for newspapers affected the market that news associations and news agencies inhabited, and vice versa. The way in which these two markets interacted made them difficult to operate in and to regulate. The promise of reduced costs encouraged newspaper publishers to cooperate, but excluding rivals from membership in an association precluded spreading costs more widely even as it increased the value of the news reports by making access to them exclusive. Depending on the nature of their local market, newspaper publishers had different news requirements and likewise different views about the relative importance that any news association ought to ascribe to exclusivity and cooperation. News association managers had to meet the needs of their members, who were also their directors and owners, while keeping an eye on the long-term interests of the association. From a managerial perspective, debates over exclusivity and cooperation were about market value and market share. Keeping a news report exclusive increased its value to newspaper editors by restricting competition among newspapers. This in turn increased the value of membership in the association, but it also limited the share of the market that the news association could serve. If cooperation and market share were constrained to increase exclusivity and the market value of the news reports, the excluded newspapers might form a rival organization or patronize a competitor. Alternatively, by carefully controlling membership, managers could prevent the emergence of a strong competing news association or agency or encourage the existence of a weak but viable rival to stave off accusations of restraint of trade or monopoly. From the 1850s until World War I, news associations and agencies in different countries also cooperated with each other to reduce costs and serve disparate markets, but during the 1920s and 1930s, as nationalism made the supply of news less multilateral but radio increased its global distribution, the tensions cooperation had engendered in the supply of news domestically also appeared on the international stage. These difficulties did not eliminate cooperation as much as they caused a rearrangement of existing alliances.

Although at times multiple news associations existed in a few national markets, such as Australia, there was almost always a large news association, such as the PA or AP, and a rival private or publicly traded news agency, such as

Reuters (established in 1851). Another example of a news agency is the United Press Association, which was also established in the nineteenth century and sold its news reports to the American press. These agencies were started by entrepreneurs and owned by investors not necessarily affiliated with any particular newspaper. Other news agencies grew out of vertical integration by newspaper chains, such as the United Press (UP), which was formed by and supplied the Scripps-Howard chain of newspapers in the United States, or the International News Service (INS), which was similarly formed by and served the newspapers of William Randolph Hearst. The savings achieved by cooperation were in theory obtainable from a news agency that sold news reports to newspapers at a profit, but in practice news agencies suffered from two flaws.

The first concerned transparency. Newspaper publishers that patronized news agencies were perennially concerned about the profits that the agencies made at their expense, whereas cooperative enterprises, which were owned by their publisher-members, could be monitored and run on a not-for-profit basis. The problem of transparency also undermined international cooperation between news agencies and news associations. In 1925, newspapers in Britain achieved a greater level of transparency by purchasing Reuters through the PA. The model of linking the press to Reuters was subsequently exported throughout the British Empire. The second and more significant disadvantage associated with the agency model was that it could not adjust the balance between exclusivity and cooperation to adapt to market conditions as effectively as news associations. Whereas for-profit news agencies were encouraged to charge newspapers for the privilege of having the news exclusively, news associations run by and for newspapers and on a not-for-profit basis could start small and provide leading newspapers throughout the country with exclusive access at no extra charge to encourage participation. As the market matured, associations could control membership to contrive competition, whereas private for-profit news agencies were locked into different relationships with their subscribers and shareholders. Likewise, if rivals became too powerful, or if concerns over restraint of trade increased and the specter of regulation loomed large, associations could expand their membership to suit the environment.

Through competition policy, intellectual property law, and telecommunications regulation, legislatures, judiciaries, and other emanations of the state, such as the British Post Office, played an active role in determining the boundaries of cooperation and exclusivity. In general, the state in both Britain and the United States pursued an active if largely implicit policy of subsidizing the supply of news. As explained in Chapter 2, in the United States, a federalist political economy permitted the creation of agreements between telegraph companies and news associations that facilitated the creation of exclusive associations.[4]

---

[4] R.F. Bensel, *The Political Economy of American Industrialization, 1877–1900* (Cambridge: Cambridge University Press, 2000), pp. 289–90.

Mechanisms for exclusion came up against state-based rules respecting competition policy, the limits of freedom of contract, and judicial understanding of news as a democratic necessity. Chapter 3 shows how state-based corporate law affected the extent to which different forms of organization were viable. In 1897, the Illinois Supreme Court found the AP in restraint of trade, which proved ruinous to the corporation, and the modern incarnation of the AP owes its existence to the New York Membership Corporations Law (1895), which legalized the association's method of organization. Federal law was also influential. The U.S. Supreme Court in *INS v. AP* (1918) granted the AP a right that protected its method of organization, whereas in *AP v. US* (1945), the Supreme Court found the AP in violation of antitrust law, which in effect transformed the association into a public utility.[5]

In the United Kingdom, the case of which is discussed in Chapters 4 and 5, the trend went in the opposite direction: government control of telegraphy generated a comparatively inclusive form of cooperation. Only in the interwar period, as the prevailing institutional arrangement shifted to favor broadcasting over the press, did private solutions akin to those in the United States emerge. The nationalization of telegraphy in 1868 shaped the organization of the PA, as well as the nature of property rights in news, and influenced the structure of the news market in Britain. Nationalization preserved the historical postal subsidy to the press, but it also privileged newspapers published in the provinces over those published in London. Maintenance of this regime until World War I was intended to preserve the level playing field that policy makers sought to establish by the Telegraph Act of 1868. Such regulation, although far from maintaining a level playing field, did help protect the status quo by preventing publishers from adopting private solutions to limitations hindering their abilities to collect and distribute news. As a consequence, policy intended to ensure a plurality of news outlets also rendered the apparatus for news provision relatively slow compared to methods employed in the United States.[6]

Telecommunications policy in Britain continued to shape the structure of the news market until World War II. Toward the end of the nineteenth century, increased use of the telephone, which was not nationalized until 1911, undermined the settlement established by the Telegraph Act of 1868. World War I brought about its demise. After the war, and despite the best efforts of the press, the long-standing subsidy for news shifted to broadcasting. The nature of the relationship between organizations that generated content and those that distributed it was central to debates about the role of broadcasting in news collection, as it had been in 1868 with the nationalization of telegraphy and the use of telephony thereafter. According to the representatives of the press, combining content and conduits for distribution in the hands

---

[5] 248 U.S. 215 (1918) and 326 U.S. 1 (1945).
[6] This order of events parallels that described by I. de Sola Pool, *Technologies without Boundaries*, ed. E. Noam (London: Harvard University Press, 1990), p. 93.

of one organization violated principles of free trade and amounted to unfair competition. The threat of the BBC, which attempted to purchase Reuters on the eve of World War II, and concentration of the newspaper industry in the hands of a few press barons, prompted publishers to adopt American solutions to problems of news collection. After the Supreme Court's decision in 1945, the AP and the PA looked alike.

In organization and operation, news associations and agencies lacked the managerial hierarchies characteristic of the large manufacturing firms that also emerged during the nineteenth century, but in Britain and the United States, government policy affected the structure of the news industry in much the same way as it affected other areas of economic activity. The similarities and differences between the structure of the news market in the United States and the United Kingdom reflected long-standing policy paradigms and institutional arrangements. In the United States, news agencies and associations were large, vertically and horizontally integrated, and loosely regulated. The history of American news agencies and associations began with attempts to centralize and coordinate production and pricing, followed by the pursuit of economies of scale and scope, and resolved in oligopoly.[7] Antimonopoly market regulation was the distinguishing feature of American policy. By preventing restraint of trade and enforcing price competition, policy makers sought to establish free markets and free competition. In the United Kingdom, the state allocated authority to entrepreneurial firms, encouraged loose combinations, and discouraged predatory mergers to shield small firms.[8] Loose organizational arrangements, comparatively greater state intervention, and cooperative self-government characterized the British market. During the nineteenth century, the attempts of small British firms to limit competition in large markets through agreement were often ineffective, but in the news business the influence of government policy ensured that similar attempts were successful.[9]

Domestic regulation not only constrained the national operation of news agencies and associations but also affected the way in which they operated overseas. Throughout the British Empire, Reuters encountered the same difficulties it confronted in the British Isles. As shown in Chapter 6, the so-called

[7] L. Galambos, "The Triumph of Oligopoly," in D. Schaefer and T.J. Weiss (eds.), *American Economic Development in Historical Perspective* (Stanford, CA: Stanford University Press, 1994), pp. 241–253.

[8] F. Dobbin, *Forging Industrial Policy: The United States, Britain, and France in the Railway Age* (Cambridge: Cambridge University Press, 1994), pp. 3–4.

[9] H. Mercer, *Constructing a Competitive Order* (Cambridge: Cambridge University Press, 1995), p. 32; T.A. Freyer, *Regulating Big Business: Antitrust in Great Britain and America, 1880–1990* (Cambridge: Cambridge University Press, 1992); L. Hannah, *The Rise of the Corporate Economy* (London: Methuen, 1983), p. 11; L. Hannah, "Mergers, Cartels and Concentration: Legal Factors in the U.S. and European Experience," in N. Horn and J. Kocka (eds.), *Recht und Entwicklung der Großunternehmen im 19. und frühen 20. Jahrhundert* (Göttingen: Vandenhoeck & Ruprecht, 1979), pp. 306–16; L. Hannah, "Managerial Innovation and the Rise of the Large-Scale Company in Interwar Britain," *The Economic History Review*, 27:2 (May 1974), 253.

imperial news agency found it difficult to sell its news at a profit throughout the empire. In Australia and South Africa in particular, Reuters encountered considerable resistance from the press. For Reuters, like so many British companies, India served as the principal source of overseas profit. To compensate for its lackluster performance selling news, Reuters diversified its business before World War I. During the war, these businesses failed. Only after the war did the company establish a profitable business supplying commercial information and news. It also pursued a new strategy abroad and at home. To overcome the unwillingness of newspaper publishers to support the agency's profitability, and to encourage transparency, Reuters sought to bring the newspapers of the empire into partnership with it. It did this first in South Africa, then in Britain, Australia, and India. After the formation of the Reuters Trust in 1941, the principal newspaper associations of Australia, India, and New Zealand became partners with the newspapers of the British Isles.

The American regulatory environment and the AP's method of domestic operation also shaped the way in which it gathered news abroad. The AP's unique competitive advantage lay in its method of organization: it secured the exclusive right to the news from its various newspaper-members before publication. Access to the news of newspapers around the United States at this early stage in the newspaper production process enabled the AP to forestall rival news organizations and made it a desirable association for American publishers to join. The association's foreign allies, such as Reuters, also had early access to the news. When, in *INS v. AP* (1918), the AP sought a property right in news, it did so not to prevent freeriding on its news reports, but to protect the critically important exclusive right it had to the news reports of its members before publication. This is why the decision in *INS* protected the AP's method of organization. Neither the AP's domestic rivals nor its foreign allies employed this method of operation. Instead, they frequently copied the news from local newspapers after publication and then sent it back to headquarters. Outside the Americas, where the AP had no members, it also gathered news by this method. After the Supreme Court delivered its decision in *INS*, however, AP executives felt obligated to discontinue this practice abroad. This meant that the AP was hamstrung. Meanwhile, the UP, the association's principal rival, took foreign news from published papers with impunity and began scooping the AP. As is made clear in Chapter 7, to rectify this difficulty the AP, like Reuters, sought to export its model of organization abroad, but this required altering the cartel arrangements it had maintained with its allies overseas since the nineteenth century. The banner of free trade was only a disguise for furthering this agenda. Debates over the international supply of news between the 1840s and 1940s were not about the benefits of free trade as opposed to cooperation, although outwardly this was how they were occasionally portrayed. Instead, they were about the form that cooperation ought to take. Cooperation was attacked under the guise of free trade, but it resumed under the pretense of press freedom.

At root, this is a story about property told through the lens of business history. Property is said to reside not in the consumption of benefits but in control over access to them. Seen this way, excludability is the essence of property. Property rights reflect the relationships created by private claims to regulate access to the benefits of particular resources.[10] This book explains how businesses sought to exert proprietary control over news through private contracting. The absence of a formal property right encouraged businesses to devise methods of organization and other strategies to establish common property in news to the exclusion of others.[11] The state regulated these activities. The concept of a freely competitive marketplace of ideas, so cherished by the Victorians, was always a fiction. A belief that press freedom necessitated freedom from state intervention was theoretically incoherent and practically false.

---

[10] K. Gray, "Property in Thin Air," *Cambridge Law Journal*, 50:2 (1991), 294.
[11] See generally E. Ostrom, *Governing the Commons: The Evolution of Institutions for Collective Action* (Cambridge: Cambridge University Press, 1990).

2

Conceiving Cooperation among American Newspapers, 1848–1892

John Sayward's scoop was big news, especially in Bangor, Maine. It ran in the Saturday issue of the *Whig and Courier*, published February 24, 1849 and Sayward, the paper's editor, deployed a large bold font to announce it. The "First Dispatch of Foreign News from the East!", Sayward explained, was obtained only with considerable effort. The news from Europe, which crossed the Atlantic aboard the royal mail steamship *Europa*, was the first foreign news ever to pass by telegraph from St. John, Nova Scotia westward. After the *Europa* arrived at Halifax on the evening of February 21, a relay of horses carried the news 144 miles to Digby through a recent and heavy fall of snow, the heaviest, it was said, that had been experienced in fifty years. The news did not arrive in Digby until four o'clock the following morning. There it was delayed nearly twelve hours, a consequence of the utter impossibility of breaking a passage for a steamer through the ice with which Digby Bay was jammed. Only with the full force of the engine and paddle wheels, and with the assistance of twenty men, was a channel finally made by which the steamer could pass through the gut between Bay View and Victoria Beach, out into the Bay of Fundy, and onward to St. John, whence the news was finally telegraphed to Bangor, and thence to points south.[1]

Sayward, however proud of his scoop he may have been, was not responsible for the journalistic effort entailed in this race for the news through the Great White North. He was but a beneficiary of an intense rivalry among the newspapers of New York City for exclusive news. During the "newspaper revolution" of the 1830s and 1840s, the penny press of Moses Beach, James Gordon Bennett, Benjamin Day, and Horace Greeley supplanted the existing

---

[1] Bangor (ME) *Whig and Courier*, February 24, 1849. See also J.W. Regan, "The Inception of the Associated Press: The Pony Express that in 1849 Forwarded European News from Halifax to Digby, to be Conveyed by Vessel to St. John, and thence telegraphed to New York," *Transactions of the Nova Scotia Historical Society*, 19 (January 5, 1912), 5.

mercantile press of New York. The newspaper market grew dramatically and newspaper circulation increased rapidly. Publishers of daily newspapers found that nonpartisan news, more than editorials or advertising, increased circulation, which motivated greater expenditure in newsgathering.[2] The average number of stories about an event published in dailies within a week of its occurrence increased from 45 to 76 percent between 1820 and 1860. Stories taking more than a month to appear dropped from 28 to 8 percent.[3] Editors of newspapers increasingly obtained the news before local elites, who previously benefitted from first access to the news owing to their social status. The reading rooms and coffee houses of Boston, New York, and other ports, which had served as the nexus of newsgathering in the country, were obsolete.[4] According to Horace Greeley, publisher of the New York *Tribune*, by 1851 the editorial was comparatively unimportant; "the telegraphic dispatch," said Greeley, "is the great thing."[5]

As much as the telegraphic dispatch mattered, exclusive possession of the news mattered more. Editorial minions raced for news on land and at sea. By 1831, five schooners belonging to the New York papers darted about New York harbor to obtain foreign news from incoming ships.[6] Scoops obtained through such enterprise were of considerable value. James Watson Webb, publisher of the New York *Courier and Enquirer*, spent more than $5,000 annually (nearly $130,000 in today's prices) to maintain his schooner, but claimed it paid for itself in added subscriptions.[7] The New York publishers' littoral engagement became a seaborne struggle, until James Gordon Bennett of the *Herald*, who spared no expense in newsgathering, and pulled even fewer punches when

[2] J.L. Crouthamel, "The Newspaper Revolution in New York, 1830–1860," *New York History*, 45 (1964), 91–113; Crouthamel, *Bennett's New York Herald and the Rise of the Popular Press* (Syracuse, NY: Syracuse University Press, 1989), pp. 19–42; M. Schudson, *Discovering the News: A Social History of American Newspapers* (New York: Basic Books, 1978), pp. 17–22.

[3] M. Emery, E. Emery, and N.L. Roberts, *The Press and America: An Interpretive History of the Mass Media*, 9th ed. (Boston: Allyn & Bacon, 2000), p. 110.

[4] Compare with R.D. Brown, *Knowledge is Power: The Diffusion of Information in Early America, 1700–1865* (Oxford: Oxford University Press, 1989).

[5] F. Hudson, *Journalism in the United States, from 1690 to 1872* (New York: Harper & Brothers, 1873 reprinted London: Routledge, 2000), p. 548. This book, which has become a classic in American journalism history, favored the New York press and the New York *Herald* in particular. See marginalia in Annual Report of the New York Associated Press, May 31, 1873, William Henry Smith papers (hereafter W.H. Smith), MIC 22 1/7, Ohio Historical Society (hereafter OHS).

[6] Editors had already used schooners to intercept news for at least several years. W.H. Hallock, *Life of Gerard Hallock: Editor of the New York* Journal of Commerce (New York: Oakley, Mason & Co., 1869), p. 12; Hudson, *Journalism in the United States*, p. 365.

[7] R.A. Schwarzlose, "Harbor News Association: The Formal Origin of the AP," *Journalism Quarterly*, 45 (1968), 253–60. All prices listed parenthetically are in dollar prices from 2010 and have been calculated using the consumer price index of S.H. Williamson, "Six Ways to Compute the Relative Value of a U.S. Dollar Amount, 1790 to Present," MeasuringWorth, 2011. See www.measuringworth.com/uscompare.

editorializing, deployed his schooner off Montauk Point, the most eastern tip of Long Island, and subsequently threatened to rendezvous with European steamers 150 miles off shore.[8] The pursuit of the news on land was just as frenzied, and editors made elaborate arrangements to have fresh and ready horses stationed throughout the countryside to speed news to New York.[9]

The electric telegraph was a technical means by which newspaper publishers could extend their contest for the news. By 1846, bold Bennett made arrangements for the transmission of telegraphic dispatches from Washington to New York for reporting on Congress. He also established a connection to Boston, whence reports could be sent from transatlantic ships, and the New York harbor race was pushed north. The Boston *Daily Times*, which Moses Beach, publisher of the New York *Sun*, also owned, obtained the news from the harbor and a representative from the New York papers then assembled a report for transmission to New York.[10] The Mexican-American War of 1846 further stimulated initiatives to obtain the news first. Likewise, the European revolutions of 1848 encouraged greater enterprise in obtaining foreign news and the consistent arrival of transatlantic steam mail services after January 1848 regularized it.[11] For New York publishers, foreign news, like foreign goods to New York merchants, was occasionally more important than news from the American hinterland, and news from the markets and bourses of Europe was consistently in high demand.[12] Once the telegraph connected Halifax with Maine, the field of battle moved north yet again from Boston to the Maritimes.

Finding they could go no farther north, the New York publishers competed on the opposite side of the Atlantic. During the height of the June Days uprising, Henry J. Raymond, then associate editor of Webb's *Courier and Enquirer*, and soon to be publisher of *The New York Times*, employed one R.H. Gould to serve as his contact in London. Arrangements with Gould provided exclusive dispatches for the *Courier and Enquirer* until Bennett's *Herald* also employed a man in England. Raymond claimed to have no fear of "competition of this sort," provided Gould's dispatches continued to be "more full, embracing more points etc. than any other," but by October 1848, the scrimmage had moved from London to Liverpool, and it appeared the game of harbor hopscotch conducted on the eastern seaboard would be replicated across the ocean. Raymond instructed Gould to retain a man at Liverpool who could retrieve dispatches sent from London and relay them to the United States more rapidly. He wrote again to Gould a month later, only to explain that the intensity of the rivalry in

---

[8] Crouthamel, *Bennett*, p. 45; A.M. Lee, *The Daily Newspaper in America: The Evolution of a Social Instrument* (New York: The Macmillan Company, 1973), p. 491.

[9] M. Blondheim, *News over the Wires: The Telegraph and the Flow of Public Information in America, 1844–1897* (London: Harvard University Press, 1994), p. 19.

[10] Blondheim, *News over the Wires*, p. 53.

[11] F.E. Hyde, *Cunard and the North Atlantic, 1840–1973: A History of Shipping and Financial Management* (London: The Macmillan Company, 1975).

[12] R.G. Albion, *The Rise of New York Port: 1815–1860* (London: Charles Scribner's Sons, 1939).

the Maritimes had further increased. The nub of the matter was a technological one, explained Raymond, for at "Halifax, from which point hereafter we shall get all our foreign news, the 'first come' at the Telegraph office, has the use of the wires." By December, Raymond was victorious. His competitors in New York caved and took their dispatches from the *Courier and Enquirer*. "The despatches from London," wrote Raymond triumphantly to Gould on December 18, 1848, "now appear in the New York papers by arrangement with us, and without any breach of faith with the Company."[13] Ruinous competition was the rationale for cooperation.

If struggling for scoops was a pastime for New York publishers, so too was cooperation; but, in practice, cooperation was just another mechanism for exclusion. By banding together, the small group of New York publishers who had been racking up expenses in contest with each other could obtain the news collectively, share it with each other exclusively, and even resell it, having already split the costs among themselves, to publishers who lacked the resources to deploy schooners and men on either side of the Atlantic. Additionally, the money each New York publisher saved through cooperation could be redeployed to develop journalistic features that demonstrated enterprise, which in turn increased circulation. The extent of cooperation among New York publishers during the 1830s and 1840s suggests that the era of "personal journalism," as some historians have called it, may have been more vituperative than it was competitive.[14] Indeed, the very fact that journalism was personal, and that the publishers of New York City were part of a small community, very likely made cooperation viable.

Although the benefits to be had from exchanging news were enticing, arranging for it, and maintaining exclusivity when doing so, was complicated and costly. Newspapers around the country had long exchanged published news via mail, which the Post Office subsidized.[15] By 1830, the Post Office annually distributed about 16 million newspapers. Until Congress modified the rates in 1845, the number of newspapers sent via post grew at an average of 2.3 million copies each year.[16] According to one estimate, in 1837, every American

[13] H.J. Raymond to R.H. Gould, June 27, 1848 and November 28, 1849, Henry J. Raymond papers, misc., New York Public Library (hereafter NYPL).

[14] *Contra*, for example, the classic history of American journalism, F.L. Mott, *American Journalism: A History of Newspapers in the United States through 260 Years, 1690 to 1950* (New York: Macmillan, 1947). Indeed, if the population of New York in 1840 was more than 300,000, if only 50 percent of the population could read, and if in 1849 the daily circulation of the *Herald* and the *Tribune* was approximately 28,000, as an independent authority corroborated at the time, then the market for readers was fairly open. Perhaps the market for advertising was more competitive.

[15] P. Starr, *The Creation of the Media: Political Origins of Modern Communications* (New York: Basic Books, 2004), pp. 84–92; R.R. John, *Spreading the News: The American Postal System from Franklin to Morse* (London: Harvard University Press, 1995).

[16] R.B. Kielbowicz, *News in the Mail: The Press, Post Office, and Public Information, 1700–1860s* (New York: Greenwood Press, 1989), p. 71.

daily received an average of seven newspapers each day from which it could clip news.[17] Newspaper editors cut articles from the papers that arrived in the mails and then reprinted them, often with few alterations, in their own publication. According to one analysis of newspapers published between 1820 and 1846, about half the news was taken from other papers.[18]

Exchanging news by post after publication meant that it was accessible to all, and offered little opportunity for exclusivity. Once published, news was regarded as public property, and free for others to use. James Gordon Bennett realized he could gain an advantage over his rivals by exchanging news before publication. He printed "news-slips" that were sent by express mail to newspapers in the interior of the country. These news-slips, which reached publishers one mail in advance of the regular issues of the *Herald*, placed the paper receiving the service under obligation to ensure that the *Herald* in turn received all the important news from their territory before the other New York papers.[19] American newsgathering organizations worked on a similar principle.

Telegraphy increased the incentive for New York publishers to cooperate. Initially, the telegraph was expensive to use, and telegraphic news dispatches contained little more than mere morsels. When it opened in January 1846, the New York to Philadelphia line charged $0.25 for every ten words ($8 in today's prices). A ten-word telegram from Baltimore to Milwaukee cost $1.40 ($40). In 1853, charges in California were as high as $2.00 for ten words ($60). For the publishers of New York, this type of dispatch, although dear and a necessary staple, provided no special evidence of enterprise. Bennett was willing to split the costs of telegraphic dispatches from Boston and Washington, DC with his rivals Beach, Greeley, and Raymond.[20] The publishers also combined their efforts to obtain telegraphic dispatches concerning the Mexican-American War.

Bandwidth limitations also encouraged cooperation. Before the introduction of duplex technology in the 1870s, which doubled bandwidth, only one telegram could be sent on a line at a time.[21] In the late 1840s, telegraph lines were consequently confused and congested, and, as Raymond wrote to his man Gould, the first to the telegraph head had a great advantage over all others, especially if the line was kept occupied by transmitting chapter and verse until the news came to hand. Messages limped along, often becoming garbled

---

[17] J.D. Stevens and H.D. Garcia, *Communication History* (Beverly Hills, CA: Sage Publications, 1980), p. 119.

[18] R.B. Kielbowicz, "News Gathering by Mail in the Age of the Telegraph: Adapting to a New Technology," *Technology and Culture*, 28 (1987), 29.

[19] J.M. Lee, *History of American Journalism* (New York: Houghton Mifflin Co., 1923), p. 200.

[20] The Associated Press, undated, Melville Stone papers (hereafter Stone), box 8, folder 532, Newberry Library (NL).

[21] Duplex had a long history, but only in January 1872 did George B. Prescott manage to apply it successfully to long-distance telegraphy. *Proceedings of the Western Associated Press* (hereafter *Proceedings*) (Detroit, 1872), pp. 28–9.

in the process. Like a disorganized railroad minus the collisions, messages from way lines entered the main line and frequently delayed others in the process of transmission.[22] While a message was on the wire, no other message could be sent and consequently all the operators on the line were unavailable despite being paid. Therefore, it cost as much to send a message 50 miles as it did to send it 500, which prevented a significant reduction in the price of telegrams.[23] To improve the service, make matters more equitable, and increase profits, telegraph companies instituted a time-sharing scheme so that operators served each customer in turn and no individual could control access to the line for more than fifteen minutes.[24] "In the heat of the fight, the telegraph came in as a mediator and regulator," observed Frederic Hudson, managing editor of the New York *Herald*. Time-sharing diminished the advantages of primacy in newsgathering, but editors soon realized that their reporters were duplicating dispatches.[25] Under the New York Telegraph Act of 1848, journalists were entitled to transmit "intelligence" of "general and public interest" ahead of regular messages, but this clause did not necessarily grant members of the New York press priority over other journalists.[26] In 1849, the principal dailies of New York formed the Harbor News Association.[27] Bennett and Greeley joined, as did Moses Beach of *The Sun*, Erastus Brooks of *The Express*, Gerard Hallock and David Hale of the *Journal of Commerce*, Raymond of *The Times*, and Webb of the *Courier and Express*. By 1856, the members had consolidated their Harbor News Association and drew up articles of association for what became known as the New York Associated Press (NYAP). Soon they had their own boat stationed off the southern tip of Newfoundland, at Cape Race.[28]

Forming a mutual association by which telegraphic news could be pooled and exchanged before publication provided a platform that not only reduced redundancy of effort and cut costs, but also, and perhaps most importantly, protected exclusivity. Ostensibly, the purpose of the NYAP was to reduce the cost members incurred collecting news, but in fact, admitted Raymond, the object was to

---

[22] A.F. Harlow, *Old Wires and New Waves: The History of the Telegraph, Telephone, and Wireless* (London: D. Appleton-Century Co., 1936), pp. 149–50.

[23] As quoted in E. Gabler, *The American Telegrapher: A Social History, 1860–1900* (London: Rutgers University Press, 1988), p. 53.

[24] Blondheim, *News over the Wires*, pp. 62–3.

[25] Hudson, *Journalism in the United States*, p. 610. Blondheim, *News over the Wires*, p. 63.

[26] R.R. John, *Network Nation: Inventing American Telecommunications* (Cambridge, MA: Harvard University Press, 2010), p. 91.

[27] Precisely when the newspapers of New York began cooperating is the subject of debate. New York publishers cooperated as early as 1846, but arrangements prior to 1848/1849 appear to have been ad hoc. Whether 1846 or 1848 is the preferred date, it is clear that competition for news via telegraph precipitated cooperation. See R.A. Schwarzlose, *The Nation's Newsbrokers: The Formative Years from Pretelegraph to 1865*, vol. 1 (Evanston, IL: Northwestern University Press, 1989), pp. 89–107; Blondheim, *News over the Wires*, chapter 3.

[28] "News Yacht off Cape Race," *The New York Times*, November 6, 1857.

prevent competition.[29] The association's bylaws reflected its object. Members were obliged to provide all their breaking news to the association and were barred from sharing it with newspapers outside. They were also barred from receiving regular telegraphic dispatches from private correspondents and from competing organizations. Except for scheduled events, such as conventions, political meetings, trials, executions, public dinners, and sports, members were prohibited from making arrangements to receive special news by telegraph without first informing the other members of the association, and offering to share it with them. To prevent cheating, publication was collectively embargoed until an agreed time of release. No other newspapers could be admitted to the association without the unanimous consent of all, although the news could be sold to other parties on an affirmative vote of six-sevenths of the membership.[30]

Exclusive access to telegraphic news before publication provided members of the association with an advantage over those New York papers that were denied access to the association's telegrams. Even if lesser publishers copied the news after it had first been published, readers were aware of imitation. Indeed, imitation was a form of flattery that worked to the benefit of the original publishers, who regarded the practice with equanimity.[31] By the 1860s, the association constrained entry into the New York newspaper market. Before purchasing the New York *Sun* in 1868, Charles Dana entertained establishing a new newspaper in New York, but failure to obtain membership in the NYAP dissuaded him. "It was then ascertained that, owing to the opposition of two or three members" of the NYAP, wrote Frederic Hudson of the New York *Herald*, "the news paper could not have the telegraphic news of the institution, and without that news the contemplated paper could not succeed; indeed, it would be folly to bring out the first number."[32]

Association also protected the valuable country circulation of the New York publishers, which the telegraph threatened to undermine.[33] Thanks to favorable postal rates, by the 1830s, metropolitan papers circulated widely throughout the countryside. "In consequence of the facility of the mails, and the cheapness of the city papers," complained one upstate New York editor at the time, "the circulation of our country papers is rapidly diminishing, and ere long many of them must be consigned to oblivion."[34] The advance of the railroad

[29] Schwarzlose, *Newsbrokers*, 1: p. 101.
[30] General news association of the city of New York, October 21, 1856, Stone, box 8, folder 529, NL; NYAP articles of association, October 21, 1856, Manton Marble papers (hereafter Marble), vol. 15, Library of Congress (hereafter LOC).
[31] Report from the Select Committee on Newspaper Stamps, 558 (1851), p. 393, l. 2644–48. See also F.L. Mott, *The News in America* (Cambridge, MA: Harvard University Press, 1952), p. 98.
[32] Hudson, *Journalism in America*, p. 679.
[33] For the role the telegraph played in this process see H. Innis, "Technology and Public Opinion in the United States," *The Canadian Journal of Economics and Political Science*, 17 (1951), 1–24.
[34] M.W. Hamilton, *The Country Printer: New York State, 1785–1830* (New York: Columbia University Press, 1936), p. 237.

enhanced the country circulation of metropolitan papers.[35] By the 1850s, New York weeklies, such as Greeley's *Tribune*, had attained a large following outside New York City.[36] The arrival of the telegraph at secondary cities in the 1850s and 1860s threatened to disrupt this pattern of trade and newspapers in rural districts surrounding the telegraph head combined to establish their own telegraphic news associations.[37] By the time city papers reached the country by post, local publications had already received and published the important national and international news. Using cooperation to regulate telegraphic news distribution helped the metropolitan publishers compensate for losses in circulation by reselling to their brethren in the American hinterland the news they had collectively obtained. Just as canals and railways extended the reach of New York producers and merchants into the Midwest, the telegraph opened these markets to the NYAP.[38]

Despite the efforts of the NYAP, the comparatively modest requirements of most American newspapers meant that the majority of publishers outside New York continued as they had for decades to rely for much of their news on the exchange of newspapers via post. Weeklies mailed from New York continued to play an important function for much of the nineteenth century, as did the growing business of stereotype plate syndicates.[39] A large majority of the press outside New York required only brief reports, which were published in regular editions as opposed to extras, therefore they could wait until the papers of the NYAP members appeared on the street before having their own agent copy and telegraph them the news. For the most part, these brief reports were only sent over the wires at what was called "report hours" – that is, an hour or so before the papers went to press – therefore great haste in the reception of news at New York, as a distributing point, was of secondary importance, and in most cases out-of-town papers could and did wait for news until New York papers were in the streets.[40]

The resale market for the NYAP news reports was limited. In 1854, the whole income of the NYAP from outside sources for general news was approximately $10,000. By 1862, the revenue made from all papers outside the association and credited in weekly exhibits averaged $1,067 per week, or about $55,000 per annum (a real increase over 1854 of approximately $40,000),

[35] Kielbowicz, *News in the Mail*, p. 63.

[36] H.W. Baehr Jr., *The New York Tribune since the Civil War* (New York: Dodd, Mead & Co., 1936), p. 21.

[37] Kielbowicz, *News in the Mail*, pp. 109, 152; R.A. Schwarzlose, "The Nation's First Wire Service: Evidence Supporting a Footnote," *Journalism Quarterly*, 57 (1980), 555–62.

[38] S. Bruchey, *The Roots of American Economic Growth, 1607–1861* (New York: Harper & Row, 1965), pp. 154–67.

[39] Kielbowicz, "News Gathering by Mail." On syndicates see Lee, *Daily Newspaper*, pp. 510–12 and D.S. Claussen, "Newspapers, Local," in D.H. Johnston (ed.), *Encyclopedia of International Media and Communications*, vol. 3 (London: Academic Press, 2003), p. 280.

[40] D.H. Craig, *Annual Report, New York Associated Press* (New York, 1862), 9.

that is within a fraction of one-half of its entire expenses.[41] This left $1,287 weekly to be assessed on the six morning papers that were then members of the association; an average to each of $214 (or $5,000 in today's prices). The significant savings to the New York publishers that the NYAP provided is apparent when one recalls that in the 1830s, James Watson Webb of the New York *Courier and Enquirer* spent $130,000 per annum in today's prices maintaining a schooner in New York harbor. However much the New York publishers benefited from association, they also were able to bear the principal financial burden for gathering it. They then resold the news to publishers throughout the country at an affordable price, which increased the public's access to international news.

CONDUITS, CONTENT, AND COLLUSION: THE COMBINATION OF THE NYAP AND WESTERN UNION

The New York publishers controlled access to international news by securing preferred treatment from telegraph companies. In 1848, the NYAP provided capital to fund construction of a line connecting Nova Scotia with Maine in exchange for exclusive access to the line.[42] It also signed collusive contracts with other nascent telegraph companies, such as the New England lines of Henry O'Rielly. Such connections, boasted the New York *Herald*, meant rivals "cannot receive a single word of news over the Halifax wires ... nor can any other party, under any but the most urgent necessity, and then only with the consent of the Association."[43] In reality, the existence of numerous telegraph providers kept the barriers to entry relatively low. As part of a broader campaign against the New York City press that went back to 1845, Abbott & Winans, a company first established independently of newspaper interests for the collection of commercial information, allied with the owners of the Morse telegraph patents, which enabled it to mount an effective campaign against the New York papers. In turn, the New York newspapers launched a campaign of public vitriol in their pages against the inefficiency and underhandedness of the Morse telegraph system, and instead sought close relations with Cyrus Field's American Telegraph Company and Ezra Cornell's New York & Western Union Telegraph Company. The fortunes of the NYAP were also tied to the American and Western Union telegraph companies, which, happily for the New York newspapers, and perhaps in part owing to their favorable publicity, became the dominant antebellum telegraph providers. As the Morse system and its allies suffered loses, so too did Abbot & Winans, and the news agency disappeared

---

[41] Confidential. Associated Press. Annual report of the general agent, January 1, 1862, 8, NYPL.
[42] J. Rens, *The Invisible Empire: A History of the Telecommunications Industry in Canada* (London: McGill-Queen's University Press, 2001), p. 14. Regan, "The Inception of the Associated Press," 18. American Telegraph Company to NYAP, October 26, 1865, Greeley papers, box 1, LOC.
[43] August 21, 1852. As quoted in Harlow, *Old Wires*, p. 194.

in 1855.[44] The success of the NYAP depended on the political economy of American telegraphy, and especially the New York Telegraph Act of 1848, which facilitated the entry of new telegraph providers and weakened Morse's patent-rights-based empire.[45]

The disparate ownership of the nascent telecommunications network, and the limited reach of the network of each company, increased the costs of coordinating the exchange of news among a large group of publishers, which kept participation in these early news organizations small, personal, and regional.[46] As the telegraph network expanded, and ownership of it was consolidated, it became possible to construct a more far-reaching news network. This task fell to Daniel H. Craig, who was appointed general manager of the NYAP in 1851. Craig, a resourceful, if occasionally imprudent and impertinent entrepreneur who raced against the New York papers at Halifax, was highly successful in his new post until he fell afoul of his paymasters in 1863 for surreptitiously starting his own financial news business.[47] Under Craig's management, the NYAP became a clearinghouse, albeit limited in size and scope, for domestic and international news. Craig placed agents in the nation's important urban centers to collect domestic news from client newspapers. Editors of these papers gathered news of their regions and supplied it to the nearest agent of the NYAP who relayed it to New York. The agents in turn supplied the report the association generated to the newspapers.[48] While he was in office, Craig undertook a national campaign to recruit different newspapers as clients of the New York association. Although editors around the country were reluctant to combine into a single telegraphic news organization, Craig spent much of his time and effort convincing newspaper publishers throughout the country of the benefits they could derive from cooperation and attempting to devise a system of newsgathering that met their diverse needs.[49] Much of the Midwestern press, unable to pay the cost of telegraph fees or employ a correspondent on the eastern seaboard, depended on the NYAP, which reduced the cost of an international

[44] Schwarzlose, *Newsbrokers*, 1: pp. 84–5.

[45] John, *Network Nation*, chapter 3; Schwarzlose, *Newsbrokers*, 1: pp. 177, 188.

[46] S.R. Brooker-Gross, "News Wire Services in the Nineteenth-Century United States," *Journal of Historical Geography*, 7 (1981), 167–79; V. Rosewater, *History of Cooperative News-gathering in the United States* (London: D. Appleton and Co., 1930).

[47] Craig's circular, August 15, 1863; Craig to Chittenden, September 12, 1863, Gordon Lester Ford papers, box 15, folders 8 and 1, NYPL; "Reminiscences of Craig and the Associated Press," *Flake's Semi-Weekly Bulletin*, Marble, vol. 23, LOC.

[48] Blondheim, *News in the Mail*, pp. 6, 148. For details of these arrangements, see St. Louis publishers' agreement with NYAP, undated (1859); WAP-NYAP contract, September 17, 1864, Stone, box 8, folder 529, NL.

[49] "Answer of Daniel H. Craig, organizer and manager of the New York Associated Press, 1850 to 1867, and originator and promoter of machine or rapid telegraphing, to the interrogatories of the U.S. Senate Committee on Education and Labor at the City of New York, 1883" (New York, 1883). See obituary in the New Orleans *Daily Picayune*, January 6, 1895.

news report to between $30 and $40 a month (or approximately $800 in today's prices).[50] Those who could not be convinced, Craig threatened to take the report either by withholding it from them or providing it to competitors at discounted rates.[51] Agreements between the NYAP and Western Union gave teeth to these threats.

After the Civil War, concentration in telegraph ownership, and cooperation between Western Union, the principal telegraph provider, and the NYAP, entrenched the dominant position of both organizations. During the 1860s, Western Union, under the leadership of the indefatigable network builder William Orton – he reportedly died from overwork – acquired considerable control over the burgeoning American telegraph network.[52] Although Western Union initially collected and transmitted news independently of the press to increase throughput during off-peak hours, it relinquished this line of business in return for a monopoly in distribution and control over the sale of commercial information.[53] Western Union also agreed to refrain from transmitting news for any rival news organization on terms more favorable than those granted to the NYAP. For its part, the NYAP and all its members and subsidiary organizations agreed to employ only Western Union to transmit their dispatches.

The economics of networks encouraged Western Union to help the NYAP grow. Telegraph traffic traveled via "circuits," as they were called, although circuits did not always form a loop in practice. Circuits connected locations. The principal cost of transmission was the initial writing up and dispatch; therefore, the greater the number of newspapers on a particular circuit, the smaller the cost to Western Union per message transmitted.[54] Western Union, observed one publisher, invited the press "to combine together all along the line and, by dividing the cost, get the news at a very low rate."[55] Rivalry among news agencies reduced interconnectivity and threatened to generate costly duplication in telegraphing for Western Union. To send two different press reports to the same territory, as opposed to one, obliged twice as much preparation, diminished

---

[50] Lee, *Daily Newspaper*, p. 503.

[51] Craig to Hicks, December 8, 1862, W.H. Smith, MIC 22 1/7, OHS.

[52] "Death of William Orton," *The New York Times*, April 23, 1878.

[53] This arrangement, and the creation of the Gold & Stock company, which was jointly controlled by the NYAP and Western Union, is deserving of greater investigation. See *Proceedings*, pp. 25–7.

[54] Under arrangements with the telegraph companies that had been in existence at least since the mid-1880s, it was necessary to send an identical report to not less than five points to get the advantage of press association telegraph rates. Regular special newspaper rates were much higher. Stone to F. Sulles, November 3, 1910, AP01.2, Kent Cooper papers (KC), box 8, folder 7, AP. Edward McKernon to Martin, January 24, 1917, AP01.2, KC, box 7, folder 7, AP; Martin to V.S. McClatchy, January 26, 1917, AP01.2, KC, box 13, folder 3, AP.

[55] As quoted in Schwarzlose, *Newsbrokers*, 1: p. 110.

Western Union's profits, and interfered with its commercial business.[56] Orton understood the advantages that would accrue to Western Union if rivals of the NYAP could be forced out of business or absorbed.[57] Consequently, when newspapers employed opposition wires to transmit their news, the NYAP compelled those papers to use only Western Union or to forego the association's report. In turn, Western Union officials used the news report of the NYAP as leverage to compel newspaper publishers to transmit only over Western Union telegraph lines.[58] Opportunistic behavior was rare. Publishers that benefitted from the arrangement could be prevailed on to cajole recalcitrant papers into line, even publicly in their pages.[59]

Western Union helped the NYAP to increase the wordage of its news reports, outstrip its rivals, and bolster its ranks, all of which increased the number of newspapers that transmitted over the telegraph company's wires. For the NYAP, Western Union transmitted 18,000 words per week from New York to Baltimore, Philadelphia, and Washington, DC, at the rate of $.25 per word and $0.05 for each "drop" at a different station along the telegraph circuit. Western Union charged the American Press Association, a rival of the NYAP, more than twice as much as it charged the NYAP for an equally laborious and larger service. In cities in which rivals threatened NYAP affiliates, Western Union temporarily carried a special service at a nominal rate or made a weekly rebate from its bills to the association.[60]

Although Western Union's control of the American telegraph network was always incomplete, the reach of alternative telegraph networks was smaller, and the services they offered rivals of the NYAP were limited. The American Press Association, for example, briefly relied on the Atlantic & Pacific Telegraph Company, but found its telegraph network inadequate.[61] James Goodsell, president of the American Press Association and editor of the New York *Graphic* (in which he let loose his venom on the NYAP and Western Union), understood that there could be no effective challenge to Western Union and the NYAP "until wires free from its control connect every city and town in the Union." The telegraph, wrote Goodsell, was "not a local but eminently national affair, and to attempt to compete with the Western Union by building an opposition telegraph from Portland to Washington would be as hopeless as it would be

[56] Green to W.H. Smith, Mach 22, 1882, Western Union papers (WU), 203A-G4, p. 198, Smithsonian Institute (SI).
[57] Orton to Bowles, November 17, 1868, WU, 197B-4, p. 461, SI.
[58] Orton to Simonton, November 7 and 21, 1867 and May 1, 1868, WU, 197A-2, p. 166, 286, SI; 197B-3, p. 424, SI.
[59] See, for example, Orton to Simonton, February 11, 1868, WU, 197B-3, p. 114, SI.
[60] Orton to Simonton, May 3, 1870, WU, 198B-7, p. 254, SI; Orton to Simonton, October 25, 1873, WU, 199B-12, p. 415, SI; Orton to E. Brooks, March 27, 1877, WU, 201B-19, p. 98, SI; Orton to R. Smith, September 18, 1874, WU, 199B-12, p. 354, SI; Orton to R. Smith, November 16, 1874, WU, 199B-12, p. 466, SI.
[61] Orton to J. Medill, June 9, 1876, WU, 200B-16, p. 490, SI.

to undertake to compete with the Union Pacific Railroad by building a new road from Portland to Quebec."[62] Without access to a telegraph company with national facilities, Goodsell had to rely on Western Union.[63]

At times Western Union's cozy relationship with the NYAP caused considerable public outcry. The combination of Western Union and the NYAP was widely perceived to adversely affect the free flow of news and did in at least a few documented instances.[64] According to Gardiner G. Hubbard, the combination was more powerful than the "French Directory, because, in an era when public opinion is omnipotent, it can give, withhold, or color the information which shapes that opinion."[65] Congressman Charles S. Sumner of California, who inveighed that Western Union and the NYAP were "banded together in the strong bond of mutual plunder and rapacity against the people," was very likely displeased on behalf of the publishers in his constituency, who had grievances with the NYAP.[66] Henry George, the famous radical, contended that the combination possessed a monopoly of public opinion after the NYAP mistreated the newspaper for which he worked.[67]

Newspaper editors complained in their pages about the NYAP and the telegraph company, and about the potential their close connection created for misleading the public, but between 1850 and 1880 such criticism appeared infrequently.[68] According to the Boston *Advertiser*, the public was "little interested in the question where or by what agency the press get their news," but it is unlikely that apathy accounts for collective quietude.[69] It is more likely that the country's major newspaper publishers, who benefited from the combination, had good reason to avoid criticizing it in their columns. In return for favorable treatment, the NYAP suppressed accusations against Western Union while editorials that favored the company were distributed gratis to all sections of the country. According to members of the association, in addition to the patronage the NYAP gave the telegraph company had also to be

[62] New York *Graphic*, January 29, 1875, as quoted in House Judiciary Committee, "In the matter of the Western Union Telegraph Company," 43rd Cong., 1875, HJ-T2, RG233, p. 32, National Archives (NA). I am grateful to R.R. John for this reference.

[63] Agreement between Pacific and Atlantic Telegraph Company and the APA, June 1870, W.H. Smith, MIC 22 1/7, OHS.

[64] Blondheim, "Rehearsal," 309–18.

[65] S. Rep. No. 48–577, pt. 1, at 17 (1884). "Gardiner G. Hubbard," New York *Times*, December 12, 1897.

[66] As quoted in Harlow, *Old Wires*, p. 333. For Sumner's motivations, see Orton to Simonton, June 9, 1876, WU, 200B-16, p. 497, SI. Western Union and the NYAP differed over the service to California; the former wanted to expand it; the latter to curtail it. See WU, 201A-17, SI.

[67] Schwarzlose, *Newsbrokers*, 2: pp. 25, 28; Henry George papers, NYPL.

[68] See, for example, Milwaukee *Daily Sentinel*, February 17, 1870; Milwaukee *Daily Journal*, September 1, 1883. *Southwestern Advocate* (New Orleans), November 5, 1874; Denver *Rocky Mountain News*, January 29, 1875. Blondheim, "Rehearsal," 306, fn. 15.

[69] December 1, 1866. See also "The New York Associated Press and the Western Associated Press," Cleveland *Herald*, December 3, 1866.

added the members' powerful influence actively exerted to prevent passage in Congress of proposals for the government ownership of telegraphy and to hinder the emergence of new telegraph providers.[70] Members of the association mounted their own propaganda campaign in which they lauded the benefits of cooperation and counteracted accusations of monopoly or unfairness. "But for this co-operative system," went the argument of one such article, it would be impossible that the news of the world should be "placed in the hands of every one who cares to read it every day at a trifling cost." Indeed, "the co-operative system" the association provided "was the only one by which a large portion of the American press could live." Government intervention, claimed one news association executive, would have increased the cost of news to the smaller provincial papers and undermined plurality.[71]

Even if public outcry over the relationship between Western Union and the NYAP had been more widespread, the judiciary lacked extensive power to regulate the way in which the telegraph company priced its services. In telecommunications, as in other areas of American business, the courts, not administrative or legislative bodies, were the principal agents of regulation. The judiciary regulated telegraphy through tortious liability, message priority, access to rights of way, and even the price of government-generated telegrams, but judicial powers were insufficient to impose common carrier obligations, and the principle received no federal endorsement until passage of the Mann-Elkins Act in 1910, despite passage of the National Telegraph Acts beginning in 1866 and the Butler Amendment in 1879.[72] The judiciary established that telegraphy constituted interstate commerce, albeit intangible,[73] but the courts could only

---

[70] Orton to Simonton, February 6, 1868, WU, 197B-3, p. 92, SI. *Proceedings* (Detroit, 1872), 10–11.

[71] "Wm. Henry Smith...," *The Courier Journal* (Louisville, KY), March 8, 1884, W.H. Smith, Mss 2, box 6, folder 2, OHS.

[72] M. Keller, "Regulation of Larger Enterprise: The United States Experience in Comparative Perspective," in A. Chandler and H. Daems (eds.), *Managerial Hierarchies: Comparative Perspectives on the Rise of the Modern Industrial Enterprise* (London: Harvard University Press, 1980), pp. 168–9; S. Skowronek, *Building a New American State: The Expansion of National Administrative Capacity, 1877–1920* (Cambridge: Cambridge University Press, 1982), p. 122. On several occasions during the 1850s and 1860s, American and English courts affirmed the duty of a telegraph company to treat all customers equally and without discrimination. See *McAndrew v. Electric Tel. Co.*, 17 Com. Bench R. 3 (1855); *Camp v. Western Tel. Co., Am. Law Reg.*, 6:7 (May 1858); 1 Metcalfe (Ky.) 164; *Parks v. Alta California Tel. Co.*, 13 Cal. 422 (1859); *Birney v. New York and Wash. Tel. Co.*, 18 Md. 341 (1862); and *New York and Wash. Tel. Co. v. Dryburg*, 32 Pa. 298 (1860). By 1865, it was clear that if a telegraph company held itself out to carry messages in the ordinary way, it took on itself a public employment analogous to that of a common carrier. T.W.D., "The Law of Telegraphs and Telegrams," *American Law Register* (1852–1891), 13 (February 1865), 199. The courts affirmed the principle at all levels throughout the nineteenth century. See *Grinnell v. Western Union Tel. Co.*, 113 Mass. 299 (1873); *Telegraph Company v. Texas*, 105 U.S. 460 (1881); *Thompson et al. v. Western Union Tel. Co.*, 64 Wis. 531 (1885).

[73] On interstate commerce see: *Pensacola Tel. Co. v. Western Union Tel. Co.*, 96 U.S. 1 (1877); *Telegraph Co. v. Texas*, 105 U.S. 460 (1881); *Western Union Tel. Co. v. Pendleton*, 122 U.S.

nullify onerous conditions, and could neither require telegraph companies to publicize their rates or profits nor set rates.[74]

Congress, although voluble, passed no legislation to regulate the telegraph. Executives of the NYAP and Western Union were repeatedly summoned to testify before congressional judiciary committees, and, by the end of the nineteenth century, seventy-five bills in favor of the creation of a governmental postal telegraph passed through Congress.[75] House and Senate committees debated government ownership of telegraphy on nineteen separate occasions, and seventeen times recommended a bill for approval, but ratification remained elusive.[76] Tarbell suggested that the franking privileges Western Union gave to government officials amounted to bribes and accounts for congressional reluctance to legislate against the telegraph company.[77] Maybe congressional representatives, who typically approved the demands of the press with respect to postal rates, were reluctant to incur the wrath of the nation's publishers.[78] By employing the First Amendment as both a sword and a shield, the press further complicated the prospect of congressional intervention. When the Senate Sub-Committee on Post Offices and Post Roads asked William Henry Smith, then general agent for the association, whether, given the public interest with which it was affected, it might be regulated by government, he strategically deployed press freedom to protect business interests. "Not unless you change the Constitutional guarantee of liberty of the press," replied Smith. "Regulation is inconsistent with liberty."[79] Congress passed a few bills, but judicial interpretation and inadequate enforcement dulled their bite.[80]

Although further regulation was not forthcoming, the prospect of it made the presidents of Western Union anxious and encouraged them to modify their

---

347, 356 (1887). This principle was subsequently extended to the telephone. *Muskogee Nat. Tel. Co. v. Hall et al.*, 118 F. 382 (1902). On intangibility; see F.H. Cook, "The Application of the Commerce Clause to the Intangible," *University of Pennsylvania Law Review*, 58 (April 1910), 411; "What is Commerce," *Harvard Law Review*, 24 (January 1911), 230–1; H.L.W., "What is Interstate Commerce?," *Michigan Law Review*, 8 (June 1910), 662–4; "Application of the Commerce Clause to the Intangible," *Columbia Law Review*, 14 (February 1914), 147–9. Compare with R.F. Bensel, *The Political Economy of American Industrialization, 1877–1900* (Cambridge: Cambridge University Press, 2000), pp. 321–33.

[74] R. Cassady Jr., "Legal Aspects of Price Discrimination: Federal Law," *Journal of Marketing*, 11 (January 1947), 260.

[75] See, House Judiciary Committee, "In the matter of the Western Union Telegraph Company," 43rd Cong., 1875, HJ-T1 (43), RG233, NA; I. Tarbell, *The Nationalizing of Business, 1878–1898* (New York: Macmillan, 1936), p. 38; D. Hochfelder, "A Comparison of the Postal Telegraph Movement in Great Britain and the United States, 1866–1900," *Enterprise & Society*, 1 (2000), 739–61.

[76] Harlow, *Old Wires*, p. 333.

[77] Tarbell, *Nationalizing*, pp. 39, 42.

[78] W.E. Fuller, "The Populists and the Post Office," *Agricultural History*, 65 (1991), 3.

[79] "The Associated Press," San Francisco *Daily Evening Bulletin*, March 8, 1884.

[80] Viz. the National Telegraph Act (1866), the Butler Amendment (1879), and the Anderson Act (1888).

relationship with the NYAP. If Western Union charged a rate to outside papers that none of them could pay, and if the NYAP refused to furnish news to some of these papers on any terms, or only on terms that were prohibitive, then, feared Orton, Congress might legislate to establish a government telegraph. "While the New York Associated Press may be justified in saying whom it will, or will not serve," wrote Orton to the general manager of the NYAP, "the Western Union, as a public corporation, is bound in honor, as it can be compelled in law, to render like service on like terms."[81] Orton suggested broadening the membership, lest "in addition to competing lines, we must also resist the antagonism of a portion of the press, hostile to us because of their exclusion from participation in your news."[82] The refusal of the NYAP to fix a uniform rate for its news, or to offer it equally to all parties, said Norvin Green, Orton's successor, devolved on Western Union, as its assumed ally, "more odium and antagonism in Legislative bodies, the popular mind, and the outside press, than any one thing in the history of this Company." When it suited his purposes, Green, like Orton, privately insisted that Western Union had "obligations as a public institution to render like service for like rates" and that "the system of the old Press Associations selling their news exclusively at certain places" caused trouble and encouraged rivals.[83] For this reason, and so that it could "make free trade in news," Western Union debated establishing its own news bureau.[84] Orton and Green feared regulation, but such statements, however concerned they make them appear, were not intended to encourage competition, but to protect, if not increase, Western Union's dominance by expanding that portion of the newspaper market that the NYAP served.[85]

THE ADVENT AND GROWTH OF REGIONAL COOPERATION

The problem with collusion between the NYAP and Western Union lay with the former's insistence on limiting the extent to which its news could be resold. If all newspapers had equal access to the NYAP, they might have benefited from a price reduction. Such was the arrangement in England.[86] Indeed, Western Union had an incentive to encourage widespread distribution of NYAP news so as to increase utilization of its network. Although members of the NYAP recognized the advantages of spreading their news and their costs more widely, they were reluctant to do so lest they diminish the value that accrued to the news reports from exclusivity.

[81] Orton to Simonton, June 9, 1876, WU, 200B-16, p. 497, SI.
[82] Orton to Simonton, April 4, 1870, WU, 198B-7, p. 217, SI; Orton to R. Smith, September 18, 1874, WU, 199B-12, p. 354, SI.
[83] Green to W.H. Smith, March 22, 1882, WU, 203A-G4, p. 198, SI.
[84] N. Green to D. Stone, January 5, 1882, WU, 203A-G4, p. 124, SI.
[85] Orton to Bowles, July 22, 1876, WU, 200B-16, np, SI.
[86] See Chapter 3.

Coordinating exchange and cooperation between the newspapers of the East Coast and those of the burgeoning Midwest was especially difficult. During the 1850s, New York was the nerve center of America's news network, which allowed Daniel Craig to build a fairly far-reaching organization under the auspices of the NYAP, but the Civil War neutralized New York's natural geographic advantage and the city's great publishers had to adapt the governance of their association to meet the demands of a lively Midwestern press. Beginning in the 1840s, the press of the Midwest grew rapidly. In western Pennsylvania, Ohio, Indiana, Illinois, Michigan, Missouri, and Kentucky, the number of dailies increased from 32 in 1840 to 72 in 1850 and 103 in 1860. The Civil War and war news, which often broke in the middle of the country, not on the eastern seaboard, further stimulated the growth and journalistic enterprise of the newspapers throughout the Ohio and Mississippi River Valleys.[87] Before the war, many of the smaller Midwestern publications were happy to fill their pages primarily with advertisements. In the *Daily Pittsburgh Gazette*, for example, advertising accounted for 87 percent of content in 1850 and 83.4 percent in 1860. That year, only 4.5 columns of 32 were devoted to news, but the events of the Civil War caused publishers to modify these proportions.[88]

The New York publishers preferred to employ their own correspondents to cover the war, rather than permit the NYAP to undertake such tasks on their behalf, and consequently the quality and breadth of the news reports of the association suffered. The New York *Herald*, for example, spent $500,000 covering the war and had sixty-three reporters in the field, while the NYAP had only ten.[89] Employing a correspondent during the Civil War cost between $1,000 and $5,000 per annum, or between $17,000 and $90,000 in today's prices.[90] Cooperation had limits. Members of the NYAP were willing to combine their efforts to avoid superfluous expenditure, but they were equally determined to pursue a valuable scoop. By pursuing their own news independently, the New York publishers inadvertently encouraged the enterprise of their Midwestern counterparts who found they could not rely on the NYAP. The growth of the press outside New York during and after the Civil War contributed to a decrease in the country circulation of Greeley's weekly New York *Tribune* from more than 200,000 at the end of the Civil War to 80,000 by the 1870s.[91] The daily newspapers of the growing Midwestern cities, such as the Chicago

---

[87] Baehr Jr., *The New York* Tribune, p. 22; Innis, "Technology and Public Opinion," 14–15; W. Cronon, *Nature's Metropolis: Chicago and the Great West* (London: Norton, 1991); D.W. Meinig, *The Shaping of America: A Geographical Perspective on 500 Years of History*, vol. 3: *Transcontinental America, 1850–1915* (London: Yale University Press, 1998). Lee, *Daily Newspaper*, p. 506.

[88] Lee, *Daily Newspaper in America*, p. 319.

[89] Huntzicker, *The Popular Press*, p. 140.

[90] W. Huntzicker, *The Popular Press, 1833–1865* (Westport, CT: Greenwood Press, 1999), p. 139.

[91] Baehr Jr., *The New York* Tribune, p. 125.

Tribune, Cincinnati *Commercial*, and Toledo *Blade*, consequently desired a greater say in the preparation of the news report compiled in New York.[92]

The ensuing battle between the Midwestern and eastern presses was not a byproduct of sectarianism. The quality and timeliness of the New York report was only partly to blame for the aggravation and mutiny of the Midwestern press. The principal problem was that publishers of large Midwestern newspapers, such as Murat Halstead of the Cincinnati *Commercial*, wanted more news by telegraph than the proprietors of small Midwestern papers could afford. The system of obtaining news from the NYAP precluded the possibility of catering adequately for these disparate needs. Given the limited staff and technology at small Midwestern papers, there was insufficient time between the delivery of news, say at midnight, and the hour of publication in the morning to have the paper produced in time. Telegraph companies, like railroads, set prices differently to compensate for elastic demand in long-distance telegraphy between major cities, and inelastic demand in local markets. Local dispatches were charged a high rate compared with charges on through-wires. Papers at Chicago, Cincinnati, St. Louis, and other large Midwestern cities, could take a report as full as the New York papers possessed and publish it simultaneously with its appearance in New York, and without extravagant cost. It was the distribution of news to smaller points by telegraph that was inconvenient, and, in proportion, expensive. If the journals of the large cities withdrew from the arrangement with the smaller places, and took a report directly from New York, it was likely that the high cost of transmitting the news would preclude the papers of many smaller towns from obtaining the reports. This aspect of telegraphic news distribution, known to railway historians as the long- and short-haul problem, meant that subdividing the report at major hubs saved telegraphing costs and was a convenience to the smaller papers, which received a digested report of the news made up by the regional parent association. Consequently, several organizations formed throughout the country to do just this and to overcome local coordination problems between large and small papers.[93]

The disparity in demand between the burgeoning Midwestern urban press and their smaller, rural counterparts led to a revolt in 1862, during which the urban publishers in the Midwest pressed the NYAP to discontinue its policy of selling its news widely and demanded the right in their area of publication to decide on the admission of new applicants.[94] Thereafter, newspapers outside New York that were already members of the NYAP obtained the exclusive

[92] For examples of early complaints, see Cleveland *Herald*, August 41, 1859 and Milwaukee *Daily Sentinel*, November 20, 1862. Contract between NYAP and WAP, September 17, 1864; NYAP agreement with Chicago papers, March 24, 1865, W.H. Smith, MIC 22 1/7, OHS; J.H. Wade to D.N. Stone et al., October 9, 1865, Greeley papers, box 1, LOC.

[93] Existing trade associations played an important role in this process. See, for instance, "Charter and by-laws of the Texas Editorial and Press Association" (Jefferson, TX, 1875).

[94] Craig to G.B. Hicks, December 8, 1862, W.H. Smith, MIC 22 1/7, OHS.

right, in each city or town, to decide which applicants would receive the news reports, with the understanding that – should any paper cease to be a member – the publishers among the remaining members in each city or town would have added to their bills a sum equal to the amount previously paid by the retired paper. Although the NYAP delegated this power, Midwestern publishers continued to demand even greater say; and, at a meeting on November 22, 1865, they determined to charter their own Western Associated Press (WAP).[95] Unlike the NYAP, which never incorporated, the WAP incorporated in Michigan. The Michigan charter, in addition to tightening the bonds of membership, authorized the WAP to procure "intelligence" from "all parts of the world by telegraph or otherwise."[96] The larger publishers, recounted the members in 1877, broke away so "that arrangements should be made allowing newspaper establishments with large resources and enterprising dispositions to obtain more news by telegraph than the proprietors of papers with small revenues."[97] Approximately fifty newspapers joined the association at the outset. The membership declined during the 1870s to slightly less than 40 and then increased to nearly 60 by 1892, although by this time the WAP served an additional 100 newspapers that paid subscriptions for smaller reports.[98]

As regional associations emerged, political decisions at the state level affected their structure and organization. The WAP first received a corporate charter in Michigan, although it subsequently moved to Chicago through a special act of the state legislature "to provide for the incorporation of associations engaged in the publication of newspapers, periodicals, books and other matter."[99] Similar charter acts permitted the Midwestern regional associations to incorporate with a small capital stock that allowed for the creation of membership shares. Each member held one share as well as one vote. The WAP issued a capital stock of $1,000 divided into shares of $10 each. All the stock stood on the same basis, the value of which was fixed and did not vary with the value of the property of the corporation or its dividend paying ability. Ordinarily, the purchase of a share of stock is sufficient to enable one to participate in the profits and management of a concern, but this was not the case with WAP. Not only was a prospective member required to be elected and purchase a share of stock, but the member, in addition to paying the $10 value of the stock, also

[95] Western Associated Press minutes, undated, Robert McCormick papers, box 9, Cantingy, IL. See also D.W. Curl, *Murat Halstead and the Cincinnati Commercial* (Boca Raton, FL: University Press of Florida, 1980), p. 36.
[96] *Laws of Michigan, 1865*, Ch 299.
[97] *Proceedings* (Detroit, 1877), 29.
[98] *Proceedings* (Detroit, 1867), 6. Membership was fifty-one in 1887. WAP annual meeting, October 26, 1887, V. Rosewater papers, box 20, folder 13, American Jewish Archives (AJA).
[99] *Acts of the Legislature of the State of Michigan* (Lansing, MI: John A. Kerr & Co., 1865), pp. 647–8. In 1867, the New York State Associated Press incorporated under a special act of the New York legislature (chapter 754).

had to pay an amount equal to what would be the member's pro rata share in the property of the association. This share was determined on the basis of the newspaper's circulation, which served as a method for approximating its reproduction of the association's news. In effect, a new member was compelled to purchase equality with the other stockholders. These membership requirements were intended to ensure that the prospective member made up to the existing stockholders the amount that the admission of the new member lessened the value of their interest in the property. The amount a new member was compelled to pay was independent of the amount of news the member proposed to take and of the assessments levied on the member.

Insofar as prior to the sale of the news it was part of the property of the corporation, each stockholder was interested in it equally, each owning the same amount of stock. The WAP was in effect a mutual benefit association, therefore the price charged to members for the news furnished was the cost of collection with a minimum sum added for expenses, and it was from subscribers that the WAP derived its profits. The greater amount of matter taken by one paper entailed no more expense on the corporation than the lesser amount taken by another, both being paid and assessed for at cost. A large paper, which deployed its own reporters and therefore took a smaller amount of news from the association, might bring in proportionately greater revenue to the association, owing to the fact that its clientele was larger and consequently its pro rata payment for reproducing the news of the association was higher.[100] Data concerning the operations of the association is unfortunately scarce, but between 1879 and 1886 assessments averaged $272 per paper per month, approximately $6,500 in today's prices.[101]

A board of directors of seven members transacted the business of the WAP and an executive committee comprising members of the board supervised its actions. The board determined assessments and could suspend members from receiving the dispatches of the association by a vote of two-thirds of the board. Between 1865 and 1888, 168 positions were available, but only 28 different publishers held the post. The board was constituted according to newspaper wealth and circulation. Richard Smith, of the Cincinnati *Gazette*, and W.N. Haldeman, of the Louisville *Courier*, served on the board every year during this period. Joseph Medill, of the Chicago *Tribune*, a director of long-standing, was initially appointed "permanent secretary."[102] H.N. Walker, of the Detroit *Free Press*, also held a seat on the board throughout the 1870s. For many years, Haldeman, Medill, and Smith comprised the executive committee, and they, along with Walker, occupied four of the seven seats on the board. The

---

[100] A.H. Belo to executive committee, February 16, 1892, Victor Lawson papers (hereafter Lawson), in Minutes of executive committee, February 22, 1892, pp. 65–74, box 2, folder 4, NL.

[101] Assessment figures, 1879–1886, Delevan Smith papers, box 13, folder 7, Indiana Historical Society (IHS).

[102] "The publishers in council...," Milwaukee *Daily Sentinel*, August 10, 1864.

three other board positions afforded a degree of turnover, but were limited to publishers from the major Midwestern cities. The management of the association was similarly stable. William Henry Smith, an Ohio Republican and confidant of Benjamin Harrison, was general agent for the lifetime of the association and a significant, but overlooked figure in the history of American journalism.[103] Smith, in his capacity as general agent, not only played a critical role in the organization of the newsgathering apparatus of the country; as a lead investor in Otto Mergenthaler's linotype machine, he also contributed to a revolution in newspaper publishing.

The WAP's method of organization was designed to protect exclusive access to the news. According to Murat Halstead:

There are no means whatever of obtaining the telegraphic news within the territory of the Western Associated Press, or that which is tributary to it, except through our regular agents, and the newspaper that, for a violation of the rules or other cause, is refused the news, can not obtain it, as there is no opposition news agency, and our contracts give us for our territory, a monopoly of the news of the world, on the wires from Liverpool to San Francisco.[104]

Applications for the news report were referred to local boards, which were entitled to fix a bonus chargeable to new members based on an estimate of the value of the telegraphic news report franchise in that town. Local boards could also refuse to admit an applicant. In cases of dispute, a vote of two-thirds of the WAP's full board was required to overrule the decision of local members or to suspend members. In other regional organizations, similarly restrictive arrangements governed the admission of new members.[105] E.W. Scripps, the publisher of Midwestern newspapers aimed at working-class readers, later recalled that the WAP was a "monopolistic and close corporation," although Scripps was no stranger to the practices of profit pooling, price fixing, collusion, and contract exclusivity.[106] In one instance, the *Pioneer-Press* declined to admit a rival paper at St. Paul, Minnesota, and the WAP, despite a petition from forty-two citizens of that city, refused to provide it with a news service.[107] From 1874, perhaps to avoid such local squabbles, and to ensure the WAP had

---

[103] O. Hoogenboom, "Smith, William Henry," *American National Biography Online* (February 2000).

[104] *Proceedings* (Detroit, 1867), 3.

[105] Charter and bylaws of the Kansas and Missouri Associated Press, January 31, 1883, 01.2, box 2, folder 7, AP corporate archives (AP); New England Associated Press secretary's record, June 5, 1869, 01.2, box 3, folder 10, p. 4, AP; "North-western Associated Press," 1887, Rosewater, Mss 503, box 20, folder 13, AJA.

[106] Scripps to R. Howard, September 27, 1912, Roy Howard papers, University of Indiana, Bloomington (UIB). E.E. Adams, "Collusion and Price Fixing in the American Newspaper Industry: Market Preservation Trends, 1890–1910," *Journalism and Mass Communication Quarterly*, 79 (2002), 416–26.

[107] *Proceedings* (Detroit, 1877), 5.

coverage in strategically important locations, power to decide on membership applications rested with the full board of the WAP. This alteration also reflected the considerable power of the board.

Other regional organizations, which emerged throughout the country to contend with similar local coordination problems, formed the makings of a federated structure of news associations. The New York parent association separately served the New England Associated Press, which had its own subsidiary, as well as the New York State Associated Press. The press of Baltimore, western Pennsylvania, Philadelphia, and Washington, DC were served directly by, and were largely subsidiary to, the NYAP. The WAP relayed news from the NYAP to the Northwestern Associated Press, which served the territory occupied by the Northwestern Telegraph Company, an ally of Western Union with lines in Wisconsin, Minnesota, and the Dakotas. The WAP also served the Kansas and Missouri Associated Press, which included the papers in the states named and those published at Denver, Cheyenne, Pueblo, and Santa Fe. The California Associated Press included the papers of the Pacific Coast. Newspapers in the south, although loosely organized under the auspices of the Southern Associated Press, contracted on an individual basis with the NYAP. The papers of the south were decidedly the poorest in the country and the news served there was not nearly as extensive as that provided in the west.[108]

Holding together this loose federation of news associations was problematic. In 1875, the coalition of news associations served approximately 350 of the daily newspapers of the United States out of a total of 458, or 76 percent of the market; but in practice, recurrent disagreements prohibited the federation of news associations from operating as a unified body.[109] The members of the WAP often complained about the provision and quality of the news reports the NYAP provided, the extent of the territory assigned to the different organizations, and the way in which the NYAP apportioned expenses.[110] The NYAP was also subject to internal divisions. The New York *Herald, Tribune,* and *World,* which outstripped the *Express, Journal of Commerce, Sun,* and *Times,* chaffed under the power of an association constituted of less enterprising

---

[108] House Judiciary Committee, "In the Matter of the Western Union Telegraph Company," 43rd Cong., 1875, HJ-T1, RG233, p. 5, NA. Associated Press State of New York, "Charter, By-Laws and Contracts of the Associated Press of the State of New York," (Elmira, NY, 1888). For information on the Northwestern Associated Press, see "North-western Associated Press," 1887, Rosewater, box 20, folder 13, AJA; Lee, *History of American Journalism,* p. 344.

[109] Testimony of W.B. Somerville, House Judiciary Committee, "In the Matter of the Western Union Telegraph Company," 43rd Cong., 1875, HJ-T2 (43), RG233, 11, NA.

[110] O. Gramling, *AP: the Story of News* (Port Washington, NY: Kennikat Press, 1969, c. 1940), pp. 71–7; Schwarzlose, *Newsbrokers,* 2: pp. 39–47; P.R. Knights, "The Press Association War of 1866–1867," *Journalism Monographs,* 6 (1967). "The Associated Press of New York and the Western Associated Press," Cleveland *Herald,* November 30; 1866, see also December 1, 1866.

and influential papers, but which to a degree directed their expenditure and controlled the content of their columns.[111] Serious though these problems appeared, the prospect of outright competition was too harrowing to allow a complete rupture in cooperation. Instead, agreements were invariably renegotiated and hatchets promptly buried.[112]

Such protests and renegotiation led to a liberalization of agreements between the NYAP and subsidiary associations, which greased the wheels of cooperation. By 1870, in return for an agreed compensation, the NYAP daily placed all the news that it gathered at the disposal of the local agents of the other press associations. These agents then made up their own reports for the several associations they represented, and Western Union transmitted their reports from New York to the principal cities of the country. The news of these principal subsidiary associations was retransmitted to the papers in the various sub-associations from convenient points such as Chicago, Cleveland, St. Louis, and so forth. Any news received by any member of the NYAP or its subsidiaries was bound by the terms of its membership to send a copy of it to the central organization to which it was immediately responsible. Western Union arranged for a telegraphic circuit to distribute the news to the several associations. Special services to each paper, or to two or three papers combined, were charged at separate rates. Such "specials," as they were called, could be sent from any point in the country.[113]

The NYAP divided the newspapers it served into two classes of customers, one of which comprised the western, New England, New York State, Brooklyn, Canadian, and California press; the other included the press of Baltimore, Philadelphia, Washington, DC, and the south. For a round sum and the exchange of their own news, the newspapers of the first class purchased from the NYAP the cable and domestic news that originated outside their own territory. They maintained their own agents and paid the telegraph company for tolls. The associations of the second class were tributary to the NYAP, and were governed by the rules of the latter, to which they paid a sum in gross. Although the archival record is sparse, the cost to the NYAP in 1872 of the news the western and New England press purchased from it was $195,402 (or $3.7 million in today's prices). On the sale of this news, the NYAP received, in addition

---

[111] Gramling, *AP*, p. 64.

[112] Manton Marble, publisher of the *World*, caused these difficulties. See "Meeting of Executive Committee," November 27, 1866, Marble, vol. 14, LOC; Blondheim, "Rehearsal," p. 313; M. Beach, meeting NYAP, December 4, 1866, Marble, vol. 14, LOC; H. White to M. Marble, December 14, 1866, Marble, vol. 14, LOC; M. Marble to J. Medill, January 4, 1867 and M. Marble to J. Medill, R. Smith, M. Halstead, January 8, 1867, Marble, vol. 14, LOC. Relations between Marble and Dana, of the *Sun*, were strained during the 1880s. See Charles Dana papers, box 116, NYPL. J.G. Bennett also threatened to leave the association. See Bennett to NYAP, June 29, 1867, and unsigned to M. Marble, August 25, 1867, Marble, vol. 15, LOC.

[113] Testimony of W. Orton, House Judiciary Committee, "In the matter of the Western Union Telegraph Company," 43rd Cong., 1875, HJ-T2 (43), RG233, NA.

to the use of all the domestic news collected by the independent associations in the United States, a total of $214,361.71, which made for a net profit to the New York association of $18,960 (about $360,000).[114] Throughout the 1870s, payments from the WAP to the NYAP averaged $42,000 per annum and included a news report of western events transmitted gratis. As a means of comparison, in 1873, William Henry Smith estimated that the WAP could obtain the same news independently for $45,000 per annum.[115] Disagreements over the price of news between the WAP and the NYAP continued to bedevil their relationship until the 1890s.[116]

Opportunism among the New York publishers partly accounts for continued disagreements with the members of the WAP, but technological constraints, which impeded the transmission of news, and the policy of Western Union in favor of the NYAP, were also to blame. Contracts between the several news associations and Western Union were for a set number of words per annum. The associations were allowed to distribute several thousand words per month for which they were charged a set rate per word and an excess charge applied for words sent over the agreed limit. The original contract made between the WAP and Western Union in January 1867 covered 6,000 words per day for $60,000 per annum, but news reports would frequently overrun the 6,000-word limit, which caused the WAP to purchase an additional service of 2,700 words per day for a further $20,000 per annum. This provided for a report of 8,700 words per "secular day," of which 5,200 were sent from the east and 3,500 from the west. For the transmission of this report, the WAP paid Western Union $80,000 per annum in monthly installments (approximately $1.25 million). For all additional words, the charge was $.03 per word.

Commercial news, which was the type of news most in demand, but also the most labor-intensive and expensive to transmit, consumed 4,000 to 4,500 of the 8,700 words allowed in the WAP's contract with Western Union until ciphers were devised to diminish the wordage required by commercial reports. Congressional reports and general news were condensed in the small balance of the word allowance, and the use of coded dispatches for commercial information reflected an increased demand among publishers for a greater quantity of general news.[117] In 1869, the WAP, dissatisfied with the report the NYAP

---

[114] Report to the board of directors, with W.H. Smith's comments, May 31, 1873, W.H. Smith, MIC 22 1/7, OHS.

[115] Report to the board of directors, May 31, 1873, W.H. Smith, MIC 22 1/7, OHS.

[116] See, for example, W.H. Smith to Simonton, June 22, 1874, and Simonton to Smith, June 26, 1874, W.H. Smith, MIC 22 1/7, OHS.

[117] Dispatching commercial information required care to ensure that the data was accurately transmitted as well as knowledge of the markets and of the ciphers necessary for transmission. For an example of these dispatches, see the Cleveland *Herald*, April 7, 1866. *Proceedings* (Detroit, 1870), 17. *Proceedings* (Detroit, 1871), 7; *Proceedings* (Detroit, 1872), 11.

provided from Congress, attempted to send its own correspondent to cover events at the capitol, but Western Union refused to extend any facility to the WAP on favorable terms for obtaining news outside its territory or to enable the association to exchange news directly with the Canadian, New England, New York State, or Southern news associations. Although Western Union advised the NYAP to be less exclusive, it also placed the WAP in a position in which it was, according to the board, "in a measure obliged to accept the proposition made by the New York press."[118] When the NYAP and telegraph company renewed their contract in 1877, telegraph rates charged were based on the distance from New York. A Gotham-centric view of telegraphy meant that tolls charged from Chicago and its environs were $.025 per word, whereas those from New York and the north-Atlantic coast were $.01 per word. The relationship between Western Union and the NYAP, said William Orton, the Western Union president who was forced to defend it before the House Judiciary Committee, was similar to that between American railways and steel companies. Just as railway companies varied freight rates based on the amount of business received, so did the telegraph company. Western Union, according to Orton, had "as many different rates" as it had press contracts.[119]

Dispatches, although they comprised the important news without embellishment, continued to press on the contracted wordage limit. Agents of the WAP were enjoined to observe the greatest care in condensation of their reports, but experience showed it to be impossible without sacrificing important news. An increase in foreign news during international crises put the number of words the association transmitted over the amount originally expected. The rapidly expanding network of international cables also contributed added wordage. The cost to dispatch oversized reports consumed reserves and imposed restrictions on the number of words transmitted. Occasional events of great importance made it impossible to condense the news report to meet what increasingly appeared to be an arbitrary word count.[120]

Western Union's limited facilities in the west after the Civil War, and a consequent obligation to divide the service into an eastern and western report, precluded the flexibility necessary to take advantage of a paucity of news in one section by omitting words in that class and adding them to the other. Keeping the New York report within limits was manageable, but the newspapers of the

---

[118] *Proceedings* (Detroit, 1869), 9–11.

[119] House Judiciary Committee, "In the Matter of the Western Union Telegraph Company," 43rd Cong., 1875, HJ-T1, RG233, pp. 37–40, NA; M. Klein, *Unfinished Business: The Railroad in American Life* (Hanover, NH: University Press of New England, 1994), pp. 122–35.

[120] For example, see the Cleveland *Herald*, March 7, 1865 and the Milwaukee *Daily Sentinel*, November 12, 1866. See also *Proceedings* (Detroit, 1870), 15 and *Proceedings* (Detroit, 1876), 6. Between June and July, the total number of words transmitted from the west dropped from 208,625 to 88,337 and did not return to normal levels until November.

west desired more news from their region. Even with close economy and the aid of telegraphic ciphers to reduce the size of the commercial report, there was still excess on the western service, said William Henry Smith, so rapid was "the increase of the country, and so great the demand for the news of this section."[121] A proposed increase in the daily minimum by 10,000 words was only a palliative measure.[122]

By the 1870s, members of the WAP believed their contracts with Western Union restricted the extent of the news reports. Reporting the Franco-Prussian War precipitated a considerable increase in the quantity of telegraphic dispatches. That year, European news consumed more than 250,000 words, an increase of 190,000 words more than the amount contemplated when the WAP was founded. Added to this was an additional 25,000 words transmitted via the cable connecting the United States with Cuba, which was soon extended to Jamaica, Panama, Puerto Rico, and St. Thomas.[123] After the war, the wordage continued to rise. Extraordinary events, such as the agitation in Brooklyn during the infamous Beecher-Tilton scandal in 1872, created a heavy excess of words. In June 1876, the WAP received an excess of 108,500 words, which doubled the size of the report, and the cost of transmission consumed the gains of the previous eight months. Consequently, significantly less news was transmitted between July and October. The Russo-Turkish War occasioned another considerable increase in the number of words the WAP had to transmit over and above its agreed maximum, which meant it had to pay at a higher excess rate.[124]

While the western portion of the country grew, the news reports of the WAP remained stagnant. Demographics and geography had little impact on the proportion of words transmitted from the east and west for use by the WAP. In 1868–1869, when the WAP was entitled to transmit 226,000 words per month, on average it sent 148,000 words from the east and 83,200 from the western cities, a ratio of 1.78. This ratio remained the same throughout the decade, and in 1881–1882 it was 1.6. New York was by far the most important source of news for the WAP; Chicago came in a distant second, followed closely by St. Louis, then New Orleans, and Cincinnati. Cities such as Cleveland, Louisville, and San Francisco were of tertiary importance. By contrast, the NYAP made increasing use of news from the west. Initially, the New York papers had little use for the news report of the western association, but in 1871 they decided to take 40,000 words a month and by 1874 they took the report of the WAP in full (see Table 2.1).[125]

---

[121] *Proceedings* (Detroit, 1871), 2.
[122] *Proceedings* (Detroit, 1875), 8–9.
[123] *Proceedings* (Detroit, 1870), 15.
[124] *Proceedings* (Detroit, 1875), 16; *Proceedings* (Detroit, 1876), 6.
[125] *Proceedings* (Detroit, 1874), 15–16.

TABLE 2.1. *Words transmitted for use by the WAP, 1868–1881*

	1868–1869	1870–1871	1872–1873	1874–1875	1876–1877	1878–1879	1880–1881
New York	1,902,997	2,099,611	1,775,370	2,048,842	1,981,499	1,951,398	2,412,825
Total from East	1,964,096	2,159,400	1,833,531	2,099,708	2,025,434	2,025,718	2,464,699
Chicago	315,721	162,320	206,994	245,656	205,025	253,323	433,364
Cincinnati	184,505	223,017	193,958	140,149	182,404	121,486	148,232
Cleveland	83,641	120,303	106,329	118,015	121,134	126,581	64,072
Indianapolis	7,338	31,973	67,895	82,332	64,220	55,607	45,277
KY, TN, AR			99,174	114,297	58,176	107,228	65,703
Louisville	194,823	138,948	148,959	64,075	50,576	49,342	93,689
New Orleans			139,011	263,690	227,213	167,561	28,408
Pittsburgh	49,722	44,107	77,623	88,579	53,334	138,851	66,458
St. Louis	226,867	169,622	200,318	188,622	240,366	210,581	271,821
San Francisco		21,263	58,833	51,091	113,183	103,811	57,509
Total from West	1,062,617	935,126	1,303,202	1,375,350	1,326,802	1,338,863	1,548,875
Grand total	3,026,713	3,094,526	3,136,733	3,475,058	3,352,236	3,364,581	4,013,574

Source: Compiled from the *Proceedings of the WAP.*

FROM REGIONAL TO NATIONAL COOPERATION: THE
IMPORTANCE OF LEASED LINES

Disputes between the NYAP and the WAP over territory, such as the right to
serve different newspapers in the oil fields of Titusville, Pennsylvania, or concerning the compilation of news from far-western cities, such as Cheyenne and
Denver, illustrated the impracticality of imposing geographical restrictions on
the collection and distribution of news.[126] According to William Henry Smith,

> our work should extend farther to the West and to the Southwest, for those sections are
> by nature and commercial intercourse closely allied to this great central section. But we
> are hampered by the dog-in-manger policy of the New York Associated Press, which
> excludes us.[127]

As the Midwest grew, and as Chicago increased in regional importance, newspapers aligned with New York, such as those in Nebraska, New Orleans, and
Texas, instead desired direct connections with the WAP.[128] If any news was sent
directly to the WAP from NYAP territory, special arrangements had to be made
at large cost for service and tolls, as during the 1875 session of the congressional committee to adjudicate in the case of the "Vicksburg Massacre" and the
negotiations of the Black Hills (Allison) Commission with the Sioux. The obligation to route news via New York delayed transmission between locations,
as from New Orleans to Chicago, and was practical evidence of the need for a
direct connection between the publications of the two locations. Technological
constraints also gave rise to the NYAP's imperious decision to sell without consent direct to the San Francisco *Chronicle* the news report of the WAP, which
the latter claimed as its exclusive property, again affirming the customary property right that existed in unpublished news.[129] Members of the WAP believed
these limitations worked contrary to the natural flow of information and commerce as well as their interests. They sought an abolition of "sectional distinctions in the service" and a more flexible system of distribution and collection,
but because such an arrangement would have made unpredictable demands on
operators and increased labor costs, Western Union refused.[130]

Given the frequency with which such problems arose, there grew up among
various publishers a demand for a nationwide arrangement that would better unite the interests and operations of the eastern and western associations.
As early as 1869, Joseph Medill, publisher of the Chicago *Tribune*, wrote to

---

[126] *Proceedings* (Detroit, 1871), 21–24; *Proceedings* (Detroit, 1872), 25.

[127] *Proceedings* (Detroit, 1875), 17.

[128] *Proceedings* (Detroit, 1873), 19; *Proceedings* (Detroit, 1874), 17; *Proceedings* (Detroit, 1875), 6.

[129] *Proceedings* (Detroit, 1876), 18–22, 24. On early newsgathering in California, see J.D. Carter, "Before the Telegraph: the News Service of the San Francisco *Bulletin*, 1855–1861," *Pacific Historical Review*, 11 (1942), 301–17.

[130] *Proceedings* (Detroit, 1875), 3.

Manton Marble, proprietor of the New York *World*, with considerations on the formation of a nationwide association with "absolute control" in the "hands of the press" so as to prevent it from falling under the influence of "stock gamblers" or Western Union, but archives contain no further mention of it.[131] In 1874, the WAP suggested a "national organization" on the "principle of the Federal Union." Each regional association would appoint one representative to act as manager of a central organization with headquarters at New York, to collect and distribute the news of the world, making an equitable distribution of the expenses of the central organization. Under the arrangement, each association would manage its internal business in its own way, subject to the general rules of the central management. Although the Boston publishers received the suggestion favorably, the New York publishers demurred.[132] In 1879, several representatives from the various associations again considered the possibility of a national association, but failure to arrive at an agreement that suited all parties prohibited action.[133] Despite such disagreements, the industry, by virtue of its cost structure and the economies of scale associated with news provision, was prone to consolidation.

Changes in the telegraph industry provided further impetus to consolidate the activities of the NYAP and the WAP. When Jay Gould, the infamous speculator and industrialist, gained control of Western Union in 1881, James Gordon Bennett Jr., scion of the great penny press provocateur and publisher of the New York *Herald*, along with John J. Mackay, the silver bonanza king, backed construction of a new trans-Atlantic cable and domestic telegraph company with which they could compete against Western Union. To rein in Bennett Jr., and competition from his new Postal Telegraph Company, Gould put Western Union behind the WAP.[134] Combined, the WAP and Western Union forced the NYAP to concede the establishment of a joint-executive committee comprising it and the WAP that consisted of five directors.[135] It helped that Gould owned the New York *World*, and that Cyrus Field, Gould's business partner, owned

---

[131] Medill to Marble, June 30, 1869, Marble, vol. 22, LOC.
[132] R. Smith to Medill, December 13, 1874, W.H. Smith, MIC 22 1/7, OHS.
[133] Minutes of meeting of representatives of various newspaper associations, January 5, 1880, W.H. Smith, Mss 2, box 3, folder 6, OHS; *Proceedings* (Detroit, 1880), 9. The rationale for consolidation is adumbrated in Dickinson, "Points in Favor of a Combination of the four Associated Press Associations of the United States," undated, Delevan Smith papers, box 13, folder 9, IHS.
[134] C. Dana to G. Jones, September 23, 1882, G. Jones papers, box 1, NYPL. Delevan Smith, memorandum, undated, box 13, folder 21, Delevan Smith papers, IHS. Statement for the plaintiffs, *Press Publishing CO. et al. v. WAP*, undated, Delevan Smith papers, IHS; *The Globe* (Atchison, KS), December 28, 1880; "Mr. Gould's latest scheme," St. Louis *Globe-Democrat*, September 20, 1882; "Gould and the newspapers," San Francisco *Daily Evening Bulletin*, September 27, 1882; M. Klein, *The Life and Legend of Jay Gould* (Baltimore: Johns Hopkins University Press, 1997), pp. 312–402.
[135] Eckert to Smith, undated, Delevan Smith, box 13, folder 8, IHS. Schwarzlose, *Newsbrokers*, 2: pp. 93–7.

the New York *Mail and Express*. Field was also the principal financier behind the Atlantic Telegraph Company, which laid the first trans-Atlantic cable in 1858. In 1882, the same year as the formation of the Standard Oil trust, the first major consolidation in American industry, the NYAP and the WAP also formed a combined executive.[136] Newspapers in other regional associations, including those in the northwest, south, and far west, were not represented. William Henry Smith managed the affairs of the combination. Having briefly exercised considerable influence on the structure of the news industry, Gould sold off his newspaper properties and focused his effort on his railways.[137] This episode further demonstrates how the structure of telecommunications and the organization of the news industry were interrelated.

Technological change made practicable the creation of the joint-executive committee as well as a rearrangement of newsgathering facilities and expenses free from sectional interests. A change in the ownership of Western Union coincided with the widespread use of quadruplex telegraphy, which allowed four separate signals (two in each direction) to be transmitted and received on a single wire at the same time.[138] The telegraph network had also grown considerably from a total of 50,000 miles in 1860 to more than 100,000 miles in 1880.[139] A significant increase in the scope and bandwidth of the telegraph network permitted Western Union to lease lines to its users on a considerable scale.[140] Western Union had leased its own lines since the 1870s, but only to a limited extent and principally to free space for the transmission of the commercial news reports it produced. During the 1870s, the perfection of quadruplex telegraphy initially caused Western Union to reduce the number of wires it leased to private parties on routes between towns and cities where the company had many wires and maintained offices.[141] But in the 1880s, having discovered that it was much more profitable to allow users to handle their own dispatches than to handle the report in-house, Gould encouraged the use of leased lines.[142] Leased lines also did away with the need for a cozy relationship between the telegraph company and the news association, which helped to quiet accusations of monopoly and diminish the telegraph company's regulatory concerns. In theory, any news organization could lease lines from Western Union; but in practice, to lease lines was tantamount to vertical

---

[136] N. Lamoreaux, *The Great Merger Movement in American Business, 1895–1904* (Cambridge: Cambridge University Press, 1985), p. 1.

[137] M. Klein, "Gould, Jay," *American National Biography Online* (February 2000).

[138] Gabler, *American Telegrapher*, pp. 53–4.

[139] Lee, *Daily Newspaper*, p. 494.

[140] The lease was for $15,000 per annum, the wire to be used from 17:00 until "good night" was received for the morning papers. Agreement, December 22, 1882, C. Field papers, box 3, folder 5, NYPL.

[141] Orton to Simonton, December 4, 1874, WU, 2004–14, p. 91; Orton to Simonton, December 3, 1875, WU 200B-15, p. 295, SI; Schwarzlose, *Newsbrokers*, 2: pp. 111–12.

[142] R.B. DuBoff, "The Telegraph in Nineteenth-Century America: Technology and Monopoly," *Comparative Studies in Society and History*, 26 (1984), 578; John, *Network Nation*, p. 190.

integration for news organizations and it raised dramatically the capital required to enter the newsgathering business at a competitive level. In this regard, news associations were similar to other American firms, such as American Tobacco, Armour, McCormick Reaper, and Singer Sewing Machine, which also began to integrate vertically during the 1880s.[143]

The de facto vertical integration of news associations into telegraphy incurred a corresponding increase in costs as well as pressures to increase productivity. Between 1871 and 1882, payments to Western Union increased in real terms by $35,600, or 36 percent, and reached a height of $116,844. Between 1882 and 1888, payments to Western Union nearly doubled and so did labor expenses.[144] It was not until the use of leased wires, reflected Charles Diehl, an early staff member of the WAP, that the news association "began to employ newspapermen of training and the highest grade of telegraph operators."[145] To work at maximum capacity, and to keep the eight operators busy on a quadruplex line, none of the receivers could break the circuit. The system thus acted "as a police by driving the operators up to their work. No man can loiter over his key while seven others are watching him." By the mid-1880s, the three quad wires connecting Boston and New York carried almost 3,000 messages daily; the ordinary circuits could only claim an average of 300 to 1,000 telegrams in the same period.[146]

For the news associations, growth in expenditure encouraged attempts to raise productivity by increased capital intensity, which propelled innovation. The pressure that had to be applied to create manifold copies of dispatches, which was at times so great that operators were plagued by cramps, led to the widespread usage of typewriters. The operators of the NYAP-WAP adapted their typewriters to receive directly from the Morse telegraph instrument, an innovation the telegraph companies had thought impossible. The use of typewriters enabled receiving operators to stay ahead of senders, as the receiver could write forty words, while the sender could not make better time than thirty, and typically achieved twenty-five words per minute. In this way, the typewriter prevented logjams and permitted a steady flow of news. In the New York office, where the most copies were required, the chief operator ingeniously substituted a hard rubber roller used in creating manifold copies for a brass one and by this improvement could make thirty copies as easily as one on

---

[143] R.R. John, "Elaborations, Revisions, Dissents: Alfred D. Chandler Jr.'s, "The Visible Hand" after Twenty Years," *The Business History Review*, 71 (1997), 158. A. Chandler, *The Visible Hand: The Managerial Revolution in American Business* (London: Harvard University Press, 1977); N.R. Lamoreaux, Great Merger Movement; John, "Elaborations, revisions, dissents."

[144] Derived from *Proceedings* and Estimated income and expenditures for twelve months on basis of present assessments, January 1, 1892, Delevan Smith, BV 1801 – Register 1891–1892, pp. 101–2, IHS.

[145] C.S. Diehl, *The Staff Correspondent* (San Antonio, TX: Clegg, 1931); *AP Annual Report* (1937–1938), 53.

[146] Gabler, *American Telegrapher*, pp. 53–4.

common paper.[147] This trend continued throughout the nineteenth and into the twentieth century. By 1933, the AP had more than 3,000 automatic telegraph printers in operation, which made it the fourth largest operator of printer equipment in the world. Western Union, the largest, operated approximately 7,000 machines; AT&T was second; and then the Postal Telegraph Company, which operated a slightly larger number of machines than the AP.[148]

The ability of news associations to construct and operate private networks radically altered the business of news collection in the United States. Most importantly, it allowed a solution to a growing bottleneck in news supply. Private networks did away with the inflexible system of news distribution that characterized the period before 1875 and nullified the vexatious limitation Western Union imposed on wordage. Circuits connecting important locations were readily made and adjusted to reflect the natural flow of news, which permitted a unification of the associated press systems in such a manner as to secure the most effective service at a minimum cost. Under the old system, for example, news originating in the western part of the country had to be sent to the NYAP and then resent to the WAP. The leased wire system removed the risk of delay en route to New York so that items could be sent first to Chicago and then rushed eastward.[149] Leased lines also permitted the manager at a distant news center to be in constant and near-instant communication with the head office at Chicago or New York. This was called "talking over the wire," which facilitated the transfer of information and improved the news report.[150]

With leased lines, the associations paid to transmit their reports by the hour instead of by the word, which caused an increase in economies of scale and, by extension, in the size of the news reports. The NYAP-WAP initially leased lines connecting the cities up and down the east coast and also with western cities, such as Denver, Grand Rapids, Minneapolis, and St. Paul, but the service to Pacific coast papers was still conducted via non-leased wires and remained particularly expensive until 1890.[151] The extent of the association's leased-line network was only 10,000 miles in length – by 1948 the AP

[147] The thin tissue was slightly oiled and between each sheet a specially prepared carbonized paper was laid. The copyist wrote with an agate stylus so that the carbon under the pressure combined with the oil of the tissue to form printer's ink wherever the stylus moved. See Beard to W.W. Clapp, January 25, 1887, NEAP, folder 4, Baker Library (hereafter Baker), Harvard University. Williams, "The Associated Press," 8–9; Smith, "The press as a news gatherer," 532; Report of the joint executive committee, undated (1891?), Delevan Smith, box 13, folder 3, IHS. Compare with W. Alpin, "At the Associated Press Office," *Putnam's Magazine*, 16 (July 1870), 23–30. See also J. Yates, *Control through Communication: The Rise of System in American Management* (Baltimore: Johns Hopkins University Press, 1989).
[148] WJM to K. Cooper, December 20, 1933, Series I, box 20, folder 3, AP.
[149] "Interrogation of W.H. Smith," Delevan Smith, box 13, folder 3, IHS.
[150] Williams, "The Associated Press," 9.
[151] WAP expenditures, June 30, 1890, Delevan Smith, BV 1801 – Register 1891–1892, p. 124, IHS.

operated nearly 300,000 miles of wire in the United States – and a considerable quantity of news, estimated in excess of 500,000 words, was sent via Western Union on non-leased lines.[152] Nevertheless, between 1882 and 1891, news copy that entered New York from Baltimore, Philadelphia, and Washington, DC increased from 9,000 to 15,000 words daily, and by 1891, the New York office handled between 75,000 and 100,000 words each day.[153] Midwestern publishers also benefited. Members of the WAP received 750,000 words in 1866 and more than 7 million in 1882. By the late 1880s, the news dispatches were comprehensive enough to constitute between 80 and 100 percent of news copy in Midwestern small town dailies, although the increase in the size of the news report did not immediately translate into an improvement of the service. At first, a large number of worthless items were received daily and not used by any paper in the country.[154]

Exclusive access to the news reports of the NYAP or the WAP had always been an asset, but as the size and quality of the news reports improved from the late 1870s to the 1890s, membership became increasingly valuable. In 1870, William J. Swain, son of William M. Swain, a co-founder of the Philadelphia *Public Ledger*, invested $6,000 (more than $100,000 in today's prices) to obtain membership for the Philadelphia *Public Record*.[155] In 1877, the WAP franchise at Terre Haute, Indiana, the nation's fifth largest producer of distilled liquors and gristmill products with a population of more than 25,000, was worth $1,500 and "sundry considerations of a private nature" (approximately $33,000 in today's prices).[156] By contrast, an 1884 report estimated the value of a franchise in New York at $250,000 ($5.9 million).[157] The book value of these franchises, although subject to debate, was of considerable significance in newspaper valuations. For example, of the $350,000 paid for the New York *World* in 1879, the NYAP franchise was estimated at $250,000.[158] Franchises provided a modicum of stability to the value of a newspaper property, and publishers were concerned to protect their value.[159]

[152] W.H. Smith, "The Press as a News Gatherer," 531, 533; L.R. Campbell and R.E. Wolseley (eds.), *Newsmen at Work: Reporting and Writing the News* (New York: Houghton Mifflin Co., 1949), p. 42.

[153] Meeting of the joint executive committee, January 25, 1883, Delevan Smith, box 1, folder 2, IHS.

[154] Blondheim, *News over the Wires*, p. 170; Schwarzlose, *Newsbrokers*, 2: p. 119; Smith, "The Press as a News Gatherer," 532.

[155] Lee, *Daily newspaper*, p. 509.

[156] M. McCormick, *Terre Haute: Queen City of the Wabash* (Charleston, SC: Arcadia Publishing, 2005), p. 55; *Proceedings* (Detroit, 1880), 4.

[157] Starr, *Creation of the Media*, p. 184.

[158] "Journalistic Enterprise," *Georgia Weekly Telegraph* (Macon, GA), October 21, 1881. Speed to Field, August 1, 1883, C. Field, box 5, folder 4, NYPL. Franchises were considered valuable assets in court. See *Metropolitan Nat. Bank v. St. Louis Dispatch Co. et al.* 36 F. 722 (1893).

[159] Watson R. Sperry (*Morning News*, Wilmington, DE), to Field, March 28, 1884, C. Field, box 5, folder 4, NYPL.

Although they were valuable, exclusive franchises encouraged the formation of rivals. As in other industries at the time, consolidation and vertical integration, although conducive to the generation of market value, did not permit market control.[160] In 1882, Charles Dana, publisher of the New York *Sun*, who disliked Gould and refused to be party to any agreement in which Gould had a hand, led a splinter group of disaffected New York publishers, including Joseph Pulitzer of the *World* and Whitelaw Reid of the *Tribune*, to take control of the United Press Association (UPA) to rival the NYAP. The UPA, which claimed to be a descendant of the American Press Association that vexed the NYAP in the 1870s, was allied with the International Telegram Company, a subsidiary that bought foreign news abroad and sold it to the UPA in New York. John P. Walsh, the infamous Chicago banker – he nearly died in a penitentiary – allegedly controlled the UPA before the New York syndicate under Dana's leadership took up Walsh's bank debts.[161] Although disagreements among the New York members of the NYAP were long-standing, and defections had occurred in the past, invariably the prospect of going it alone was too frightening, and mutinous members returned to the fold.[162] Although the defection in 1882 was more damaging to the NYAP than previous disputes, it was short lived.[163]

Rivalry between the NYAP-WAP and the UPA was brief, but intense. The UPA was a joint-stock company, with a capital stock of $1 million, which distinguished it from the associational structure of its principal rivals and forebears. The newspapers that took its service were clients, not partners or members. The UPA sought to undermine the NYAP-WAP by appealing to the mass of smaller papers throughout the country. With its vast resources and expensive machinery, claimed the UPA, the NYAP-WAP furnished to its clients in Boston, Chicago, Cincinnati, New York, and other cities "an amount of material sufficient to swamp even such omnivorous journals as the New York *Herald*, the Chicago *Tribune* and the Cincinnati *Enquirer*, but the service to the second-class cities is abridged and unsatisfactory to the last degree." This strategy appeared to be successful in New England, but "it was the stupidity that was shown by the [NYAP-WAP] in keeping out such papers as the Boston *Globe* in New England and the Chicago *Herald* in the West," wrote Walter Phillips, manager of the UPA, "that made it possible for The United Press to grow up."[164]

---

[160] The influx of competition after consolidation was widespread. Lamoreaux, *Great Merger Movement*, p. 139.

[161] E.W. Scripps to R. Howard, Howard, UIB; Statement of Haldeman, undated, Lawson, box 113, folder 730, NL; Confidential statement made by Mr. Reid to Mr. Bennett, June 30, 1891, W.H. Smith, Mss 2, box 13, vol. 31, OHS; E.H. Butler to M.E. Stone, February 5, 1908, Edward Butler (Butler) papers, E.H. Butler Library, Buffalo State College (hereafter Buffalo).

[162] Marble, vols. 14, 15, LOC.

[163] Dana to Jones, September 23, 1882, George Jones papers, box 1, NYPL.

[164] For the quote, see Phillips to Stephen O'Meara, 31 Mar. 1890, NEAP, folder 15, Baker. On the relative success of the UPA, see Lawson to McLaughlan, November 1, 1893, Lawson, box 113,

The service provided by the UPA was insufficiently different from that of the NYAP-WAP to justify to publishers the added expenditure. Instead, the rivalry between the two organizations undermined cooperation and increased expenses. "After you have both wasted several hundred thousand dollars by the competition," wrote Norvin Green of Western Union to Charles Dana, "you will realize the folly of obtaining duplicate news reports not only by cable but from all quarters of the country at a double expense … and you will then agree on terms to unite your interests and work in harmony."[165] Green had the interests of Western Union in mind, as well as the benefit it would obtain from a single organization dedicated to the use of the company's wires, but his admonition proved accurate. The leased lines of the two organizations overlapped and their news reports often contained duplicate matter.

By 1885, three years after Dana's secession, the NYAP-WAP joint-executive committee and the UPA were ready for peace. The two parties contrived a secret stock swap that provided for an exchange of news that expanded the UPA's news coverage. The UPA was to be "a conservative competitor who does not demoralize business," wrote Delevan Smith, a senior director on the WAP board. Maintaining the corporate identity of the UPA warded off potential rivals and provided a service to those newspapers otherwise excluded from the news reports of the NYAP-WAP. The contract prevented rivals of the members of the NYAP-WAP from receiving comprehensive news reports. The UPA sold the news it received cheaply from the NYAP-WAP at a profit and disbursed these profits to its shareholders. The stock swap was kept secret, therefore the clients of the UPA could receive a modified and reduced report of the news provided to members of the NYAP-WAP. Profits from this arrangement were distributed among those newspapers party to the secret agreement and in rebates to members. An agreement between the UPA and the NYAP-WAP joint-executive committee enabled the adjustment of differences among members, sub-associations, and clients of the UPA throughout the country.[166] For example, on the Pacific coast, where the California Associated Press was determined to go into business independently of the NYAP-WAP, the UPA rejected every overture made by the Californians. Its inability to make an alliance with the UPA at any time during the two years that it attempted to establish itself in opposition to the NYAP and WAP forced the Californian association to go out of business and the NYAP-WAP was enabled to renew its undisputed sovereignty on

folder 730, NL. "The United Press A.D. 1882," NEAP, folder 1, Baker. Confidential statement made by M. Reid to Mr. Bennett, June 30, 1891, W.H. Smith, box 8, folder 11, OHS. William Henry Smith, Statement of the general manager, undated, Delevan Smith, box 13, folder 17, IHS. Fletcher to Clapp, January 24, 1890; Hartford *Courant* to Clapp, March 26, 1887, NEAP, folder 5 and folder 8, Baker. See also letters in folders 11 and 12. W.H. Smith to Clapp, April 8, 1887, NEAP, folder 15, Baker. See Schwarzlose, *Newsbrokers*, 2: pp. 131–6.

[165] Green to Dana, October 27, 1882, WU, 203A-G4, p. 355, SI.

[166] Phillips to O'Meara, March 31, 1890, NEAP, folder 15, Baker; W.H. Smith to Halstead, undated, Delevan Smith, box 13, folder 10, IHS.

the Pacific coast. During the time that the modus vivendi with the UPA was in operation, there were many occasions when, if the UPA had not been bound to the NYAP-WAP by the joint committee agreement, it could have made a permanent alliance with one of the regional organizations.

Despite advantages, these agreements among the several news organizations were insufficiently binding to prevent opportunistic behavior. More importantly, they also failed to provide sufficient protection for exclusive franchises. It was difficult to police the agreement, and publishers not privy to the details of it were suspicious of the transfer payments made among the different factions. The UPA continued to sell franchises, cut rates, and give its news to rivals of the NYAP-WAP.[167] Certain newspapers, in contravention of association bylaws, received the UPA report in addition to that of the NYAP-WAP. Members of the NYAP-WAP were angry to discover that their supposedly exclusive news was shared with publishers outside the association. Victor Lawson, publisher of the Chicago *Daily News* and a principal member of the WAP, was especially upset that the Chicago *Herald*, his main rival, received the NYAP-WAP news report gratis.[168] When, in 1891, the WAP's contract with Western Union came up for renewal, Lawson and a group of other Midwestern publishers called for an investigation of the agreement between the UPA and the joint-executive committee, which led to a collapse of the secret agreement. Lawson's goal was to form a new agreement that secured his paper, and those of his friends, exclusive possession of the news but also encouraged cooperation and discouraged opportunistic behavior. In 1892, Lawson set out independently to form the AP as an organization distinct from the internecine wrangling among the WAP, NYAP, and the UPA.

Between 1848 and 1892, newspaper publishers throughout the United States searched for private solutions to the problems and potential telegraphy presented for newsgathering. They sought to devise a new institutional arrangement as gathering news by post gradually became antiquated. Cooperation, which at first was a local affair run by the newspapers of New York, grew to a nationwide endeavor largely controlled by the newspapers of Chicago. Technological constraints may have generated the incentive to cooperate, but it was the lure of exclusivity that prompted the newspaper publishers of New York to combine their efforts. The collusive combination of Western Union and the NYAP – of conduits and of content – reinforced exclusivity, but at the expense of increased cooperation. As the nation's newspaper press and telegraph network expanded, exclusivity artificially constrained the free flow of news and invited competition. Technological limitations created a bottleneck in the supply of news that at once furthered regional cooperation but undermined nationwide integration. Leased lines eliminated this bottleneck in supply, which

---

[167] W.H. Smith to Clapp, NEAP, folder 1, Baker.
[168] Associated Press papers having UP franchises, undated, Delevan Smith, box 13, folder 19, IHS.

enabled publishers to begin coordinating the establishment of a nationwide news association. Alongside these technological developments, state-based legislation allowed for the creation of exclusive news associations, and the threat of federal regulation encouraged greater inclusivity but left room for private initiative. The state was permissive, not absent, and allowed the press to seek a balance between cooperation and exclusivity while attempting to forge a new institutional arrangement for the supply of news by telegraph.

3

Cooperation, Competition, and Regulation in the United States, 1893–1945

Although the increase in competition that telegraphy generated during the 1840s encouraged newspapers to cooperate, the limited reach of the nascent communications network, and the consequent costs of coordination among a large group of publishers, kept participation in these early news organizations small, personal, and regional. Limited telegraph bandwidth, and then opportunistic behavior, prevented the loose federation of news associations that emerged after the Civil War from establishing a comprehensive nationwide organization. Yet, by 1897, the operations of the Associated Press not only encompassed the territory from the East Coast to the West, it had eliminated potential rivals and consolidated its control over the newsgathering business of the country. The path to the establishment of a nationwide news association lay not through merger or horizontal integration, but through the maintenance of exclusivity and the elimination of competitors.

THE FORMATION AND ASCENDANCE OF THE AP

Following disagreeable revelations about the secret agreements between the WAP and UPA, Lawson and several Midwestern publishers fulminated a rearrangement of relations that would better serve their interests and protect their exclusive franchises. Their efforts culminated in December 1892 with the incorporation of the AP in Chicago, which that year surpassed Philadelphia as the second largest city in the United States.[1] The AP charter entitled the association to not only to "buy, gather and accumulate information and news; to vend, supply, distribute and publish the same," but also "to purchase, erect, lease operate, and sell telegraph and telephone lines and other means of transmitting news; to publish periodicals; to make and deal in periodicals." The

[1] Mott, *American Journalism*, p. 561.

46

AP reserved the right to erect and operate telegraphs for fear that relations with Western Union might sour or that Western Union might either raise its rates or enter the news business.[2] In other respects, the new association was much the same as the WAP, save that Lawson was in charge. Initially, Lawson and his friends contemplated the continuance of an integrated two-firm solution, believing that closer cooperation between Chicago and New York might advantageously stifle competition from hostile third parties. During the winter of 1892–1893, Lawson drew up the bylaws of the AP in conjunction with executives of the UPA.[3]

Although members from the New England, Southern, Western, and other regional organizations entertained the formation of "one grand national organization" with a federated structure centered in New York, Lawson, perhaps nervous about going it alone, was reluctant to agree to plans for a "National Associated Press."[4] Instead, in October 1892, he and several other Midwestern publishers signed a secret and exclusive three-way agreement with the Southern Associated Press and UPA to divide the American news market. Adolph Ochs, then publisher of the Chattanooga (TN) *Times* (he purchased the New York *Times* in 1896), represented the Southern Associated Press, and William Henry Smith and William Penn Nixon, publisher of the Chicago *Inter-Ocean*, established in 1872 as the political organ of the "Stalwart" ring of the Republican party of the west, represented the UPA.[5] In effect, this secret agreement meant that the remaining members of the NYAP – the *Herald*, the *World*, and the *Times* – were cut out, which precipitated the demise of the NYAP and its absorption by the UPA.[6]

There were several benefits to Lawson and his Midwestern friends of these modifications to the status quo. It ensured better protection for their franchises; the AP gained undisputed possession of the Midwestern territory and retained rights to gather and sell news anywhere; and, perhaps most importantly, combination secured exclusive access to the news reports of Central News, which was allied with several of the newspapers of New York, and Reuters, the two principal British foreign news services transmitted to the United States. Exclusive access to these news reports, wrote Lawson, meant "no effective competition

---

[2] McCormick to W. Kirkland, May 4, 1943, and unsigned memo (perhaps McCormick), undated, McCormick, box 9, Cantigny.

[3] Memo pertaining to a new joint-association, undated (c. October 10, 1892), Lawson, box 2, folder 4, pp. 188–91, NL; Lawson memo, undated, Lawson, box 2, folder 4, p. 238, NL. Concluding correspondence relating to the work of the conference committee, July 1, 1895, Lawson, box 112, folder 729, p. 73, NL; Digest of verbatim board minutes, December 11, 1912, AP01.1, series III, box 3 folder 26, p. 247, AP.

[4] SAP volume, September 20, 1892, pp. 25–9, Adolph Ochs papers, 34a, NYPL.

[5] Agreement, October 24, 1892, Lawson, box 2, folder 4, p. 245, NL; Lawson to G.G. Howland, October 25, 1892, Lawson, box 2, folder 4, p. 251, NL. Lee, *History of American Journalism*, p. 375.

[6] Lawson to H. Mends, October 26, 1892, Lawson, box 2, folder 4, pp. 255–9, NL. Schwarzlose, *Newsbrokers*, 2: p. 167.

[was] therefore possible against it."⁷ The disadvantages of this arrangement were similar to those that plagued earlier interlocking agreements: UPA papers in AP territory would receive the AP report in addition, and a division of territory precluded the possibility of unified effort and consequently constrained economies. These disadvantages rapidly vitiated the advantages derived from the perpetuation of agreements. Coordination in New York between the former members of the NYAP and the UPA proved complicated, the exchange of stock among members of the UPA and the AP was problematic, and the division of territory was divisive. By March 1893, Lawson anticipated a war with the UPA, although he remained keen for peace.⁸ In July, the UPA, which united the principal papers of New York behind it, declared war.⁹ Only thereafter did Lawson become convinced that the AP, as he wrote to Charles H. Grasty of the Baltimore *Evening News* in December 1894, was "designed to be the one dominant, controlling, national news-gathering organization."¹⁰

In the ensuing battle between the AP of Chicago and the UPA of New York, the different business models of the two organizations were a decisive factor. The UPA was an openly commercial organization. Although both the AP and UPA incorporated as corporations for profit, the AP issued stock to overcome differences among its members, not to declare dividends. The AP service was rendered at cost; therefore, there were no disbursements. Members of the AP argued that the pursuit of profit offered no protection for consumer interests. Instead, wrote Lawson, "the open and avowed purpose of making dividends on its capital" meant that at the UPA "the temptation to excessive assessment is obvious."¹¹ According to members of the AP, the UPA executives were financiers "of the typical Wall Street kind," "mercenary sharks," and speculators in pursuit of a trust "more lucrative than the sugar, the oil, the cordage, or any other of the numerous modern monopolies which have grown fat at the expense of legitimate trade of the country."¹² It would "not only be dangerous to the rights of the clients," wrote Lawson to Harrison Gray Otis, president and general manager of the Los Angeles *Times*, but "the service itself would inevitably deteriorate."¹³

The UPA countered that it was impracticable, if not impossible, for the AP to coordinate the exchange of news before publication among the numerous

⁷ Lawson to M.H. de Young, October 26, 1892, Lawson, box 2, folder 4, pp. 261–5, NL.
⁸ Lawson to Driscoll, March 9, 1893, Lawson, box 2, folder 5, pp. 211–14, NL; Lawson to Driscoll, May 18, 1893, Lawson, box 2, folder 5, pp. 317–19, NL; Lawson to Driscoll, June 7, 1893, Lawson, box 2, folder 5, pp. 358–60, NL.
⁹ Report of the executive committee, July 28, 1893, Lawson, box 2, folder 5, pp. 178–93, NL.
¹⁰ Lawson to Grasty, December 17, 1894, Lawson, box 3, folder 6, NL.
¹¹ Lawson to Eggleston, March 8, 1900, Lawson, box 4, folder 9, pp. 38–41, NL; Lawson to McLaughlan, November 1, 1893, Lawson, box 113, folder 730, NL.
¹² "The United Press...," undated, Rosewater, box 20, folder 17, AJA. J.E. Scripps, "The Associated Press v. The United Press," September 11, 1893, Rosewater, box 20, folder 17, AJA.
¹³ Lawson to H.G. Otis, July 30, 1895, Lawson, box 3, folder 6, p. 919, NL.

and various newspapers of the country on an ostensibly cooperative basis. The cooperative model, wrote Walter Phillips, manager of the UPA, was "a cumbersome piece of machinery." "It is like attempting to steer a ship with a multitude of rudders.... No railroad, no newspaper, no bank, no insurance company, no business has ever succeeded in which several hundred men had equal shares in the management and meddled alike in its affairs." Rather than promote an alternative method of governance for a nationwide organization, Philips favored a "federation of the various associations, each to preserve its autonomy and to govern itself in its own fashion."[14] This was a strategic blunder. For Lawson and other members of the AP, the debate had shifted. Federation was inconceivable; the question was which model of newsgathering would predominate.[15]

The vituperation of the AP and the UPA obscured the advantages and disadvantages of their respective methods of governance and organization. In fact, the AP was more monopolistic than the UPA. The AP granted so called first-class papers exclusive franchises that covered a geographic area 120-miles in diameter. Within their territory these members could veto applications for admission. First-class members, who took the entire news service and paid full tolls, rendered by their corps of correspondents a larger service to the AP than others, who covered only the local news of their city. Voting privileges protected these exclusive franchises from alteration. Each first-class member took eight voting shares, whereas other newspapers were allowed only one each. Additionally, contracts were made for more than ninety years to protect franchise rights from changes in administration. The "absolute mutuality of financial interests" among first-class members, wrote Lawson to M.H. de Young, editor of the San Francisco *Chronicle*, ensured "permanence of our franchises."[16] Other newspapers included in the association, wrote Lawson, had "no voice at all."[17] Second-class members were mostly foreign-language newspapers. They had no exclusive rights. Third-class papers took a limited service, called a pony report.[18] All members, however, were required to send exclusively to the AP – and before publication – all the breaking news within their territory, or within a thirty-mile radius from their place of publication. Members caught violating the rules of the AP could be fined, suspended, or expelled.

The UPA also provided exclusive franchises, which it sold to clients, but the AP's method of organization better protected these privileges. Being motivated by the pursuit of profit, the UPA was encouraged to serve all customers at a reasonable rate, or to charge a high rate for exclusive access, whereas

---

[14] "The United Press," June–July, 1895, Rosewater, box 20, folder 17, AJA.

[15] Lawson to S. O'Meara, February 6, 1897, Lawson, box 3, folder 7, p. 977, NL.

[16] Lawson to de Young, October 26, 1892, Lawson, box 2, folder 4, NL.

[17] Lawson to A. Bechhoffer, February 2, 1894, Lawson, box 2, folder 5, NL.

[18] Minutes of stockholders meeting, October 22, 1892, Lawson, box 113, folder 730, NL.

members in the AP with exclusive rights benefited from a system of assessments in which rivals were excluded without any increase in payment.[19] The tendency to extort high payments for exclusivity, a practice the UPA had employed since the 1880s, caused the AP to create a bylaw that prohibited members from receiving the news of any businesses declared "antagonistic" to the association. Aside from curtailing the development of rival associations, this bylaw reduced the likelihood that newspapers would be obliged to purchase exclusive franchises at extortionate prices, and not for the value of the news they entailed, but simply to prevent rivals from buying them.[20]

Exclusive franchises encouraged newspapers to join the AP, adhere to its bylaws, and fight for its ascendancy. Franchises were tangible assets and property rights of value beyond the news they entailed. In 1896, Lawson, perhaps optimistically, valued an AP franchise in Chicago at $11,000, or nearly $300,000 in today's prices.[21] Much of this value derived from exclusive possession of the news reports of the AP. "The exclusive character of the news," wrote Charles W. Knapp, president of the St. Louis *Republic*, was "an essential element of its value, and incentive to its collection."[22] Publishers wielded their exclusive contracts to prevent the emergence of rivals. From Omaha, Nebraska to New Bedford, Massachusetts, and numerous locations in between, members objected to the admission of rivals on an equal basis.[23] In other instances, incumbent members refused to admit new papers without compensation in the form of entry fees or rebates for the money already invested in the association.[24] Lawson had to plead with Joseph Pulitzer to waive his exclusive rights and admit William Randolph Hearst's *Journal of Commerce* as well as Adolph Ochs's New York *Times*.[25] Pulitzer actively prevented Hearst from obtaining an AP franchise in New York, and although he eventually agreed to admit the *Journal*, Pulitzer came to regret it as "one of the stupidest mistakes."[26] He also admitted the New York *Times* to membership, but not without stipulating that it be of secondary status and that its franchise could never pass to Hearst.[27]

[19] F.W. Lehmann, *Laws of the Associated Press* (New York, 1909), p. 41.

[20] See, for example, F.B. Noyes to Swayne & Swayne, February 28, 1898, AP01.1, correspondence of Noyes, box 1, folder 1, AP.

[21] Lawson to Rocky Mountain News Printing Co., July 23, 1896, Lawson, box 3, folder 7, NL.

[22] Knapp and Diehl to members, September 14, 1900, Ochs, box 53, folder 9, NYPL.

[23] Rosewater to Stone, May 3, 1895, Rosewater, box 19, folder 17, AJA; Edmund Anthony & Sons to Fletcher, August 8, 1890, NEAP, folder 12, Baker.

[24] Rosewater to Stone, May 2, 1897, Rosewater, box 19, folder 17, AJA; Stone to Rosewater, August 12, 1895, Rosewater, box 19, folder 17, AJA.

[25] Lawson to Pulitzer, November 20, 1895, Lawson, box 3, folder 7, pp. 362–4, NL; Lawson to Knapp, January 14, 1896, Lawson, box 3, folder 7, p. 446, NL; Lawson to Pulitzer, March 5, 1896, Lawson, box 3, folder 7, p. 539, NL; Lawson to Knapp, October 3, 1896; Lawson to Campbell, October 10, 1896, Lawson, box 3, folder 7, p. 725, 730, NL.

[26] Lawson to Pulitzer, July 17, 1896, Lawson, box 3, folder 7, pp. 678–80, NL; Pulitzer to RP, September 28, 1907, Joseph Pulitzer papers, Mss 37044, box 6, LOC.

[27] Lawson to Nicholson, February 26, 1897, Lawson, box 4, folder 8, pp. 311–13, NL.

The protection that the AP's method of organization afforded enabled it to attract a critical mass of members quickly. After several of the principal American dailies joined the association, other publishers desired to be connected to the same network for the exchange of news. In the contest of the 1890s, such "network effects" helped the AP to beat the UPA. In 1895, the UPA had 338 members to the AP's 396. By 1897, the AP had 637 members.[28] That year, the executives of the UPA filed for bankruptcy. The New York *Sun*, the principal member of the UPA, continued to operate a wire service known as the Laffan News Bureau, named after William Laffan, its manager, who had joined the *Sun* in 1877.[29] In 1900, the Laffan News Bureau and the AP signed a collusive agreement that prevented the Laffan News Bureau from selling its news to members of the AP, except for several select newspapers, and the AP in return agreed not to suspend those select members allowed to take the Laffan Service. Despite this separate peace, the *Sun* was barred from membership in the association until Frank Munsey purchased it in 1916.[30] The paper disappeared shortly thereafter, when, in 1920, Munsey merged it with the New York *Herald*.

THE LEGAL LIMITS OF EXCLUSIVITY: *INTER-OCEAN V. AP* AND THE MEMBERSHIP CORPORATIONS LAW OF NEW YORK

If exclusive access to the news reports of the AP strengthened the competitive position of its members, it also increased the strength of the association. It was a long-standing explicit policy of the AP to guarantee the news to a limited number of newspapers and to build them thereby into strong, substantial, permanent, and paying members of the association, which in turn increased the permanency and power of the AP.[31] Despite the benefits it initially provided, exclusivity created two problems over time: first, attempting to prevent certain publications from access to its news reports brought the AP into conflict with the courts and with competition policy; and second, although it ensured the market value of members' franchises, it prevented the association from growing or expanding the share of the market it could serve. Those publications left without an AP news service patronized rivals.

During the 1890s, associations, whether commercial cartels or labor unions, occupied a central role in debates over the limits of the liberty of

---

[28] Schwarzlose, *Newsbrokers*, 2: p. 248.

[29] C. Stone, *Dana and the Sun* (New York: Dodd, Mead & Co., 1938), p. 44.

[30] W.L. McLean et al. to W. Laffan, September 20, 1900, 01.2, AP; Baehr Jr., *The New York Tribune*, p. 226.

[31] Occasionally, however, the AP became attached to a loser, as in Taunton (MA). See F.R. Martin to B.H. Anthony, May 9, 1923, AP01.2, KC, box 7, folder 10, AP.

contract and the boundaries of the public interest, and the rules of the AP, in part owing to the democratic qualities attributed to news, were also subjected to judicial and legislative scrutiny.[32] The collapse of the UPA in 1897, and the resultant inability of certain newspapers to obtain news of the Spanish-American War, coverage of which cost the AP more than $7 million in today's prices, increased demand for state intervention among those newspapers excluded from the association. To counteract pilfering of its news reports, the AP offered rewards of $20,000 ($500,000) leading to the arrest and conviction of those caught misappropriating its news.[33] In 1898, Kentucky, Tennessee, and Texas passed bills to compel the AP to admit any applicant.[34] Speaking with respect to the bill in Kentucky, one State Representative said the AP was a "monopoly" that "seeks to control public thought itself."[35] State legislatures in Mississippi and Nebraska subsequently passed similar laws.[36]

Other newspapers excluded from the AP challenged the legality of its bylaws in court. In 1891, Dunlap's News Company, a private news agency, brought a suit against the NYAP, which had threatened to discontinue its service to newspapers if they patronized Dunlap's.[37] Dunlap's sought an injunction against the restraint imposed by the New York association. Dunlap's argued that collecting and distributing the news was a "public business," and therefore the New York association was under an "obligation to serve the entire public." Additionally, Dunlap's alleged that having the report of the NYAP was "essential for the proper conduct of a newspaper," and that it was critical to "the interest of the public" that newspapers be at liberty to employ all sources of information. The court denied Dunlap's application for an injunction. "Exclusive dealing" was an "ordinary limitation." The association "had a perfect right to limit the sale of the news collected by its members to those who contracted exclusively with them," and the claim of Dunlap's amounted to nothing more than an attempt to enhance its business.

In the case of *Mathews*, which the New York Court of Appeals decided in 1893, the publishers of the Buffalo *Express* and of the Buffalo *Courier* brought proceedings against the New York State Associated Press, a separate

[32] R.J.R. Peritz, *Competition Policy in America, 1888–1992* (Oxford: Oxford University Press, 1996), p. 28.

[33] Stone to members, November 10, 1898, Lawson, box 112, folder 729, p. 141, NL. Stone to AP, January 1, 1898, Lawson, box 112, folder 729, p. 119, NL.

[34] *AP Annual Report* (1898–1899), 3–4, 71. See also *Laws of Kentucky, 1898*, No 172 in *Carroll's Kentucky Statutes* (1936), ss. 883a-1 to 883a-4 and *Michie's Tennessee Code* (1938), Mss 6759–6761. W.F. Swindler, "The AP Anti-trust Case in Historical Perspective," *Journalism Quarterly*, 23:1 (March 1946), 47.

[35] "Exposes News Trust," *Inter-Ocean* (Chicago), February 8, 1898, Ochs, vol. 35b, NYPL.

[36] Lehmann, *Laws of the Associated Press.*

[37] *Dunlap's Cable News Co. v. Stone et al.*, 15 N.Y.S. 2 (1891). Dunlap's was in cahoots with Dalziel's, which collected news internationally and briefly competed with Reuters in Britain.

organization but similar in most respects to the NYAP, for an injunction to prevent their suspension from the association after they were both found to be taking the news reports of the UPA.[38] The bylaw, wrote Judge Peckham for the court, had a "tendency to strengthen the association and to render it more capable of filling the duty it was incorporated to perform"; therefore, it seemed "most appropriate that the members of such [an] association should not take news from any other." The latest decisions of the courts in the United States showed a "strong tendency to very greatly circumscribe and narrow the doctrine of avoiding contracts in restraint of trade," wrote Judge Peckham, who himself led the trend, and the bylaw of the association was not in restraint of trade "as the courts now interpret that phrase"; so the application for an injunction failed. The fact that Judge Peckham approved of such rules in *Mathews*, only to adopt a literalist interpretation of the Sherman Act in *Trans-Missouri* four years later, highlights the distinction that existed between the restraints doctrine and competition policy.[39]

Outside New York, the restraints doctrine was still seen as a means to preserve competition. In 1894, in a dispute between the AP and the Washington News Co. (1894), the important question, as in *Mathews*, was whether the AP could prevent the *Evening News* from receiving the news report of a rival organization. The District of Columbia Court of Appeal was unable to see that in receiving the news of a competitor the *Evening News* injured the AP. Taking two news reports, held the court, granted nothing to the competitor that it took away from the AP, and therefore did not tend to divide the business of the AP. Additionally, the court reasoned that to prevent the *Evening News* from receiving other news reports would "give a monopoly to the complainant." The court said that the contracts of the AP reduced competition and so were unenforceable. Unable to prevent the *Evening News* from receiving the report of a competitor, the AP discontinued its service to the paper altogether.[40]

However distinct the restraints doctrine and competition policy may have been in Judge Peckham's mind, the two became increasingly blurred during the 1890s. Peckham's opinion in *Mathews* was mentioned repeatedly in antitrust cases adjudicated later in the decade, including *Knight* and *Addyston Pipe*.[41] Thanks to Peckham, the rules of the AP were welcome in New York,

---

[38] *Mathews v. AP*, 32 N.E. 981 (1893). The New York State Associated Press was different from the NYAP insofar as it incorporated in 1867 under a special act of the New York legislature (chapter 754 of the laws of 1867).

[39] Compare *Mathews v. AP*, 32 N.E. 981 (1893) and *U.S. v. Trans-Missouri Freight Association*, 166 U.S. 290 (1897). See H. Hovenkamp, *Enterprise and American Law, 1836–1937* (London: Harvard University Press, 1991), p. 285.

[40] As quoted in *AP Annual Report* (1894–1895), 42–54.

[41] *U.S. v. E.C. Knight*, 156 U.S. 1 (1895) Record, Brief for the appellant, p. 25; *Addyston Pipe v. U.S.*, 175 U.S. 211 (1899). Transcript of Record, p. 306.

but the restraints doctrine was interpreted differently in other jurisdictions.[42] A new theory emerged during the late 1890s that held when a firm or a group of firms acting together dominated a market, such that buyers in the market lacked adequate alternatives, then price increases or refusals to deal could be inherently coercive.[43] The Supreme Court of Illinois applied this theory in *Inter-Ocean v. Associated Press*.[44]

The AP had suspended the *Inter-Ocean* for subscribing to news reports from the Laffan News Bureau, among other organizations, in contravention of the AP's bylaws, and the *Inter-Ocean* sought an injunction to prohibit implementation of the suspension. There is reason to suspect that the expulsion of the *Inter-Ocean* from the AP was politically motivated. Since its formation in 1872, the *Inter-Ocean* – which predated Lawson's establishment of the *Daily News* in 1875 – had passed to Herman Kohlsaat, who had purchased it with the backing of Charles T. Yerkes, the notorious speculator and Chicago's streetcar boss. In addition to being a source of competition for Lawson, Yerkes, who became chief owner of the *Inter-Ocean* in 1897, used the paper to attack Lawson's *Daily News* and Medill's *Tribune*, who protested against Yerkes's schemes for Chicago's streetcar system. Whatever the reason behind the expulsion of the *Inter-Ocean*, the Supreme Court of Illinois sided with Yerkes.

The court's rationale for circumscribing the AP's behavior rested on two pillars. The first derived from the AP's charter. The clause in its articles of incorporation that enabled it to erect, operate, and purchase telegraph lines, said the court, made the business of the AP "essentially public in its nature." A telegraph company was "bound to treat all persons and corporations alike, and without discrimination in its business of receiving and transmitting messages." Additionally, "where one is the owner of property which is devoted to a use in which the public has an interest, he in effect grants to the public an interest in such use, and must, to the extent of that interest, submit to be controlled by the public for the common good as long as such use is maintained." By reason of its ability to construct telegraph lines, the AP "voluntarily sought corporate existence to engage in an enterprise which invested it with, among others, the power of eminent domain," and, "a corporation so engaged" was "amenable to public control." In effect, the AP could be regulated like a public utility.

The second pillar of the court's holding was that the news reports of the AP were an essential facility for newspapers. No newspaper, held the court, could independently obtain the same amount of information provided by the AP and no paper could be regarded as a newspaper of worth unless it had access

[42] See, for example, the suit of the Washington, DC *Evening News. AP Annual Report* (1894–1895), 42–54; "Associated Press defeated," New York *Times*, June 10, 1894. Hovenkamp, *Enterprise*, pp. 272, 281. C.K. Burdick, "Origin of Peculiar Duties of Public Service Companies," *Columbia Law Review*, 11 (1911), 764.
[43] Hovenkamp, *Enterprise*, pp. 290, 295.
[44] *Inter-Ocean v. AP*, 184 Ill. 438 (1900).

to and published the reports of the association. The news provided by the AP was "of vast importance to the public, so that public interest is attached to the dissemination of that news"; consequently, all newspapers desiring to buy such news for publication were entitled to purchase it without discrimination against them. The court concluded that the association's exclusive dealing obligations restricted trade and tended toward a monopoly capable of dictating the character of news furnished to the public. In contrast, in 1901, a year after the decision of the Illinois Supreme Court in *Inter-Ocean* was handed down, the Supreme Court of Missouri, when adjudicating a similar case, found no authority to hold that business that was otherwise without a public interest became so merely by reason of its extent.[45]

Although these cases are now forgotten, at the time they became part of the larger debate over the distinction between businesses held to be private and those clothed with a public interest, which questioned the degree to which the trusts that dominated certain facets of American enterprise could be regulated and, by extension, be declared a public calling.[46] By arguing that the AP bylaw prohibiting members from receiving news from other organizations tended to create a monopoly, the Illinois Supreme Court in effect held that the AP sought to monopolize the patronage of newspaper publishers. A sufficient number of publishers were brought into membership so that the magnitude of the association made it impossible for those newspaper publishers denied admission to acquire and transmit successfully the same volume and variety of news at similar cost. By this reasoning, the relative difference in the cost of gathering news determined the existence of a monopoly in a press association, but it was unclear at what point the variation in expenses of competitors produced illegality or if size automatically had an adverse effect on competition.[47] The scope, volume, and variety of the news report, productivity of the association, and other factors affected the cost of gathering news, therefore the court's test was a problematic, although practicable, measure of monopoly. Seen in this light, the right to regulate was not highly principled, but a question of degree.

To escape the Illinois Supreme Court's decision in *Inter-Ocean*, the AP changed domicile. After the trial, members of the AP threatened to abandon the organization if it violated their exclusive contracts, and newspapers excluded from the association instituted suits against it. In an attempt to augment his position in the competitive Chicago newspaper market, William Randolph Hearst, the ascendant newspaper baron, sought to force the entrance into membership of certain of his papers then excluded from the association by means

[45] *Star Publishing Co. v. AP*, 159 Mo. 410, 60 .W. 91 (1901).

[46] "Associated Press as a Public Calling," *Harvard Law Review* 13 (April 1900), 681–2; B. Wyman, "Competition and the Law," *Harvard Law Review* 15 (February 1902), 431–2; B. Wyman, "The Law of the Public Callings as a Solution to the Trust Problem. II," *Harvard Law Review*, 17 (February 1904), 299.

[47] As Lawson observed. Lawson to Stone, March 21, 1900, Lawson, box 4, folder 9, pp. 51–8, NL.

of the Illinois courts.[48] Fortunately for the AP, the rules governing property and contract rights varied from state to state. The United States Constitution of 1787 created a national market for free trade, but – at least until the New Deal – the peacetime operation of the Constitution's federal system ensured that the rules governing property rights varied from state to state and different rules governing identical property claims frequently existed side by side.[49]

New York was a more attractive domicile for the AP's practices and afforded the AP the opportunity to sidestep the ruling of the Illinois Supreme Court.[50] Judge Peckham's judgment in *Mathews* and advantageous legislation made incorporation in New York attractive to the AP. The Membership Corporations Law (1895), a revision of existing statutes that authorized the incorporation of nonpecuniary organizations, such as agricultural, cemetery, fire, hospital, and library corporations, as well as boards of trade, enabled the AP to reestablish its method of organization in the Empire State.[51] John G. Johnson, the celebrated corporate lawyer who acted for companies in most of the great American antitrust cases at the turn of the century, such as *Knight*, *Northern Securities*, *Standard Oil*, and *American Tobacco*, suggested to Lawson that the AP reincorporate under the New York law.[52] Melville Stone, the first general manager of the AP, disingenuously claimed it was George Jacob Holyoake and the Rochdale cooperative stores that inspired him to move to New York in 1900, but the bylaws of the AP were significantly less egalitarian than those of the Lancashire weavers.[53] "The purpose of this whole operation," acknowledged

[48] Report of the Board of Directors to the members, September 10, 1902, APo1.4B, Series IX, box 54, folder 903, AP.

[49] T.A. Freyer, "Business Law and American Economic History," in S.L. Engerman and R.E. Gallman, *The Cambridge Economic History of the United States*, vol II: *The Long Nineteenth Century* (Cambridge: Cambridge University Press), p. 436.

[50] For mention of intentions to leave, see Report of the Board, June 30, 1900, Rosewater, box 19, folder 17, AJA; On other suits see C. Knapp to members, June 29, 1900, Ochs, box 53, folder 7, NYPL and Wilson to Knapp, July 21, 1900, Rosewater, box 19, folder 17, AJA, as well as *News Publishing Co. v. AP*, 114 Ill. App. 241 (1904).

[51] The law provided that "Any corporation ... organized under this article for the purpose of gathering, obtaining and procuring information and intelligence, telegraphic or otherwise, for the use and benefit of its members, and to furnish and supply the same to its members for publication in newspapers owned or represented by them may admit as members thereof, other associations, partnerships and individuals engaged in the same business or in the publication of newspapers, periodicals or other publications, upon such terms and conditions, not inconsistent with law or with its certificate of incorporation, as may be prescribed in its by-laws." *Laws of New York, 1895*, Ch. 559, as amended by *Laws, 1901*, Ch 436. The news agency proviso and similar special clauses of the Law were eliminated in a general amendment of 1926, which provided, however, that all rights already existing under these clauses should be preserved. *Laws, 1926*, Ch. 722, s. 3. See also R.C. Cumming, *Membership and Religious Corporations of New York* (New York, 1896), pp. 75–154; Swindler, "AP Anti-trust Case," p. 49.

[52] J.G. Johnson to Lawson, April 25, 1900, APo2.A, box 5, folder 2, AP. "John G. Johnson, Noted Lawyer, Dies," *The New York Times*, April 15, 1917. See 156 U.S. 1 (1894); 221 U.S. 1 (1911); 221 U.S. 106 (1911).

[53] M.E. Stone, *Fifty Years a Journalist* (London: Heinemann, 1922). *AP Annual Report* (1919–1920), pp. 157–8.

Stone in private, "is to protect our friends in their rights."[54] "Unfortunately," wrote E.F. Mack of the Montreal *Gazette* to Stone, Canadian law did not provide for the incorporation of membership associations. The Canadian news association had to be formed under the joint-stock companies act, and was therefore liable, like the AP of Illinois, "to be declared a public service corporation."[55] Such international comparison exemplifies how critical the state was to the successful formation of the AP.

The Membership Corporations Law of New York prohibited the creation of shares, but its provisions allowed for a type of corporate structure whereby control might be concentrated by means of the votes of bondholders, despite the equal distribution of membership voting rights. The new corporation issued bonds that paid no interest but which, like shares in the Illinois association, entitled the holder to vote for the board. The reason for granting them a voting privilege, albeit limited to the election of members of the board of directors, was to allay the apprehension of the papers paying large assessments who feared that the small papers might numerically control the organization and seek to alter the character of the news service so as to make it undesirable for those paying a considerable proportion of the bills.[56] The vast number of small papers, which were not bondholders at all, had one vote each, but first-class members received forty bonds of $25 each. The bonds were made small to make the voting power of bondholding members large. These members consequently had one vote on the board and one vote for each bond, or a maximum voting power of forty-one, which meant that bondholders held a total of 6,150 votes.[57] The association never had more than 1,400 members, therefore bondholders, if they voted together, could outvote normal members by a large margin.[58] This "protected suffrage," as one member called it, enabled the bondholders to determine the board of directors.[59] On all other matters raised in general meetings, vote was by a poll of members.

The voting structure purposefully engendered stable and conservative government. "As the British House of Lords is a body of hereditary peers," said Adolph Ochs, the famous proprietor of the New York *Times*, and a leading member of the AP, "so perhaps it may be said the bondholders of the A.P. are."[60] The analogy between the private governance of the association and the public government of the British Parliament was apt. As one AP member put

[54] Stone to Ochs, June 7, 1900, Ochs, box 53, folder 7, NYPL.
[55] E.F. Mack to Stone, October 27, 1910, 01.2, early operating records, series 1: correspondence of Stone, AP.
[56] Noyes to C.L. Brown, April 29, 1926, AP01.2, KC, box 27, folder 7, AP; Memo by Stone, March 1, 1927, AP01.2, KC, box 27, folder 7, AP.
[57] McClatchy, Suggested defects in the bylaws, June 15, 1900, Rosewater, box 19, folder 17, AJA.
[58] In every year, from 1937 to 1942, the bondholder vote for each nominee director greatly exceeded the membership vote. Brief for the US, p. 16, *AP v. US*, 326 U.S. 1 (1945).
[59] McKelway to W. Hester, May 26, 1900, McKelway, box 5, NYPL.
[60] Ochs, address to annual meeting, April 25, 1927, Oswald Garrison Villard papers, Ms AM 1323, O.G., folder 2883, Houghton Library, Harvard University.

it, the board of directors was "a sort of perpetual body."[61] Lawson served as a director and member of the executive committee for more than twenty-eight years; Ochs served for twenty-four. Frank Noyes, publisher of the Washington, DC *Star*, was president of the AP for thirty-eight. By bringing other important East Coast papers into the AP, Noyes had played a pivotal role in the fight with the UPA during the 1890s and he therefore enjoyed a prominent place in the government of the association.[62] The directors appointed in 1902 served an average of 15.5 years.[63] In theory, the House of Lords is removed from the pressures of politics, and therefore capable of disinterested decision-making, just as the bondholders of the AP were intended to adjudicate internal political disputes. In practice, bondholders, like peers, had agendas of their own. For example, Ochs, even more so than other board members, typically sided with incumbents in membership disputes.[64]

The board was responsible for the admission of new members. A bylaw that prohibited the board from admitting a new member over the protest of an incumbent circumscribed its powers only slightly. John G. Johnson, and the eighteen other eminent corporate lawyers in various parts of the country that counseled the AP on its relocation to New York, advised that the perpetuation of an absolute veto power on the admission of a new paper in a prescribed district was likely to be in restraint of trade.[65] Although a member's protest could stop the board of directors from approving an application, applicants had to have a right to apply to the corporation as a whole; the bylaws could only stipulate by what vote a member could be admitted. The new bylaws therefore made a four-fifths majority necessary for admission over a right of protest. "This feature," said Ochs many years later, "is the one particular appeal we make to public confidence in this organization that it is not a monopoly."[66] The right of protest, however, was as effective as the lost right of veto. It was, said Charles Diehl, an early AP executive, "deemed practically impossible that any such percentage of the total membership could be brought together to vote unanimously to over-ride the protest right of a member."[67] In some respects, the protest right was better than the lost right of veto. To be

[61] Pape to Clark, January 16, 1920, Butler papers, Buffalo.
[62] Lawson to Noyes, January 29, 1894, Lawson, box 2, folder 5, p. 663, NL.
[63] *AP v. US*, 326 U.S. 1 (1945), brief for the US, p. 17. Unsigned, Directors of New York corporation, undated, AP01.2, KC, AP.
[64] P. Cowles to Cooper, December 28, 1927, AP01.2, KC, box 4, folder 2, AP. On Ochs, see Ochs to Martin, March 5 and Martin to Ochs, March 6, 1917, AP01.2, KC, box 9, folder 10, AP. Compare Martin to Ochs, May 15, 1917, with McClatchy to Stone, May 16, 1917, and O.G. Villard to Martin, May 17, 1917, AP01.2, KC, box 9, folder 4, AP; H.S. Thalheimer to Martin, May 2, 1918, AP01.2, KC, box 9, folder 12, AP.
[65] J.P. Wilson to Knapp, July 21, 1900, Rosewater, box 19, folder 17, AJA.
[66] Ochs, Application for Membership, Baltimore *Sun* – pm, verbatim minutes, 1924, AP01.2, KC, box 22, folder 12, AP.
[67] C. Diehl to B. Merrill, May 29, 1924, AP01.4B, series 1, box 1, folder 1, AP.

approved for admission, the applicant had to obtain a written waiver of protest from incumbents in the same district, which meant newspapers no longer had to file protests at all, enabling them to avoid at least some of the odium associated with objection. Silence, explained St. Claire McKelway of the Brooklyn *Eagle*, did not give consent.[68]

In practice, the right of protest was frequently superfluous, it being almost always the policy of the AP board to vote against the application of a potential competitor to an incumbent member.[69] Rights of protest were limited to those publishers who had possessed them as members of the Illinois association. It required a seven-eighths vote of all the members to grant protest rights, which made it difficult to expand the list of protest holders, and it was practically impossible after the membership was enlarged. Consequently, although the membership grew, the number holding protest rights remained the same until 1928. In 1915, a total of 131 cities had 237 members holding de jure protest rights out of a total membership of 900.[70] Yet, "with never a deviation for twenty-five years," observed Lawson in 1924, protest right, or not, neither the board nor the membership ever "installed an additional membership in the home field of an original member."[71] This long-standing policy, observed Kent Cooper, who was appointed AP general manager in 1925, had "so ingrained itself into the fabric of the organization" that non-protest members were convinced they had de facto protest rights.[72]

Between 1900 and 1928, 103 applications for membership subject to protest rights were submitted to the vote of the members. Only six obtained the requisite four-fifths vote for admission. All six were located in cities other than those in which the papers of the protesting members were published. Of the ninety-seven applicants refused admission, twenty-five were taken in after the extent of protest rights was reduced during the 1920s; sixty-three were never admitted. After 1928, protest rights were extended by bylaw to all members of five years' standing. During the years 1929–1941, only four applications involving protest rights were submitted to a vote of the members and all were rejected.[73]

---

[68] McKelway to W. Hester, May 26, 1900, St. Claire McKelway papers, box 5, NYPL.

[69] On a few occasions, however, the board had to plead with members to admit applicants at strategic locations, e.g. Noyes to H.S. New, February 7, 1901; Noyes to W.D. Brickell, June 13, 1902; Noyes to M. Bickham, June 14, 1902, APo1.1, correspondence of Noyes, box 1, folder 1, AP.

[70] Noyes to McClatchy, October 21, 1915, APo1.2, KC, box 18, folder 5, AP.

[71] Lawson, Application for Membership, Baltimore *Sun* – pm, verbatim minutes, 1924, APo1.2, KC, box 22, folder 12, AP.

[72] Cooper to Dealey, November 28, 1924, APo1.2, KC, box 15, folder 4, AP.

[73] *US v. AP*, 52 F. Supp. 362 (1943), complaint, pp. 37–9; J.H. Lewin, "The Associated Press Decision: An Extension of the Sherman Act," *The University of Chicago Law Review*, 13 (1946), 258. In the antitrust suit against the AP, C.B. Rugg, in his argument on behalf of the government, placed considerable emphasis on these figures. Rugg to F. Biddle, July 12, 1943, box 17066, file 134–51–1, NA.

HOW PROPERTY RIGHTS REINFORCED EXCLUSIVITY:
THE CASE OF *INS V. AP*

As *Inter-Ocean* demonstrated, the validity of the AP's internal rules turned on competition policy, which in turn hinged on conventions concerning news as a tradable article. According to custom, when members gathered news that they shared with an agent of the AP, the news was without public interest as long as it was within the knowledge only of the newspapers by which it was collected.[74] When, in 1866, the newspapers of California applied to the NYAP for the news reports of Chicago, Daniel H. Craig, general manager, observed that these reports "are the property of our Association until published."[75] The news reports of the WAP were its "exclusive property," claimed Joseph Medill, publisher of the Chicago *Tribune*, in 1876, and "could not be sold or given away without consent."[76] Numerous examples from before and after these pronouncements affirm that publishers throughout the country shared the view that unpublished news was "property."[77] "Our experience has taught us," wrote Lawson to Clark Howell of the Atlanta *Constitution*, in 1897, "that if we desired to keep our news 'exclusive' we must guard the copy."[78]

The importance of protecting copy, which is unpublished news, explains why the AP went to great lengths to ensure against leaks in the process of transmission. Attempts to purloin the news before publication were widely deprecated and punished. The AP sent out bogus dispatches to reveal those publishers who, although not members of the association, intercepted its telegrams to gain access to the news before publication.[79] The association offered financial rewards for the identification of spies and disloyal telegraphers who facilitated interception.[80] It even established rules dictating the spatial arrangements of its members' newsrooms to prevent telegraphers working for rival

---

[74] Before publication, but after it was shared among members of the AP, news was similar to an expressed, but not communicated idea. Ownership of such ideas, observes Bouckaert, is tantamount to ownership of a moveable. Published news is akin to ideas that are expressed and communicated, the ownership of which the author must share with others. B. Bouckaert, "What is Property?," *Harvard Journal of Law & Public Policy*, 13 (1990), 16.

[75] D.H. Craig to NYAP executive committee, January 1, 1866, Marble, vol. 12, LOC.

[76] Medill, R. Smith, and W.H. Haldeman to E. Brooks, August 12, 1876 in *Proceedings* (Detroit, 1876), 24.

[77] Bylaws, October 21, 1856, Stone, box 8, folder 529, NL; Agreement, 1859, Stone, box 8, folder 529, NL; Smith to Clapp, 1 May 1888, NEAP, folder 15, Baker.

[78] Lawson to Howell, December 27, 1897, Correspondence of Noyes, 01.1, box. 1, vol. 1, AP.

[79] Baird cites several such examples. See D. Baird, "Common Law Intellectual Property," 411–29; "Property, Natural Monopoly, and the Uneasy Legacy of *INS v. AP*," John M. Ohlin Law & Economics Working Paper, No. 246 (June 2005); www.law.uchicago.edu/Lawecon/index.html. For an early example of this practice, see W.H. Smith to Clapp, October 14, 1890, NEAP, Mss 1874–1890 N547, folder 2, Baker. See also "A little joke on the U.P.," November 12, 1894, New York *Press* and "Associated Press Nails News Theft," *New York Times*, November 28, 1914.

[80] Stone to members, January 1, 1898, Lawson, box 112, folder 729, p. 119, NL.

news associations from pirating the news reports before publication.[81] The courts long upheld the customary protection of unpublished news and the Supreme Court affirmed it in *Board of Trade v. Christie Grain & Stock Co.* In that case, the Chicago Board of Trade collected quotations of grain prices and distributed the quotations under contract to its customers. The Board of Trade sought to enjoin the unauthorized use of its quotations by the Christie Grain & Stock Company. In its defense, the Company claimed that the Board had no property rights in the price quotations, but the Court determined otherwise. The Court held that the Board was entitled to have its collection of price quotations, like trade secrets, protected by law. The Board did not lose its property rights in the quotations by communicating them to others in confidential and contractual relations.[82]

By contrast, published news was customarily regarded as "public property."[83] In 1851, Thomas Milner Gibson, chairman of the parliamentary Select Committee on Newspaper Stamps, asked Horace Greeley, publisher of the New York *Tribune*, whether he had cause to "complain of piracy in the United States; for instance, of one publisher who has not himself been at the expense of obtaining news, copying immediately from another?" To which Greeley replied: "It is sometimes talked of for effect's sake; yet, on the whole, I would rather that those who do not take it should copy than not ... the evening journals all copy from us, and we rather like it."[84] The practice of benefiting from a difference in time zones to republish published news was common; indeed, it had been standard practice since the telegraph first spanned several time zones, which helped to liberate newspapers in the hinterland from their reliance on the mails and to curtail the country circulation of widely distributed city publications.[85] In 1890, William Henry Smith had cause to complain of news being

---

[81] H.P. Heatherington to F.R. Martin, January 17, 1913, AP01.2, KC, box 8, folder 1, AP; E.G. Pipp to Stone, November 13, 1914, AP01.2, KC, box 8, folder 1, AP; R.R. Buvinger to AP, September 30, 1917, AP01.2, KC, box 8, folder 7, AP. Apparently the courts upheld this practice, although competitors contested its legality. M.E. Stone to J.E. Atkinson, October 29, 1910, Early operating records, AP01.2, Stone correspondence, AP.

[82] 198 U.S. 236 (1905). The principle advanced in *Board of Trade* may be traced back to *Kiernan v. Manhattan Quotation Tel. Co.*, 50 How. Pr., 194 (1876). In England, it dates from at least *Prince Albert v. Strange*, 1 Mac. & G. 25, which was affirmed in *Jeffreys v. Boosey*, 4 H.L. Cas. 815, 867, and subsequently in *EXTEL v. Gregory*, [1896] 1 Q.B. 147 and *EXTEL v. Central News*, [1897] 2 Ch. 48. In subsequent opinions, the American courts cited these cases frequently. See, for example, *Dodge v. Construction*, 183 Mass. 62 (1903). There are numerous parallels between the history of news associations and boards of trade. See J. Lurie, *The Chicago Board of Trade, 1859–1905* (Urbana, IL: University of Illinois Press, 1979).

[83] For a full exegesis of this point, see Brief for Defendant Respecting Complainant's Appeal, *AP v. INS*, 240 F. 983 (1917).

[84] Report from the Select Committee on Newspaper Stamps, 558 (1851), p. 393, l. 2644–48. See also Mott, *News in America*, p. 98.

[85] See, generally, Innis, "Technology and Public Opinion," 1–24. For specific examples, see G.N. Belknap, "Oregon Sentinel Extras – 1858–1864," *Pacific Northwest Quarterly*, 70 (October 1979), 178–80 and J.D. Carter, "Before the Telegraph: The News Service of the San Francisco

copied from newspapers in Boston, which appeared in eleven o'clock or noon editions, and then telegraphed for use in New York where papers appeared on the street between half past twelve and half past one.[86] In 1895, T.T. Williams, business manager of the San Francisco *Examiner*, and a member of the AP, beseeched Lawson for relief from the practice of M.H. de Young, who admitted to taking messages from the New York *Sun* after publication and printing them in his San Francisco *Chronicle*; yet, Lawson offered none. "After news is printed and issued it is of course public property, and any newspaper can do just what Mr. de Young claims he is doing," wrote Lawson to Williams. "The difference in time in favor of the Pacific Coast makes it of course an entirely practicable matter for the newspapers of that section if they deem it worth their while to go to the expense."[87] In *Tribune Co. v. AP*, Judge Seaman upheld this custom, affirming literary property to be "protected at common law to the extent only of possession and use of the manuscript and its first publication by the owner."[88] Although "there was a stable system of customary property rights in news," the custom was that there was no private property right in published news, the taking of which was permitted and customary.[89]

An appreciation for the customary distinctions that existed with respect to rights in unpublished and published news sheds light on the landmark, and controversial, case of *International News Service v. AP*.[90] In that case, the AP accused INS, the private news agency of William Randolph Hearst, of bribing employees of newspapers to furnish the AP's news before publication for transmission to INS's clients, inducing members of the AP to violate the association's bylaws by permitting INS to obtain news before publication, and copying news from public bulletin boards on which pages of the forthcoming paper were displayed before publication and from early editions of AP newspapers and selling it either bodily or after rewriting. The first two claims concerned the taking of news before publication. In the district court, Judge Augustus Hand held that these practices constituted tortious interference with contracts; Judge Hand affirmed the custom prohibiting the taking of exclusive unpublished news.

Bulletin, 1855–1861," *The Pacific Historical Review*, 11 (1942), 301–17. See also "The Evening Papers," *Fourth Estate*, 3:65 (May 23, 1895), 8.
[86] Smith to Clapp, May 21, 1890, NEAP, Mss 1874–1890 N547, folder 2, Baker.
[87] Lawson to Williams, August 20, 1895, Lawson, box 3, folder 7, pp. 85–9, NL.
[88] 116 F. 126 (1900). For further corroboration of these points see F.S. Siebert, "Rights in news," *The Journalism Bulletin*, 3 (November 1927), 45–54.
[89] *Contra* R.A. Epstein, "International News Service v. Associated Press: Custom and Law as Sources of Property Rights in News," *Virginia Law Review*, 78 (1992), 94–5 and Epstein, "The Protection of 'Hot news': Putting Balganesh's 'Enduring Myth' about *International News Service v. Associated Press* in Perspective," *Columbia Law Review Sidebar* 111 (May 30, 2011), http://www.columbialawreview.org. For a further elaboration of this principle, see *US v. AP*, 52 F. Supp. 362 (1943), Memorandum in Behalf of the Chicago *Times*, and R.J. Finnegan, "The Copy of a Free Press is Not Commerce," July 6, 1943, Field Enterprises, box 39, folder 498, NL.
[90] *INS v. AP*, 248 U.S. 215 (1918).

The important question before the Supreme Court in *INS* was whether the news was similarly protected after publication; that is, as Hand put it, "whether abandonment to the public has been so complete that no further justifiable cause remains for protecting these business interests from competitive interference."[91] As stated in the original complaint, and as Hand understood, what was of value to the AP, was "the power to control the sale of news [it had] gathered until sufficient time [had] elapsed to enable to it be published by the newspapers" it supplied.[92] By reducing the time difference that had historically existed between unpublished and published news, and consequently the territory in which the AP's news was exclusive, INS's practice of copying news from bulletins confused the distinct customs attaching to these hitherto separate categories of news.

To reinstate the customary distinction between published and unpublished news, Hand perceived that despite the existence of publicly available bulletins on the East Coast, "the news is in effect unpublished and unavailable for use by competing news agencies until the time for general publication has elapsed." To substantiate this interpretation, Hand required no recourse to concepts of property. Instead, he predicated his argument on the theory of an "implied contract arising from the relations of the parties." As with lectures, plays, or trade secrets, the real basis for invoking equitable aid, wrote Hand, is that "one who has, with labor and expense, created something which, while intangible, is yet of value, is entitled to such protection against damage as is not inconsistent with public policy." Accordingly, the creators of intangibles, without claiming any property right, possess rights, not simply against the individuals with whom they contract, but against their competitors as well, which, however limited, protects the value of their labor and expense.[93] The U.S. Supreme Court also came to a similar conclusion, but it invoked arguments about property to get there.

According to one recent interpretation, the decision of the U.S. Supreme Court, which precluded a direct competitor from misappropriating time-sensitive factual information, was concerned principally with establishing a formal mechanism to overcome the collective action problem of collecting news in the face of an incentive to free ride on the efforts of others.[94] This conclusion

---

[91] 240 F. 983 (1917). Epstein rightly notes that this is the important question, and that it was problematic, but he contends that the decision was in keeping with custom, "International News Service," pp. 112–17.

[92] 240 F. 983 (1917). The bill of complaint stated: "An essential part of the plan of operation of the complainant accordingly is that news collected by it shall remain confidential and secret until its publication has been fully accomplished by all of complainant's members."

[93] This interpretation differed from earlier analogous decisions, such as *EXTEL v. Central News* and *Dodge v. Construction*.

[94] *Contra* S. Balganesh, "'Hot News': The Enduring Myth of Property in News," *Columbia Law Review*, 111 (2011), 419–95. Additionally, there is no evidence to support Balganesh's claim that the propensity to pilfer published or unpublished news increased before or during World War I or that worries about freeriding became "rampant." Balganesh, "Hot News," 29.

ignores the fact that the AP existed for the exchange of news *before* publication, not after, and that the collective action problem it confronted was not one of freeriding, but of exchanging among its members news they each held exclusively. This distinction is critical. Only if it is apparent that the AP sought to protect the exchange of news among its members does it become clear, as demonstrated later, that the AP sought a property right to constrain the activities of the United Press (UP), its principal rival, and not to prevent freeriding by Hearst's INS. Hand's decision, and that of the Supreme Court, sought to preserve the customary treatment of unpublished and published news despite the fact that technology, by allowing for more rapid publication, had narrowed the gap in time on which the distinction between them was predicated.[95]

It is likely that the AP pursued a property right in news to protect the exclusive rights it held with its members.[96] The connection was apparent to AP executives. It could not have been lost on them after 1901, when, in a case involving the St. Louis *Star* against the AP, the Supreme Court of Missouri observed that unless there was "property" that could be said to be "affected with a public interest," there was no monopoly and no basis to allege that a monopoly existed.[97] When, in 1942, the Department of Justice sued the AP for violation of the Sherman Act, the association, relying on *INS*, argued that newsgathering produced private property that it could not be obliged to share with competitors.

In the years immediately preceding *INS*, the AP had increased cause to fear further regulation and to seek greater protection for its method of operation. After 1911, the state and federal courts' consistent enforcement of a "per se" rule against cartel practices, as well as the Supreme Court's sanction of increased state and federal regulatory activism, boded ill for the AP.[98] In 1913, Arkansas passed a law aimed at the AP (which caused the board concern) that sought to prevent all newsgathering associations from giving exclusive franchises to a single newspaper in any city; a similar bill was introduced in Illinois. Also in 1913, Oregon Congressman Abraham William Lafferty, known at the time for his prosecution of the Oregon and California Railroad in what became known as the Oregon land fraud scandal, introduced a bill in Congress which provided that the AP or associations of such character be placed under the jurisdiction of the Interstate Commerce Commission. The business of the

---

[95] But see Balganesh, "Hot news." The interpretation developed here also differs from that in B. Westley, "How a Narrow Application of 'Hot News' Misappropriation Can Help Save Journalism," *American Univ. L. Rev.*, 60 (February 2011), 691–730.

[96] Other companies have employed similar strategies. See, for example, the recent case of *Copad SA v. Christian Dior SA* [2009] Bus. L.R. 1571. I am grateful to G. Dinwoodie for this reference.

[97] *Star Publishing Co. v. AP*, 159 Mo. 410 (1901).

[98] Members were concerned about the decision in *Standard Oil* (224 U.S. 270 [1912]). See *AP Annual Report* (1912). Freyer, "Business Law," pp. 475–6; Peritz, *Competition Policy*, pp. 60–1.

AP was not "commerce at all," replied Melville Stone, "we say it is purely a personal service."[99]

The AP also received a beating at the hands of the press. William H. Irwin, the muckraker, attacked the AP in the pages of *Harper's Weekly*.[100] The *American* of Austin, Texas took issue with the association's method of incorporation. The AP, claimed the *American*, did "business under an assumed name, like the burglar, the highwayman, the confidence man and the assassin." It was not a "corporate name"; instead, it was a "hunting and fishing club," which "fishes for suckers and is always hunting an opportunity to bilk them."[101] After passage of the Clayton Act (1914), part of which was intended to prevent exclusive dealing agreements, Thomas Watt Gregory, the southern progressive United States Attorney General, investigated the bylaws of the AP. Gregory opined that it was "no violation of the Anti-Trust Act for a group of newspapers to form an association to collect and distribute news for their common benefit ... and determine who shall be and who shall not be their associates." But the bylaws that prevented members from obtaining news from other sources, Gregory contended, constituted a restraint of trade.[102] The association removed the offending clauses from its articles, which eradicated the mechanism employed to prevent rival associations from auctioning exclusive franchises, although in practice the AP had never made use of this bylaw and instead had sought out other means to prevent members from taking alternative services, such as prohibiting members from maintaining an operator of a competing service in the same building as the AP operator. Although Gregory's opinion was fairly innocuous, publicly complaints about the AP continued.[103]

In addition to these regulatory threats, the AP faced growing competition from the UP, which was established in 1907. The UP, like INS, was a product of vertical integration by an existing newspaper chain.[104] As Kent Cooper put

[99] Digest of verbatim board minutes, April 21, 1913, AP01.1, series III, box 3, folder 26, pp. 255–6, AP; "News Control Bill Signed," New York *Times*, February 14, 1913.

[100] W. Irwin, "What's Wrong with the Associated Press," *Harper's Weekly*, March 28, 1913, and "The United Press," *Harper's Weekly*, April 25, 1914. See also M.E. Stone, "The Associated Press. Criticism and Reply," *Collier's*, June 6 and 11, 1914.

[101] "Contemptible Conduct," *American*, December 6, 1914, AP01.2, KC, box 15, folder 1, AP.

[102] Opinion of T.W. Gregory, March 12, 1915, AP01.4B, Series IX, box 61, folder 952, AP.

[103] *AP Annual Report* (1915–1916), p. 46. "Gregory Replies to 'Sun' Complaint," New York *Sun*, March 17, 1915. Much to the consternation of the AP, the UP, like the UPA, sold exclusive contracts to newspapers. Howard to J.G. Scripps, August 17, 1911, Howard, UIB. *AP v. US*, 52 F. Supp. 362 (1945). K. Roberts, "Antitrust Problems in the Newspaper Industry," *Harvard Law Review*, 82 (December 1968), 332.

[104] Regarding the INS and vertical integration, see W.R. Hearst to F.E. Mason, February 5, 1928, 77/12/c, box 34, folder 27, and W.R. Hearst to H.H. Stamburg, 77/12/c, box 35, folder 2, Bancroft Library (hereafter Bancroft), Berkeley. E.W. Scripps to E.F. Chase, March 5, 1903, Howard, UIB. For an interesting statement on the benefits and disadvantages of such vertical integration, see J.C. Harper to Howard, August 13, 1912, Howard, UIB.

it years later, there was "really only one press association. The others, so called, really are rich publishers selling news."[105] The UP was therefore more of a threat to INS than it was to the AP. Indeed, as early as 1927 there were rumors that the two organizations might merge, which they finally did in 1958.[106] In the face of a growing challenge from the UP, Hearst, being the largest bond-holder in the AP in addition to owning INS, may have reasoned that the enemy of his enemy was his friend.[107] The *INS* decision, although it created little dif-ficulty for Hearst, who continued to receive the news reports of the AP, created problems for the UP, which before the decision frequently rewrote local news from papers that belonged to the AP. As Roy Howard, general manager of the UP, understood it, the *INS* decision made it illegal for the UP to continue this practice.[108] Howard acknowledged to Melville Stone that the decision was binding on the behavior of the UP. "I am very happy over it," gushed Stone when reporting Howard's acknowledgement to the AP board, "it accomplishes a great deal. In some respects it is better, I think, than the Supreme Court decision."[109]

After *INS*, the AP credit notice, which all members of the association were (and still are) obliged to publish, was enforceable:

The Associated Press is exclusively entitled to the use for republication of all news dispatches credited to it or not otherwise credited in this paper and also the local news published herein. All rights of publication of special dispatches herein are also reserved.[110]

In 1923, Oswald Garrison Villard, then owner and editor of *The Nation*, opined that the attempt of the AP to make the bylaws of its members bind-ing on other organizations and the employees of individual member papers pressed the bounds of reason. It was, confided Villard to Roy Howard, "in direct restraint of trade and tends toward a monopoly."[111] Publicly, Villard struggled to understand why after the decision "Hearst's disciplining was never brought up in the Board of Directors or in the annual meeting of the members," but the reason may be that through *INS* Hearst had done the AP an admirable

[105] Cooper to Eastman, November 17, 1921, AP01.2, KC, box 14, folder 11, AP.
[106] Unsigned to P. Cowles, May 26, 1927, AP02.A, box 24, folder 10, AP.
[107] According to J.F. Neylan, Hearst's lawyer and representative respecting association matters, Hearst's investment in the AP in 1934 was worth between $3 and $3.5 million. Neylan to Hearst, March 15, 1934, BANC Mss C-B 881, box 190, Bancroft. In 1926, Hearst had fifteen papers in the AP, which entitled him to 460 votes. Papers owned by Hearst, April 16, 1928, Ochs, box 54, folder 1, NYPL.
[108] Howard to J.E. Perry, March 31, 1917, Howard, UIB.
[109] Digest of verbatim board minutes, January 23, 1924, AP01.1, series III, box 3, folder 27, p. 654, AP; Verbatim board minutes, AP01.1, series III, sub-series 4, box 19, folder 57, pp. 303–7, AP.
[110] Publishing the second sentence of the credit notice was optional. See, for example, membership letter to R.A. Conevery, April 6, 1931, AP01.2, KC, box 4, folder 7, AP.
[111] Howard to T.L. Sidlo, November 27, 1923, Howard, UIB.

TABLE 3.1. *Distribution of daily morning and evening newspapers among the major news services, 1941*

	News service	Number of newspapers	Circulation
Morning	Regular AP members	302	15,780,201
	UP but not AP	56	835,706
	INS but not AP	6	18,627
Evening	Regular AP members	887	18,812,988
	UP but not AP	412	4,980,109
	INS but not AP	91	1,508,227

Source: US v. AP, 326 U.S. 1 (1945), Transcripts of record, vol. III, p. 1074.

service.[112] In 1927, it appeared to Kent Cooper, then AP general manager, that the case had made a franchise in the AP "far more valuable."[113] The limited right generated by the decision was sufficient for the AP. "Our sole interest in retaining exclusivity of our news," wrote Cooper, "can well be confined to the stipulation that it is exclusive as against a competitor, rather than as against any one."[114] The exclusive right to the news of its members had been a source of advantage for the AP, which *INS* protected. By the 1940s, the AP was exclusively entitled to the local news of morning newspapers having 96 percent, and afternoon newspapers having 74 percent, of the country's total circulation in these respective fields (see Table 3.1).[115]

COMPETITION CONTRIVED AND COOPERATION EXPANDED: THE AP AND THE UP

Although necessary to its formation and initial success, exclusivity brought the AP into conflict with the law; but, whereas the association could escape the ruling of state legislatures and courts in certain instances, and in other instances gain their favor, there were no safe harbors in which it could hide from the winds of competition. By prohibiting a considerable proportion of the nation's newspapers from joining the association, the AP intentionally encouraged establishment of a viable rival. It was "foolish to think that in this day of cheap telegraphy we can absolutely stifle competition," wrote Lawson in 1892. "The next best thing, and the practical thing, is to in a large degree control it." Lawson envisioned forming a secondary organization "so as to give a limited service to papers outside our Association – a service which we can at

[112] O.G. Villard, *Some Newspapers and Newspaper-Men* (New York: Alfred M. Knopf, 1923), p. 53.
[113] Cooper to Patterson, January 28, 1927, Kent Cooper papers, box 1, Lilly Library, University of Indiana, Bloomington (hereafter LL).
[114] Cooper to Noyes, December 11, 1928, AP01.2, KC, box 4, folder 2, AP.
[115] Brief for the US, *US v. AP*, 326 U.S. 1 (1945), p. 105.

all times shape and control – and thus prevent the growth of a new competing association to serve that portion of the market that had been excluded from the AP."[116] In particular, this tertiary news agency could be used to serve Lawson's three nearest competitors, the Chicago *Evening Mail*, the *Evening Dispatch*, and the *Globe*.[117] An organization called the Telegraphic News Company was formed for this purpose, but appears to have been short lived. There is evidence to suggest that subsequently INS occasionally served this function.[118]

The board of the AP purposefully regulated entry to the association to maintain a weak competitor, which helped it to avoid legal sanctions. "All the value to be expected from the competitive relationship might be reasonably expected in a mutual association where each member would have not only a right, but an influence to make that right felt, to demand of the management the proper character of service at all times," wrote Lawson to Harrison Gray Otis of the Los Angeles *Times-Mirror* in 1894.[119] "If there are other associations they will not be competing associations."[120] The AP regulated competition through the valve of membership and thereby ensured the viability of a weak rival. This practice was not unique to the AP. Du Pont, for example, intentionally limited its market share, and encouraged the existence of weaker firms, to discourage regulation of its business.[121] To oblige the AP to give its news report to all, observed Lawson after *Inter-Ocean*, would remove the stimulus to competition.[122] In 1921, Ochs similarly argued that given that the service of the AP was "so good as to be indispensable to a newspaper," "the opening of the door to every applicant" would mean that the AP would "at once become a monopoly because every existing paper would seek admission." This was one of the "dangers" which the AP had confronted for many years; consequently, said Ochs,

the Board of Directors have carefully considered every application and refused admission to a considerable number who could be adequately served by competing associations. There has been a definite purpose to avoid anything like the destruction of competition either through a wholesale admission of applicants or by any other process.[123]

116 Lawson to Barr, November 2, 1892, Lawson, box 2, folder 4, pp. 286–7, NL.
117 Lawson to de Young, January 17, 1893, Lawson, box 2, folder 5, pp. 30–3, NL.
118 Lawson to Barr, November 2, 1892, Lawson, box 2, folder 4, pp. 286–7, NL. See also J.W. Scott to W.C. Reick, January 28, 1895, Lawson, box 3, folder 6, pp. 293–4, NL. On cooperation between INS and AP, see Cooper to Noyes, December 11, 1928, AP01.2, KC, box 4, folder 2, AP; Neylan to Noyes, February 25, 1928, AP01.2, KC, box 4, folder 1, AP; Neylan to Hearst, March 9, 1934, BANC Mss C-B 881, box 190, Bancroft. INS was also friendly with UP, and Neylan maintained a close and friendly relationship with Roy Howard. See BANC Mss C-B 881, boxes 42, 52, 82, 83, and 92, Bancroft.
119 Lawson to H.G. Otis, July 30, 1895, Lawson, box 3, folder 6, p. 919, NL.
120 Lawson to Otis, September 24, 1894, Lawson, box 3, folder 6, pp. 20–1, NL.
121 Galambos, "The Triumph of Oligopoly," pp. 241–53.
122 Lawson to Stone, March 21, 1900, Lawson, box 4, folder 9, pp. 51–8, NL.
123 Ochs to L. Young, March 11, 1921, Ochs, box 53, folder 12, NYPL.

The members of the AP were less concerned to increase the share of the market served by their association than they were to protect their franchise rights. Had they been eager to control the market they would have permitted all newspapers to join. "I have no objections to the existence of the United Press," confided Kent Cooper to Ochs, "in fact, I believe it has a real mission to fill, for I want The Associated Press to have competition."[124] Controlling access to the association moderated competition between the AP and its rivals. Open entry, it was argued, would have led to monopoly; competition was contrived.[125]

Despite Lawson's best intentions, members clung to their exclusive franchises sufficiently to prevent the AP from admitting new members in important locations, which invited the establishment of a stronger rival than originally desired. These restrictions encouraged E.W. Scripps, whose chain of newspapers catered to the Midwestern working-class, to establish a competing agency.[126] Scripps initially formed an agency to serve his several newspaper properties, and in 1907, he amalgamated several regional organizations to form the UP; that year, it had 367 clients.[127] The UP, a commercial concern that paid dividends, was known for its attention to the human-interest angle and for its "bright and snappy" stories; the reporting of the AP was regarded as prosaic.[128] An enterprising spirit and dedication to serving the afternoon newspaper field, in which the AP service was especially wanting, made the UP a success.[129] Its client base grew from 300 in 1907 to 515 in 1914. That year, the AP had 895 members out of a total daily newspaper population of approximately 2,500.

Competition from the UP obliged the AP to improve its reports, generate new services, and liberalize its organization.[130] In 1908, a year after the UP was established, members of the AP began pressing for reforms to expand

---

[124] Cooper to Ochs, June 14, 1926, Ochs, box 54, folder 2, NYPL.

[125] See R.H.K. Vietor, *Contrived Competition: Regulation and Deregulation in America* (Cambridge, MA: Harvard University Press, 1994).

[126] V. Trimble, *The Astonishing Mr. Scripps: The Turbulent Life of America's Penny Press Lord* (Ames: Iowa State Press, 1992); O. Knight, *I Protest: Selected Disquisitions of E. W. Scripps* (Madison: University of Wisconsin Press, 1966); C. McCabe, *Damned Old Crank: A Self-Portrait of E. W. Scripps* (New York: Harper, 1951); M.A. McRae, *Forty Years in Newspaperdom: The Autobiography of a Newspaper Man* (New York: Brentano's, 1925). E.W. Scripps to Chase, March 5, 1903 (cataloged with correspondence from 1912), Howard, UIB.

[127] On the formation of the UP see Scripps to Howard, September 27, 1912, Howard, UIB. J.A. Morris, *Deadline Every Minute: The Story of the United Press* (Garden City, NY: Doubleday, 1957), p. 54.

[128] Richard Hooker to F.R. Martin, January 6, 1923, AP01.2, KC, box 1, folder 5, AP; CAP to Garges, September 17,1925, AP01.2, KC, box 13, folder 7; Edson K. Bixby to Cooper, March 8, 1927, AP01.2, KC, box 8, folder 13, AP. See also, D.M. Owens, "The Associated Press," *The American Mercury*, 10 (April 1927), 385–93.

[129] Most of Scripps' papers were published in the afternoon, whereas the most powerful members of the AP were morning papers. Lee to Butler, December 29, 1910, Butler papers, Buffalo.

[130] For evidence to this effect, see particularly W.F. Brooks to Lowell, December 3, 1930, and generally AP01.2, KC, box 4, folder 9, AP.

and democratize the association.[131] By 1912, the AP faced an annual deficit of $50,000 ($1 million in today's prices). That year, the membership accused Melville Stone of mismanagement.[132] Historians have portrayed Stone as a capable manager who led the AP to become the dominant domestic news association, but it was widely thought at the time that he was not.[133] An insurrection against him led to the appointment of several department chiefs who divided the executive work of the association into news, traffic, and finance divisions.[134] This change led to a reduction in expenditures by $100,000 ($2 million).[135]

Exclusivity limited the AP's growth and encouraged the UP, but attempts to liberalize the association had to overcome the value members ascribed to their exclusive franchises. Members in large cities assigned high values to their AP franchises.[136] Others used franchises as collateral to borrow money.[137] The promise of an exclusive AP franchise enticed purchasers to buy the *Evening Telegram* in Portland, Oregon.[138] "I can truthfully say," wrote F.W. Enwright to Kent Cooper in 1926, "that the A.P. franchise was one of the main inducements that interested me in the Lawrence [Massachusetts] *Telegram*."[139] The New York *Daily News* purchased the New York *Commercial Bulletin*, for $500,000 ($6.5 million in today's dollars) solely for the AP franchise.[140] Newspapers, such as the Chicago *Daily News* and the *Dispatch* of St. Paul, Minnesota, sold their AP bonds to investors.[141] In at least one instance, the AP upheld an exclusive franchise to bolster the sales value of the newspaper that owned it.[142] On the contrary, the refusal of AP membership could dissuade even well-heeled would-be publishers from going into business. In 1919, Henry Ford dropped his scheme to start a new evening newspaper in Detroit after the AP refused to

---

[131] *Report of the Special Committee to the Board of Directors and Members of the Associated Press* (New York, 1908).

[132] His removal had long been foretold. See R.W. Patterson to Rosewater, March 8, 1893, Rosewater, box 20, folder 17, AJA; Lawson to Driscoll, August 1, 1895, Lawson, box 3, folder 6, pp. 928, 1/3 – 2/3, NL; Lawson to Driscoll, May 15, 1896, Lawson, box 3, folder 7, pp. 618–19, NL; Ochs to George, April 10, 1899, Ochs, box 53, folder 5, NYPL.

[133] Contra D.P. Nord, "Stone, Melville Elijah," *American National Biography Online* (February 2000).

[134] McRae to E.W. Scripps, March 29, 1916, Howard, UIB. *AP Annual Report* (1912–1913), 3–4.

[135] "A Study of Efficiency of the Business Management of the Associated Press," April 1, 1913, 01.48, AP. Cooper, Statement to the members of the AP, April 25, 1932, Roy Howard papers, box 65, LOC.

[136] In 1911, the AP franchise of the Boston *Transcript* was valued at $1 million ($23 million) and the value of the franchise of the Indianapolis *News* was fixed at $500,000 ($12 million).

[137] Howard to J. Scripps, August 17, 1911, Howard, UIB.

[138] E.B. Piper to Stone, November 21, 1916, AP01.2, KC, box 13, folder 3, AP.

[139] Enwright to Cooper, August 18, 1926, AP01.2, KC, box 7, folder 9, AP.

[140] Address to the AP, undated (1927), Howard papers, box 14, LOC.

[141] C.K. Blandin to J.F. Neylan, June 17, 1926, AP01.2, KC, box 27, folder 5, AP.

[142] A.H. Rogers to B.H. Anthony, October 2, 1925, AP01.2, KC, box 7, folder 9, AP.

grant him a full news report. "As an A.P. franchise was a chief asset," reported *Editor & Publisher*, "the proposition fell through."[143]

For the publishers of newspapers in cities with small- to medium-sized populations, exclusive territory was an advantage. A leased wire report in a town of 16,000, such as Muscatine, Iowa, at an expense of $59.50 ($1,400) a week was a heavy undertaking, but it increased "newspaper prestige and worth."[144] Even for large papers, the AP was a considerable expenditure. In 1916, payments to the AP constituted the largest fixed editorial expenditure on the balance sheets of the New York Mail & Express Company, publisher of the *Evening Mail*.[145] In dozens of cities across the country, members objected to the admission of competitors on an equal basis, refused to admit applicants without compensation for the money already invested in the association, and benefited from the advantage exclusive access to the AP reports provided over rivals.[146] Incumbents argued that the admission of a new member would damage their competitive position, and consequently the interests of the association. According to the manager of the *Daily Sun*, electing an additional member in Parsons, Kansas "only embarrasses the old member and in the long run will not strengthen the AP."[147] In Bryan, Texas, wrote A.J. Buchanan, editor of the *Eagle*, customers would "get a far inferior service" with two papers than they would with "one good prosperous paper."[148] Likewise, in Springfield, Illinois,

[143] "Ford Drops Scheme for New Paper," *Editor & Publisher*, February 1, 1919, p. 24. I am grateful to Michael Stamm for this reference.

[144] F.D. Throop to Stone, April 14, 1913, AP01.2, KC, box 6, folder 4, AP.

[145] Memo from managing editor, June 19, 1916, Mail & Express papers, box 2, NYPL.

[146] L. Withington to AP, September 5, 1914, AP01.2, KC, box 7, folder 7, AP; E. McKernon to F.R. Martin, December 22, 1917, AP01.2, KC, box 7, folder 7, AP; Cooper to Lawson, November 11, 1921; F.G. Smith to Cooper, November 7, 1921, AP01.2, KC, box 4, folder 11, AP. Ochs to Martin, March 5, 1917, AP01.2, KC, box 9, folder 10, AP; Application for Membership, undated (1914), AP01.2, KC, box 15, folder 1, AP; Application for Membership, undated (1915), AP01.2, KC, box 12, folder 12, AP; Secretary to A.L. Miller, April 26, 1915, AP01.2, KC, box 7, folder 12, AP; E.J. Kiest to Board of Directors, February 3, 1914, AP01.2, KC, box 15, folder 3, AP; D. Gideon to Board, September 22, 1926, Ochs, box 54, folder 3, NYPL; Assistant Secretary to R.J. Smith, April 26, 1913, AP01.2, KC, box 17, folder 5, AP; Rosewater to Stone, May 3, 1895, Rosewater, box 19, folder 17, AJA; E. Anthony & Sons to Fletcher, August 8, 1890, NEAP, folder 12, Baker; Resolution of the Western Division Advisory Board, April 24, 1917, AP01.2, KC, box 13, folder 3, AP; Cooper to Stone, September 8, 1916, AP01.2, KC, box 11, folder 4, AP; L.D. Starke to Martin, August 3, 1917, AP01.2, KC, box 16, folder 7, AP; Application for Membership and Night Report, April 26, 1917, AP01.2, KC, box 14, folder 4, AP; Cooper to G.E. Dunham, April 28, 1921, AP01.2, KC, box 9, folder 15, AP. E. Howard to Stone (Wichita Falls [TX]), September 18, 1917, AP01.2, KC, box 15, folder 12, AP; F.W. Hardy to Cooper, October 4, 1927, AP01.2, KC, box 5, folder 6, AP. Rosewater to Stone, May 2, 1897, Rosewater, box 19, folder 17, AJA; Stone to Rosewater, August 12, 1895, Rosewater, box 19, folder 17, AJA. Martin to Stone, September 25, 1913, AP01.2, KC, box 13, folder 7, AP.

[147] F. Motz to F.R. Martin, December 7, 1917 and Motz and C.M. Reed to P. Cowles, November 28, 1917, AP01.2, KC, box 6, folder 8, AP.

[148] A.J. Buchanan to AP, 7 December 1916, AP01.2, KC, box 14, folder 12, AP.

wrote J. David Stern, editor and publisher of the *News-Record*, there were "three papers where two ought to be."[149] The AP, wrote one senior manager of the association, "always considered the representations of an existing member as to whether the town would support two newspapers."[150] Insofar as the quality of the association's news reports depended on the quality of its membership, protecting incumbent members was important. Until the AP developed a significant staff of its own reporters in the 1930s, the exclusive right to a member's local news was a contribution, said the directors, "quite as valuable as the weekly sum he pays as his share of the expenses of the organization."[151]

Although Noyes claimed in public that a new member should be elected when it was "to the benefit of the association generally," ascertaining what advantaged the association involved determining whether a city could support more than one newspaper.[152] In these market studies, the AP considered the contribution of the newspaper to the news reports, the industrial development of the area, and the quality of the population in the area of circulation.[153] "A large percentage of colored population," wrote S. Lover, president of Norfolk, Virginia *Dispatch* to the AP board, "would permit of no argument for the development of another paper in this field."[154] A large "foreign population of non-readers," such as "Lithuanians, etc.," claimed Edgar E. Bartlett of the *Register-Gazette* in Rockford, Illinois, meant that the AP service could not "possibly be of the same relative value as in some other city."[155] Free newspapers and publishers that undersold members were barred, as were newspapers that threatened existing collusive arrangements among incumbent members in particular regions.[156]

[149] J.D. Stern to Martin, January 22, 1919, AP01.2, KC, box 5, folder 10, AP.
[150] E.g. Martin to K.G. Colby, September 28, 1923, AP01.2, KC, box 7, folder 10, AP; F.D. Throop to Stone, December 3, 1913, AP01.2, KC, box 6, folder 4, AP; F. Motz to F.R. Martin, December 7, 1917 and Motz and C.M. Reed to Cowles, AP01.2, KC, box 6, folder 8, AP; M.S. Shaw to Stone, February 26, 1914, AP01.2, KC, box 5, folder 7, AP; A.J. Buchanan to AP, December 7, 1916, AP01.2, KC, box 14, folder 12, AP; J.D. Stern to Martin, January 22, 1919, AP01.2, KC, box 5, folder 10, AP; J.O. Abernathy to Noyes, April 9, 1926, AP01.2, KC, box 12, folder 2. J.S. Elliott to C.W. Jones, July 12, 1928, AP01.2, KC, box 8, folder 3, AP.
[151] Complaint, par. 72, R. 20, admitted R. 126, 141–2, *US v. AP*, 326 U.S. 1 (1945).
[152] "Denies Monopoly of News Can Exist," *New York Times*, May 12, 1914.
[153] P.A. Bryant to Cooper, August 13, 1925, AP01.2, KC, box 11, folder 5, AP. Regarding local industry see, for example, Hildreth & Rogers Co. to AP, October 1, 1923, AP01.2, KC, box 7, folder 10, AP.
[154] S.L. Lover to board of directors, September 29, 1917, AP01.2, KC, box 16, folder 7, AP. See also V.B. Imes to AP, August 30, 1923, AP01.2, KC, box 8, folder 6, AP.
[155] E.E. Bartlett to Cooper, June 17, 1925, AP01.2, KC, box 4, folder 11, AP.
[156] The board refused admission to a one-cent paper in Newark (NJ) that undersold incumbent members. See Ochs to Martin, June 27, Martin to McClatchy, July 21, and Noyes to Martin, August 3, 1917, AP01.2, KC, box 9, folder 12, AP. According to its bylaws (Art. 13, s. 1), the AP refused to admit newspapers distributed gratis. See L.P. Bennett to Stone, May 15, 1917, AP01.2, KC, box 9, folder 4. See J.C. Fisher to L.B. Sheley, June 21, 1916, and Sheley to F.R. Martin, AP01.2, KC, box 4, folder 11, AP. See also J.D. Stern to Frederick Roy Martin, March 17, 1919, AP01.2, KC, box 5, folder 10, AP.

"Spite" papers – newspapers started for political purposes – were unlikely to gain admission. According to George Shaw of the Dixon, Illinois *Telegraph*, an AP member, the Dixon *Leader*, was "a spite paper" formed by "politicians, who style themselves Progressives," and "you know about how long such an enterprise usually lasts."[157] By contrast, the *Telegraph* was the official newspaper of Dixon, by act of the city commissioners, and of Lee County, by act of the Board of Supervisors.[158] Its founder was "present at the founding of the Republican Party and the paper has been steadfast ever since."[159] The Republican *Star* of Miles City, Montana, complained that the proposed Democratic upstart in town was a "purely party organ" that "must of necessity drive" the *Star* from the field to survive.[160] The Oklahoma City *Capital*, claimed E.K. Gaylord, president of *The Daily Oklahoman* and the *Oklahoma City Times*, was "for a political purpose only" and would not be heard of "after election day."[161] Colonel C. Copley's *Courier* of Elgin, Illinois was refused admission on the grounds that Copley, being the principal owner of the gas and electricity business in the Congressional district, was, according to Richard Lowrie and Lyman F. Black of the Elgin *Daily News*, "using his own newspapers to protect his public utility franchises and to promote his financial and political schemes."[162] By favoring established and successful newspapers with exclusive membership, the AP indirectly reinforced the status quo among American newspapers, and perhaps encouraged their depoliticization. Whichever newspaper was predominant, whether Republican, Democratic, or, as was more often the case, apolitical, it received membership in the AP and the others labored under a double disadvantage: first for having smaller circulations, and then by being denied the AP news reports.[163]

The right of members to protest the admission of a potential rival hindered expansion in strategic locations, prevented cooperation, interfered with the apportionment of assessments, and stymied innovation. For example, an inability to modify the relationship between members that published their papers in

---

[157] G. Shaw to Stone, February 7, 1914; M.S. Shaw to Stone, February 26, 1914, AP01.2, KC, box 5, folder 7, AP; F.E. Sterling to AP, February 9, 1914, AP01.2, KC, box 5, folder 7, AP.

[158] G. Shaw to AP, February 7, 1914, AP01.2, KC, box 5, folder 7, AP.

[159] W.B. Binton to AP, February 9, 1914, AP01.2, KC, box 5, folder 7, AP. A.P. Armington, cashier of the Dixon National Bank, G.J. Downing, the city's grocer, and W.C. Durkes, cashier for the City National Bank of Dixon, submitted similar letters to the AP on behalf of the *Telegraph*. AP01.2, KC, box 5, folder 7, AP.

[160] L.T. Bennett to Stone, May 11, 1917. See also J.D. Scanlan to Stone, May 11 and Martin to Ochs, May 15, 1917, AP01.2, KC, box 9, folder 5, AP.

[161] E.K. Gaylord to AP, July 1, 1920, AP01.2, KC, box 12, folder 10, AP. The application of the *Capital* was rejected. Cooper to Gaylord, October 7, 1920, AP01.2, KC, box 12, folder 10, AP.

[162] R. Lowrie and L.F. Black to AP, April, 1921, AP01.2, KC, box 5, folder 7, AP.

[163] Such behavior comports with theoretical thinking on networks. E. Noam, "The Tragedy of the Common Network: Theory for the Formation and Breakdown of Public Telecommunications" in E. Noam and A. NiShuilleabhain (eds.), *Private Networks Public Objectives* (Amsterdam: North Holland, 1996), p. 60.

the morning and those that published in the evening constrained the ability of the AP to compete effectively with the UP, which offered a service tailored to the evening newspaper sector.[164] Evening papers subscribing to the UP consistently scooped papers taking the AP service, which dictated when morning papers received the news reports and when evening papers had their turn.[165] Morning papers had historically held the most votes in the AP and they refused to permit the evening papers open access to the news report, although evening papers for much of the time between 1893 and 1945 constituted the larger portion of the membership numerically.[166] The rules that governed when morning papers and evening papers received the news reports consistently favored morning papers and consequently did not keep pace with changes in newspaper production and competition, especially after World War I.[167] The pace of newspaper production and distribution quickened, which created new fields of competition and demands to publish at different times. A stopgap amendment to the bylaws of the AP in 1927 appeased morning and evening members temporarily, but the issue was still the subject of debate in 1941.[168]

The organization of the AP also inhibited its ability to adapt to the emergence of radio broadcasting. As the number of stations increased during the early 1920s, newspapers that could afford to do so established radio stations of their own.[169] Smaller newspapers, which could not afford their own broadcasting stations, feared that if larger members of the AP broadcasted the association's news reports, such broadcasts would diminish their circulation.[170] The management of the AP was concerned that if these members found their own news being used in competition against them, they would be reluctant to supply news to the association. Additionally, if the news of the AP was broadcast, and immediately aired in the territory of the paper that provided it, the exclusive right the AP claimed over its members' news, and which the association had only recently secured through the decision in *INS*, would be

[164] The distinction between morning and evening papers had long posed a problem for American news associations. See WAP Annual Report, 1868, p. 2, W.H. Smith papers, IHS.

[165] Hodams to McCormick, November 3, 1914, McCormick, box 7, Cantigny; Butler to Stone, June 19, 1913, Butler, Buffalo. Lee, *History of American Journalism*, p. 279.

[166] Schwarzlose, *Newsbrokers*, 2: p. 169; FDW to J. Pulitzer Jr., January 20, 1914, Joseph Pulitzer Jr. papers, reel 34, LOC. Ochs speech, undated, Ochs, box 53, folder 11, NYPL.

[167] McClatchy to McKelway, May 5, 1899, McKelway, box 2, NYPL.

[168] Minutes of the AP board, November 28, 1927, McCormick, box 7, Cantigny; *AP Annual Report* (1941–1942).

[169] M. Stamm, *Sound Business: Newspapers, Radio, and the Politics of New Media* (Philadelphia: University of Pennsylvania Press, 2011); M.V. Charnley, *News by Radio* (New York: Macmillan Co., 1948), p. 4. Several newspapers combined to form an organization called Press Wireless. J. Pierson to J.S. Steele, October 16, 1936, Roderick Jones (Jones) papers, series 1, box 43, Reuters Archive (RA).

[170] Bickel to Howard, August 18, 1932, Howard, box 71, LOC. Noyes to members re radio questionnaire, April 11, 1933, McCormick, box 11, Cantigny. *AP Annual Report* (1933–1934), pp. 24–7.

undermined.[171] Indeed, to prevent such eventualities in the northeast of the country, Cooper urged executives of the Canadian news association, which was then experiencing similar difficulties with broadcasting, to seek out a property right in news to prevent AP news reports sent to Canada from being rebroadcast within range of American listeners.[172] In addition, members of the AP board were also concerned that if the association entered the broadcasting business it might, as it was in the *Inter-Ocean* case, be classified as being akin to a common carrier.[173]

The consequent unwillingness of the AP to supply independent radio stations caused these stations to lift the association's news from published newspapers for broadcasting, which forestalled the distribution of newspapers to outlying districts and threatened to curtail the circulation of AP members. Such threats gave the AP reason to test the doctrine established in *INS*, which the circuit court for the ninth district upheld in 1935, but the decision had little impact on broadcasting.[174] For fear that "it would be dangerous legally," said Cooper, or that it would be perceived as being in restraint of trade, according to Noyes, the AP board refused to consider entering into an agreement with the other news agencies to control broadcasting collectively.[175] Uncertain how to respond, the AP was noncommittal, which led to confusion, infractions, and discontent among the membership, and left the field open to INS and the UP, which made great use of broadcasting.[176] Concerns

---

[171] Ochs and F.W. Lehmann, November 24, 1924, APo1.2, KC, box 23, folder 5, AP. See also, J.H. Tennant to Cooper, April 22, 1930, APo1.2, KC, box 10, folder 6, AP.

[172] AP board minutes, April 17, 1925, APo1.1, series III, box 18, pp. 465–70, AP; J.F.B. Livesay, "Report of the Management on Property Right in News," undated (November 23, 1925), APo2A.3, box 14, folder 2, AP; G. Allen, "New Media, Old Media, and Competition: Canadian Press and the Emergence of Radio News, 1922–1941," in G. Allen and D.J. Robinson (eds.), *Communicating in Canada's Past: Essays in Media History* (Toronto: University of Toronto Press, 2009), p. 56.

[173] Digest of verbatim board minutes, October 3, 1928, APo1.1, series III, box 3, folder 28, p. 994, AP.

[174] See *AP v. KVOS, Inc.* 80 F.2d 575 (1935).

[175] Digest of verbatim board minutes, October 7, 1931 and April 24, 1933, APo1.1, series III, box 3, folder 29, pp. 1117, 1127, AP.

[176] *AP Annual Report* (1932–1933), pp. 76–8. See, for example, Butler to Cooper, December 11, 1925, Butler papers, Buffalo; Glenn to Cooper, December 21, 1925 and similar letters in Cooper, box 1, LL; Noyes to members re radio questionnaire, April 11, 1933, McCormick, box 11, Cantigny. Some allowances were made. Noyes to members, March 21, 1933, Howard, box 77, LOC. Howard to Bickel, August 15, 1932, Howard, box 71, LOC; Elliot to members, October 21, 1935, McCormick, box 7, Cantigny; Bickel to Howard, May 20, 1934, Howard, box 94, LOC; Bailie to Sayler, June 17, 1941, Howard, box 178, LOC. Hearst also encouraged INS to broadcast. E.J. Gough to Hearst, September 24, 1930, Hearst papers, BANC 77/121c, box 36, folder 2, Bancroft. In 1924, the AP's refusal to permit the broadcasting of election returns caused some members to use the UP. Martin to Lawson, August 11, 1924, Lawson, box 113, folder 736, NL. In 1925, when the UP made elaborate plans to broadcast the baseball World Series, Cooper was obliged to make similar arrangements. Cooper to Noyes, August 13, 1925, Cooper, box 1, LL.

about the success of the UP, the collapse of the radio bubble caused by the economic depression, and a corresponding belief that broadcasting presented less of a threat to newspaper revenues, not to mention the threat of antitrust proceedings, finally prompted the AP to relax its attitude to broadcasting during the 1940s.[177]

Similar difficulties arose in the development of a news photo service, which relied on wireless telegraphy to transmit photos from Europe to New York and telephone wires to transmit photos within the United States. In 1925, the Scripps-Howard newspaper interests, and by extension, the UP, established Acme Photos. The entry of the UP into the field compelled the AP to enter. The problem, as with radio, was that nearly 98 percent of the AP membership could not afford to purchase the new technology.[178] Large city papers that could afford the new technology used the photos that the association supplied in competition with smaller members.[179] The issue remained a source of contention until the late 1930s, when improvement of wirephoto technology, including development in the AP laboratory of a receiving apparatus for smaller papers, brought down the price and allowed for an increase in the number of papers making use of the service.[180]

Many of these problems derived from the central issue of exclusive franchises, which had long been a fundamental component of the association's organization and governance. By the 1920s, the "era of cooperative competition" may have been in full bloom, but within the AP the boundaries between exclusion and cooperation were still subject to negotiation.[181] To persuade members to relinquish the value of their exclusive franchises, and to increase the share of the market the AP could serve, required modifying the association's constitution. Kent Cooper, who was appointed head of the traffic department in the shake-up of 1912, led the charge. Cooper, a young upstart from Indiana and the son of George William Cooper, a Democratic congressman, initially worked for the UP, before moving to the AP in 1910.

---

[177] For an overview, see Cooper to editors, November 12, 1932, APo2A.3, box 14, folder 9, AP. Cooper to board, May 16, 1940, APo1.2, KC, box 25, folder 6, AP. By 1946, the AP served 675 stations, which generated an additional income of $5 million. O. Gramling to Connecticut state members, December 4, 1946, APo1.2, KC, box 25, folder 11, AP. The AP refused, however, to permit the BBC to broadcast AP news abroad, and insisted that it be limited to the British Isles. Meeting of the Board, October 3, 1946, APo1.2, KC, box 26, folder 6, AP.

[178] J.F. Neylan, circular, June 14, 1934, Howard, UIB. Knox to Pape, April 1, 1935, Cooper, box 2, LL; J.F. Neylan, circular, June 14, 1934, Howard, UIB; Edwards to Harte, March 28, 1935, Cooper, box 2, LL.

[179] Smith to McCormick, March 21, 1935, McCormick, box 11, Cantigny; Macy to members of New York, March 16, 1935, Howard, box 100, LOC.

[180] Cooper report to board, December 31, 1939, McCormick, box 6, Cantigny; *AP Annual Report* (1937–1938), p. 39; *AP Annual Report* (1939–1940), p. 60.

[181] See Peritz, *Competition Policy*, pp. 76–89.

Already in 1911, owing to the growth of the UP, members of the AP board acknowledged that exclusive franchises prevented the association from bringing in new members in strategically important locations.[182] Although Stone acknowledged that the AP suffered from franchise restrictions, he was convinced that exclusivity was necessary to maintain the appearance of competition. "The moment you break down the protest rights," said Stone to the AP board, "the Associated Press becomes indeed a monopoly because the instant that is done every paper in the United States will scramble into the Associated Press."[183] By excluding a certain portion of the press, Stone hoped to keep the UP as a weak competitor and to prevent regulation; but by being overly exclusive, he ran the risk of being accused of restricting trade. In 1915, in response to the Clayton Act, a serious attempt to reform the rules of the association began, but in 1917 Stone expressed concern that the AP was "growing a little too ambitious." The AP, said Stone, is "always face to face with the danger of being charged with being a monopoly" and "anyone who was in control of a monopoly would have to walk with a good deal of care." Although Stone welcomed the decision of the Supreme Court in *INS*, he feared that it was "very far reaching," and "if the effect is to be such as to destroy our competition or hamper it in such measure that it will make us seem a monopoly, I think it will be very dangerous."[184]

The advance of the UP, however, convinced the AP's board that it had more to fear from ossification in the face of a strong rival than it did from legal sanctions. The UP's success, and the ability for newspapers to obtain a competitive report from another organization aside from the AP, undermined the value of exclusive franchises, which made it easier for the association to reduce them in size and number. Beginning in 1915, Cooper and Noyes led a movement to reduce the geographic reach of protest rights. "Fairness to the general membership," wrote Cooper, now required that members protesting the admission of a new member beyond a ten-mile limit, or "home territory," should at least pay to the general funds the amount that such a member would pay to that fund if elected.[185] Threats of increased assessments brought about a reduction in the size of exclusive territories and the number of members exercising protest rights. By June 1916, of the original 131 cities with 237 members holding protest rights, 41 cities with 87 members continued to

---

[182] See the comments of Lawson and Herman Ridder in Digest of verbatim AP board minutes, April 24, and October 4, 1911, AP01.1, series III, box 3, folder 26, pp. 206, 212, AP.

[183] Digest of verbatim AP board minutes, April 23, 1913, AP01.1, series III, box 3, folder 26, p. 259, AP.

[184] Digest of verbatim AP board minutes, October 4, 1917, AP01.1, series III, box 3, folder 26, p. 354, AP.

[185] *AP Annual Report* (1916–1917). Management had made similar threats before. Stone to Butler, April 11, 1903, Butler, Buffalo. Noyes to McClatchy, October 21, 1915, AP01.2, KC, box 18, folder 5, AP.

exercise protest rights outside a ten-mile limit; yet, owing to these 87 members there were more than 150 papers, not in the local fields of AP newspapers, that the board could not elect.[186]

In 1921, the directors recommended that members relinquish their protest rights beyond ten miles. In 1923, Stone again raised concerns with this movement. "In the morning field at least," said Stone to the AP board, "we are today pretty nearly a monopoly in this country." As a result, "we are so standardizing The Associated Press papers that I think it is inevitable that there should be consolidations, and that in some cases they should cease to exist." On a trip across the country, observed Stone, "you get on a train to go from here to Chicago and buy papers at Schenectady and Utica and Syracuse, and everything in those papers except the local news is precisely the same."[187] But Stone's power in the association had been in decline since 1912. After he retired as general manager in 1921, his concerns carried less weight than they had. By 1925, only half of the original members granted protest rights still wielded them beyond their "home territories," which permitted the board to elect a considerable number of small papers to membership.[188] In 1931, Roy Howard showed how inflated the AP franchise valuations still were when he purchased the New York *Evening Telegram* and then refused the news report of the AP, relying instead on the UP report, and thereby, commented Howard, "giving the theory of the value of an A.P. membership a death blow."[189]

To further liberalize the association, between 1925 and 1930 Cooper increased the news staff from 332 to 600, or 45 percent, which made the AP less dependent on its members for news, and therefore protests by incumbent members against the admission of new papers on competitive grounds carried less weight.[190] In 1930, the AP had eighty-one domestic bureaus and the UP had forty-five. There were five states in which the AP had no bureau, but twenty in which the UP had none. In only two cities, Fresno, California, and Hartford, Connecticut, did the UP have an office where the AP did not.[191] By 1935, the AP had eighty-seven domestic bureaus and 7,483 full and part-time correspondents in the US and Canada, excluding member paper employees.[192] In addition, it also maintained 50 full-time correspondents abroad, 112

[186] Noyes to McClatchy, October 21, 1915, AP01.2, KC, box 18, folder 5, AP; Noyes to Otis, June 24, 1916, Noyes correspondence, box 2, vol. 2, AP.

[187] Digest of verbatim board minutes, April 23, 1923, AP01.1, series III, box 3, folder 27, pp. 630–2, AP.

[188] *AP Annual Report* (1922), p. 27. Cooper to Lawson, March 10, 1925, Lawson, box 113, folder 737, NL.

[189] Howard to W. Miller, April 16, 1931, Howard papers, UIB.

[190] Unsigned, private to the board, AP01.2, KC, box 2, folder 6, AP; Paul Cowles to H. Le B. Bercovici, July 1, 1930, AP01.2, KC, box 3, folder 2, AP.

[191] WJM to Cooper, May 22, 1930, AP01.2, KC, box 3, folder 3, AP.

[192] Lloyd Stratton to John A. Park, AP01.2, KC, box 3, folder 2, AP.

part-time correspondents, and bureaus in the major capitals of Asia, Europe, and South America.[193]

Although management initiatives partly account for members' willingness to be more inclusive, during the interwar period numerous newspapers throughout the country closed, which weeded out exclusive territories and reduced the value of franchise rights. Whereas in 1909, 689 cities had competing daily newspapers, in 1929 only 288 cities had two or more dailies.[194] By 1945, the bulk of the dailies in towns with 50,000 or fewer people lacked local competition.[195] Urbanization increased city circulation, which diminished regional competition, and correspondingly reduced the value of exclusive territory outside a newspaper's "city of publication," particularly among morning newspapers.[196] The majority of Americans did not live in major cities until 1920, but thereafter a sixty-mile protest territory was of comparatively small importance in many locations.[197] But in a "sparsely populated inter-mountain country," wrote Thomas F. Kearns of the Salt Lake *Tribune*, a sixty-mile protest area was far less advantageous than a fifteen-mile protest area in "almost any other section of the country."[198] The circulation of some newspapers remained predominantly rural. Less than a third of the circulation of the Dallas (TX) *Morning News*, for example, was in the city of Dallas. For most of the members of the AP board, however, city circulation was more important. Twelve of the fifteen AP directors had city circulations on their papers that varied daily from 50 to 88 percent. Of these twelve, five achieved more than 70 percent of their circulation within their city of publication.[199]

In 1925, the year Cooper was appointed general manager, 119 of the 614 members that joined the AP in 1900 had either resigned or merged with other titles. The total membership was 1,198, which meant, according to Cooper, that 703 new members came into the organization "very largely through waivers given by the charter members." Only 205 of the 495 remaining charter

[193] Cooper to W.B. Preston, March 26, 1932; Unsigned to John R. Whitaker, February 17, 1931, AP01.2, KC, box 3, folder 2, AP.

[194] T.A. Pilgrim, "Newspapers as Natural Monopolies: Some Historical Considerations," *Journalism History* 18 (1992), 3.

[195] *Survival of a Free, Competitive Press: The Small Newspaper: Democracy's Grass Roots*, Report of the chairman, Senate small business committee, 80th Cong., 1st session (1947), p. 20. See also R.B. Nixon, "Trends in U.S. Newspaper Ownership: Concentration with Competition," *International Communication Gazette*, 14 (1968), 186; and Pilgrim, "Newspapers as Natural Monopolies," 3.

[196] R.A. Easterlin, "Twentieth-century American Population Growth," in S.L. Engerman and R.E. Gallman (eds.), *The Cambridge Economic History of the United States*, vol. 3: *The Twentieth Century* (Cambridge: Cambridge University Press, 2000), pp. 522–3.

[197] Freyer, *Regulating Big Business*, p. 7.

[198] Thomas F. Kearns to Cooper, October 3, 1925, AP01.2, KC, box 16, folder 2, AP.

[199] G.B. Dealey to board, January 17, 1925, AP01.2, KC, box 15, folder 4, AP.

TABLE 3.2. *AP membership, leased lines, and annual revenue, 1900–1940*

	A.M. papers	P.M. papers	Total daily members	% total U.S. dailies	Leased lines (ml.)	Revenue ($ in millions)*
1900	256	356	612	26	29,063	56,600**
1910	309	508	817	32	44,000	64,600
1920	482	715	1,197	51	64,800	58,500
1930	415	872	1,287	63	220,000	134,000
1940	–	–	1,367	67	300,000	176,000

* In dollars at constant 2010 prices. ** Revenue is 1902–1903, not 1900.
Source: Compiled from Cowles to Garretson, April 14, 1930, AP, KC, 01.2, 3/3; AP *Annual Reports*; and A.J. Field, "Communications," in R. Such and S.B. Carter (eds.), *Historical Statistics of the United States*, vol. 4: *Economic Sectors* (Cambridge, 2006), pp. 1055–9.

members had any right of protest.[200] Although membership increased, the percentage of papers that received a leased wire report, namely the larger papers, remained almost static at 59 percent of the membership (see Table 3.2).[201] In 1927, there were 2,001 daily newspapers published in the continental United States, 1,926 of which received news reports, or 96 percent. Of this total, 1,169 (58 percent) were members of the AP. The total listed clientele of the Scripps-Howard service was 662; and the Hearst-owned service, 338. Of the number taking UP and INS services, 30 percent were AP members. Of those subscribing to the Scripps-Howard service 24 percent were AP members; and 37 percent of Hearst's clientele were members in the AP.[202] By 1942, the AP served 1,274 newspapers and the UP served 981. In addition to having the larger membership numerically, the AP served papers constituting 81 percent of the daily morning market, with 97 percent of the nation's circulation, and 59 percent of the evening newspapers, with 77 percent of the circulation. By 1981, despite the merger of the UP and the INS to form United Press International (UPI), the AP was even stronger: out of a total population of 1,749 newspapers, 1,327 took the AP reports, of which 1,045 took only the AP. Of the total population, 406 took only UPI, and 279 took both, leaving it with a total of

[200] Cooper to Stahlman, March 2, 1925, AP01.2, KC, box 14, folder 6, AP.
[201] Calculated from *AP Annual Report* (1920–1921), p. 4. Annotated membership role, March 31, 1925, AP01.2, KC, box 2, folder 3, AP. Few charter members switched from taking a pony report to taking a leased one as the majority of members started with leased wires, but classification was and is difficult. Unsigned to Noyes, March 31, 1925, AP01.2, KC, box 2, folder 3, AP.
[202] M. Garges to Cooper, March 4, 1927, Ochs, box 54, folder 5, NYPL. Hearst owned 445 bond votes, while the board in total held only 365, and he had protest rights in thirteen memberships. Application for membership, Baltimore *Sun* – pm, verbatim minutes, 1924, AP01.2, KC, box 22, folder 12, AP. For figures: Proxy Committee, Address to the Associated Press Members, AP01.2, KC, box 27, folder 8, AP; Noyes to members, June 29, 1926, AP01.2, KC, box 27, folder 5, AP. Unsigned, Papers owned by Hearst, April 16, 1926, Ochs, box 54, folder 1, AP.

685 subscribers. By the 1960s, UPI was running at a loss as American evening papers folded and merged with morning papers. In 1991, it filed for bankruptcy, owing $60 million.[203]

FREEDOM OF THE PRESS AND FREEDOM OF CONTRACT: *AP V. US*

While a process of liberalization was underway at the AP, the "anti-monopoly moment" of the late 1930s precipitated a flood of regulations that spilled over into the supply of news.[204] The legislatures of Missouri and New York, although historically safe havens for the AP, considered bills to regulate the press and specifically the association.[205] These bills failed, but antitrust prosecutions under the Sherman Act also increased after 1938, as did the assault on exclusive trading practices.[206] In 1942, Wendell Berge and Charles B. Rugg, the great trustbusters, began an investigation of the AP under the direction of Francis Biddle and Thurman Arnold of the Department of Justice.[207] The war was also allegedly behind the investigation. "During war time nothing can be more important than the dissemination of all available information through every newspaper source, news items and photographic services alike," wrote Thurman Arnold, then Assistant Attorney General, to Robert McLean, publisher of the Philadelphia *Bulletin* and president of the AP. "If our information is correct," continued Arnold, "the present operation of the Associated Press is a direct and substantial restriction on the freedom of the press, which in the public interest should be removed."[208]

A related motivation for the investigation was a growing concern in official circles respecting the dwindling number of independent newspapers throughout the United States and a belief held in certain quarters, albeit difficult to substantiate empirically, that, by withholding its news reports from certain publications, the AP was partially responsible for growing concentration in the industry. Thurman Arnold was convinced that "no first-class newspaper, except perhaps in the most unusual circumstances, can have an even chance with its competitors – or, for that matter, a chance at survival – without the service

[203] Papers concerning acquisition of UPI, September 11, 1981, LN95/1/876110, RA; B. James, "A Pledge to Avoid Censorship," *International Herald Tribune*, 25 June 1992.

[204] A. Brinkley, *The End of Reform: New Deal Liberalism in Recession and War* (New York: Alfred A. Knopf, 1995), p. 106; T.K. McCraw, "Regulation in America: a Review Article," *The Business History Review*, 49 (1975), 161–2.

[205] N.W.H., "Recent Legislative Proposals to Classify Newspapers and Magazines as Public Utilities and to Regulate them Accordingly," *Virginia Law Review*, 17 (1931), 705–9.

[206] Vietor, "Government Regulation of Business," pp. 975–88. K.J. Curran, "Exclusive Dealing and Public Policy," *The Journal of Marketing*, 15 (1950), 142.

[207] Robert McCormick argued vociferously that the suit was politically motivated, but his fellow AP board members disagreed. Digest of verbatim minutes, January 6, 1942, AP01.1, series III, box 3, folder 29, p. 1142, AP.

[208] T. Arnold to R. McLean, February 11, 1942, AP01.4B, series I, box 11, folder 139, AP.

TABLE 3.3. *Cities with one daily, all dailies under common control, and with competing dailies, 1920–1942*

	Cities with dailies	Cities with only one daily		Cities with only dailies under common control		Cities with competing dailies	
		Number	% of total	Number	% of total	Number	% of total
1920	1,292	724	56.0	743	57.5	549	42.5
1930	1,402	1,002	71.5	1,114	79.5	288	20.5
1936	1,457	1,056	72.5	1,206	82.8	251	17.2
1937	1,460	1,083	74.2	1,230	84.2	230	15.8
1938	1,458	1,094	75.0	1,249	85.7	209	14.3
1939	1,437	1,080	75.2	1,241	86.4	196	13.6
1940	1,426	1,092	76.6	1,245	87.3	181	12.7
1941	1,431	1,098	76.6	1,280	89.5	151	10.5
1942	1,403	1,100	78.4	1,276	90.9	127	9.1

Source: *US v. AP*, 326 U.S. 1 (1945), Transcript of record, vol. III, p. 1066.

of the Associated Press."[209] The Department of Justice did its best to marshal evidence of this trend in support of its case against the AP (see Table 3.3 and Table 3.4). Once the claim against the AP became public knowledge, newspapers and commentators weighed in, and the nub of the matter quickly became press freedom. Among the most sophisticated and influential observers was the First-Amendment scholar and Harvard law professor Zechariah Chafee, who argued that the bylaws of the AP "abridge liberty of the press."

Chafee contended that denying a newspaper access to the news reports of the AP was akin to having a city with only one newspaper. "The biggest injury caused by the close restrictions on AP membership is not to the excluded newspapers, but to the citizens who are deprived of the chance of getting the best news in those newspapers." Concentration in the newspaper industry was bad enough. There were, Chafee lamented, 1,245 cities in the United States with either a single newspaper or single ownership of a morning and evening newspaper and only 181 cities with any apparent rivalry between newspapers. "The AP barriers against the admission of new papers are an important cause for this shrinking of competition," wrote Chafee, and "the plain way out of this difficulty is that the AP should regard itself as a public service open to all who will pay the price."[210] Members of the AP, especially those that represented smaller newspapers throughout the country, countered that forcing open the association would undermine the value of the news reports and compel local

[209] Hearings respecting H.R. 110, May 5, 1947, AP01.4B, series IX, box 57, folder 936, AP.
[210] Chafee, "How the Associated Press can Uphold Liberty of the Press," undated (c. 1943), AP01.4B, series IX, box 52, folder 882, AP.

TABLE 3.4. *Urban and nonurban circulation of U.S. daily and Sunday newspapers, 1920–1940 (%)* *

	A.M. papers		P.M. papers		All dailies		Sunday papers	
	Urban**	Other	Urban	Other	Urban	Other	Urban	Other
1920	52.7	47.3	67.2	32.8	61.2	38.8	49.9	50.1
1930	55.1	44.9	67.2	32.8	62.4	37.6	46.1	53.9
1935	55.7	44.3	66.6	33.4	62.4	37.6	46.1	53.9
1940	55.3	44.7	66.9	33.1	62.0	38.0	45.8	54.2

* Computed from Audit Bureau of Circulation figures for English-language daily and Sunday papers as reported in *Editor & Publisher* "International Year Book Numbers" for 1920–1921, 1931, 1936, and 1941.

** This was the classification the Audit Bureau listed as "City Zone." It was the circulation in the urban area of the city of publication, which the Audit Bureau designated in consultation with the newspapers. It was recognized that these areas tended to expand during the period.

Source: US v. AP, 326 U.S. 1 (1945), Transcript of record, vol. III, p. 1052.

papers to rely more heavily on the reports of large regional publications. In private, Robert McLean, president of the AP, confided to the AP's counsel that it was "hard to quarrel with [Chafee's] philosophy that 'the ideal of the duty of a business [is] to serve all potential customers' in the public interest." Chafee had "taken the Government case with its fallacies and its errors and wrapped it so cleverly in the mantle of a dignified philosophy that it makes the document a rather dangerous piece of writing." Chafee's persuasive analysis, however, did not preclude "a reasonable control that the processes of expansion shall be orderly and that newcomers shall prove their stability and character before admission," but "I confess," wrote McLean, "that we have not succeeded in fulfilling that ideal ideally."[211]

For men like Chafee, arguments about the adverse effects the AP had on newspaper concentration were the product of genuine conviction, but for mandarins in the Department of Justice they may have simply been politically expedient. Several high-ranking members of the AP were convinced that political motives at the highest levels of government had prompted the investigation.[212] It seemed to AP members to be more than mere coincidence, that the AP, although repeatedly subject to scrutiny since its incorporation in 1900, was only officially investigated by the Department of Justice four months after Marshall Field III's pro-Roosevelt paper, the Chicago *Sun*, was denied membership in the association. Apparently, Frank Knox, the newspaper editor and publisher who served as Secretary of the Navy under Roosevelt and for most

[211] McLean to T.N. Pfeiffer, April 2, 1943, AP01.4B, series IX, box 54, folder 903, AP.

[212] See, for example, H. Harte to G.F. Booth, September 16, 1943 and December 28, 1943; Booth to Mclean, October 30, 1943, AP01.4B, series II, box 14, folder 178, AP.

of World War II, also backed the publication of the *Sun*.[213] According to Turner Catledge, Field's editor, "it was early in 1941 that Field resolved to start a newspaper ... Roosevelt was trying to move the nation toward support of England and Colonel McCormick was fighting him tooth and nail.... The *Tribune's* influence on the American heartland was great, and to Field and others who thought the United States must fight Nazism, McCormick's daily tirades were agonizing."[214] Colonel Robert McCormick, a long-standing board member of the AP and an ardent critic of the New Deal, fought adamantly against Field's admission to membership. He and Hearst, who owned the morning and evening editions of the *Herald American*, refused to waive their protest rights. Reportedly, Louis S. Weiss, attorney for Field (and a naming partner of the famous New York firm of Paul, Weiss, Rifkind, Wharton & Garrison) contacted Francis Biddle to complain of the situation.[215] "The case was brought at the instigation of Mr. Roosevelt, because he wanted to get the AP membership in Chicago for the Chicago *Sun*," complained George F. Booth, publisher of Worcester, Massachusetts *Telegram* and a member of the AP board, to Robert McLean, then president of the association. "The matter can be dressed up in all sorts of ways with fancy words and one can put perfume on it, but the suit was brought as a holdup."[216]

In *AP v. US*, as in *Inter-Ocean* and *INS*, the freedom of contract came up against the freedom of the press. The AP argued that newspaper "copy" before it was printed was not an article of commerce, but the property of the association, and therefore the courts could not compel members to share it with anyone against their will. According to the Chicago *Times*, a member of the association, "the exclusive ownership of copy prior to its publication in those who write and produce it is the very essence of freedom of the press," and to undermine it was destructive of initiative and industry.[217] Yet, to the judges of the United States Court of Appeals, private property in the news reports generated by the association was decidedly secondary to the public's interest in news. When the case came before the Second Circuit, Judge Learned Hand, a well-known advocate of freedom of the press, argued that the production of news is inevitably subject to "personal impress," which gave the lie to claims of objectivity and made it impossible to treat two news services as interchangeable. It being "only by cross-lights from varying directions that full illumination can be secured," wrote Hand, to deny any paper the benefit of any news service of the first rating was to deprive the public of important information.

[213] Unsigned (McLean?), "Chronology of the Government's Anti-Trust Suit against the Associated Press," undated, AP01.4B, series VII, box 34, folder 655, AP.
[214] T. Catledge, *My Life and The Times* (New York: Harper & Row, 1971), p. 126.
[215] McLean memo, March 1, 1942, AP01.4B, series I, box 11, folder 139, AP.
[216] Booth to McLean, June 4, 1945, AP01.4B, series IX, box 53, folder 888, AP.
[217] "Appeal! Why AP Must Appeal to the Supreme Court," Chicago *Times*, November 1943, p. 6.

In the marketplace for ideas, where supposedly only by free competition would the truth be revealed, the report of the AP was an essential facility. This assertion was different from claiming that the news reports of the AP were essential for producing a successful newspaper. Instead, the report of the AP had to be freely available to ensure that the public was adequately informed. In this respect, the size of the AP was determinative. A reporter and editor were free from obligations in the name of public interest to supply the news they collected, but the AP, "a vast, intricately reticulated, organization," according to Hand, was not.[218]

In *AP*, the Supreme Court affirmed Hand's opinion and privileged competition in the newspaper market over competition in the newsgathering market.[219] The exclusionary bylaws of the association, and all aspects of its protest rights, were found in restraint of trade. There could be no restrictive practices with respect to membership. The consequent consent decree required that the AP bylaws contain a positive declaration that, in passing on applicants, the elective body would not consider the competitive effect of an election either on the applicant or the member, although the association was allowed to retain the exclusive right to the news of its members.[220] The "inability to buy news from the largest news agency" wrote Justice Black for the court, meant that a newspaper without the news service of the AP was "more than likely to be at a competitive disadvantage." The bylaws of the AP, which "aimed at the destruction of competition," made it so difficult for newspapers in competition with incumbent members to gain access to the news that "the opportunity of any new paper" was seriously limited. For Justice Frankfurter, who also wrote a concurring opinion, the particular interest that the public had in the business of the AP made regulation necessary. The business of the press, and of the AP, was "the promotion of truth regarding public matters," wrote Frankfurter. "Restraints upon the promotion of truth through denial of access to the basis for understanding," he continued, called "into play considerations very different from comparable restraints in a cooperative enterprise having merely a commercial aspect."

The interest of the public is to have the flow of news not trammelled by the combined self-interest of those who enjoy a unique constitutional position precisely because of the public dependence on a free press. A public interest so essential to the vitality of our democratic government may be defeated by private restraints no less than by public censorship.[221]

---

[218] 52 F. Supp. 362 (1943). Thurman Arnold made a similar point to the AP in private. See Unsigned (perhaps McLean?) memo, July 22, 1942, AP01.4B, series IX, box 52, folder 876, AP.

[219] 326 U.S. 1 (1945).

[220] M.A. Blanchard, "The Associated Press Antitrust Suit: A Philosophical Clash over Ownership of First Amendment Rights," *The Business History Review* 61 (1987), 43–85.

[221] 326 U.S. 1 (1945) at 1427–28.

For Frankfurter, business practice and censorship were two sides of the same coin, and both required careful monitoring to prevent against encroachments on press freedom.

Justice Roberts, writing for Justice Stone, and Justice Murphy, who wrote separately, all dissented. Roberts observed that there was no evidence the AP intended to destroy competition. He also objected that the size of the association had no apparent bearing on the question of restraint. Converting the AP into "a public utility subject to the duty to serve all on equal terms," opined Roberts, was "government-by-injunction with a vengeance," which might "well result not in freer competition but in a monopoly in AP."[222] The implications of the decision were far-reaching for the news industry and for jurisprudence. Although refusal to deal when part of a scheme to dominate the market or suppress competition might be unlawful, in *AP* the court found no suppression of competition in the gathering of news; instead, it predicated its decision on the interests the public had in the service of the association.[223]

From the 1890s to the 1940s, American courts repeatedly found that the dominance of the AP and its refusals to deal with certain news outlets were detrimental to the public interest. In their decisions, judges favored small newspapers over large newspapers and, consequently, over rivalry between newsgatherers. This propensity reflected a desire to maintain a plurality of newspapers to uphold "free trade in ideas," which became "commercial canon" before it became a metaphor for the constitutional protection of political speech.[224] It may appear to be contradictory that the court simultaneously prohibited competitors from misappropriating the AP's news and prohibited the AP from refusing to deal, but the courts understood the prohibitions to be distinct, and a clear conception of the disparate markets to which they applied makes them reconcilable and consistent. In *Board of Trade v. Christie*, for example, the United States Supreme Court drew a clear distinction between the rules and contracts of the Chicago Board of Trade and the property right it had in the market information it generated.[225] By protecting the AP from misappropriation, the court confined itself to the newsgathering market; its prohibition against refusals to deal applied to the newspaper market. Forcing open the AP undermined the possibility to control admission, and by extension to self-regulate competition in the newsgathering market. After *AP*, more newspapers subscribed to the association than before, which increased the economies accruing to membership and in turn entrenched the dominance of

---

[222] This is the same argument Lawson and Ochs had made, and it cuts against the prevalent view that the wire services were common carriers. See I. de Sola Pool, *Technologies of Freedom: On Free Speech in an Electronic Age* (Cambridge, MA: Belknap Press, 1984).

[223] P.W. Bruton, "United States v. Associated Press," *University of Pennsylvania Law Review*, 92 (December 1943), 210.

[224] Peritz, *Competition Policy*, pp. 100–1.

[225] (198 U.S. 236 [1905])

the AP.[226] Provided it could be kept in check, size had considerable advantages, including an increased supply of news for public consumption at a cheaper price. The enforcement of American antitrust laws, although intended to preserve competition, encouraged big business. In all events, it is clear that the suit in 1945 was hardly a "watershed departure by government from its largely laissez-faire attitude toward media economic concentration," but rather the continuation of an established tradition of regulation.[227]

International comparison helps to establish the relative strength of the Supreme Court's property rights action. In Britain, after the nationalization of telegraphy in 1868, the Post Office stipulated that all newspapers be included in the formation of any nationwide news association. By World War II, however, the British Press Association embraced private practices that were less cooperative and more exclusive, whereas the AP became more akin to a regulated public utility. Convergence appears to have been partly purposeful. In the private papers of Justice Frankfurter, who concurred in *AP*, is an editorial in which he underlined passages that suggested the AP ought to be open to all like the British association.[228] In Britain, the Press Association avoided the difficulties of balancing exclusion and cooperation, but it paid the price in terms of its reliance on the limited speed of the Post Office telegraph department. As early as the 1880s, news associations in the United States used leased lines widely, but to preserve its policy of maintaining a level playing field among the press, the British Post Office denied the Press Association such facilities until the 1920s. The comparatively weak American state privileged exclusivity over cooperation. The stronger British state enforced cooperation at the expense of exclusivity.

---

[226] Counsel for the government recognized that the UP and INS benefited from the membership restrictions of the AP. *AP v. US*, 326 U.S. 1 (1945), brief for the US, p. 79.

[227] *Contra* Pilgrim, "Newspapers as Natural Monopolies," p. 5.

[228] "The Problem of the Associated Press," *The Atlantic Monthly*, 114 (1914), 132–7 with Frankfurter's marginalia, Felix Frankfurter papers, reel 12, Harvard Law School.

4

The "Rationalist Illusion," the Post Office, and the Press, 1868–1913

The American state regulated news associations through competition policy to protect newspaper plurality. In Britain, the state also sought to protect plurality but it did so through telecommunications policy. By nationalizing telegraphy, Parliament sought to create and maintain a level playing field for competition among provincial publishers while subsidizing their newsgathering collectively. These policies, the intellectual origins of which may be traced to the Enlightenment, continued until World War I.

Government control of telegraphy delayed vertical and horizontal integration and encouraged the perpetuation of several specialized newsgathering organizations which were loosely combined through various agreements. In this way, the structure of the newsgathering market in Britain was similar to that of British manufacturing. If America was the land of the trust, then Britain was the land of the gentlemen's agreement; but whereas the attempts of small firms to limit competition in large markets through agreement during the nineteenth century were often ineffective, the influence of government policy ensured that those among news organizations worked.[1]

Decisions concerning the regulation and operation of telecommunications reflected a particular policy paradigm respecting the press as well as a long-standing industrial policy against mergers in favor of "restrictive agreements," the effect, if not purpose, of which was to protect small firms.[2] Restrictive practices and arrangements were also strategically attractive to company managers as alternatives to monopoly.[3] The readiness of British firms to resolve

---

[1] Mercer, *Constructing a Competitive Order*, p. 32. Freyer, *Regulating Big Business*; L. Hannah, *Rise of the Corporate Economy*, p. 11; Hannah, "Mergers, Cartels and Concentration," pp. 306–16.

[2] Dobbin, *Forging Industrial Policy*, pp. 197–212. S. Pollard, *The Development of the British Economy 1914–1990*, 4th ed. (London: Edward Arnold, 1992), p. 4.

[3] As described in L. Hannah, "Mergers in British Manufacturing Industry, 1880–1918," *Oxford Economic Papers*, 26 (1974), 1–20.

disputes by arbitration, and to continue to cooperate, rather than to force mergers or pursue litigation, meant British courts had a significantly smaller role with respect to competition policy and property rights in news than in the United States.[4] The British Post Office, the administrative body charged with the operation of telegraphy, and then an important department of state, frequently decided competition and property rights issues as well, which obviated the need for judicial intervention. The PA was established in reaction to the nationalization of telegraphy in 1868, and the effects that Post Office control of telegraphy had on the method of news collection and distribution in Britain. Consequently, it was fundamentally different in organization and operation from the early American news associations, which formed to contend with the way in which telegraphy affected market competition.

FORGING THE SETTLEMENT OF 1868

The determination to grant the Post Office control of telegraphy was in part a response to the conviction that a cartel of telegraph companies overcharged users and provided them with an inadequate service. This reflected the mid-Victorian view that cartels worked against the public interest, although they were accepted as part of liberal economic life by the end of the nineteenth century.[5] The Electric and International, the Magnetic, and the United Kingdom telegraph companies, all of which incorporated during the 1840s and 1850s, controlled telegraphy throughout the country. According to a government report of 1868, "the three principal telegraph companies are, and have for some time been, in perfect agreement as to the rates they shall charge for messages," and the consequences were apparent.[6] Statistics illustrated the point: in 1859, according to another government report, upward of five million messages were sent in the United States at an average charge of between 1s 4d and 1s 8d, which produced, exclusive of press messages, revenue of £400,000. In the United Kingdom in the same year, 1,575,437 messages were sent and the average charge was 3s 6d, which, inclusive of press messages, produced revenue of £275,704. Accordingly, the British companies received £.18 per message, whereas the Americans earned £.08, which suggests that the British companies were comparatively unproductive, monopolistic, or both.[7] According to Post

---

[4] As described in M. Keller, "The Pluralist State: American Economic Regulation in Comparative Perspective," in T. McGraw (ed.), *Regulation in Perspective: Historical Essays* (London: Harvard University Press, 1981), p. 64. Compare with S. Skowronek, *Building a New American State*, p. 122.

[5] M. Keller, "Regulation of Large Enterprise: the United States in Comparative Perspective," in A. Chandler Jr. and H. Daems (eds.), *Managerial Hierarchies: Comparative Perspectives on the Rise of the Modern Industrial Enterprise* (Cambridge, MA: Harvard University Press, 1980), p. 163.

[6] "Electric Telegraphs Bill," *British Parliamentary Papers* (BPP), 1867–1868 (272), XLI.737, p. 21.

[7] S. Broadberry, *Market Services and the Productivity Race* (Cambridge: Cambridge University Press, 2006), pp. 172–3. It appears, however, that in 1865–1866 the cost of maintaining telegraph

Office statistics at the time, which accounted for population, the Americans sent four times as many messages as the British.[8] Such aggregate data is open to various interpretations, but it does provide a sense of the information underlying Parliament's decision-making. Despite the alleged shortcomings of the telegraph companies, between 1855 and 1866, Britain's miles of telegraph wires nearly doubled from 43,720 to 80,466; the number of stations open to the public increased from 678 to 2,151, or nearly six offices for every 100,000 people; and the number of public messages grew from slightly more than 1 million per year to more than 5 million.[9]

The absolute growth of telegraphy in Britain, despite its lackluster relative performance, and a general reluctance among policy-makers at the time to encourage the usurpation of private undertakings, has led some historians to conclude that passage of the Telegraph Act of 1868 was a product of the political influence of different user-groups.[10] No business group made more public pronouncements about the inadequacy of the service the companies rendered than the provincial press, even though it was the mercantile classes that made the most use of the telegraph.[11] Since 1848, the major British telegraph companies had supplied news, and newspapers were beholden to them for it.[12] The Electric Telegraph Company, established in 1846, started a service of news messages to increase throughput during lulls in paid-for telegram traffic, much like Western Union in the United States. Whereas the American press quickly gained control of its own newsgathering, in Britain, whether by choice or compulsion, the press left the task to the telegraph companies. The news services of the Electric provided coverage of general parliamentary, sporting, stock exchange, and commercial news. In 1852, formation of the International Telegraph Company, a subsidiary of the Electric that controlled cables on the European continent, provided the means to supply the British press and other customers with reports from Europe. By 1854, the Electric served more than 120 provincial newspapers.[13] Newspapers could purchase a service of approximately 6,000 words when Parliament was in session and 4,000 words daily at

wires was cheaper in Britain than in either Belgium or Switzerland. "Electric Telegraphs," *British Parliamentary Papers* (BPP), 1867–1868 (202), XLI.555, p. 128.

[8] "Electric Telegraphs," p. 86.

[9] "Electric Telegraphs," pp. 73–4, 126, 158.

[10] On the unwillingness to commit to government control, see H. Perkin, "Individualism Versus Collectivism in Nineteenth Century Britain: A False Antithesis," *The Journal of British Studies*, 17 (1977), 105–18. For the pressure-group, thesis see J.L Kieve, *The Electric Telegraph* (Newton Abbot: David & Charles, 1973).

[11] "Report from the Select Committee on the Electric Telegraphs Bill," *BPP*, 1867–68 (435), XI.1, p. 3.

[12] W. Tegg, *Post and Telegraphs, Past and Present: With an Account of the Telephone and Phonograph* (London: William Tegg & Co., 1878), p. 218.

[13] Manager's Memoranda, March 4, 1915, Press Association papers (hereafter PA), Ms 35362/8, p. 129, Guildhall Library (hereafter GL); Kieve, *Electric Telegraph*, p. 72; Tariff of Charges, November 1, 1868, TGE 3/5, BT Archives (hereafter BT).

other times of the year for less than £17 per month (or approximately £1,300 in today's prices). Although in 1865 the British telegraph companies collectively raised rates, which caused complaints from a variety of user groups, especially newspapers, the charge was, said one Post Office official, "unquestionably low."[14]

Publishers of daily provincial papers complained that the news service provided by the companies was expensive, contained telegrams editors found superfluous, omitted others concerning topics of importance, and was often transmitted illegibly.[15] According to the Edinburgh Chamber of Commerce, which lobbied on behalf of the Scottish press, it was a criticism often repeated that "the inexperience, want of intelligence, or carelessness of the staff of the telegraph companies" meant the manuscripts furnished to the press were "inaccurate and often unintelligible, so that in every newspaper office much valuable time [was] nightly wasted in the irritating and wearisome occupation of deciphering and reducing to intelligible order the news received from the telegraph offices."[16] Francis D. Findlay, proprietor of the Belfast *Northern Whig*, and other newspaper publishers, claimed the telegraph companies wielded a "despotic and arbitrary" power in the collection of news.[17] What little evidence there is suggests that, for the companies, the gathering of news was an economical, logical, and profitable extension of their principal line of business. On average, between 1857 and 1859, newsgathering constituted less than 2 percent of the British and Irish Magnetic Telegraph Company's annual expenditures. However, even according to internal company documents, the press messages were frequently written illegibly.[18] But Post Office officials did not rely on criticisms of the accuracy of the telegraph companies as a rationale for government control. "I have never concurred with those who accused them of habitual inaccuracy in the transmission of messages," said Frank Ives Scudamore, the official principally responsible for the Post Office campaign, when he testified before the select committee on the Telegraphs Bill in 1868. "I think they have done their work uncommonly well, and in the first instance at very great pecuniary risk, and in spite of very great difficulties indeed." The problem, said Scudamore, lay not with individuals, but with "the system."[19]

[14] "Electric telegraphs bill," p. 17.
[15] H. Weaver to All Stations, October 1867, TGE 3/5, BT. Representatives of the press made abortive attempts to improve the service through negotiations with the telegraph company. See J. E. Taylor et al. to EITC, October 19, 1865, POST 81/115, BT. See also R.N. Barton, "New Media: The Birth of Telegraphic News in Britain," *Media History* 16 (2010), 379–406.
[16] "Electric Telegraphs," p. 51.
[17] "Report from the Select Committee on the Electric Telegraphs Bill," p. 102.
[18] "Electric Telegraph Companies," *BPP*, 1860 (434), LXII.189, p. 13. In 1866, the telegraph companies' Intelligence Department earned £30,318 on an expenditure of £6,581. Intelligence Department Income Statement, 1866, TGE 3/2, BT. Regarding the illegibility of messages, see H. Weaver to all stations, October 1867, TGE 3/5, BT.
[19] "Report from the Select Committee on the Electric Telegraphs Bill," p. 7.

Certainly, the complaints of the press, and the alleged inadequacy of the service the companies provided, were influential in shaping policy, but to perceive the workings of interest-group politics in the campaign for government control of telegraphy does a disservice to the idealism of the mid-Victorian generation, ignores how answers to new policy problems were designed around the principles of existing institutions, and fails to account for the fact that policy strategies persisted over generations.[20] The policy toward the press embodied in the Telegraph Act, which implemented the first major government purchase of private enterprise in modern British history, was an outgrowth of an historical belief in "the vision of human educability" characteristic of the British Enlightenment and doctrines of free trade, the combination of which gave rise to the concept of the marketplace for ideas.[21] The reasoning by which education was linked to free trade relied on the metonymy by which knowledge and print were conceived as contiguous. The conflation of print and knowledge was not merely a turn of phrase. It reflected a particular understanding of communication. "The mass of every people must be barbarous where there is no printing and consequently knowledge is not generally diffused," said Dr. Johnson, and "knowledge is diffused among our people by the newspapers."[22] If print was knowledge manifest, then knowledge could be an article of commerce, trade in which could be subjected to the principles of political economy. Hence the remark of Adam Smith, that "knowledge [was] purchased in the same manner as shoes or stockings, from those whose business it is to make up and prepare for the market that particular species of goods."[23] Taken together, these beliefs led to a conviction that the only restriction on the greater diffusion of knowledge was that imposed by the inadequacy of the means, or what E.P. Thompson called the "rationalist illusion."[24]

If print was knowledge, then it was a double-edged sword, for if it bore the impress of enlightened thinking, the people might be civilized; but if it did not, they would be misled. In 1812, Robert Southey, the poet and conservative writer, lamented how by dint of their ignorance the poor were severely subject to the fabrications that the press propagated. "The weekly epistles of the apostles of sedition," wrote Southey with rhetorical flourish, "are read aloud

---

[20] For the interest-group approach, see Kieve, *Electric Telegraph*, and J. Foreman-Peck, "Competition, Co-operation, and Nationalisation in the Nineteenth-Century Telegraph System," *Business History*, 31 (1989), 98. On the formation of industrial-policy paradigms, see F. Dobbin, "The Social Construction of the Great Depression: Industrial Policy during the 1930s in the United States, Britain, and France," *Theory and Society*, 22 (1993), 1–56.

[21] On educability and the Enlightenment, see R. Porter, *English Society in the Eighteenth Century* (London: Penguin, 1990), p. 310 and *Enlightenment: Britain and the Creation of the Modern World* (London: Allen Lane, 2000).

[22] J. Boswell, *The Life of Samuel Johnson* (London: J. Davis, 1820), p. 320.

[23] As quoted in Porter, *English Society*, p. 242.

[24] E.P. Thompson, *The Making of the English Working Class* (Harmondsworth: Penguin, 1968), p. 733.

in taprooms and pot-houses to believing auditors, listening greedily."[25] *The Times* echoed Southey's sentiments. The poverty of the "more humble classes" was such that "if they do read, or know anything of public affairs, it must be in the cheapest forms: and hence they become the dupes, to a certain extent, of the basest and most profligate of men."[26] The efforts of middle-class reformers therefore turned to ensuring that the working classes had access to cheap and useful literature. In 1826, such concerns drove the Whig Henry Brougham and his Utilitarian allies to establish the Society for the Diffusion of Useful Knowledge.[27]

Any hindrance to the distribution of print threatened to undermine the purpose of the Society for the Diffusion of Useful Knowledge, which, ipso facto, was linked with free trade, and consequently with the movement to repeal the "taxes on knowledge," which in turn was linked with reforming the postal system. The term "taxes on knowledge," which referred to those imposts levied on the production of newspapers, and especially to the notorious newspaper stamp first instituted in the reign of Queen Anne, is illustrative of the continuation into the Victorian era of the Georgian belief in a connection between the written word and knowledge. The phrase is commonly attributed to Edwin Chadwick, or *Le Père Sanitaire* as the French named him for his public health reforms. When, in 1836, after much agitation, Thomas Spring Rice, a fluent debater but lackluster chancellor, reduced the stamp duty on newspapers from 4*d* to a penny, some argued that the remaining tax was payment for the circulation of information, but advocates of total abolition of the stamp were convinced that a universal tax of a penny, as opposed to a scale of postal charges, benefited the London papers. The papers of the metropolis, they claimed, could circulate from one end of the country, and back, as well as to any place thereafter *ad infinitum*, simply by paying only a penny for a newspaper stamp. Local newspapers, having a comparatively smaller territory of circulation, received less value for the initial penny paid under the stamp duty.[28] Even after the requirement to purchase a stamp to benefit from the penny rate was repealed in 1855, the London dailies continued to buy them. In 1858, three-quarters of the 71 million newspapers the Post Office transported continued to bear the stamp, and in 1864, 44 million newspapers still bore the stamp and traveled through the Post Office without postage.[29] The large number of newspapers

[25] R. Southey, "Propositions for Ameliorating the Condition of the Poor," *Quarterly Review*, 8 (December 1812), p. 342.

[26] *The Times*, January 3, 1817, p. 2.

[27] B. Hilton, *A Mad, Bad, and Dangerous People? England, 1783–1846* (Oxford: Clarendon Press, 2006), p. 174; A. Aspinall, *Lord Brougham and the Whig Party* (London: Longmans, 1928).

[28] C. Wilson, *First with the News: The History of W.H. Smith, 1792–1972* (London: Cape, 1985), p. 68.

[29] H. Robinson, *Britain's Post Office* (Oxford: Oxford University Press, 1953), p. 174; L. Bentley, "The Electric Telegraph and the Struggle over Copyright in News in Australia, Great Britain and India," in B. Sherman and L. Wiseman (eds.), *Copyright and the Challenge of the New* (Alphen an den Rijn: Kluwer, 2012), chapter 3.

that retained the newspaper stamp after its abolition indicates the advantage it provided. According to W.H. Smith, the nineteenth-century newsagent and one informed in such matters, the abolition of the stamp might have stimulated production of newspapers in the provinces, but "every change" had "been in favour of the London press."[30]

However desirable free trade in print may have appeared, a neutral system of distribution proved illusory, but the zeal of postal reformers persisted undiminished. Aside from its fiscal rationale, the establishment in 1840 of the penny post, argued Rowland Hill, its self-proclaimed progenitor, would send knowledge to the darkest corners of the country and wash away rural ignorance.[31] Legislation pertaining to the penny post, aside from establishing a uniform rate of postage, also stipulated that newspapers could travel from one town to another free of charge, and for one penny each by the post of a post town addressed to a person within the limits of the same town.[32] As a consequence, under a postal regime, as opposed to a stamp regime, local papers could copy news from London publications and then circulate freely by hand delivery in their vicinage, thereby underselling the London papers that paid postage.[33] It is an indication of the intractability of bias in the pricing structure of communication networks generally that in the United States similar debates occurred in Congress between 1789 and 1792. Other things being equal, most Americans preferred to read newspapers that originated in the large commercial towns; therefore, the admission of newspapers into the mail free of charge, some objected, would benefit printers in those towns. American country publishers complained that "free trade" amounted to the dumping of metropolitan publications throughout the countryside.[34]

Setting aside whether the postal system privileged the London or provincial press, throughout the nineteenth century, newspapers en masse received a considerable subsidy from the Post Office. In 1860, the *Westminster Review* observed that the average cost of transmission for a newspaper was 1.25*d*, but for a letter it was 1/36th of a penny, yet they were charged alike. "Surely it is unjust to the letter sender," opined the *Review*, "to make him pay dearly in order that the newspaper sender may pay cheaply."[35] James Bruce, eighth Earl of Elgin and postmaster-general from 1859 to 1860, believed "the wide circulation of newspapers" to be "a very desirable object, as it tends to diffuse knowledge," but the same could be said of letters and books, and "the demand for special privileges in the case of newspapers," according to Elgin, was "only

[30] "Report from the Select Committee on newspaper stamps," *BPP* (558), 1851, XVII.1, p. 431.
[31] R. Hill, *Post Office Reform: Its Importance and Practicability*, 3rd ed. (London: Charles Knight & Co., 1837); R. John, "The Political Economy of Postal Reform in the Victorian Age," *Smithsonian Contributions to History and Technology*, 55 (2010), 3–12.
[32] 3 & 4 Victoria, cap. 96; s. 44.
[33] "Report from the Select Committee on newspaper stamps," pp. 224, 241–7.
[34] John, *Spreading the News*, pp. 33–5, 40.
[35] "The Post Office Monopoly," *Westminster Review*, 18 (July 1860), 79.

one of the many forms of a claim for protection."[36] Even Rowland Hill came to regard the rate charged to newspapers as too low, which, by his calculations, worked out at about one-seventh of the charge made for a letter, if the average weight of the two was compared.[37] Already in the 1830s, it took two hundred sorters in the London Post Office, with additional help from the letter carriers after they had finished ringing their bells, to get the newspapers off for the outgoing coaches in the evening.[38] By 1875, the Post Office delivered 121 million newspapers annually, and thereafter the number continued to increase. During a five-year period ending March 1891, the average annual number increased to 155 million.[39]

During the 1850s and 1860s, Post Office control of telegraphy was understood to be an extension of the process of postal reform and the pursuit of free trade in knowledge.[40] Indeed, the persuasiveness of the analogy proponents of government control drew between the penny post and the operation of the telegraph helps to account for the success of the campaign, despite the fact that Rowland Hill had fundamentally miscalculated the economics of his scheme.[41] Chadwick, a reformer for all seasons, was convinced that the analogy between letters and telegrams was "exact."[42] He believed government management would promote efficient competition and free trade in other private industries. "Great as have been the benefits derived from the repeal of protection duties on corn and other articles," claimed Chadwick in a paper he subsequently addressed to Benjamin Disraeli, then chancellor, and referred to Lord Stanley of Alderly, then postmaster-general, "I believe it will be found that they are inconsiderable as compared with the benefits derivable from the removal of excessive charges on transit, as well as fiscal and other obstructions to free inter-communication."[43] Affirmation for the pursuit of free trade

---

[36] "Sixth Report of the Postmaster General," *BPP*, 1860 (2657), XXIII.311, p. 24.

[37] Robinson, *British Post Office*, p. 356.

[38] Robinson, *British Post Office*, p. 246.

[39] J.C. Hemmeon, *The History of the British Post Office* (Cambridge, MA: Harvard University Press, 1912), p. 68.

[40] Hochfelder, "Comparison of the Postal Telegraph Movement," 739–61.

[41] Such analogical reasoning was often repeated. For one example, see the comments of F.I. Scudamore in "Electric Telegraphs Bill," p. 6. Although W.S. Jevons supported government control, he objected that the post and telegraphy were not entirely analogous. See "On the Analogy between the Post Office, Telegraphs, and Other Systems of Conveyance of the United Kingdom, as Regards Government Control," in *Methods of Social Reform* (London: Macmillan, 1883), pp. 277–92. See also Jevons' testimony in "Report from the Select Committee on the Electric Telegraphs Bill," p. 63. R.H. Coase notes the influence of the penny post on future policy in "Rowland Hill and the Penny Post," *Economica*, 6 (1939), 423–35. M.J. Daunton points out Hill's miscalculations in *Royal Mail: The Post Office since 1840* (London: Athlone Press, 1985), pp. 5–35.

[42] E. Chadwick, "On the Economy of Telegraphy as Part of a Public System of Postal Communication," *Royal Society of Arts*, 22 (1867), 227–8.

[43] Chadwick, "On the Economy of Telegraphy," 225–6; "Electric Telegraphs," *BPP*, 1867–1868 (202), XLI.555, p. 8.

through government control of telegraphy also came from abroad. According to Corr Van der Maeren, president of the Brussels Tribunal of Commerce, it was in light of the low price of telegraphy that his government stipulated, and in combination with that "other great vehicle of thought, the press," that he did "not despair seeing in our little country perfect freedom of trade."[44]

If there was a material difference between the "rationalist illusion" of the Georgians and that of the Victorians it lay in the connection that the former drew between print and knowledge and the latter drew between print and commerce. Chadwick's support for government ownership of telegraphy sprang not only from his pet obsession with repeal of the "taxes on knowledge," but also from his particular brand of political economy. In a paper read before the Statistical Society of London in January 1859, Chadwick explained the results of two different principles of legislation and administration in Europe, which he called "competition for the field" as compared with "competition within the field" of service. Competitions "within the field" of service were wasteful when they interfered with economies of scale, as in the provision of water pipes. In contrast, "competition for the field," which Chadwick proposed, meant that "the whole field of service should be put up on behalf of the public for competition." This was the "only condition on which efficiency, as well as the utmost cheapness, was practicable, namely, the possession, by one capital or establishment, of the entire field ... with full securities towards the public for the performance of the requisite service during a given period." The Post Office was an example of effective "competition for the field," which prevented "the acknowledged evils of unrestricted monopolies" while it maintained "that responsibility towards the public for efficient service," which was otherwise "thought to be only obtainable by unregulated competition within the field."[45] Chadwick applied this theory to telegraphy with fervor, and it goes some way toward explaining why, in its first iteration, the Telegraph Act did not grant the Post Office a monopoly over telegraphy, but only licensed it to purchase the assets of the telegraph companies.

Chadwick and Scudamore's views on the subject were so closely aligned that one opponent of a postal-telegraph confused them with each other.[46] Scudamore entered the service of the Post Office before his twentieth birthday and owed much to the intellectual heritage of the penny post and postal

---

44 "Electric Telegraphs," p. 55.
45 E. Chadwick, "Results of Different Principles of Legislations and Administration in Europe; of Competition for the Field, as Compared with Competition within the Field, of Service," *Journal of the Statistical Society of London*, 22 (1859), 381–420. See also the interesting interpretation and application of Chadwick's principles in R.B. Ekelund Jr. and E.O. Price III, "Sir Edwin Chadwick on Competition and the Social Control of Industry: Railroads," *History of Political Economy*, 11 (1979), 213–39, esp. 237.
46 Electric and International Telegraph Co., *Government and the Telegraphs. Statement of the Case of the Electric and International Telegraph Company against the Government Bill for Acquiring the Telegraphs* (London: Effingham Wilson, 1868).

reform generally. In Scudamore's mind, as in those of Chadwick and Rowland Hill, removing impediments to the free flow of information would further the knowledge of the populace and augment trade. "The more you can increase the means and facility of communication," said Scudamore, "the more you stimulate trade, economist capital, and facilitate every operation of commerce."[47] Even "a mere beggar in the streets," said Scudamore in one of his more dramatic moments, "who does not write a letter in a year, would be a more wretched beggar than he is if the correspondence of the country were cut off."[48] It was for these reasons, that Scudamore was convinced the transmission of news "to the press throughout the kingdom" was "a matter of national importance."[49] Indeed, one of the "principal results" the government sought to obtain through purchase of the telegraphs, wrote Scudamore, was "free trade in the collection of news for the press."[50] Only by placing the collection of news in the hands of the newspapers would every publisher be free to obtain the material they desired, the Post Office transmitting news irrespective of its contents, and only then would knowledge and trade bloom and boom throughout the land.

With the ideas of his predecessors, Scudamore comingled his creed of the "cooperative society," by which he meant efficient public institutions that demonstrated the benefits of working together.[51] The expansion of the remit of the Post Office during Scudamore's tenure to include, among other things, a system of savings banks, lent credence to this view.[52] In the "cooperative society," a public-service ethos and parliamentary accountability made government departments better equipped than joint-stock companies to be entrusted with communication. There was, of course, the peril that "a Government entrusted with a monopoly becomes lazy," said Scudamore, but he refused to "allow that that holds good with reference to the Post Office," which did "its work from day to day before the public," so that every shortcoming on its part was "discovered at once and complained of." Companies were "bound to consider the interests of their shareholders before they consider the interests of the public," whereas the "Post Office would be bound in the interest of the nation to make its system self-supporting undoubtedly, and in doing that they could not avoid making a profit; but profit is not the first object in view."[53]

---

[47] "Report from the Select Committee on the Electric Telegraphs Bill," pp. 7–8.
[48] "Report from the Select Committee on the Electric Telegraphs Bill," p. 133.
[49] Scudamore to J.E. Taylor, May 15, 1868, PA, Ms 35361/1, GL.
[50] "Report by Mr. Scudamore on the re-organization of the telegraph system of the United Kingdom" *BPP*, 1871 (304), XXXVII.703, p. 2.
[51] See C.R. Perry, "Scudamore, Frank Ives (1823–1884)," *Oxford Dictionary of National Biography Online (ODNB)* (Oxford: Oxford University Press, 2004), online ed., accessed March 13, 2011.
[52] C.R. Perry, "Frank Ives Scudamore and the Post Office Telegraphs," *Albion*, 12 (1980), 353.
[53] "Report from the Select Committee on the Telegraph Bill," *BPP*, 1868–1869 (348), VI.651, pp. 8, 11, 14. For similar pronouncements see "Electric Telegraphs," p. 18.

Scudamore was not alone in his favorable opinion of public departments, which was pervasive among Post Office employees in the decades following the establishment of the penny post. According to Frederick E. Baines, an officer of the Post Office, the postal system was in the hands of government "for the express purpose of facilitating the communication of the country, and not as a source of revenue only"; therefore, he concluded that the Post Office was better suited to control telegraphy as well. Baines, like Scudamore, owed a debt to Rowland Hill. Through the influence of Frederic Hill, to whom Baines was related by marriage, Rowland Hill, Frederic's brother, obtained for Baines a clerkship in the correspondence branch of the General Post Office.[54] Even William Stanley Jevons, the great political economist, was convinced that public ownership was preferable to private control. "In the hands of private persons" monopoly, said Jevons, would tend toward higher prices. Any monopoly of telegraphy was better "in the hands of the Government than in the hands of a private company."[55]

The view that the telegraphs, when under government control, would be operated in the public interest and not necessarily for pecuniary gain was reflected in the Telegraph Act of 1868. It was pronounced in the preamble, which noted that a "cheaper, more widely extended, and more expeditious System of Telegraphy" would be of "great Advantage to the State, as well as to Merchants and Traders, and to the Public generally."[56] When, after the passage of the Act, the telegraph department showed a marked and growing deficit, Post Office officials relied on this preamble as evidence that Parliament had not intended the postal-telegraph to be a source of financial gain but of public benefit. "No words can well be plainer than these, or show more clearly that the intention of the Legislature was to consult public convenience, and not to purchase the telegraphs as a mere commercial speculation," wrote Lord John Manners, postmaster-general, in 1875.[57] William Preece, chief engineer, acknowledged that the Post Office lost approximately £300,000 per year providing a cheap service to the press, but, he said, "the benefit which the public derive from the dissemination of accurate news was worth this additional charge on taxes."[58] As a consequence, successive suggestions to raise the rate charged for press messages made little progress.[59]

The low tariff charged for press telegrams reflected the public-service ethos of the Telegraph Act. Between the hours of 6 p.m. and 9 a.m., any publicly registered newspaper, newsroom, club, or exchange room paid 1s for a message

---

54 "Electric Telegraphs," p. 42; S. E. Fryer, "Baines, Frederick Ebenezer (1832–1911)," rev. Anita McConnell, *ODNB*.

55 "Report from the select committee on the Electric Telegraphs Bill," pp. 63–4.

56 The Telegraph Act, 1868, c. 110.

57 "Post Office Telegraphs," *BPP*, 1876 (34), XLII.371, p. 9.

58 As quoted in Hochfelder, "Comparison of the Postal Telegraph Movement," p. 756.

59 See Kieve, *Electric Telegraph*, pp. 219–20.

of 100 words, and between 9 a.m. and 6 p.m. for a message of seventy-five words. An additional charge of 2*d* was levied for every "drop" of 100 or 75 words at an additional address. It was the low "drop," or duplicate rate, that generated considerable economies for the press. In this way, a report sent to all daily provincial papers cost each slightly less than 2.25*d* per 100 words, or nearly 4*s* per column of solid minion type.[60] To appreciate how economical this tariff was, recall that in 1870 Western Union charged the NYAP £4.47 for messages of 100 words (or $.25 per word) between New York and Washington, DC.[61] Scudamore, who was responsible for determining the tariff, was clearly predisposed to the publishers' propositions for a low rate, but, as one news association executive reflected in 1915, "I don't think the Government quite knew what it meant when it granted the two-penny duplicate rate."[62]

COOPERATION AND EXCLUSION UNDER
A POSTAL-TELEGRAPH REGIME

The tariff and privileges for the press that passed with the Telegraph Act, the way in which the legislation was enforced, and the manner in which the Post Office operated the telegraph, all had significant long-term consequences for the gathering and distribution of news in Britain. The collection and distribution of news was centrally conducted by the companies before the passage of the Act, and – for policy and practical reasons – the Post Office refused to assemble news reports on behalf of the press, therefore, a new organization for this purpose had to be devised or else provincial publishers risked repeating their efforts, increasing their expenditure for telegraphic dispatches unnecessarily, and burdening the postal telegraph department.[63] The only organization capable of generating such news reports that existed prior to the passage of the Act, aside from the apparatus of the telegraph companies, was Reuters, a London-based news agency established in 1851. Reuters benefited from an exclusive agreement with the Electric and International, which purchased the agency's foreign news reports for resale to the provincial press while leaving it free to sell its news directly to London publishers.[64] After passage of the

---

[60] Supplementary Report of the Committee of Provincial Daily Newspaper Proprietors, June 26, 1868, PA, Ms 35356/1, GL.

[61] See Chapter 1.

[62] Scudamore consulted with the press when setting the tariff. See Supplementary Report of the Committee of Provincial Daily Newspaper Proprietors, June 26, 1868, PA, Ms 35356/1, GL. The comment was from Edmund Robbins, general manager of the PA. See Manager's Memoranda, March 4, 1915, PA, Ms 35362/8, p. 130, GL.

[63] As Scudamore acknowledged on several occasions. See, for example, "Report from the Select Committee on the Electric Telegraphs Bill," p. 26; and Scudamore to J.E. Taylor, May 15, 1868, PA, Ms 35356/1, GL.

[64] "Transmission of News by Telegraph," undated, p. 16, TGE 3/3, BT. D. Read, "Truth in News: Reuters and the Manchester *Guardian*, 1858–1964," *Northern History*, 31 (1995), 285.

Telegraph Act, Reuters was keen to supply both domestic and international news to the provincial press, but from the perspective of provincial publishers, and of Post Office officials, the prospect of replacing the telegraph companies with another organization separate from the press threatened to perpetuate the same problems of which the publishers had complained. Several provincial publishers found Reuters's service of foreign news to be as unsuited to their needs as that of the telegraph companies.[65] A considerable portion of Reuters's news, said Francis Findlay of the Belfast *Northern Whig*, was "so absolutely valueless to the Irish Press, that we do not even take the trouble to insert it."[66] It was clear, acknowledged Scudamore, that "the Newspaper Proprietors have long desired, and would greatly prefer, to appoint their own collectors of news."[67]

Provincial publishers preferred to undertake their own newsgathering, but doing so required them to form their own organization. The demand of provincial publishers for a greater quantity and higher quality of telegraphic dispatches meant that the cost of their news reports as compared with those of the telegraph companies would increase. Unless all the publishers, newsrooms, and exchanges that had patronized the telegraph companies purchased their news from this press-controlled organization, the economies from which the publishers had benefited before government control would dissipate. "If the Press all come into our association, as we hope they will," said John Edward Taylor, proprietor of the Manchester *Guardian*, before the select committee on the Telegraph Bill, "we have very little doubt that the news may be supplied at a very small increase, if any, upon the present rate; but should only a small proportion come into the association, of course the cost must be raised."[68] The incentive to cooperate was obvious, but obstacles to coordination stood in the way.

Whereas in the United States the press navigated the obstacles that hindered cooperation on its own, which led down a path to exclusivity, in Britain the Post Office facilitated the formation of an inclusive press association among newspaper publishers in the provinces. According to the Telegraph Act, only the publishers of publicly registered newspapers, or the proprietors of newsrooms, clubs, or exchange rooms were entitled to the highly discounted tariff for telegrams that the Act instituted. This proviso undermined the possibility of any organization not backed by the press, such as Reuters, from supplying news to provincial publishers directly, encouraged the provincial press to form an association of its own and protected it from competition. The assistance that

[65] Regarding publishers' thoughts on Reuters, see Memo of C.V. Boyes, January 21, 1865, TGE 3/2, BT and "Report by Mr. Scudamore on the Re-organization of the Telegraph System of the United Kingdom," p. 14.

[66] "Report from the Select Committee on the Electric Telegraphs Bill," p. 102.

[67] Scudamore to J.E. Taylor, May 15, 1868, PA, Ms 35356/1, GL.

[68] Testimony of J.E. Taylor, "Report from the Select Committee on the Electric Telegraphs Bill," pp. 91–7.

Scudamore gave the provincial publishers was partially self-serving.[69] The Post Office, like Western Union in the United States, had an incentive to encourage the formation of a dominant organization. If more than one news association or news service existed, it would increase the work of, and expense incurred by, the Post Office.

Granting provincial publishers a de facto monopoly over the supply of news to newsrooms and exchanges also facilitated the creation of a provincial news association. Newsrooms and exchanges, where people gathered to read the news, threatened the circulation of provincial newspapers. Additionally, once telegraphic news dispatches appeared in newsrooms, newspapers could copy them without having paid for them. There were papers that sent reporters to newsrooms expressly for this purpose.[70] It had therefore been a source of considerable consternation among publishers that the telegraph companies also sold news reports to newsrooms and exchanges.[71] Although the Telegraph Act promised newsrooms the same low tariff as newspapers, to control competition and to spread more widely the expense incurred in gathering their own news, provincial publishers were adamant that they should control the supply of news to the newsrooms and exchanges.[72] Privately, Scudamore consented. "If the agency which the Press are about to establish does in fact work in a satisfactory manner," wrote Scudamore to George Harper of the Huddersfield *Chronicle* and the Provincial Newspaper Society, "it will by force of circumstances have a practical monopoly of the collection of news and will become a sole agency for the exchange rooms, clubs and newsrooms."[73] Being assured of the patronage of the newsrooms and exchanges throughout the country, provincial publishers were incentivized to join any proposed cooperative association to benefit from a corresponding reduction in the cost of their news. In the autumn of 1868, the leading provincial dailies – including the Birmingham *Daily Gazette*; Cork *Examiner*; Dundee *Advertiser*; Edinburgh *Scotsman*; Glasgow *Herald* and *North British Daily Mail*; Leeds *Mercury*; Liverpool *Courier*, *Daily Post*, and *Mercury*; Manchester *Guardian* and *Examiner*; Newcastle *Northern Daily Express*; Nottingham *Journal*; Sheffield *Independent*; and Yorkshire *Post* – established the Press Association (PA).[74] In 1870, with a few exceptions, the proprietors of all the daily morning and evening papers in the country outside London were members of the association. Additionally, 130 proprietors of tri-weekly, biweekly, and weekly papers were also members, and nearly the same

[69] Supplementary Report of the Committee of Provincial Daily Newspaper Proprietors, June 26, 1868, PA, Ms 35356, GL.
[70] "Provincial Newspaper Society…," July 25, 1868, PA, Ms 35357, GL.
[71] Intelligence department, October 1, 1867, TGE 3/5, BT; Fisher to Montrose, March 6, 1868 in "Report from the Select Committee on the Electric Telegraphs Bill," appendix 3, pp. 25–6.
[72] "Report from the Select Committee on the Electric Telegraphs Bill," pp. 95, 214.
[73] Scudamore to Harper, July 25, 1868, PA, Ms 35357, GL.
[74] Meeting of the Committee for Establishing a News Association, September 15, 1868, PA, Ms 35356/1, GL.

number, although nonmembers, were subscribers. The association also served eighty chambers of commerce and public newsrooms, nearly 100 provincial sporting houses, and more than sixty London clubs.[75]

Although the economies to be gained from association were enticing, forming a cooperative organization inclusive of the nation's provincial press was hardly a fait accompli. But the process was considerably easier and far less confrontational in Britain than it was in the United States, and there was never any attempt to exclude a portion of the press through membership strictures or to grant certain publications advantages over others. Instead, "all Provincial Newspaper Proprietors who require Telegraphic News" were encouraged to join.[76] The PA was to be "a co-operative association on a thoroughly Republican basis of 'Liberty, Equality and Fraternity.'"[77] The committee charged with its organization "therefore endeavoured to make such arrangements as will meet the wants of all," certain that the association could "never be worked for individual profit, or become exclusive in its character."[78] The policy of the Post Office, which granted equal access to telegraphy to all publishers and encouraged the formation of a cooperative provincial press association, made it difficult to create an exclusive association even if a portion of the provincial press had desired it. Without a mechanism for excluding certain publications from the association, such as franchise rights, there was little incentive for publishers to share with each other the news they had gathered and possessed exclusively. Additionally, there was no tradition among British newspapers of exchanging news exclusively by post, as there was in the United States, and even if there had been such a tradition, the unwillingness of the telegraph companies to permit the provincial papers to undertake their own newsgathering precluded the possibility of any system of exclusive sharing among the press. The determination of the press to rely on independent press association correspondents, as opposed to sharing news copy exclusively before publication, made coordination easier.

That the daily newspaper market in the United Kingdom was considerably smaller than in the United States, both in terms of the number of publications as well as the distance between them, also made coordination considerably easier. As early as 1836, provincial publishers banded together to form the Provincial Newspaper Society, now called the Newspaper Society, which protected the trade's interests.[79] In 1865, leading provincial dailies met to demand

[75] "Report of the Second Annual Meeting of Shareholders," May 11, 1870, PA, Ms 35372/1, GL.
[76] Supplementary Report from the Committee of Provincial Daily Newspaper Proprietors, June 26, 1868, PA, Ms 35356/1, GL.
[77] Meeting of the Proprietors of the Provincial Daily Newspapers, September 29, 1868, PA, Ms 35356/1, GL.
[78] "Report of the Committee of the Provincial Daily Newspaper Proprietors," June 29, 1868, PA, Ms 35356/1, GL.
[79] Newspaper Society, *The Newspaper Society, 1836–1936; A Centenary Retrospect* (Birmingham: Silk & Terry, Ltd., 1936). For an early mention of the activities of the Provincial Newspaper Society, see "Caution to Newspaper Proprietors," Liverpool *Mercury*, August 3, 1838.

TABLE 4.1. *Daily newspapers published in Britain, 1846–1915*

	Daily papers		Daily papers
1846	14	1885	156
1855	21	1890	160
1860	36	1895	164
1865	53	1900	211
1870	79	1905	200
1875	116	1910	168
1880	139	1915	172

Source: Benn's Newspaper Press Directory (London).

of the telegraph companies the right to gather their news independently.[80] That year, the number of daily papers published, exclusive of those in London, was twenty-nine in England and Wales, eleven in Scotland, and twelve in Ireland.[81] The rest of the 1,000-odd other publications, which appeared at varying intervals throughout the country, were, according to Taylor of the *Guardian*, "very little interested" in telegraphic news reports (Table 4.1).[82]

The absence of a London-led effort to establish an association for the collection of news, akin to that among the publishers of New York, left the provincial press to establish an organization of its own free from the meddling of the metropolitan press. Absent the need to admit these divergent groups to membership, coordination among newspapers was easier. There was little love lost between the provincial and London press, which competed against each other more than the New York press did with the press of the American hinterland, and a clear separation between the two classes of newspaper with respect to newsgathering obviated the need for any press association to cater simultaneously to the widely divergent demands of urban and rural publications.

There was comparatively little competition among the London press before the late 1850s, which largely explains why there was no similar struggle for news in the Big Smoke as there was in the Big Apple.[83] Until at least the repeal

---

[80] There was some disagreement between daily and weekly provincial publishers insofar as the latter group perceived in telegraphy a threat to their circulation, but these problems were quickly overcome. See Undated, LN 1026, 1/014539, RA.

[81] Provincial daily papers at this time had circulations ranging from 20,000 to 50,000 copies daily. Newspaper Telegraphic Company, September 20, 1865, PA Ms 1/35357, GL; A.J. Lee, "The Management of a Victorian Local Newspaper: the Manchester *City News*, 1864–1900," *Business History*, 15 (1973), 134; A. J. Lee, "The Structure, Ownership and Control of the Press, 1855–1914," in G. Boyce et al. (eds.), *Newspaper History from the Seventeenth Century to the Present Day* (London: Constable, 1978), pp. 120–2.

[82] "Report from the Select Committee on the Electric Telegraphs Bill," pp. 93–4.

[83] Contra D. Read, *The Power of News: The History of Reuters*, 2nd ed. (Oxford: Oxford University Press, 1999), p. 6.

of the newspaper stamp in 1855, *The Times* dominated the London newspaper market and other London dailies did not threaten its position.[84] Government subsidies as well as the invidious "taxes on knowledge" protected *The Times* from competitors. Between 1841 and 1855, the first fourteen years of John Delane's editorship of *The Times*, the circulation of the paper increased from 20,000 to 58,000, which was three times the aggregate circulation of the whole of the rest of the daily London papers published at the time.[85] The circulation of the *Morning Advertiser*, the second largest publication, was under 7,000.[86] Other London papers could barely compete let alone cooperate with *The Times*. After 1848, the telegraph companies met the demand for and controlled the supply of provincial news. Following the successful completion of a submarine telegraph between England and France in 1851, Reuters supplied the foreign news needs of the London press, which it supplemented with its own correspondents. A market solution to the provision of domestic and foreign news reports diminished further the likelihood of the London press attempting to form a news association.[87]

By far, however, it was the organization of telecommunications under the Post Office that had the greatest effect on the manner in which the PA collected and distributed news. After passage of the Telegraph Act, the provincial press gained the right to collect and edit its news reports, but the Post Office retained control over its distribution and, however economical the press tariff under the Telegraph Act was, the number of words transmitted determined the price of the message sent. "Our function begins and ends with the delivery of our news to the Post-Office," explained John Lovell, first general manager of the PA. "That done, we are helpless, having no further control over it."[88] Not having control over the distribution of its news report, and paying by the word, constrained the way in which the PA could distribute its news report to its members. "Having to pay for every line of news we transmit," explained Lovell, "it would have been improvident and foolish to have transmitted useless news; and therefore we were thrown back upon one of two courses – either to make up batches of news at various rates, and supply those, or else to adopt

---

[84] I. Asquith, "The Structure, Ownership and Control of the Press, 1780–1855," in *Newspaper History*, p. 104. After competition among the London press increased, but before the completion of a trans-Atlantic telegraph cable, Reuters did compete with the London press to obtain news from the United States arriving by ship, and he helped to fund a telegraph cable connecting Cork and Crookhaven to meet the steamers sooner. See Read, *The Power of News*, pp. 39–40

[85] In the late 1830s, the government considered lowering the stamp duty to encourage competition against *The Times*. This had the adverse effect, causing *The Times* circulation to escalate to more than 50,000 copies by 1855. By this time, most of its competitors from 1836 had folded. O. Woods and J. Bishop, *The Story of The Times* (London: Michael Joseph, 1985), pp. 55–6.

[86] H. Herd, *The March of Journalism: The Story of the British Press from 1622 to the Present Day* (London: Allen & Unwin, 1952), p. 153.

[87] Compare with L. Hannah, "Visible and Invisible Hand in Great Britain," in *Managerial Hierarchies*, p. 64.

[88] J. Lovell to members, March 3, 1870, PA, Ms 35357, GL.

the system of fixing a price to each article of news, and allowing the consumer to choose what best fitted his own wants and means." Different publishers demanded different services of news, which led Lovell to opt for the latter method of distribution and pricing, but doing so raised the difficult question of how to address through the Post Office the different services to the association's many members and subscribers.[89]

Addressing different messages anew for multiple users entailed unnecessary repetition and was wasteful of words estimated to cost approximately £3,000 per year (£235,000 in today's prices). To avoid this expenditure, the PA divided its news reports into a large number of distinct classes, including foreign news, general morning news, parliamentary, and sports news. It then furnished the Post Office on a biweekly basis with lists containing any modification in the distribution of the report. The Post Office in London instructed the postmasters of the towns in which the offices of the papers were situated to modify the news report accordingly under the corresponding heading in the lists supplied to them. In the same manner lists were also supplied to each station that had to submit news to other offices. For example, if an order were received from the PA to supply the London corn market report to the South Shields *Gazette*, the postmaster of Shields was instructed to enter the *Gazette* under the heading "London Corn Report," and the postmaster of Newcastle was instructed to enter South Shields in the list at that office. The corn report was then sent from London to Newcastle headed "Press Association, London Corn," and the postmaster there would, with reference to the list, send it to the postmaster at South Shields, who in turn performed a similar operation and forwarded it to the *Gazette*.[90]

The benefit of this system was that it afforded greater differentiation and the servicing of individual needs, but dividing the news report into different classes and relating any modification in the distribution of the report to the various telegraph centers of the Post Office engendered considerable waste and placed artificial restrictions on the development of the news reports. "The returns I receive from all parts of the country," wrote Lovell to his disappointed members in March 1870, "reveal a state of telegraphic derangement, which can only be described as disastrous both to newspapers and to newsrooms."[91] The system of distribution presented few problems for daily morning papers, which were for the most part published simultaneously. It was different with the daily evening newspapers. Published at different hours, in different towns

[89] "Report of the Committee of the Provincial Daily Newspaper Proprietors," June 29, 1868, PA, Ms 35356/1; "Report of the Second Annual Meeting of Shareholders," May 11, 1870, PA, Ms 35372/1, GL.

[90] "Report by Mr. Scudamore on the Re-organization of the Telegraph System of the United Kingdom," p. 82; "Report of the Second Annual Meeting of Shareholders," May 11, 1870, PA, Ms 35372/1, GL; Post Office London to Post Office Dundee, February 4, 1870, POST 104/29, Royal Mail Archives (RM).

[91] J. Lovell to members, March 3, 1870, PA, Ms 35357, GL.

and issuing sometimes one, two, or three editions daily, requiring also news, as Lovell put it, "during the most barren period of the day," and often, in cases where they were the offspring of a weekly paper, demanding, in addition to their ordinary news, a special supply during the whole of the twenty-four hours on Fridays, and perhaps no news at all on Saturdays – it was difficult to devise subdivisions which met their varied wants without descending to a minuteness which would have overloaded the tariff with detail, and rendered the instructions to the Post Office too complicated. The weekly papers also, published at all hours, and issuing second and sometimes third editions at intervals, which almost constituted them biweekly journals, presented difficulties that may have been less serious in degree, but were, according to Lovell, "equally embarrassing in kind." The complication was still further increased by the necessity that existed for providing for the special requirements of the press of Ireland and Scotland, where remoteness from London and local circumstances produced an entirely new set of wants, and also for the even more special and peculiar wants of the commercial newsrooms, mechanics' institutions, and other public institutions scattered up and down the whole of the country.

In the United States, paying for the distribution of news per word had also curtailed the growth of press association news reports and created a bottleneck in supply until leased lines became widely available in the 1880s. In Britain, absent leased lines and an all-inclusive service of news for which papers collectively paid assessments, the problem was more severe. The gross cost to the association of the particular news was ascertained or estimated and this cost was then apportioned pro rata: first to each class of customers and then to each customer in each class. This was called the cost of collection. Wherever a given head of expenditure, as in the case of the salaries of parliamentary reporters, could be traced to a specified source, it was charged to the class of news giving rise to it, and wherever expenditure, as in the case of rent, applied equally to all classes of news it was made an establishment charge and spread equitably over the whole tariff. To the cost of collection was added the cost of transmission. Where the number of words to be supplied was conjectural, as with foreign and parliamentary news, a basis was estimated by taking in the former case a half-year's supply to *The Times* and in the latter case the supply during the previous session. Where the number of words was under the control of the association, as was the case with general news, arbitrary figures were taken.[92] The number of newspapers that subscribed to each class of news that the PA supplied therefore determined the amount of revenue that the association received from subscriptions, but the number of words transmitted, not the number of newspapers taking a particular service, set the cost incurred to provide it. The number of words in the news report changed with the events of the day, therefore the fixed annual sum charged by the PA to its members did not always reflect the cost of providing the service. By 1872, Lovell had cause to

[92] Lovell to editors, October 28, 1869, PA, Ms 35372/1, GL.

complain to his members that a growth in the foreign news service meant the original estimates of the cost of transmission were "considerably exceeded."[93]

Unlike in the United States, where newspapers paid assessments levied on the basis of the potential number of purchasers in their respective areas of circulation, the PA charged members that took the same class of news the same rate, and not a variable rate that reflected their differing abilities to pay. Although "it was a fundamental rule of the association that the charges to all members should be uniform," said Lovell at the second annual meeting of the association's shareholders in 1870, "at the same time, the means and needs of the subscribers varied," which created a "double necessity" of having a uniform tariff and varied news supplies.[94] The assumption ruling the news reports was that newspapers would take, as indeed they were required to take, basic services of home and foreign news. According to a newspaper's requirements, the PA supplemented these news services with additional dispatches and special reports. In this way, the PA struck, and maintained, a rough balance among the newspapers with small (less than 20,000 copies), medium (20,000 to 40,000), and large (more than 40,000) circulation. Several smaller newspapers took a large variety of services and several larger ones preferred to gather their own news, which meant the balance was inexact. The principle that all newspapers, irrespective of the number of customers in their areas, should pay the same price for the same service was valid only if the PA could keep the price at a figure acceptable to the bulk of subscribers. The revenue from a modest general service, plus specials, was sufficient to maintain a system of newsgathering that was not too expensive for the small paper, while at the same time securing necessary additional revenue from the bigger papers.

The fine balance among newspapers and between the revenue and expense of the PA made its rate structure inflexible. The rates charged for different classes of news were pegged to the price of the association's base service, therefore the PA could not easily alter its rates. A hike in price would have caused some members, particularly smaller newspapers, to downgrade their services. If, in response to an increase in tariff, six subscribers went from the largest class of foreign news provided by the PA to the second largest, the diminution in revenue would have been larger than the new amount the PA received. As the service increased in size, it was not sold at a price that covered the cost to obtain, handle, and supply it. Each newspaper could make its own selection of what service it obtained, therefore, the larger newspapers, which could rely on their own correspondents and cut down their orders from the PA to a minimum, gained an advantage at the expense of the mass of smaller newspapers that, out of necessity, more generously supported the association. The smaller newspapers took fewer dispensable services, therefore they found cancelling them difficult, and therefore could save less than their larger brethren

---

[93] Lovell to editors, November 25, 1872, PA, Ms 35372/1, GL.
[94] "Report of the Second Annual Meeting of Shareholders," May 11, 1870, PA, Ms 35372/1, GL.

when retrenchments were necessary. Had revenue from the smaller papers diminished, the PA would have found it difficult to make up the difference by charging the larger papers an increased rate.[95]

The Telegraph Act established an inclusive but constrained provincial press association tasked with gathering domestic news. The limited allocation of press telegram rates and the establishment of the PA effectively barred Reuters from entering the provinces. Reuters encouraged provincial papers to take its news in London, which they could then transmit independently to the provinces, but the PA secured the assurance of provincial proprietors that they would not contract with Reuters except under the auspices of the association. Provincial publishers agreed to this restriction on their freedom to avoid a bidding war for Reuters's news.[96] Mounting an effective challenge to Reuters had been part of the rationale for forming the PA. The association's board entertained competing with the agency, but was encouraged to form an alliance after it discovered that Reuters had established exclusive news exchange agreements with the principal news agencies of Europe and North America.[97]

A long-term exclusive arrangement between the PA and Reuters protected both organizations from competition. A contract signed between Reuters and the PA in 1870 was the first in a series of ten-year agreements that lasted, with few amendments, until 1925. The PA gained exclusive rights to Reuters's news outside London, while Reuters retained control over the London market.[98] In return, the PA agreed not to gather foreign news independently of Reuters or to support other foreign news providers. The PA also paid Reuters £3,000 per annum (or approximately £214,000 in today's prices) for foreign news and provided Reuters with its news reports, which Reuters controlled exclusively outside the British Isles. The terms of this agreement were based on and were nearly the same as those that had existed between Reuters and the telegraph companies before 1868.[99] In 1884, the PA agreed to raise its fixed payment to Reuters to £8,000 (£621,000) and Reuters obtained the right to request speeches and special reports from the PA, provided it did not incur the association any extra expense, for distribution abroad.[100] In return, although Reuters retained the right to supply foreign commercial information to private

---

[95] PA board minutes, January 8, 1889, PA, Ms 35358/6, GL.

[96] Director's Letter Book, PA, Ms 35414, GL.

[97] See Chapter 6. Minutes of the Committee of Management, September 16, 1868, PA, Ms 35357; PA board minutes, October 17 and 19, 1868, PA, Ms 35358/1, GL; W. Saunders to A.C. Wilson, Director's letter book, November 23, 1868, PA, Ms 35414, GL; Cartel agreements, April 20, 1867, LN288/883501, RA.

[98] PA board minutes, March 22, 1869, PA, Ms 35358/1, GL. Reuters declined requests from competitors of the PA for access to its news. Reuters's board minutes, August 4, 1875, box 288, RA.

[99] F.J. Griffiths to PA, February 24, 1869 in PA board minutes, March 2, 1869, PA, Ms 35358/1, GL.

[100] Agreement of 1884, PA, Ms 35441, GL.

subscribers in the provinces, it lost the right to serve newspapers, newsrooms, exchanges, or public institutions, which curtailed the development of its domestic commercial services.[101] After the agreement of 1884, the fixed rate paid by the PA did not change until 1904, when the PA agreed to pay Reuters an additional £5,000 (£402,000) for special news services, in addition to the standard foreign news report Reuters provided.

Their agreements for the exclusive exchange of news and the allocation of territory enabled the PA and Reuters to counter rivals. To confront Dalziel, an American-backed news agency that briefly aggravated established relations in Britain and the United States during the 1890s, Reuters and the PA agreed to the joint development of a foreign supplementary news service.[102] Dalziel was quickly overrun, but the foreign supplementary service became a cornerstone of the agreement between Reuters and the PA. All major international news coverage after 1890 was conducted under this arrangement at joint expense, but the association retained the right to restrict its size, and special service telegrams were issued in the provinces under the byline of the PA, or as being "from our own correspondent," instead of under Reuters's name.[103] These special dispatches, which were optional for subscribers to the PA, supplemented the stories that went in the regular service. In the case of a shipwreck, for example, the general service consisted of not more than half a dozen words including where the ship went ashore and the number of passengers and crew saved or drowned. For the special service, correspondents reported details of the wreck – how it happened, by what means the survivors were saved, and so forth, in a coherent, graphic and circumstantial account, which could require hundreds of words.[104]

The foreign supplementary service enabled the PA to exercise greater control over the way in which Reuters collected foreign news. "The interests of the two Companies," wrote Edmund Robbins, then general manager of the PA, to Reuters in November 1894, "are so identical that if one fails the other is bound to be affected."[105] The PA had occasionally complained that Reuters's agents wrote prosaically and were ill-acquainted with the "new style" of journalism, but, according to Robbins, the special service permitted the association to transform Reuters's news report "from a mere official service into a living flesh-and-blood chronicle of the leading events throughout the world."[106]

[101] See Chapter 5. Fleetwood-May, "Reuters' Commercial Services in the United Kingdom," August 14, 1957, LN 954/013299, RA.
[102] PA board minutes, November 5, 1890, PA, Ms 35358/6; PA board minutes, January 5, 1897, PA, Ms 35358/7, GL.
[103] PA board minutes, June 4, 1889, PA, Ms 35358/5, p. 229, GL.
[104] "General Instructions for the Guidance of Correspondents," May 1, 1905, LN 807, 1/980830, RA.
[105] PA board minutes, October 3, 1894, PA, Ms 35358/7, GL.
[106] PA board minutes, December 2, 1890 and November 5, 1890, PA, Ms 35358/6, pp. 17–23, 30, GL.

Reuters also benefited from the special service. It charged the PA pro rata for the special service and not a flat monthly rate, therefore payments tracked expenses, and by having the PA share the cost of sending out a foreign correspondent, Reuters obtained news at half the expense, which it could then sell to the London papers at full price. It was a sore point with the metropolitan press that their regular subscription service became purely routine, while all the important news was put in the special service and charged for separately. Between 1891 and 1914, Reuters's profits from the special service averaged 23 percent of its total domestic news service profits.[107]

Despite the advantages of the foreign supplementary service, incomplete combination and the limitations of the postal-telegraph department precluded the PA and Reuters from operating in tandem. The PA and Reuters agreed to an annual limit for the share of special-service expenses undertaken by the association, but the cost incurred to cover world affairs often exceeded the agreed amount. Reuters had an incentive to increase the size of the reports and to sell them to the London press to generate profits, but the PA, by dint of the pricing system devised under the Telegraph Act, was obliged to keep Reuters's reports within the agreed word limit. On numerous occasions, such as covering the failing health of the Russian Czar in 1895, the PA resisted Reuters's attempts to increase the size of its news service on the grounds that the cost of transmission was too large.[108] The association had "no wish to cripple the service in any way," wrote the board of the PA to Reuters, but it did desire to "protect itself."[109] Reuters had to wait for the approval of the PA before it could dispatch correspondents and on several occasions the consequent delay enabled the London press to forestall Reuters in the field. Attempts to dispatch correspondents without the consent of the PA, as in the case of the Turko-Greek War, incurred the anger of the association's board, and Reuters was obliged to foot the bill.[110]

Aside from fending off competitors, agreements between the PA and Reuters for the exclusive exchange of news and the division of territory better enabled both organizations to extract higher payments from London publishers. In 1877, John MacDonald, editor of *The Times*, complained that Reuters supplied provincial papers through the PA, "at absurdly low rates," with the same foreign news for which the London papers paid heavily. This disparity, according to MacDonald, tended "unquestionably to injure our country circulation."[111] Of course, part of the reason it appeared to the London press that their provincial competitors, such as the Manchester *Guardian*, received the news so cheaply

[107] RAGH to NLJ, DCF, et al. re: PA Analysis, November 1, 1963, CR box 4, RA.
[108] PA board minutes, February 8, 1895, PA, Ms 35358/7, GL. See also Manager's memoranda, March 10, 1911, PA, Ms 35362/2, p. 146, GL.
[109] PA board minutes, November 25, 1892, PA, Ms 35358/6, p. 199, GL.
[110] PA board minutes, undated, PA, Ms 35358/8, p. 23, GL.
[111] John MacDonald to Paul Reuter, February 5, 1877, LN87/3324, RA.

was that the PA insisted on charging all its members the same for a like service of news. When Reuters requested a further increase to provide for the mounting costs of covering General Gordon's escapades at Khartoum, the London press, led again by MacDonald, revolted and threatened to form an agency of its own. Eventually the London papers agreed to a "war clause," which entitled Reuters to an increased payment from the London papers before, during, and after any great political disturbance; and even *The Times*, which held out to the end, finally conceded defeat after Reuters's threatened to shut off its service of telegrams.[112] The competitive advantage of *The Times* in the London market derived from its extensive use of foreign correspondents, which in part explains its hostility to Reuters; but, additionally *The Times* had also taken to reselling portions of its foreign news service to the provincial press, which made it a rival of the agency. In 1889, the PA, which then comprised nearly all of the 160 daily newspapers published outside London, paid Reuters £8,000, whereas each London paper paid an annual subscription to Reuters of £1,600 (£145,000), or one-fifth of the total paid by the PA.

The connection between the PA and Reuters also enabled the association to extract larger payments from the London press. The PA charged each of its members the same amount for like service, so that large provincial newspapers, such as the Glasgow *Herald*, Liverpool *Post*, and Manchester *Guardian* received Reuters's news reports at very low rates. Likewise, the revenue that the PA received for its news reports from the London press helped to stabilize its otherwise precarious pricing system. In 1885, for example, there was, on the tariff services supplied to members, a net loss of £7,673 (£678,000), but the revenue of £7,382 (£652,000) from the London papers, together with revenue from special reporting, turned this loss into a profit of £3,743 (£330,000).[113] This was as true in the 1880s as it was on the eve of World War I. By then, whereas the leading provincial morning newspapers paid approximately £400 per annum (£29,327) for all their news services from the PA, the London papers paid an average of £558 (£31,000), and some papers, such as the *Daily Telegraph*, paid as much as £650 per annum (£51,000). "The fact was," reflected Robbins in 1916, "the Press Association lived on the London papers."[114]

As long as the Post Office continued to moderate competition among the provincial press and between the provincial press and the London press, the PA could continue to rely on the London publishers to fund services of domestic

[112] The war clause enabled Reuters to raise the cost of subscriptions by £66 a month, or 50 percent, which became payable one month after the outbreak of the war and lasted until one month after the end of the war, so that when the national dailies were paying £1,600 for the basic foreign telegrams service, the war clause annual basis was £750, paid from month to month. "War on Reuter: London Papers and News Agency at Loggerheads," *The Milwaukee Sentinel*, June 30, 1885. Reuters board minutes, June 10 and 24 and July 8, 1885, and January 6, 1886, box 289, RA.
[113] PA board minutes, PA, Ms 35358/4, 280, GL.
[114] Manager's memoranda, August 10, 1916, PA, Ms 35362/9, 710, GL.

and foreign news. Between 1870 and 1894, the PA showed only minor annual losses on five occasions. For Reuters, the market arrangement was also satisfactory, although slightly more perilous. Caught in its domestic market between the upper and nether millstones of the provincial and London press, Reuters sought revenues overseas and diversified its business. In doing so it was exposed to greater risk.[115] To the casual observer in the 1870s and 1880s it may have appeared that the goals of postal reformers had been achieved. Although newspaper publishers frequently complained that the news distribution apparatus of the Post Office was slow and cumbersome, the provincial newspapers, collectively organized under the auspices of the PA, suffered from this arrangement equally. An abundant quantity of news reached most parts of Britain at little cost to provincial publishers, who also benefited from the riches of their London counterparts, which arguably helped to stave off concentration and maintain plurality. Although powerful, the PA was constrained, which limited integration among news providers, but the association was sufficiently robust to purchase minor organizations supplying news to newsrooms and clubs, which increased economies of scale.[116]

PRIVATE WIRES, TELEPHONY, AND THE DISSOLUTION OF THE SETTLEMENT OF 1868

The settlement of 1868, however satisfactory it may have been, rested on shifting sands. It was a change in Post Office policy that eventually disrupted the status quo. Under the Telegraph Act of 1868, the Post Office, in keeping with the practice of the telegraph companies, was permitted to rent to any publisher, proprietor, or occupier for the use of their newspaper, newsroom, club, or exchange a "special" wire during a period of no more than twelve hours per day at a rate not exceeding £500 per annum. A staff of the Post Office worked these "special" wires and had full control over the service, so that in practice such wires were rarely used and provided only a limited advantage to those publications that could afford them. The Post Office did grant licenses for the distribution of news by companies, such as the Exchange Telegraph Company (Extel), to which a license was first granted in 1872 for transmitting the price of stocks within the limits of a particular town. Initially, Extel was only a news distributor, not a news collector. It benefited from the exclusive right to be represented on the floor of the London Stock Exchange. Each Extel subscriber had a ticker tape instrument in its office that was controlled from a central office in each town. Extel distributed to registered newspapers and clubs as well as to private persons, such as members of stock exchanges, therefore it was not entitled to receive telegrams at the press rates granted by the Act of 1868.

---

[115] See Chapter 5.
[116] See PA board minutes, January 4, 1870, PA, Ms 35358/1, GL and PA agreement with W. Wright, January 30, 1870, PA, Ms 35442, pp. 31–5, GL.

The Post Office had always refused to allow a news agency or association to have use of private wires for the transmission of news between towns.[117] It was held that this activity had been expressly assigned to the postmaster-general in 1868. In 1881, Henry Fawcett, the economist and postmaster-general, laid down the rule on the subject: "One of the objects sought to be gained by the representatives of the Provincial Press during the inquiry into the Telegraph Bill of 1868," wrote Fawcett, "was that the country papers might be placed upon an equality as regards the time, cost, and method of obtaining their news." Were the Post Office to relinquish control over the task of distributing the news, "the effect would be to create rival lines of telegraph for Press telegrams with varying rates, and would give rise to endless complaints and dissatisfaction." The Post Office applied the same rule in 1883 and again in 1887, at which time it was similarly observed that allowing anyone but the Post Office to carry on the business of transmitting news between towns would threaten "the strict impartiality and the absence of undue preference and priority contemplated in the Telegraph Acts."[118]

At the end of 1887, however, the Post Office made a radical new departure under the heavy-handed leadership of Henry Cecil Raikes, then postmaster-general. Raikes' "despotic manner" and his determination "to secure the optimum provision of postal services," reports one biographer, made him few friends in the Post Office or among the public, but enabled him to achieve considerable financial savings in his department, and may account for his decision to grant a private wire to the Manchester *Guardian*, which the newspaper was permitted to staff and operate between its London and provincial offices twenty-four hours a day.[119] The decision was made out of a concern for the deficit of the Post Office telegram department, which had grown since its inauguration, and for protecting the monopoly of the Post Office over telegraphy, without which the revenue of the telegraph department might have suffered a further blow.[120] In 1893, when the Post Office reconsidered its concession to the *Guardian*, it acknowledged that there was "a great deal to be said in favour of the news being transmitted in a uniform manner by means of the public wires, so that one newspaper should not be able to secure an undue advantage over another," but if the Post Office did not supply the wires, it risked the prospect of a private

[117] The purpose of these wires was not, as Kieve claimed, "to enable competition as well as co-operation between newspapers." *Electric Telegraph*, p. 217.

[118] The Telegraph Act 1868, c. 110, ss. 15–16. Tariff of charges for newspaper messages, December 30, 1865, BT; Minute of the postmaster-general upon the report of the committee on certain matters connected with the transmission of press messages, October 26, 1907, POST 30/4322C, pp. 24–5, BT.

[119] N.D. Daglish, "Raikes, Henry Cecil (1838–1891)," *ODNB*, accessed August 2, 2011. See also R. Coase, "The British Post Office and the Messenger Companies," *The Journal of Law and Economics*, 4 (1961), 33.

[120] On the subject of protecting the Post Office monopoly, see Coase, "The British Post Office," pp. 12–65.

provider meeting the demands of the press, undermining its monopoly, and taking the revenue.[121] It is unlikely that newspapers located 200 or 300 miles outside London would have been able to secure the necessary wayleaves to erect private wires of their own. It is considerably more likely that Raikes was anxious to increase the revenue of the Post Office telegraph department.

The volte-face in Post Office policy undermined the equality among provincial papers that the Telegraph Act had achieved, and therefore threatened both the system of news delivery and market structure that developed after 1868. The PA "represented very strongly" against the "injustice" of granting private wires. It was, said Robbins of the PA, "a policy of favour and preference for the rich, and was utterly opposed to the spirit of the Act of Parliament." Inasmuch as it enabled these wealthy papers to withdraw from the association, it made it difficult for the PA to continue to supply the news to its remaining members at a moderate price, and so meant "ruin to all the smaller Provincial newspapers." Post Office officials acknowledged as much. According to one in-house report, "the consequences of granting these private wires have been great and far-reaching. The wealthier papers have been able to outstrip their poorer competitors, who could not afford a private wire." The difference in time of delivery that a private wire afforded was so great that papers in possession of them were able to sell editions in towns other than those in which they were published, and with news not yet delivered over the wires operated by the Post Office to the local newspapers of those towns.[122]

Granting private wires would not have been so detrimental to poorer provincial papers had the postal-telegraph department been quicker in sending out the news reports of the PA. The unpredictable ebb and flow of news at the different offices throughout the country created variable demands on telegraphers and unforeseeable, as well as expensive, labor requirements, which the Post Office was ill-equipped and unwilling to meet. For example, on the basis of the hours stipulated in the Telegraph Act of 1868, and because it threatened to interrupt the staff tea hour, the Post Office refused the requests of the PA to undertake preparatory work before 6 p.m. Such preparatory work, had it been undertaken, might have eased the onslaught of press work which arrived at that time.[123] "In the public interest the demand for so expeditious a transcription of Press messages should be resisted," argued several Post Office officials. "It should be made clear to the Press," continued this internal memorandum, that the Post Office "cannot provide an excessive staff to meet the fluctuations

---

[121] Minute of the postmaster-general upon the report of the committee on certain matters connected with the transmission of press messages, October 26, 1907, POST 30/4322C, p. 26, BT.

[122] Minute of the postmaster-general upon the report of the committee on certain matters connected with the transmission of press messages, October 26, 1907, POST 30/4322C, p. 27, BT.

[123] The Post Office refused for twenty years to act on this suggestion. For the tea-break excuse, see PA board minutes, February 4, 1908, PA, Ms 35358/13, pp. 277–80, GL. The Post Office finally acquiesced in 1908. PA board minutes, July 7, 1908, PA, Ms 35358/14, pp. 182–3, GL. On the PA's relief, see Manager's memoranda, June 25, 1912, PA, Ms 35362/4, p. 90, GL.

of the traffic, and that sufficient time must be allowed for the transcription of news in an economical manner."[124]

Although the British system of postal telegraphy for distributing press messages was quicker than the government system of France and cheaper than that in Germany, it was slow and expensive in comparison to the private system in the United States.[125] According to calculations carried out by Western Union in 1880, the British Post Office delivered to the press 285 million words at an average rate of £.03 per hundred words to each paper served. In the same year, Western Union delivered 605,474,452 words of regular AP matter at an average rate to each paper served of £.02 cents per hundred words, not to mention the additional 55,725,478 words of special press matter it delivered to individual papers at an average rate of £.013 per word. On the basis of an average of two papers to each place served, the British rate was more than twice as high as that of Western Union, although Western Union covered territory that was twenty-five times larger than that of Britain. Under the tariff schedule that went into effect in March 1884, the press rate between points on the American east and west coasts was £.07 per word during the day and £.04 per word at night, which made Western Union's average special rate lower than that of the Post Office on a distance basis. As a consequence, the service of the AP more than doubled between 1870 and 1880 at an increased cost of about 20 percent, whereas the PA, by contrast, had to struggle to keep its news report within strict word limits.[126]

The large advantage in terms of time of dispatch that newspapers with private wires gained not only disrupted the level playing field sought under the Telegraph Act, it also challenged the established customary system of property rights in news. Newspapers in possession of a private wire could copy news from newspapers published in London, which appeared on the streets before newspapers in the provinces, and then wire it bodily to their provincial offices, thereby preempting the reports of the same news that was sent by the Post Office wires. Post Office regulations prohibited matter distributed at press rates from being redistributed on private wires, which mitigated the problem with respect to news reports of the PA, but the practice was widespread with respect to Reuters's news reports, which the agency shared with the London press before they arrived in the provinces. In 1888, in an early instance of this practice, the Belfast *News Letter* regularly published telegrams from Reuters by taking them from the evening editions of the London papers. Reuters requested the

[124] Minute of the postmaster-general upon the report of the committee on certain matters connected with the transmission of press messages, October 26, 1907, POST 30/4322C, p. 28, BT.

[125] PA board minutes, July 4, 1893, PA, Ms 35358/6, 262–63, GL; J. Medill to W.H. Smith, September 2, 1874 in *WAP Annual Report* (1874), pp. 18–19. See, generally, R. Millward, *Private and Public Enterprise in Europe: Energy, Telecommunications and Transport, 1830–1990* (Cambridge: Cambridge University Press, 2005).

[126] "The newspaper service of the Western Union Tel. Co.: letter from W.B. Somerville, supt. press transmission, December 1883" (1883).

News Letter to cease doing so, but it persisted. Reuters's telegrams, argued the *News Letter*, were published hours previously in the evening newspapers and "when they thus become public property they may be used by any newspaper." Reuters appealed to the good nature of the newspaper's editors:

Even supposing as you state that our telegrams become public property when published in the newspapers, it seems a breach of equity for a journal of the standing of the Belfast *News Letter* to appropriate gratuitously material that is obtained at considerable sacrifice by the Company and your contemporaries who also support the service.[127]

Failing a copyright law available to them, Reuters's solicitors proposed publishing the telegrams in a journal, subsequently entitled *The Epoch*, which would be subject to statutory copyright, and in March 1890, the company sent a letter to the *News Letter* advising that its telegrams were now copyrighted.[128] Despite these precautions, the second Boer War, and the increased demand for foreign news it precipitated, caused a significant growth in the use of private wires. In 1899, the Manchester *Evening News* hired a private wire and engaged in independently collecting and wiring Reuters's news from London, much to the dismay of the Manchester *Evening Mail*, which continued to rely on the PA for its report of Reuters's news.[129] It is hardly coincidental that a bill to amend and consolidate the law relating to literary copyright was read in the House of Lords that April. This bill, originally advanced by Robert Lord Monkswell, proposed that protection with respect to foreign news be granted for twelve hours, but as this would have legitimized pilfering after the grace period and thereby enabled evening papers to publish news of the morning sheets and morning sheets to copy from evening papers of the day before, both Reuters and the PA contended that the bill was worse than no protection at all, and they argued that the interval ought to be extended to twenty-four hours, but compromised on eighteen.[130]

The problem this use of private wires presented was similar to that which the AP confronted in the landmark intellectual property case of *INS*, but it was materially different insofar as neither the *News Letter* nor the *Evening News* were competitors of Reuters or the PA in the way that INS was of the AP.[131]

---

[127] Copies of this correspondence appear in PA board minutes, January 12, 1888, PA, Ms 35358/5, pp. 111–13, GL.

[128] Reuters's board minutes, November 20, 1889 and March 26, 1890, box 289, RA.

[129] The Manchester *Guardian* and Manchester *Evening News*, although owned by separate companies, had been closely associated since the foundation of the *Evening News* in 1868. Their offices were in the same building in Manchester, they shared a London office and, presumably, a private wire. On April 26, 1924, they amalgamated. PA board minutes, March 7, 1899, PA, Ms 35358/8, pp. 284–7; Manager's memoranda, May 6, 1924, PA, Ms 35362/16, p. 4371, GL.

[130] *Hansard*, HL Deb April 18, 1899, vol. 69, c. 1431; Manager's memoranda, July 4, and September 5, 1899, PA, Ms 35358/9, pp. 20, 47, GL; "Report from the select committee on the House of Lords on the Copyright Bill," 1899 (362), VIII.539, l. 1647–49, 2653–55, 2611–18, 2629–31.

[131] It was materially different from *Exchange Telegraph Company v. Gregory & Co.* [1896] 1 Q.B. 147, which was a case of intentional interference with contractual relations and the

This important difference meant that the nub of the issue was one of membership rights and obligations, and not one of unfair competition, for which there was no tort in the United Kingdom. So, prosecution fell to the PA rather than the courts. If members of the PA were permitted to publish Reuters's news before it came over the Post Office wires, the value of Reuters's news to all the shareholders not in possession of private wires would decrease.[132] "The Association," wrote the board of the PA to its solicitor, "has paid a large sum in order to secure a monopoly which would thus become of little practical value." The object of the PA, explained the board, was "to put all provincial newspapers on the same level and to prevent one subscriber obtaining a particular class of news earlier than another subscriber who may have a private wire or other means of communication not open to other newspapers." The PA, advised counsel, could put a stop to such practices by demanding that members adhere to their obligations to the association.[133]

Despite such admonitions, any prohibition on the practice was difficult to enforce, and newspapers continued to make illicit use of their private wires. In the case of Manchester, as long as the *Evening News* continued the practice, its rivals felt obliged to follow suit. "Whilst we are perfectly willing to abide by the resolutions and conditions of your society," wrote the Manchester *Chronicle* to the PA, "we cannot be left behind."[134] Likewise the Liverpool *Echo* was discovered receiving Reuters's news by private wire, which put it an hour ahead of its competitors, much to the consternation of the Liverpool *Courier*, which threatened to do the same if the PA failed to provide it any protection.[135] The Birmingham *Evening Dispatch* engaged in similar behavior.[136] In 1900, the problem became worse after Alfred Harmsworth determined to publish a northern edition of the *Daily Mail* and to wire the entire contents of his London paper to Manchester for publication so that the paper printed in the provinces would be an exact replica of that published in the metropolis. This threatened to undermine the business model of the PA, as well as to do a disservice to Reuters, and the two organizations appealed to the Post Office for help. Relying on the Act of 1868, the Post Office stipulated that a press message addressed to a particular newspaper could be published in that newspaper only, and that "where a newspaper is issued in different versions

proprietary right of persons in unpublished matter, and not one of property rights in published news. Reuters took an active interest in the case. See Secretary to Nicholson & Crouch, June 14, 1895, Exchange Telegraph Company Archives (hereafter Extel), CLC/B/080/MS22970, London Metropolitan Archives (hereafter LMA).

[132] PA board minutes, March 7, 1899, PA, Ms 35358/8, pp. 284–7, GL.
[133] PA board minutes, May 9, 1899, PA, Ms 35358/8, pp. 307–13 and PA board minutes, May 7, 1900, PA, Ms 35358/9, pp. 146–50, GL.
[134] PA board minutes, June 13, 1900, PA, Ms 35358/9, pp. 175–6, GL.
[135] PA board minutes, February 6, 1901, PA, Ms 35358/9, pp. 259–60, GL and PA board minutes, January 13, 1903, PA, Ms 35358/10, pp. 179–87, GL.
[136] PA board minutes, June 10, 1903, PA, Ms 35358/10, pp. 234–8, GL.

for circulation in different places it becomes more than one newspaper."[137] This was a significant and heavy-handed intervention by the Post Office. The Manchester edition of the *Daily Mail* was technically a different newspaper and therefore, if it wished to publish the news reports of the PA and Reuters, it had to subscribe to their services separately. The Manchester edition of the *Daily Mail* duly became a member of the PA.[138] Worse than the threat of the *Daily Mail*, in 1904 the PA found that London-based private news agencies, of which there were approximately twenty that had been denied press rates under the Telegraph Act of 1868, were selling their reports to the London offices of provincial papers and that those reports were being wired privately to newspaper editorial desks throughout the country.[139]

Rather than pursue litigation to enforce the contractual obligations of its members, the PA turned to the Post Office for a solution. If the Post Office would not rescind the right of provincial papers to hire private wires, which was the root cause of the problem, then it might be prevailed on to lease private wires to the association.[140] The advantages of a leased-line system were apparent, as reference to the United States illustrated. According to a report written for the PA by Reuters's New York agent, in all larger American cities, newspapers were connected with the main offices of the telegraph companies via "loops," which the telegraph companies willingly generated at little extra cost. The 1,200-mile AP trunk line between New York and Chicago served thirty papers in eleven cities, and additional cities could be added to the line at no extra charge. For wires leased to morning papers, the AP paid £2 2s per mile per month; for evening wires the charge was £4 4s per mile per month. Messages went directly to newspapers and words were only counted afterwards, thereby avoiding delay. Foreign cables were also connected to circuits. "Owing to the readiness with which loops and special wires are supplied, scarcely is a speech of commanding importance finished before it is in its entirety before the Editors throughout the United States," Reuters's agent claimed. It was consequently unnecessary for the AP to provide its telegraphers with the manuscripts of such speeches for preparation in advance, whereas in Britain the Post Office required twenty-four hours' notice of any message more than 200 words.[141] This particular Post Office regulation was awkward for provincial editors, although the Post Office

[137] A debate in 1927 over what constituted a "separate and distinct performance" in the rebroadcasting of news by radio was analogous to the debate over what constituted a separate newspaper. See Chapter 5.

[138] See Post Office memo of January 5, 1900 in PA board minutes, February 16, 1909, PA, Ms 35358/15, pp. 173–5, GL. See also PA board minutes, October 10, 1901, PA, Ms 35358/9, pp. 86–8; PA board minutes, January 13, 1903, PA, Ms 35358/10, pp. 194, 200–1, GL.

[139] PA board minutes, February 26, 1904, PA, Ms 35358/11, pp. 18–9, GL.

[140] The PA first submitted a request for private wires in the autumn of 1900. PA board minutes, November 7, 1900, PA, Ms 35358/9, pp. 240–1, GL.

[141] A. King to Robbins, December 22, 1911, in Manager's memoranda, PA, Ms 35362/2, p. 274, GL.

was not so rigid in enforcing it when a suddenly arising event occurred; but this rule also limited competition on fast breaking items, which Robbins thought was advantageous to the PA and its members.[142] Reuters's agent attributed the comparative flexibility of the American system to competition in the provision of telegraphy. "The rivalry between the Western Union and the Postal Telegraph Companies, both of which are private organisations, results in the promptest possible service," concluded the report. "There can be no doubt that the efficiency of the Service is mainly due to the fact that there is competition in America. On this side of the Atlantic we are unfortunately baulked through the wires being in the hands of a Government department."[143] Chadwick and Scudamore's view that the Post Office provision of telegraphy would effectively create a level playing field among newspapers and advantageously generate competition among them was no longer convincing and was rapidly losing believers.

Despite the clear advantages the PA stood to gain from a leased wire system, the Post Office only intimated its willingness to provide such facilities in 1907, and no conclusive arrangement was reached before Britain was embroiled in World War I. As early as 1893, the PA had represented to the Post Office that it considered it unfair that a newspaper could possess a private wire and not a news agency, but the difficulties confronting the implementation of a leased-wire network were manifold.[144] First, it contradicted the policy of equality pursued via the Telegraph Act of 1868 even more so than the granting of private wires to individual newspapers, which arguably could be construed as falling under the clause of the Act that pertained to "special" wires. Lord Stanley, postmaster-general until 1905, refused to grant the PA leased wires unless all provincial newspapers agreed to take their news solely from the association, the logic being that if this were agreed to it would remove the possibility of any complaint of unfair preference and would unburden the Post Office of all press-related telegraph work. Not only was it impossible for all provincial newspapers to afford the high costs of the leased wire system, but even if the PA amalgamated the several smaller news agencies then extant, new ones would emerge. Indeed, these smaller firms, such as Central News, which was founded by a member of the PA in 1871, dissuaded new rivals from entering the field without demoralizing the business of the association.[145] In December 1905, Sidney Buxton, a liberal and forward-thinking politician, replaced the comparatively staid seventeenth Earl of Derby as postmaster-general, and in

[142] Manager's memoranda, March 4, 1912, PA, Ms 35362/3, pp. 264–5, GL.
[143] PA board minutes, January 4, 1905, PA, Ms 35358/11, pp. 147–9, GL.
[144] PA board reports, September 10, 1907, PA, Ms 35358/12, p. 139, GL.
[145] William Saunders, MP, newspaper owner and founding member of the PA, founded Central News in 1871. The company made most of its money from its "column-ticker" business. "The Central News diamond jubilee souvenir," 1931, LN 505/1/9071166, RA; PA board minutes, PA, Ms 35358, April 14 and 18, 1882, GL; PA board minutes, May 9 and September 7, 1905, PA, Ms 35358/11, pp. 215–25, 272, GL.

this capacity he introduced a number of important reforms, including penny postage to the United States and reduced charges for the postage of literature to blind people. Buxton also purchased several coastal wireless stations. In 1907, in a significant departure from established policy, Buxton agreed to permit the PA to lease telegraph lines. Having precipitated considerable change in the organization of postal telegraphy, Buxton went on to reform the Board of Trade. Members of the press mourned his departure.[146]

Despite a change in policy, further difficulties lay in devising a leased-wire system. Staffing the wires was particularly expensive. Large newspapers might have their own staff, but small papers could not afford one, and organized labor at the Post Office opposed the change.[147] In 1908, the Trades Union Congress (TUC) passed a resolution against handing over to newspaper proprietors and news agencies the transmission of news telegrams, and permitting them to supply their own operators. Additionally, the TUC resolved "that the State, having acquired the monopoly of the telegrams by purchase in 1868, should not give undue preference to wealthy newspaper proprietors, etc., but maintain communal ownership and work the system in the interests of the people generally."[148] Initial estimates conducted in 1908 suggested that the price of any leased wire system would be too expensive for many evening newspapers, and would therefore undermine the cooperative ethos and purpose of the PA. The proposed charge for leased lines – £7 per mile underground or overhouse and £5 per mile for overhead on a road or canal (in the region of £600 and £450 today) – would "deprive the concession of much of its value to the larger portion of newspapers published in Great Britain."[149] Unless the Post Office could reduce the price by £5,000, said the PA, it could not afford the service.[150] Considering the reduction in work a leased-wire system promised the Post Office, officials were eager for the association to lease lines, but they refused to allow the press any special dispensation or discounted rate.[151] This reluctance, aside from indicating a shift in thinking at the Post Office since Scudamore's time, was connected to the considerable deficit the Post Office telegram department continued to incur. In 1905–1906, the loss on press messages alone was £220,000; in 1908–1909, it was £205,000; and in 1910, the matter was raised before an agitated Parliament.[152] Whether or not the fee demanded by the Post Office for leased lines was in fact high was somewhat beside the point. The principal difficulty the PA confronted was convincing

[146] H.R. Young to G. Toulmin, June 29, 1911, in Manager's memoranda, PA, Ms 35362/2, pp. 299–300, GL.
[147] Proceedings of the Committee on the Transmission of Press Messages, January 28, 1907, PA, Ms 35358/12, p. 15, GL.
[148] PA board minutes, October 7, 1908, PA, Ms 35358/15, p. 6, GL.
[149] PA board minutes, January 7 and March 5, 1908, PA, Ms 35358/13, p. 252, 308, GL.
[150] PA board minutes, March 10, 1909, PA, Ms 35358/15, p. 219, GL.
[151] PA board minutes, May 19, 1908, PA, Ms 35358/14, pp. 112–3, GL.
[152] PA board minutes, March 9, 1910, PA, Ms 35358/16, pp. 195–6, GL.

its members to pay for the leased wires. The wealthy papers could obtain, or already had, their own private wires and stood to lose by funding them for the entire association, while the rest of the membership was insufficiently prosperous to meet the cost on its own.[153] Whereas the AP had confronted such coordination problems in the 1880s, the PA did not encounter them until the eve of World War I, and this too was a result of the Telegraph Act of 1868.

A pooling agreement between the PA and Extel also made it difficult for the association to take up the Post Office's offer of leased lines. Before Sidney Buxton's unanticipated decision in 1907, it appeared that the Post Office was unlikely to grant the PA leased wires. Members of the PA who lacked private wires therefore sought to encourage the association to counteract those that possessed such wires by making use instead of the telephone to distribute news. When the National Telephone Company first erected wires, the Post Office authorities were emphatic that the transmission of news would not be permitted, as this domain was the exclusive preserve of the Post Office under the Act of 1868. Indeed, postmaster-general Henry Fawcett restricted the telephone company to prevent it from competing with the postal-telegraph service, which did little to help the development of telephony.[154] Notwithstanding these precautions, short items of important news, and particularly horseracing results, were transmitted over the telephone wires, and it was impossible to stop or even control the practice. Accordingly, authorities at the Post Office, although not specifically sanctioning the practice, did not interfere, and soon it was openly acknowledged. The news services then provided by phone were largely confined to "snap-shot" reports of racing, soccer results, and cricket scores, but more and more newspapers were making arrangements for such services.[155] Extel began a service of cotton reports by telephone in 1882, shortly after the National Telephone Company erected a trunk line between Liverpool and Manchester, which was gradually extended in conjunction with the phone network. Extel organized a system of distributing racing results and other important news by phone, which coincided with a growth in popularity of organized sports, and it was thus enabled to beat all rivals who depended on the government wires for distribution of their news. As between the two methods, it was not a case of a few minutes, but sometimes nearly an hour between the receipt of the same news by telephone and by telegraph.[156]

In the summer of 1905, the PA commenced a limited service of soccer scores by phone, which was intended to supplement, and not to supplant, the telegraphic service. Equality among members was to be "preserved as far as

[153] PA board minutes, May 12, 1909, PA, Ms 35358/15, pp. 309–10, GL.
[154] Coase, "The British Post Office and the Messenger Companies," pp. 22, 61.
[155] PA board minutes, June 6, 1905, PA, Ms 35358/11, pp. 256–6, GL.
[156] Report as to the arbitrations between the parties, 1919, Extel, CLC/B/080/MS22974, LMA; PA board minutes, November 6, 1907, PA, Ms 35358/13, pp. 179–80, GL. R. McKibbin, *Ideologies of Class: Social Relations in Britain, 1880–1950* (Oxford: Clarendon Press, 1990), p. 103.

practicable by placing competing or contemporary papers alternating first," but members of the PA with private wires objected to funding the phone service, the intention and effect of which was to render their private wires less valuable.[157] Although the PA told Extel that it wished to avoid "cutting competition," and the two agencies agreed to meet occasionally to protect their interests, rivalry between them quickly escalated and caused both organizations to incur considerable expense.[158] The PA initially preferred an outright purchase of Extel, but the latter demurred, and the absence of any general corporate reporting requirements limited the possibility for hostile takeover.[159] Instead, in the spring of 1906, the two companies signed a twenty-five year agreement that created a pooling arrangement for all telephonic and tape-machine news.[160] This agreement, despite the occasional glitch, solidified the control of the PA and Extel over the collection and distribution of sporting news throughout the country and proved profitable for both organizations.[161]

Despite the advantages of the joint-pooling agreement, it also proved restrictive. All the news covered by the joint concern was telephoned from center to center, and distribution was affected by the telephone and tape machine. Extel worked the phone service by booking a series of calls on trunk wires. With expected events, wires could be booked in advance, which allowed Extel to get through to all offices in minutes; but with unexpected events, the process took longer as traffic blocked the way. In 1907, when the Post Office intimated its readiness to grant the exclusive use of leased wires to news agencies, Extel was anxious to escape from the large expense, as well as interruptions and delays, incurred using the phone. The PA and Extel stood to benefit by a substitution of the leased wire for the costly and wasteful telephone trunk call service, but, according to Extel, the PA "took violent exception to this proposition." The PA feared for its telegraphic services, as the effect of the joint-agency's use of leased wires would have been to set up a news system that superseded the press rate telegrams sent over the public wires from which the PA drew its income. The PA was also concerned that Extel intended to establish under its own control a telegraphic service that, at the termination of the joint agreement, would have been an asset for Extel. Consequently, the PA reasoned that to pay in

---

[157] PA board minutes, July 4 and September 5, 1905, PA, Ms 35358/11, pp. 229–33, 264–6, GL.

[158] PA board minutes, July 19, 1905, PA, Ms 35358/11, pp. 244–5, GL.

[159] PA board minutes, March 6, 1906, PA, Ms 35358/12, pp. 50–63, GL; D.S. Karjala, "The Board of Directors in English and American Companies through 1920" and L. Hannah, "Mergers, Cartels and Concentration: Legal Factors in the U.S. and European Experience," both in *Recht und Entwicklung der Großunternehmen*, pp. 204–24, 306–16.

[160] PA board minutes, April 17, 1906, PA, Ms 35358/12, pp. 96–102, GL.

[161] As a consequence, the PA and Extel were able to amalgamate several smaller sports news organizations, including the Golf Reporting Agency of Edinburgh. See PA board minutes, May 8, 1911, PA, Ms 35358/16, p. 303, and Manager's memoranda, May 9, 1911, PA, Ms 35362/2, pp. 212–14. See also the arrangements the PA made with Sporting Life, PA board minutes, July 31, 1912, PA, Ms 35358/17, p. 120, GL.

part for the joint wire would have been to invite an enemy in its own business. "Although it would benefit them," opined one internal Extel memo, the PA "thought that it was of more importance to them to prevent the Exchange Company from being benefited also." The matter went to arbitration, which was decided in favor of the PA insofar as leasing wires was outside the agreement concluded in 1906. Consequently, a distinction was drawn between "telegraphic" and "telephonic" transmission, and every "telegraphic" distribution was outside the scope of the joint service. Every "telephonic" and tape distribution in the provinces was inside; therefore, Extel could neither set up a new and separate telephonic and tape distribution, nor could it improve the joint service by leasing wires.[162]

By 1914, the settlement established under the Telegraph Act of 1868 was still in place, but it was crumbling everywhere and its remnants restricted the advancement of newsgathering in Britain. In 1911, Herbert Samuel, then postmaster-general, received a deputation of the press at which William Brimelow, editor of the Bolton *Evening News*, explained that

in 1868 we had our misgivings that what has happened would happen if the stimulus and incentive of competition ceased; and we only withdrew our opposition on the distinct promise of a better service than we had from the old Companies. Now – I am speaking in the main – it is worse. No great commercial concern could sustain its reputation or succeed if admissions of delays and inefficiency were made to customers to such an extent as the news agencies and the newspapers receive from the Post Office.

Samuel countered that the Post Office could not operate as a commercial concern given the "excessively cheap" rates the press was charged for telegrams.[163] Meanwhile, despite the low tariff for press messages, the services of the PA, said Robbins, still "did not pay." In 1913, all the flat-rate services were more or less conducted at a loss, as they had been for several decades, but the special service, London papers, and pooling arrangement with Extel compensated for it. So long as the business of the PA showed a profit at the end of the year, its management saw no reason to change the tariff.[164] By World War I, this system for supplying news was fragile, and the onset of war helped to bring about its collapse.

Establishing a level playing field among the provincial press was an explicit and significant policy objective underlying the Telegraph Act of 1868, but it proved largely elusive. The way in which the Post Office distributed telegrams

[162] Report as to the arbitrations between the parties, 1919, Extel, CLC/B/080/MS22974, LMA; Extel v. PA arbitration, February 13, 1912, POST 30/2401B and Memo, March 7, 1912, POST 30/2401B, BT. See also PA board minutes, June 8 and 21, 1909, PA, Ms 35358/16, pp. 5–6, 41, GL.
[163] Deputation before Samuel, December 7, 1911, PA, Ms 35362/3, pp. 176–83, GL.
[164] Manager's memoranda, October 9, 12, PA, Ms 35362/4, pp. 180–1; Manager's memoranda, May 6 and June 4, 1913, PA, Ms 35362/5, pp. 117–18, 163–5; Manager's memoranda, October 8, 1913, PA, Ms 35362/6, pp. 12–14, GL.

severely restricted the PA's method of newsgathering. This method was a relatively inclusive organization compared with the AP, but it excluded the newsrooms of the provinces and the London press. The creation of the PA also had significant consequences for the way in which foreign news was supplied to the British Isles. Reuters, despite its controlling position, was consequently placed in an uncomfortable position between the provincial and metropolitan presses. The maintenance of the settlement of 1868 required perpetuating this largely artificial balancing act by restricting the use of new technology, including quadruplex telegraphy and telephony. The ad hoc telecommunications policy of the Post Office, which changed with the political winds, disrupted established market relations and customary regimes. To contend with these alterations, the press increasingly sought private solutions to the problems of newsgathering.

5

Private Enterprise, Public Monopoly, and the Preservation of Cooperation in Britain, 1914–1941

World War I helped to precipitate the demise of the settlement achieved under the Telegraph Act of 1868, but it did not collapse until the eve of World War II. The end of war in 1918 ushered in an age of "rationalization" among newsgatherers, concentration of ownership among newspapers, and a period of increased competition in both sectors. The British government played an important part in this process by creating an environment generally conducive to rationalization and combination, particularly during the wars and especially with respect to broadcasting, even if the rationale that motivated interwar intervention was not as explicit as that which motivated the Victorians. The BBC, established as a public corporation in 1926, wielded considerable power in the market by virtue of the monopoly granted to it by the state. The threat the BBC posed to existing industry alliances undermined cooperation and precipitated merger. Seen in this light, the subsidization of the press by the British state did not disappear. Instead, it shifted to radio. The creation of the BBC marked the end of the consensus established in 1868 and signaled the start of a new policy regime with respect to news.

The war brought to fruition those changes already underway in the 1890s. The PA embraced leased lines, but it continued to rely on the London press, Extel, and Reuters to subsidize the news reports it provided to the provincial press. Only when these alternative lines of revenue dried up, was the PA forced to charge provincial newspapers differently for a like service of news. As in other areas of industrial activity, such as alcohol and chemicals, mergers occurred during the interwar period among firms previously linked by agreements.[1] Reuters and the PA merged, which in retrospect appears to have been the culmination of a fifty-five-year courtship, the operations of Extel and the PA became more closely intertwined, and the PA purchased Central News, a

---

[1] Mercer, *Constructing a Competitive Order*, p. 12.

tertiary organization that had long been the PA's foil. More so than before the war, the landscape in Britain resembled that in the United States. The British United Press (BUP), a subsidiary of the American UP, increased competition in the United Kingdom. The largest visible difference between the two countries lay in their varying responses to broadcasting.

THE CONSEQUENCES OF WORLD WAR I

On the eve of World War I, the growth of the large provincial dailies, and in particular their increased use of private wires, caused the London press concern. The large provincial papers especially cut down the circulation of the London evening papers, such as the *Pall Mall Gazette*, *Westminster Gazette*, and *The Globe*. To counteract this tendency, London publishers refused to continue sharing summaries of their news with the PA, a practice that had been in place since the 1880s. There was so much prior publication of the news material of *The Times* outside London that it damaged circulation, which caused Viscount Northcliffe to end a long-standing agreement between the PA and his paper. In certain instances, such as the explorations of Sir Robert Scott and Sir Earnest Shackleton to Antarctica, individual London newspapers actively competed with, and successfully outbid, Reuters and the PA for exclusive access to reports of the expeditions. In 1912, the Newspaper Proprietors Association (NPA), a trade organization of London publishers established in 1906, attempted to block the PA from representation on the Admiralty committee that debated the role of the press in wartime.[2]

After the outbreak of hostilities, competition between the metropolitan and provincial press became more pronounced. Difficulties and restrictions at the war front were the principal cause. Telegraph facilities between the continent of Europe and England were greatly reduced, often slow, and closely monitored. Unexpectedly, censorship and the cessation of British sporting events, as well as a hiatus in domestic political affairs, caused a 15 percent overall reduction in the size of the news service the PA provided in 1914 as compared with that of 1913. "From all the great provincial centres, the service has practically ceased, except for war items," complained Frederick Storey of the Sunderland *Echo*, to Edmund Robbins, general manager of the PA.[3] Whereas the cost of international telegrams constituted 13 percent of all telegraph and cabling expenses in 1915, by 1916 the figure had nearly doubled. By 1918 the cost reached 32 percent. This increase was attributable to real growth in the size and cost of international news as well as a decrease in domestic news.

[2] Meeting of Robbins and H. de Reuter, Manager's memoranda, January 11, 1914, PA, Ms 35362/6, p. 163, GL; Robbins to Phillips, Manager's memoranda, September 10, 1912, PA, Ms 35362/4, pp. 187–8; PA board minutes, June 25, 1914, PA, Ms 35358/18, GL.
[3] F.G. Storey to Robbins, Manager's memoranda, April 21, 1915, PA, Ms 35362/8, p. 282, GL.

The physical position of correspondents at the front further complicated reporting the war. In the pitched battles of the nineteenth century, journalists could report on events from a safe distance, but there was no obvious vantage point from which they could easily observe trench warfare. Instead, correspondents were stationed at military headquarters and the authorities took them on scheduled visits to the battle lines. With only so many beds at headquarters, representation at the front was constrained – or so went the official line – and the London papers, despite protest, were obliged to restrict their number of correspondents while the PA and Reuters were jointly allocated only one spot in the war party. A Press Committee, which included representatives of the London press, the PA, War Office, and Admiralty, made decisions about the allocation of correspondents at the front. George Riddell, publisher of the *News of the World*, was a close friend of Lloyd George, through whom he gained access to Kitchener, Churchill, and other important government officials. These contacts contributed to his considerable influence with the Press Committee and, according to the PA, enabled him to shunt the association and Reuters to the side.[4] In certain instances, such as the British expedition to Mesopotamia, the London papers compelled the PA to send only one correspondent and Reuters was cut out entirely, although it did receive a copy of all messages at its office in Bombay for sale abroad.[5] Reuters also had difficulty with the London papers over its charge for war news. In the case of the Dardanelles, London publishers refused to provide the necessary funds for Reuters to send another correspondent to the seat of operations, which pushed the agency closer to the PA and caused C.P. Scott of the Manchester *Guardian* to complain of the "aggressive attitude" of the London press.[6] Reuters in turn sought out an increased subscription from the PA. The agency, said one Reuters executive to the PA, was "not in a position to fight the London press single-handed."[7] Although the PA refused to pay an increased subscription, it did promise to back Reuters materially to keep up the standard of the service if the London press denied it further patronage.[8]

As a result of the constraints on frontline reporting, the London papers benefited from their own correspondents and Reuters's news, but the provincial papers were only entitled to one account of foreign news through the agency. Provincial publishers complained that London editors had been unfairly allocated two strings to their bow and feared that without special reports from their own correspondents readers would increasingly turn to London. Newspapers in Birmingham, Glasgow, Leeds, Manchester, and other cities constituted a

---

[4] See, for example, Manager's memoranda, November 10, 1915, PA, Ms 35362/9, p. 285, GL.

[5] Manager's memoranda, December 8, 1915, PA, Ms 35362/9, pp. 303–4 and August 20, 1917, PA, Ms 35362/10, p. 1319, GL.

[6] Manager's memoranda, June 9, 1915, PA, Ms 35362/9, p. 20, GL; PA board minutes, August 1, 1916, PA, Ms 35358/19, p. 31, GL.

[7] Bradshaw to Robbins, Manager's memoranda, July 25, 1915, PA, Ms 35362/9, p. 117, GL.

[8] Manager's memoranda, August 5, 1915, PA, Ms 35362/9, p. 143, GL.

"Northern Federation" to demand the right of a correspondent of their own at the front so as to obtain news reports in addition to that which was common to all the papers in the provinces.[9] The inequality between London and leading provincial papers also put Reuters in a difficult position. During July and August 1915, aside from the news gathered by their own correspondents, the *Daily Telegraph*, *Morning Post*, and *The Times* published an average of twenty columns of Reuters's news per week. Had Reuters been unable to sell its news in the London market, it would have lost revenue and prestige.[10]

As ever, Reuters was stuck inconveniently between the London and provincial press. In 1919, when the agency attempted to raise subscription charges to compensate for the termination of wartime government subsidies, the first question from the representatives of the London press was to what extent Reuters first intended to increase the payment of the provincial papers.[11] Although the London publishers had varying opinions of the agency, and some might have been persuaded to pay an increased fee, Reuters's managers feared that by applying for a larger payment they would aggravate tensions between the London and provincial presses, which would make Reuters's position more complicated. "The feud is between the London papers and the wealthy provincial papers," wrote W.L. Murray, Reuters secretary, to Roderick Jones, then general manager of the agency, "and we, by our application, have furnished the London newspapers with a weapon to bring the P.A. to heel."[12] In 1919, the metropolitan newspapers paid Reuters £22,500 (approximately £846,000 in today's prices), against £8,000 (£3000,000) from the PA, not inclusive of specials, which meant that the rate paid by the large provincial papers for Reuters's news as compared with their circulation was very low indeed. By comparison, the entire press of South Africa paid Reuters £24,000 (£900,000) per annum in addition to the costs of transmission. The London newspapers considered that they bore the main expenses of Reuters's service to the advantage of the provincial newspapers. They contended that the provincial publishers were in a better position to pay an increased subscription. At this time, provincial publishers received a greater number of advertisements from manufacturing firms. These firms placed large orders for advertisements with the press to reduce the amount payable under the Excess Profits Taxes, which was levied during the war on business profits over an assumed so-called normal profit.[13] The London papers were also the main supporters of the special reporting services that the PA provided. In 1917, a London morning paper paid £5 5s a week (£240) for

[9] PA board minutes, September 6, 1916, PA, Ms 35362/9, p. 732, GL.
[10] J. Scott in Manager's memoranda, August 1, 1916, PA, Ms 35362/9, p. 704, GL; Bradshaw to NPA in Manager's memoranda, August 13, 1915, PA, Ms 35362/9, p. 148, GL.
[11] Murray to Jones, June 25, 1920, Jones papers, series 1, box 33, RA.
[12] Murray to June 28, 1920, Jones papers, series 1, box 33; Giles to Jones, January 3, 1921, Jones papers, series 1, box 28; Murray to Jones, February 2, 1919; July 28, 1920, Jones papers, series 1, box 33, RA.
[13] Murray to Jones, September 19, 1919; June 26, 1920, Jones papers, series 1, box 33, RA.

the metropolitan service provided by the PA, against £1 10s (£69) paid by the provincial papers.[14] The provincial morning papers paid roughly £62 per year (£2,800) for a good telegraphed service of cricket results. These reports were not wired, but hand delivered to the London papers, two of which were charged £200 each (£9,000).[15]

Although the position of Reuters and the PA relative to the London press was contested, their position relative to other British news organizations improved. Extel was cut off from the front. An interruption in soccer and horseracing and a discontinuance of cricket more seriously affected Extel than the PA. Reuters, conversely, received special dispensation from the government Press Bureau with regard to incoming messages and censorship. During 1918, Reuters received approximately £126,000 from the government in payment for the large amount of propaganda material it sent to neutral countries during the war. These advantages gave the agency a monopoly over the prompt arrival of foreign news, particularly commercial information, which laid the foundation for the expansion of these news services after the war.[16] With Extel considerably weakened, the PA had a chance to exert greater influence over the organization of the news industry. Before the war, Extel had consistently undersold the PA in commercial intelligence, which caused the association to incur a loss on these services. After the war, the PA was able to compel the agency to set equal rates.[17] In the spring of 1918, the association began to purchase shares in Extel.[18] In 1926, the PA and Extel extended the life of their pooling contracts until 1961.[19] Although incomplete cooperation proved limiting on occasion, neither the PA nor Reuters ever sought to merge with Extel.[20] From the perspective of the PA and Reuters, there was no point, as Jones put it, in taking over competitors which they knew and could measure just to make room for new and probably stronger competition.[21]

Specialized news organizations, such as the London News Agency, incorporated in 1901, which competed with the metropolitan news service the PA provided, also suffered because of the increased working expenses the war

---

[14] Manager's memoranda, November 5, 1917, PA, Ms 35362/10, 1392, GL.

[15] Manager's memoranda, May 10, 1915, PA, Ms 35362/8, p. 235, GL.

[16] Manager's memoranda, August 1, 1917, PA, Ms 35362/10, pp. 1282–3; Sixth report of the select committee on national expenditure, copy in Manager's memoranda, PA, Ms 35362/12, p. 2149; G. Cockerill to Robbins, Manager's memoranda, September 30, 1914, PA, Ms 35362/7, pp. 169–70, GL.

[17] Manager's memoranda, November 5, 1918, PA, Ms 35362/12, pp. 2230–1, GL.

[18] PA board minutes, May 6, 1918, PA, Ms 35358/20, p. 28, GL.

[19] Manager's memoranda, November 2, 1926, PA, Ms 35362/21, p. 295, GL.

[20] For further incidents of the restrictions imposed by the PA-Extel pooling arrangement, see Manager's memoranda, May 6, 1924, PA, Ms 35362/16, p. 4384 and Manager's memoranda, November 1, 1927, PA, Ms 35362/19, GL.

[21] R. Jones to A. Burchill, July 17, 1929, Jones papers, series 1, box 36, RA. In 1925, the PA did, however, move to purchase the Sportsman News Agency, but for defensive reasons. See Manager's memoranda, January 6, 1925, PA, Ms 35362/17, p. 4594, GL.

occasioned. Before 1914, the PA considered purchasing the London News Agency, which collected local news of London for the London press, but the price demanded was thought to be exorbitant. The management of the PA was also concerned about the possibility that, if they purchased the London News Agency, the London press might be motivated to form a stronger competing agency of its own, or that it might lobby against the PA's monopoly.[22] After the war, the London News Agency was obliged to seek some form of agreement with the PA, and in 1919, the PA determined in conjunction with Extel to purchase the agency outright. To avoid hostility from the London press, the *Daily Chronicle* was invited to partake in the purchase.[23] Even so, Sir Andrew Caird of the *Daily Mail* complained that the PA's acquisition of the London News Agency illustrated that the association and Extel had a "trust," which enabled the former to control the distribution of news in the provinces and the latter to control it in London. The PA replied that its purchase had saved the London press an unnecessary subscription, although in practice the association purposefully refrained from raising the cost of the London service to avoid additional complaints.[24] The name of the London News Agency still adorns 45 Fleet Street.

The enlarged press work that war necessitated, combined with a significant diminution in staff, aggravated the financial difficulties of the Post Office. According to the Committee on Public Retrenchment, the cost of purchasing the telegraphs in 1870 cost in excess of £10 million, and the loss on working since then had been £1 million per annum. In 1911–1912, the total accumulated loss was calculated as being in excess of £21 million, or double the amount of the original purchase money.[25] In Parliament, Labour Party members demanded that the Post Office turn a profit and increase the wages of its telegraphers.[26] Other MPs complained that the press was subsidized, which it was. To counteract these views the PA argued in private that any increase in the charge for press messages would increase concentration in the newspaper industry and place control over the nation's press in the hands of a group of powerful syndicates, which would be prejudicial to the interests of the state and public.[27] Arguments from the PA to uphold the principles of the Telegraph Act of 1868 still carried weight in some quarters, particularly among those policy-makers, such as Walter Runciman, president of the Board of Trade, and Winston Churchill, then first lord of the Admiralty, who objected to a figure like

---

[22] Manager's memoranda, April 8, 1914, PA, Ms 36362/6, p. 310, GL.
[23] PA board minutes, PA, Ms 353418/1, GL.
[24] Manager's memoranda, March 9, 1920, PA, Ms 35362/13, p. 3097; Manager's memoranda, December 7, 1920, PA, Ms 35362/14, p. 3349, GL.
[25] "Final Report of the Committee on Retrenchment in the Public Expenditure," *BPP*, 1916 [Cd. 8200], XV.181, pp. 20–1.
[26] Manager's memoranda, March 4, 1915, PA, Ms 35362/8, p. 138, GL.
[27] Meeting with H. Samuel, October 6, 1915, PA, Ms 35362/9, p. 192, GL.

Northcliffe gaining control of the nation's press. Both Runciman and Churchill were reluctant to cause further concentration in the newspaper industry by an increase in telegram rates, and the tariff finally decided in October 1915, and passed in the Postal & Telegraphs Rates (Statutory Limits) Act, was consequently lower than that which the Post Office had initially proposed.[28] Indeed, in real terms the increase did not keep pace with inflation.[29]

Having been delayed several times by the protests of the press, the increase in rates was finally implemented at the end of 1919, after which it became more difficult for the PA to continue to serve its members alike. Even after the war, the Post Office telegram service remained remarkably slow and comparatively expensive. Reportedly, when Melville Stone, the AP general manager, visited England at the end of the war, he laughed at the delays the PA suffered at the hands of the Post Office. In 1918, the AP delivered its messages simultaneously, and practically instantaneously, to all of its 1,100 members.[30] In the AP offices, the operators transmitted an average of 33 words per minute, or 2,000 words per hour. In turn, secretaries typed the "copy" at a corresponding speed in the receiving offices. The AP could send an unlimited number of words over its leased telegraph network, which cost £168,000 per year (£6.7 million), or a little more than 23 percent of its annual revenue of £725,000 (£28.8 million). According to the Post Office, the output of American telegraphers was twice that of British operators and it was rare that a Post Office operative transmitted twenty-four messages per hour as they were supposed to do, although a good operator could transmit that amount in eighteen minutes. As a consequence, in 1918 the PA paid the Post Office nearly £60,000 (£2.4 million), or 32 percent of its annual revenue of £136,000 (£5.4 million), for a delayed and limited news report.[31]

FROM PRIVATE WIRE TO PRIVATE NETWORK: LEASED LINES IN BRITAIN

After the rate increase on press messages, news services telegraphed through the Post Office were sufficiently slow and expensive that more members of the PA began to demand that their services from the association be sent over their private wires. To reduce labor requirements and costs after the war broke out, the Post Office allowed press telegrams to be received at London newspaper

---

[28] Manager's memoranda, PA, Ms 35362/9, GL.
[29] During the interwar period, policy makers continued to debate the rate charged for press telegrams, but, after 1922, most of the messages the PA sent went via private wires and not through the Post Office. For information on these debates and the rates charged, see Kieve, *Electric Telegraph*, pp. 226–9.
[30] Manager's memoranda, August 6, 1918, PA, Ms 35362/12, 2374, GL.
[31] Manager's memoranda, August 27, 1918, September 30, 1918, and Janyart 6, 1919, PA, Ms 35362/12, pp. 2362–4, 2367, 2375, GL.

offices for distribution via private wire to provincial newsrooms.[32] This caused an increase in the use of private wires. The shift to private wires threatened to split the association between the haves and the have-nots. Many of the have-nots were evening papers. Some evening newspapers could have afforded private wires but they required them during the day. The Post Office, however, lacked the bandwidth to allocate lines for individual use during the day when public traffic was heavy. Whereas thirty-one of the fifty-one provincial morning papers had private wires, only fifteen of the seventy-five evening papers were similarly equipped.[33]

To survive this division in its ranks, the PA had to cease relying on the Post Office telegraph department and establish its own telegraph network for the collection and distribution of news.[34] The new telegram rates were high enough that a leased system was economical. The cost to the PA to telegraph news through the Post Office in 1913 was £51,529, of which £40,216 was for regular services. The total cost at the new rates for the same wordage was £88,000 per annum.[35] The cost of a leased-line system, inclusive of all the machinery necessary for 113 newspaper offices throughout the provinces, was estimated at a few hundred pounds less and promised advantageous economies. The great number of telegraph operators trained during the war provided labor to reduce the cost of staffing the leased-wire system despite the relatively high union density in Britain's post and telecommunications sector and the protests of the Postal and Telegraph Clerks Union, which continued to resist any movement to allow the PA to lease wires.[36] In 1920, the last year before an experimental leased-wire system came into operation, the PA paid the Post Office £57,590 to telegraph press messages, whereas in 1925 it paid just more than £12,000. That year, the total cost of its telegrams was £66,800, or about £9,300 more in real terms than before the adoption of the system. For that sum, however, the PA telegraphed much more than double the amount of matter at a great gain in speed of transmission.[37]

---

[32] PA board minutes, January 23, 1914, PA, Ms 35358/17, pp. 304–5; A.G. Leonard to Robbins, January 23, 1914, PA, Ms 35362/6, pp. 153–5; Interview with Leonard, January 26, 1914, PA, Ms 35362/6, pp. 155–7, GL.

[33] Manager's memoranda, August 1, 1916, PA, Ms 35362/9, p. 695, GL.

[34] There was no practical alternative to a leased-wire system. The telephone was unreliable, involved constant danger of serious error, and was not improving compared to private wires in rapidity of transmission. It remained impossible for wireless receiving stations in the provinces also to act as broadcasting stations, which meant wireless telegraphy was impracticable, despite its rapid development during the war.

[35] Given inflation, £88,000 from 1918 in real terms was worth approximately £42,500, or somewhat less than the rate charged in 1913.

[36] Manager's memoranda, July 29, 1919, PA, Ms 35362/13, p. 2747, Manager's memoranda, October 5, 1920, PA, Ms 35362/14, p. 3327, GL. S.N. Broadberry and S. Ghosal, "From the Counting House to the Modern Office: Explaining Anglo-American Productivity Differences in Services, 1870–1990," *The Journal of Economic History*, 62 (2002), 990.

[37] Manager's memoranda, March 9, 1926, PA, Ms 35362/18, p. 4918, GL.

The leased-wire network of the PA expanded rapidly. In 1922, a formal agreement was signed with the Post Office, and by 1924, the network was extended to Scotland. The total number of papers connected to the system at the end of 1923 was 118; namely, 40 morning dailies and 78 evening dailies, as compared with 19 morning papers and 54 evening papers at the beginning of 1923, and 7 morning papers and 11 evening papers at the start of 1922.[38] By 1925, the network ran into or through sixty-three of the seventy-two towns in England, Scotland, and Wales in which daily newspapers were published. In the nine daily newspaper towns not connected to the system, one morning and nine evening papers were published.[39] Every daily newspaper was connected to the network by 1930. Smaller newspapers and those published on a triweekly, biweekly, or weekly basis, but still members of the association, faced increased charges, which in light of the trade depression, they found difficult to meet. Weekly papers were reluctant to join the scheme and most left the association.[40]

"It has always been a matter of principle with the Press Association," said H.C. Robbins, who took over as general manager of the PA after his father retired in 1918, "that there should be no differentiation between one paper and another in sending out our services." The use of a leased-wire system undermined this guiding principle. Indeed, to price the new services over its network of leased wires the PA considered but then rejected the idea of granting exclusive franchises to its members.[41] The demise of many smaller newspapers during and after World War I made departure from a principle of equality and a leased-wire system possible. The onset of hostilities in 1914 caused a dramatic increase in the costs of running a newspaper. The price of raw materials ballooned, staffs were depleted, salaries and wages grew, and advertisement revenue diminished. Government obliged the press to publish a large number of official messages gratis while paid-for party propaganda practically ceased, which caused the papers previously kept alive by the Liberal or Conservative parties to suffer severely.[42] By 1916, eight morning and four evening newspapers had ceased to publish. High provincial newspaper mortality rates persisted during the war and throughout the early 1920s, particularly among morning papers. Expansion of the national press accompanied a decline in the provincial newspaper field (see Table 5.1 and Table 5.2). Between 1920 and 1939, the circulation of the national dailies increased from 5.4 to 10.6 million copies daily.[43]

[38] Report of the 56th annual meeting, May 6, 1924, PA, Ms, 35372/3, p. 6, GL.
[39] Manager's memoranda, September 3, 1925, PA, Ms 35362/17, p. 4749, GL.
[40] Manager's memoranda, June 13, 1923, PA, Ms 35362/16, p. 4130, GL; Manager's memoranda, June 28, 1927, PA, Ms 35362/19, GL.
[41] Manager's memoranda, September 3 and October 8, 1918, PA, Ms 35362/12, pp. 2098, 2210, GL.
[42] Manager's memoranda, September 8, 1915, PA, Ms 35362/9, p. 129, GL.
[43] G. Murdock and P. Golding, "The Structure, Ownership and Control of the Press, 1914–76," in G. Boyce, et al. (eds.), *Newspaper History from the Seventeenth Century to the Present Day*

TABLE 5.1. *Average circulation (000)*

	Daily			Weekly	
	London		Provincial	Sunday	Prov. and
	Morning	Evening	(AM & PM)	London & Prov.	sub-urban
1920	5,430	1,940	7,300	13,500	6,820
1930	8,650	2,030	7,270	15,510	7,480
1939	10,570	1,900	6,990	16,040	7,370

Source: A.P. Wadsworth, "Newspaper circulations, 1800–1954," *Manchester Statistical Society* (March 9, 1955), p. 28.

TABLE 5.2. *Number of newspapers published, 1921–1947*

	1921	1937	1947
Nationals and provincial Sundays	21	17	16
National morning	12	9	9
Provincial morning	41	28	25
Provincial evening	89	79	75
Weeklies	–	1,348	1,307

Source: Murdock and Golding, "The structure, ownership and control of the press, 1914–76," p. 132.

A considerable reduction in the number of provincial newspapers and increased competition from the London press had adverse consequences for the PA. Before 1920, a total of fifty-four newspapers took a first-class general evening service from the association, but by 1924 the number had dropped to forty-three. Morning papers disappeared at Aberdeen, Cork (2), Darlington, Dublin, Exeter, Huddersfield, Leicester, Manchester (2), Newcastle, and Plymouth, and none arose to take their place. Fewer evening newspapers closed, but the number of newspapers supporting the PA contracted appreciably over-all. The total loss of revenue to the association from newspaper stoppages and amalgamations – counting only those since the beginning of 1921 – aggregated upward of £20,000 per annum. Concentration of ownership accompanied this decline in the number of newspapers, which gave rise to a number of newspaper chains. The percentage of provincial evening papers owned by chains rose

(London: Constable, 1978), pp. 130–3; J. Curran and J. Seaton, *Power without Responsibility: The Press and Broadcasting in Britain* (London: Routledge, 1997), p. 51. For an in-depth analysis, see N. Kaldor and R. Silverman, *A Statistical Analysis of Advertising Expenditure and the Revenue of the Press* (Cambridge: Cambridge University Press, 1948), pp. 57–97; Political and Economic Planning (PEP), *The State of the Press*, No. 58 (London: PEP, 1935); PEP, *Report of the British Press* (London: PEP, 1938).

from 8 to 40 percent between 1921 and 1939. Chain ownership of morning papers also increased from 12 to 44 percent during the same period. In 1924, the London and Glasgow papers in the Rothermere publishing group, which represented the PA's largest customer, contributed more than £13,000 to the association's revenue.[44] Many of these chains were based in London, but the Berry group of Lord Camrose, in addition to owning a number of important London publications, had its greatest strength in the provinces, where it owned a large list of newspapers.[45] The Starmer group, named after Sir Charles Starmer, its managing director, had about thirty provincial newspapers.[46] Several smaller provincial chains also formed. By 1935, independent newspapers were scarce. Outside London, the remaining leading independent newspapers of the time were the Manchester *Guardian*, the Yorkshire *Post*, the Glasgow *Herald*, and the Glasgow *Scotsman*, each with their respective satellite evening journals.[47]

Shedding the obligation to serve all newspapers equally, and distributing news via leased lines, enabled a dramatic improvement in terms of rapidity of dispatch over the Post Office and also reduced the costs incurred by the PA. The tariff in 1920 fixed the price for the first-class general evening and midday special services at £168 per annum each, or 10s 8d a day. On average, these services provided twenty-four messages per day at a rate of 5.28d per message. Compared with these figures, the leased-wire service showed an advance. A first-class general evening and midday special service alike cost less than 3.5d per message; a real reduction of more than 5 percent from the price charged in 1920. By 1923, the number of words the PA dispatched over leased wires significantly exceeded those sent via the Post Office. During the first four months of the year, the principal services sent over leased wires – midday special, morning express, and Reuters – were on average 29 percent larger than those sent via the Post Office.[48]

By June, payments to the Post Office showed a 40 percent decrease when compared to the corresponding period in 1922, and 44 percent for the same period in 1913. New York prices, continental bourses, foreign rates of exchange, court circulars, lists of bankruptcies, evening paper weather reports, and other small services were all sent entirely by the PA's telegraph network. News dispatched this way traveled much faster than through the Post Office. The average transmission time by leased wire was fourteen minutes; by Post Office wire

[44] Manager's memoranda, April 8, 1924, PA, Ms 35362/16, p. 4350, GL.
[45] The Berry group's provincial properties included the Manchester *Daily Dispatch* and *Sunday Chronicle*, the Glasgow *Daily Record*, the *North Mail* and *Western Mail*, the Bristol *Times*, and the Sheffield *Daily Telegraph*. The Berry group also had an enormous interest in the weekly periodical field through its control of Amalgamated Press and other companies
[46] The largest of which were the Birmingham *Gazette*, the Yorkshire *Observer*, the Nottingham *Journal*, and the Sheffield *Independent*.
[47] PEP, *The State of the Press*; Notes on provincial papers, July 1, 1926, Jones papers, series 1, box 68, RA.
[48] Manager's memoranda, May 8, 1923, PA, Ms 35362/15, pp. 4073-4, GL.

TABLE 5.3. *Amount paid to the Post Office for wiring services and for leased wires (in £ at constant 1913 prices)*

Year	Cost	Year	Cost (Rental)
1913	54,150	1919	21,069
1914	57,492	1920	21,080
1915	48,994	1921	21,318
1916	35,482	1922	20,458 (5,902)
1917	26,143	1923	13,045 (12,720)
1918	21,163	1924	6,505 (13,116)

Source: PA, Ms 35362, GL.

TABLE 5.4. *Total messages and daily averages, 1920 and 1924*

	1920		1924		
	Total messages	Daily avg.	Total messages	Daily avg.	Change (%)
General evg.	3,771	24.2	5,948	38	+58
Midday special	3,667	23.5	5,773	37	+57.5

Source: PA, Ms 35362, GL.

it was seventy minutes and thirty-six seconds.[49] Results of the Tiverton by-election in June 1923 were received via leased wire thirty-four minutes before the quickest Post Office telegram.[50] By the end of 1923, the PA paid the Post Office £20,000 in rent and another £25,000 for matter sent via the public wires. Had the same amount of news been sent entirely by the Post Office, it would have cost the association roughly £90,000. The leased-wire system thus represented a savings of £35,000, not including the benefits that accrued to the association and its members from increased speed in transmission (see Table 5.3 and Table 5.4).

Soon it was possible for the newspapers to receive from the PA over the leased-wire system twice the supply of news it had previously received without any extra cost.[51] "Once the crippling system of public wire transmission was exchanged for our own private wire distribution," commented the PA general manager, "we were able, as the latter developed, to increase the quantities [of the service]."[52] In 1921, when the PA started using a leased-wire system, the loss

---

[49] Manager's memoranda, September 7, 1920, PA, Ms 35362/14, p. 3290, GL.
[50] Manager's memoranda, June 22, 1923, PA, Ms 35362/16, p. 4133, GL.
[51] Manager's memoranda, January 4, 1927, PA, Ms 35362/19, p. 2, GL.
[52] Robbins and Hodgson to directors, July 18, 1924, PA, Ms 35362/16, p. 4461–80, GL.

to the Post Office from the postal telegraph service was £3,728,779. By 1925, the loss had fallen to £1,645,625, a reduction in real terms of approximately £1.25 million. It would be presumptive to claim that the diminished loss was entirely attributable to the PA relieving the Post Office of about two-thirds of the press work it formerly carried, but there is no doubt that the leased-wire system had a material effect in bringing about the decrease. By the end of 1926, the PA leased 3,218 miles of wire; by 1930, the AP leased 220,000 miles.[53]

The improvement in transmission afforded by leased lines, and the ability to increase the size of the news report, allowed the PA to accommodate various changes underway during the interwar period in newspaper presentation. It was during this period that the daily press, in the chase for readers, circulation, and increased advertising revenue, adopted tabloid journalism. Toward the end of 1926, once the leased line system was fully established, an editor of the "new school," as it was called, was employed to overhaul the services so that they better met the needs of the association's members. C.L. Cranfield, the editor appointed to fulfill this task, explained that "while maintaining the tone and importance of our Mid-day Special and General Evening messages, and avoiding any suggestion of flippancy, I have sought to leaven them with more stories of interest to women and of general human interest." Plaudits for improvements in the service came from around the country. "I remember my old attempts to find something bright in the P.A. copy," wrote the editor of the Cardiff *Evening Express* to Cranfield. "It is at last clear that the P.A. understands what an evening paper wants."[54] Much to the pleasure of the PA directors, members relied on the general tariff services for the brunt of their news. The schedule for the midday special of February 24, 1927 provides an indication of the stories the PA reported:

- What to do with baby: A church crèche and pram park
- Lord Ashfield's appeal for industrial peace
- Women centenarian's advice
- The King's first levee of the season
- Bride's suicide; remarkable letter
- Stroubridge election results
- Mrs. Bruce Ismay's £20,000 necklace lost
- Father's transfusion to save son
- Girl's wedding morning shock (bigamy case)
- Tributes to Sir E. Marshall Hall
- Shire Horse Society; first woman president interviewed
- Views of Note to Soviet
- Peer's brother as amateur 'Raffles' (an exclusive)
- Lower House of Convocation and the new prayer book

[53] Manager's memoranda, March 9 and July 26, 1926, PA, Ms 35362/18, p. 4918, GL.
[54] Manager's memoranda, May 31, 1927, PA, Ms, 35362/19, GL.

- Manslaughter charge against guards officer
- Solitary confinement for zoo alligator
- Lobby correspondent on British cruiser for Nicaragua

The introduction of the leased-wire system helped precipitate a modification in the association's method of charging its members for news. Initially, the association continued its effort to charge newspapers a flat rate for transmission (a proportion of the wire rental). Papers were required, however, to take services of a minimum value. It remained the case that the various news services the PA offered were not charged to newspapers on the basis that each service should cover its cost. The basic and essential news services grew, but the charges were not increased in proportion to the additional costs, which made them unprofitable. Offered specials, which supplemented the reports in the basic services, and additional services, such as the joint-service with Extel, as well as charges to the London papers, made good the loss that would otherwise have accrued from this system of charging for the news reports. The joint-service with Extel grew substantially after 1923, when the two organizations developed a joint-commercial news service. Thereafter, and until 1938, the Paxtel service, as it was called, brought the association on average slightly more than £50,000 per annum in revenue, or 16 percent of its average total annual income. Absent these alternative sources of revenue, the standard tariff news services continued to show a loss.[55]

After 1927, the year in which the PA first obtained a considerable network of private wires, the increase in the quantity and quality of the general news services was such that the first of these supplementary sources of income – offered specials – began to fail. The revenue from specials decreased gradually after 1927 (see Table 5.5). As the standard tariff services were developed to, and maintained at, a high level, newspapers no longer wanted specials to the extent that had previously been the case. Proposals to introduce new special services failed for lack of support. "The needs of subscribers are shown to be so diverse," said H.C. Robbins in 1932, "that it is impossible under existing conditions to obtain sufficient support for a single service."[56] During 1935, cancellations and reductions in the use of specials diminished the net gain from a gross increase in tariff of £13,833 to £8,683.[57]

The emergence of newspaper chains also undermined the PA's long-standing principle of charging all papers the same rate regardless of the potential of their areas. The Southern Echo group, for example, published three evening newspapers – the *Dorset*, the *Southern*, and the *Bournemouth Echo* – and it paid the PA three times more for the same service of news, yet each newspaper circulated in a different territory with dissimilar population densities and sales

55 Secretary's memo, October 28, 1927, PA, Ms 35438, GL.
56 Circular to members, October 17, 1932, PA, Ms 35358/23, pp. 4–5, GL.
57 PA board minutes, October 8, 1935, PA, Ms 35358/23, p. 268, GL.

TABLE 5.5. *PA revenue from specials and member newspapers, 1927–1939 (£)*

	Specials	Members	Per cent of total revenue		Total revenue
			Specials	Members	
1927	51,194	128,561	24.08	60.47	212,614
1929	53,705	155,740	21.25	61.63	252,699
1931	50,063	147,460	20.61	60.71	242,875
1933	47,541	148,494	19.64	61.35	242,035
1935	43,548	156,975	17.48	63.01	249,137
1937	35,584	165,850	14.05	65.50	253,201
1939	36,058	178,391	13.74	67.99	262,393

Source: GA, Ms 35438.

potential. The Southampton *Echo* was for many years a prosperous concern and the paper at Bournemouth likewise. The *Echo* at Weymouth, however, was established to defend the western end of the Echo group's territory against the competition of the Weymouth *Press*, a small evening sheet started by the proprietors of two Channel Island papers. The Echo group eventually acquired the *Press*, which was also a PA member. Although the Weymouth paper was run at a loss, its continuance was of considerable indirect value to the Echo group, and it did not seem fair to the publishers of these papers that Weymouth, a town of about 25,000 people in a generally sparsely populated area with poor communications, should be charged as much as manufacturing centers with teeming populations. Instead, the publishers proposed that the paper at Southampton should pay full rates, the one at Bournemouth 75 percent, and the one at Weymouth 50 percent.[58]

Although proposals were made to abandon the practice whereby specials were debited and ordered per item in favor of a "super-service" that contained these extended reports at a nominal increase in charge, it was not instituted until the onset of World War II. The war precipitated a collapse in the association's revenue from other sources, such as its joint-service with Extel, which forced the PA to modify its pricing structure. The cessation of sporting activity at the start of World War II caused a dramatic reduction in the revenues of the PA. Whereas in 1938 the Paxtel service provided the PA with profits totaling nearly £30,000, in 1939 the amount had decreased to £14,981, and in 1940 it showed a loss of £31,208.[59] The war interrupted trade, which increased the cost of paper and forced a reduction of newspaper sizes. With the small size of newspapers, and the prospect of further reductions looming, even the London papers ceased to be a source of revenue on which the PA could rely. As revenue decreased, the impossibility of the PA continuing to charge all newspapers the

[58] W.A. Gleave to C. Hyde, November 14, 1927, PA, Ms 35362/19, GL.
[59] October 8, 1941, PA, Ms 35363/1, p. 83, GL.

same price for the same service, irrespective of their potential to pay, became glaringly apparent. To take the news services related to the war without any increase in the cost of their subscription to the PA, large newspapers, which could afford to rely on their own correspondents, dispensed with certain services. But smaller newspapers still relied on these services. To compensate for the loss of revenue that the PA typically received from the larger papers, the association attempted to increase the cost of its war reports and to use the profits that accrued from the increase to subsidize the services the smaller papers required. The price increase only caused more newspapers to cancel their subscriptions to less important services, so that to cover the cost of the depleted subscriptions would have required a 150 percent increase in the price of the association's main services.[60]

In 1940, a comprehensive service replaced the medley of services previously supplied and charged for separately and did away with the obligation to charge all newspapers a like fee for the same service regardless of their abilities to pay. Instead, the charge for the service was graded based on the daily net sales figures of the newspaper that took the service. To operate the net sale system, each newspaper annually declared by means of a certificate from its auditors the circulation grouping into which it fell.[61] Under the new service, the charge even for the highest classification was less than the various component services provided under the old tariff headings. The charges to those members that owned morning and evening newspapers were in many cases reduced, or left the same, and the comprehensive service was distributed at all hours, which did away with charges previously levied by the Post Office for reports taken after hours. Despite these reductions, in round figures the comprehensive service produced revenues for the PA of £180,000 from the 110 newspapers served (thirty-five morning, seventy-five evening), whereas the previous system had generated only £169,000.[62] When it proposed these revolutionary changes to its rate structure, PA management claimed that the association did not sell news; it sold the right to reproduce news. It therefore seemed equitable that those publishers who reproduced the news in a large number of copies should be charged more than those that reproduced it in a smaller number. When the long-standing influence of the Telegraph Act of 1868 came to an end, the pricing system of the PA resembled that which the AP had adopted in the 1890s.

[60] PA board minutes, November 1, 1927, PA, Ms 35358/22, pp. 20–2; PA board minutes, July 30, 1940, PA, Ms 35358/25, p. 121, GL.
[61] In the United States, the Audit Bureau of Circulations (ABC), established in 1914, conducted this necessary service. It was not until 1931 that a like organization was established in Britain. The importance of these organizations in mediating newspaper competition for advertising has been largely overlooked.
[62] PA board minutes, July 30, 1940, PA, Ms 35358/25, p. 121, Report of the special sub-committee on PA charges in PA board minutes, October 8, 1940, PA, Ms 35358/25, pp. 140–7, The Press Association Tariff for 1941, November 13, 1940, PA, Ms 35358/25, GL.

THE PA-REUTERS MERGER: A FURTHER SUBSIDY FOR
THE PROVINCIAL PRESS

The war exacerbated the consequences of bad management at Reuters. Despite the paid-for propaganda services the agency provided the British government, Reuters's business fared poorly during the war. The company had previously gathered commercial information and had conducted a private telegram business in conjunction with its news business, but in response to poor performance during the late 1880s and early 1890s, Reuters pursued a strategy of diversification in earnest. The agency developed a range of financial services. A private telegram business, which relied on the coding and packing of private telegrams with press dispatches, expanded to the remittance of small sums throughout the Empire. The growth of this business, and the need for increased capital, led to the creation of a banking business in 1910. The agency also leveraged its brand to develop a moderately successful business placing advertisements in newspapers throughout the Empire. After the outbreak of war, concerns about the potential security threat from telegraphy caused the British censor to prohibit the use of the telegraphic codes on which Reuters's private telegram and remittance services relied. As a consequence, this branch of the company's business incurred considerable losses.[63] Incompetent management, financial dislocation, and the government's determination to freeze foreign assets had deleterious effects on the company's banking business. Reuters's already depressed financial position took a turn for the worse on May 18, 1915 when Herbert de Reuter, then general manager, took his own life. The press blamed his suicide on the untimely death of his wife, but PA and Reuters's executives attributed it to the pressures of business.[64]

Shortly after Herbert de Reuters's suicide, Roderick Jones, formerly the company's representative in South Africa, became general manager. Before the war, Jones had come to the attention of the London management following his resourceful brokering of an agreement in the face of a collapse in relations between the South African press and Reuters. Jones was a calculating and ambitious man. "I was grieved for the Baron; I was disturbed for myself; again grieved for the Baron; again fevered for my career," wrote Jones after hearing of Herbert de Reuters's death. "All was in jeopardy."[65] As early as 1911, Jones had plotted to gain control of the agency. "I shall not shrink from a coup d'etat," wrote Jones to a confidant, "I hope I do not lack courage and fortitude: the fighting spirit (tempered by modern discretion) is strong within me. Most providentially bequeathed, through my mother, by my Scottish ancestors,

---

[63] Defence of the Realm Act: Losses Committee, Reuter's claim, undated, Jones papers, series 1, box 18, RA.
[64] Manager's memoranda, April 27, 1915, PA, Ms 35362/8, p. 222, GL; Williams to Jones, July 3, 1930; and Edmund Parker to Jones, July 3, 1930, Jones papers, series 1, box 51, RA.
[65] Jones, undated, Jones papers, series 1, box 47, RA.

Kennedys, Earls of Cassilis, who were always at war."[66] These were grandiose claims for anyone, let alone for the son of a Manchester hatter. For these characteristics, and his bountiful ego, historians have maligned Jones, but such ad hominem assessments do disservice to his business acumen.[67]

After his appointment as general manager, Jones set about disposing of Reuters's poorly performing bank.[68] Absent direct compensation for losses on its private telegram business, which Reuters repeatedly sought under the Defence of the Realm Act, management actively and effectively demanded the support of the Foreign Office to overcome its distress. Members of the Foreign Office accepted some responsibility for the depressed condition of the company, and Jones plotted to take advantage of this position to amputate the defunct bank. The capital structure of the company complicated the operation. Reuters raised funds for the establishment of the bank by a sizeable increase in nominal capital – from £90,000 to £500,000 – effected through a share bonus package and the issuance of new shares above par, which enabled older shareholders to part with their watered down stock at an inflated price. The whole share capital of the company was invested in the bank. The working revenue account in effect derived almost entirely from the goodwill, which the company had built up in the course of its fifty years, and was not the result of the employment of capital. The business of the news agency had as a capital basis only a reserve fund of £35,350, which was capital for the freehold properties of the company rather than for its business operations. The capital of the bank showed a loss and was entirely inoperative, which made dividends impossible. Shares of Reuters's stock dropped from £11 at the beginning of 1916 to £4 10s by the end of the year. To sell off the bank would have been to trade nearly the entirety of the company's capital. If Reuters lowered its capital, it would appear – when economic conditions improved after the war – that the agency was making considerable profits on a small share capital. Reuters's managers were concerned that this might lead to a demand by the newspapers for lower subscriptions.

To Jones there appeared to be two ways around this inconvenience: an agreement between Reuters and a new company for the sale of all the assets, exclusive of the shares in the bank; or an agreement encompassing sale to a syndicate with a voluntary winding-up of the old company. A voluntary winding-up and sale of the company to new owners was the only method by which Jones could be assured of complete control of the business. A reconstruction,

[66] Jones to Dickinson, September 3, 1911, Jones papers, series 1, box 47, RA.
[67] D. Read, "Jones, Sir (George) Roderick," *ODNB Online* (2004). Read, *Power of News*; D. Read, "Sir Roderick Jones and Reuters: Rise and Fall of a News Emperor," in D. Fraser (ed.), *Cities, Class and Communication: Essays in Honour of Asa Briggs* (London: Harvester Wheatsheaf, 1990); J. Lawrenson and L. Barber, *The Price of Truth: The Story of Reuters Millions* (Edinburgh: Mainstream Publishing, 1985).
[68] The following explanation of the events of 1915–1919 relies on J. Silberstein-Loeb, "Foreign Office Control of Reuters during the First World War," *Media History*, 16 (2010), 281–93.

or reduction, of the company's existing capital, although plausible, would have necessitated a public hearing in court, which Jones found undesirable. A voluntary winding-up, he reasoned, as opposed to some form of capital restructuring, was the most likely method to pass muster with existing shareholders. It promised them an adequate and immediate return on their investments without much negotiation. Reuters was able to put the reconstruction forward to the public as its own act. That is, the company itself promoted the new company, to which the business was sold, and not the case of a new outside purchaser coming in and buying the concern, with no guarantee of continuity in administration. Owing to Excess Profit Duty the assets in the bank appreciated (by the accumulation of the yearly bank profit) by a greater amount than if the bank was sold, therefore retaining the bank for at least two and a half years made more sense than selling.

Funding a voluntary winding-up of the company and a buyout of the shareholders required capital. This was where the Foreign Office came in. Jones lacked the means to undertake the purchase and planned to bring in the government as a source of funds. Jones allied with the Hon. Mark Francis Napier, chairman of the news agency, who was related by marriage to Prime Minister Asquith. Jones relied on Napier's contacts to convince the Foreign Office to act as surety against a £550,000 loan with which he and Napier could buy out Reuters's existing shareholders. Officials at the Foreign Office drew an analogy between their agreement with Reuters and another agreement they had recently concluded with the Anglo-Persian Oil Company. For strategic ends, the oil company had repeatedly attempted to involve government in its affairs and even offered to place itself under government "control."[69] Corporate strategy similarly motivated the agreement between Reuters and the Foreign Office, which fell in line with Jones's proposal in return for a golden share that enabled it to appoint a director and influence the agency's operations for the remainder of the war.[70]

After the shares were purchased, Jones, Napier, and a roster of characters from the ranks of "Greater Britain" – Leander Starr Jameson, Lord Glennconner, and Viscount Peel – formed a private company, Reuters Ltd., with an authorized capital of £200,000. Only 999 shares were issued. The nominees of the Foreign Office controlled the majority and they were to be retained until the loan was repaid. Jones arranged for sale of the bank in 1917 at £480,000, and by 1919, the bank loan of £550,000 was repaid and Jones and Napier held all the shares. This suggests that Jones and Napier paid only £70,000 for the news agency, or £20,000 less than the nominal capital held by the company before the formation of the bank, out of money loaned to them on assets they never

---

[69] G.G. Jones, "The British Government and the Oil Companies 1912–1924: The Search for an Oil Policy," *The Historical Journal*, 20 (1977), 647–72.

[70] For an assessment of these events that places the Foreign Office in a position of control see P. Putnis, "Reuters and the British Government – Re-visited," *Media History*, 16 (2010), 295–9.

owned and which were not so highly valued to begin with – a rather deft piece of business.

Jones' strategy all along had been to sell the company to the London and provincial press after he had gained control. He first made a concrete proposal to the press in 1919, but he had discussed his plans with the barons of Fleet Street as early as 1916. To encourage the possibility of press ownership, Jones planted hints among PA executives of a possible hostile takeover of Reuters, but members of the association were predisposed to the idea, having already debated the benefits of an ownership position and even considered an outright takeover. Indeed, the possibility of a newspaper-backed purchase of Reuters was seemingly commonplace in 1916, and it was mentioned in *The Newspaper World*, an industry trade journal.[71] Although the PA made overtures to Reuters about the possibility of a share purchase, the London press blocked this eventuality with threats to take up twice the amount of stock in any PA purchase. The PA feared that, if the London press owned a stake in Reuters, it would be impossible to continue to exact heavy payments from the metropolitan press to subsidize newsgathering for provincial papers and that joint-ownership would permit the London newspapers to manipulate smaller papers in the provinces or to demand an equal payment from the provincial press for Reuters's news (see Table 5.6). Early in 1922, Jones tried again by seeking the approval of Northcliffe, but the great press baron died several months later. Only in 1925 did the PA independently purchase a majority holding, and in 1930, it bought up most of the remaining shares. The London papers took up shares individually.[72] In 1941, the London press en masse purchased an ownership stake in Reuters equal to that of the PA.

The operations of the two organizations remained more or less distinct to avoid accusations of bias from overseas clients, but the merger of Reuters and the PA enabled the association to exercise greater control over the agency's income, which it used to make up for the diminution in its alternative sources of revenue and to subsidize the cost of providing news to its members.[73] The

---

[71] Negotiations with newspapers. Sequence of main events, September 17, 1925, LN 960 1/013632, RA. Manager's memoranda, November 1, 1916, PA, Ms 35362/10, pp. 841–2, Manager's memoranda, August 4, 1915, PA, Ms 35362/9, p. 125, Manager's memoranda, October 6, 1915 and November 7, 1916, PA, Ms 35362/9, pp. 180, 845–6, GL. *The Newspaper World*, November 11, 1916. Managers at Reuters were eager for the deal to be completed. Giles to Jones, November 29, 1925, Jones papers, series 1, box 32, RA.

[72] Manager's memoranda, December 5, 1916 and May 8, 1917, PA, Ms 35362/10, pp. 887–8 and p. 1161, GL. Jones to F.W. Dickinson, March 29, 1922, Jones papers, series 1, box 48; Jones memo, July 7, 1924, Jones papers, series 1, box 74, RA. PA board minutes, November 3, 1925, PA, Ms 35358/21, p. 252, GL; Balfour to Jones, July 15, 1926, Jones papers, series 1, box 68, RA.

[73] Jones to Henderson, May 3, 1939, Jones papers, box 1, series 74, RA. There were also difficulties associated with combining the two organizations because of their different news needs. V. Harvey memo, December 8, 1939; Rickatson-Hatt to Jones, January 10, 1940, Jones papers, series 1, box 82, RA.

TABLE 5.6. *Comparison of provincial and metropolitan subscriptions to Reuters, 1925–1948 (£)*

	PA	Metropolitan papers
1925 (pre-PA ownership)	16,000	37,000
1930 (first contract under PA ownership)	36,000	39,000
1941 (last year of PA ownership)	59,000	30,000
1942 (first year of joint ownership)	59,000	56,000
1948 (first postwar contract)	130,000	130,000

Source: Fleetwood-May, memo, November 8, 1963, CR, General PA, box 4, RA.

PA relied on Reuters as it had long relied on the revenue from the London press and its pooling arrangement with Extel. According to Jones, the provincial press received its news from Reuters at 25 to 50 percent below cost. In 1926, Reuters's revenue in Britain fell short of the bare cost alone of telegrams, correspondents, and editors, by £14,800, and in 1927 by £22,350. In turn, Reuters sought to offset the losses on its news business with sources of revenue from lucrative lines of work. Advancements in the agency's alternative departments, particularly its commercial news service, kept Reuters's in the black. By April 1931, the news service cost four times as much as the newspapers were asked to pay. Losses on the home service between 1936 and 1938 averaged £29,749. Although Jones repeatedly requested more money, the PA suffered during the economic depression of the 1930s and net trading at Reuters remained more profitable than at the association. In fact, dividend payments from Reuters to the PA helped to support the association. Between 1931 and 1938, dividends averaged £17,822 per year, yielding 5.7 percent net on the PA's shares. Between 1930 and 1939, Reuters also paid the PA £22,000 per annum for the rights to distribute the association's domestic news report abroad, whereas the PA paid Reuters £36,000 for its news of the world. Between 1926, the first year of PA ownership, and 1936, Reuters's profits from the home news services dropped from approximately £24,500 to £2,600, a real decrease of approximately £18,400.[74]

---

[74] Chairman's speech, June 5, 1928, LN 296; Young to Jones, July 17, 1936, Jones papers, series 1, box 81. See, for example, Chairman's (Jones) speech, June 4, 1935 and June 9, 1936, Jones papers, series 1, box 70. Rickatson-Hatt to Jones, July 23, 1936, Jones papers, series 1, box 81. Young to Jones, June 16, 1935, Jones papers, series 1, box 81. Memo, unsigned, December 31, 1939, Jones papers, series 1, box 81. During the period of 1926 to 1940 inclusive, a total net – i.e., net of tax – sum was paid in dividends of £297,436 paid in dividends by Reuters to the PA. LW to JEB, July 12, 1950, LN1008. Reuters's use of P.A. copy, May 25, 1939, Reuters's outward services, December 19, 1939, PA use of Reuters reports and vice versa, February 13, 1940, Jones papers, series 1, box 69. Jones notes, April 20, 1931, Jones papers, series 1, box 34. L.W. to Jones, October 6, 1939, Jones papers, series 1, box 82, RA.

Covering the great events of the day and demands from the PA to improve the news service account in part for Reuters's growing expenses, but the principal cause was increased competition, the result of which was a significant improvement in the agency's news service. As part of its competitive strategy against the Associated Press (AP), the United Press (UP) created a subsidiary in Canada, called the British United Press (BUP), to exploit the European market. In 1923, the BUP established an office in London and began to distribute foreign news. The BUP was unencumbered by restrictive agreements that prevented it from selling its news directly to the provincial press, and it posed a particular threat to the long-standing arrangement between the PA and Reuters. In addition, telegrams from Europe intended for the UP in New York, and for sale in the American market, passed through London, which enabled the BUP to sell them to the British press at reduced rates, which Reuters called "dumping."[75] Reuters's revenue from the foreign special service declined as papers began to take cheaper, livelier reports from the BUP. The services of the BUP suited the editorial policy of the evening newspapers in the provinces and in London, such as the *Evening Standard*, and provided clients with content that distinguished their papers from those publications that relied exclusively on Reuters and the PA. To meet competition from the BUP, Reuters was consequently obliged to improve and increase the volume of its general service, for which it received no additional return. At the same time, the BUP spoiled the market for Reuters's special service, from which Reuters had always expected to derive some compensation for increased general service expenditure.[76]

In 1919, the editor of the *Evening Standard* critiqued Reuters's news service as dry, semi-official, and the product of "centenarians," yet Reuters's advantage over the BUP lay in the credibility it had cultivated through trustworthy, albeit somewhat dull, reports.[77] The reports of the BUP, although punchy, were often unverified and it became something of a joke that the agency's reports had several times announced the death of Mussolini. "The British United Press seems rather to specialise in the imaginary assassination of prominent personages," quipped one director at the PA after a premature proclamation of the Duce's death, "for it is not so very long ago since it 'killed' King Boris of Bulgaria."[78]

[75] Chairman's speech, May 31, 1927, Jones papers, series 1, box 71, RA.
[76] Compare J. Buchan (deputy chairman of Reuters), "Reuters' Monopoly in Foreign News," *The Nation and The Athenæum*, December 22, 1923 and H. Bailey, "Reuters' Monopoly in Foreign News," *The Nation and The Athenæum*, December 29, 1923. See also London letter, January 15, 1924, Williams to Jones, February 1, 1924, Jones papers, series 1, box 30, RA. WWH to R. Howard, February 24, 1923, Howard papers, UIB. Unsigned, June 30, 1934, Jones papers, series 1, box 42. Jones memo, April 29, 1927, Jones papers, series 1, box 36, RA.
[77] S. Levy Lawson, Reuters's correspondent in the United States since the 1890s, was not replaced until 1918, at which point he was sixty-six years old. H. Jeans to Jones, September 19, 1922, Jones papers, series 1, box 31, RA; Murray to Jones, September 4, 1919, Jones papers, series 1, box 33, RA; PA board minutes, April 8, 1918, PA, Ms 35358/20, p. 11, GL.
[78] Manager's memoranda, February 3, 1925, PA, Ms 35362/17, p. 4604, GL; Chief editor memo, October 27, 1927, Jones papers, series 1, box 36, RA.

The newsgathering arrangements of the UP and the BUP in Europe were allegedly slipshod. It was commonly thought that the agency's correspondents clipped news from foreign newspapers, mailed them to London, and pawned them off as telegraphic cables.[79] The principal cause of concern for Reuters was not the direct threat that the BUP posed to its business, but that its advance might encourage the AP to establish a similar subsidiary, which would have certainly damaged Reuters's position.

The indirect threat the BUP posed to Reuters caused the agency to modify its style of reporting. Directors at the PA thought that Reuters should emulate the "bright human touch" that the BUP gave to its reports. "Probably Reuters were always too 'serious' in their presentation of copy," said the PA. "It was quite possible to send out brighter stuff and at the same time be accurate. The PA needed something beyond the 'little Foreign Office' style of Reuters."[80] C.L. Cranfield, news editor at the PA, claimed that Reuters's correspondents gave too little attention "to the colour and human interest that need drawing out in their stories." "If they only had Reuters' accuracy," by which he indirectly meant its resources and reach, the BUP "would excel in providing stories of special value for evening papers," warned Cranfield.[81] Jones agreed with Cranfield's assessments and confided to his editors that "we must, as nearly as possible, WIPE THE B.U.P. OFF THE MAP, by furnishing a bright and comprehensive service in a form so attractive that newspaper sub-editors will have neither the occasion nor the desire to turn to the B.U.P."[82] With this purpose in mind, Cranfield attended meetings of the consultative committee at Reuters and was in close cooperation with its chief editor. In addition, Bernard Rickatson-Hatt, who had spent five years in the United States and observed the operations of the AP as Reuters's representative in New York, was assigned to reorganize the agency's editorial department in London and of the news service generally to meet American standards.[83]

After Rickatson-Hatt returned to England from New York and surveyed the editorial department at Fleet Street, he complained of a complete lack of "all kind of incentive and driving impulse." Antiquated equipment and archaic methods of news presentation acted as a damper on the staff. Editors had

[79] Manager's memoranda, November 3, 1925, PA, Ms 35362/17, p. 4769, GL; "The British United Press," October 27, 1927, Jones papers, series 1, box 36, RA.

[80] Manager's memoranda, December 7, 1926, PA, Ms 35362/18, GL.

[81] Manager's memoranda, December 7, 1926, PA, Ms 35362/18, GL.

[82] Jones to Rickatson-Hatt, December 3, 1931, Jones papers, series 1, box 37, RA.

[83] Rickatson-Hatt was gazetted in 1915 from New College, Oxford where he read classics. Shortly afterward he transferred to the Coldstream Guards. He remained with the Guards for seven years, first in France, and during his last three years, 1919–1922, on the Intelligence Staff in Constantinople. In 1923, he joined Reuters and in the following year was sent to Egypt to cover the crisis arising out of the assassination of the Sirdar. In 1926, he accompanied Jones as private secretary around the world and afterward was attached to the New York office. In 1929, he was placed in charge of Reuters's services from North America as chief correspondent. "Reuters News Reorganization," *The Northern Whig* (Belfast), February 19, 1931.

come to regard themselves not as journalists, but as "conscientious cable transcribers." The time-honored traditions of accuracy, reliability, and good taste, so important to Reuters's reputation, had snuffed out color, speed, and enterprise from the staff and news report. During his time in the United States, Rickatson-Hatt learned the importance of "news value," as he called it, and how to determine it by American standards. His colleagues at Reuters, complained Rickatson-Hatt, remained attached to the passé practice of sending over the wire all news received at headquarters. In a report that suggested methods for reorganization, Rickatson-Hatt quoted Kent Cooper, the AP general manager, who had reportedly said: "If the public want to read about the maiden lady of Kalamazoo and not what the Polish Minister of Finance thinks about the zloty, you must give it to them or go under."[84]

News values had to change, as did the organization of the agency's newsroom and the method by which it dispatched its reports. Seniority played a larger role in rank than merit and older employees retained important positions while young and talented staff festered in unchallenging roles. Significant improvements were achieved when editors-in-charge were given authority to scrap, summarize, and rewrite incoming messages. Prior to these changes, the rule had been to send nearly everything out irrespective of its news value. This practice resulted in a daily report that was too long, with good stories buried in a mass of second-class material. The Reuters's editorial staff had not learned the importance of the inverted pyramid in news reporting – the practice of writing an article proceeding from the most to the least important bit of information, which had taken hold in the United States during the nineteenth century – and instead perpetuated that "horrible and detestable habit of putting the main point of a story at the end." Arranging stories this way around meant that before it could go to press, newspaper sub-editors had to spend substantial time rewriting copy the agency transmitted, which endlessly irritated news editors of the London papers. Another outdated practice of the editorial department was to issue stories piecemeal with "adds," "second-adds," "third-adds," and a succession of "laters." To better serve newspapers required replacing this practice with "leads" and "rewrites," which greatly reduced the need for newspaper editorial departments to aggregate the scraps sent by Reuters into a complete article. Additionally, editors at Reuters paid little attention to edition times. It was common practice to send out a message whenever it came in. This meant that feature stories that arrived at Reuters around midnight or after were completely lost to the newspapers, which had already gone to print. If these messages had been held over and issued over the wire at 6 a.m. for the evening papers then they would have had a chance of publication.[85]

---

[84] The following relies on Rickatson-Hatt to Jones, April 11, 1931, Jones papers, series 1, box 35, RA.

[85] Bettany to Jones, August 17, 1922, Jones to Jeans, September 20, 1922, Jones papers, series 1, box 31; Jeans memo, October 12, 1922, Jones papers, series 1, box 28; Bettany to Jones,

Reuters had also failed to make the changes in office storage and systematization necessary to facilitate the rapid location, combination, and arrangement of information.[86] Editors at newspapers and news agencies relied heavily on clippings as a source of reference to add to and complete stories they received by wire. Under Reuters's system, cuttings were pasted haphazardly in chronological order in large scrapbooks. In some cases, three or four countries were lumped together in one book. There was no index to these books, and considerable time was wasted finding a reference to a particular story. Where an enormous cuttings book was required for a single month for countries such as France and the United States, from which Reuters received a large service of news, the task of searching through a series of these books was slow. The reference system was so notorious that Kent Cooper of the AP made sarcastic remarks about it. By contrast, nearly every reputable newspaper and progressive news agency, including the PA, had cuttings pasted on sheets in filing cabinets under the heading of countries and subjects and persons, with a complete index of the whole to make them available for ready reference. Well-managed reference departments also kept an effective "morgue," a cabinet of biographies in alphabetical order with a separate file for each person that contained all the relevant cuttings so that whenever an obituary was required, or any message necessitated a write-up of any particular individual, the information could be found in a matter of seconds. The AP feature department prepared and printed some 2,000 biographies of notable people of all countries. They issued these sketches to their members at a nominal fee. During his time in New York, Rickatson-Hatt obtained a complete set of these biographies which formed the nucleus for the "morgue" at Reuters's headquarters and at its offices abroad. Reuters also needed a suitable cable index and library. Rickatson-Hatt's counterpart at the PA, C.L. Cranfield, who had done so much to improve the association's news service, also supervised the creation of the association's library. The state of the Reuters editorial library was so poor, said Rickatson-Hatt, it would have been a "disgrace to the Y.M.C.A. in Tooting." Not only did Reuters lack the essential reference books, it did not have a decent encyclopedia. When editors required references they had to go to the AP offices, then located in the same building, and consult the AP's edition of the *Encyclopedia Britannica*.

Besides Reuters's obsolete indexing system and antediluvian library, the system by which it received foreign cables via tube from the Post Office was also antiquated. Under the tube system, nearly every message received had to pass through the bottleneck of the Post Office, a byproduct of government control of telegraphy that caused considerable delay. The perpetuation of this old system is all the more remarkable given that American companies operating in

November 21, 1930; Jones to Rickatson-Hatt, April 14, 1931, Jones papers, series 1, box 37, W. Turner memo, October 6, 1932, Memo to Jones, November 7, 1932, Jones papers, series 1, box 35, RA.
[86] Yates, *Control through Communication*.

England had printers arranged on connections between their London offices and those of the cable companies, rather than going via the Post Office. American telegraph companies collected and delivered telegrams directly to their clients within Britain and were not required to go through the Post Office.[87] Reuters's system amused the AP. By 1911, the New York office of the AP had dispensed with such arrangements. Instead, a story that reached a cable company in New York instantaneously triggered the AP column printer, which conveyed sixty words per minute. The AP machines printed on rolls with marks on the back to make carbon copies, so that three copies of a message were printed at once. Such machines would have saved Reuters considerable time in the copying of dispatches for the agency's various departments.

The improvements Rickatson-Hatt suggested and implemented improved Reuters's news services. Editors weeded out the dull stories from the Reuters's reports, which made it cheaper to provide and more useful to newspapers. An analysis of the use of Reuters news by all the daily London papers, morning and evening, and four representative provincial newspapers during a randomly chosen day in 1932 showed that the morning papers on that day published 156 Reuters messages, which occupied 673.5 column inches, as compared with 42 from all the other news services combined, which occupied only 76 inches. Among the morning papers, Reuters's best display was in the *Morning Post* – 150.5 inches (see Table 5.7). *The Times* published 49.5 inches, as compared with 1.5 inches of material from competing agencies. The *News Chronicle* contained seventy inches from Reuters, and seven from the others, and the *Daily Mail* had twenty-nine inches, as compared with two inches from the others.[88]

Reuters gradually ousted opposition news agencies from the *Financial News* and *Financial Times*, where the commercial services of Extel had enjoyed significant play for many years. The *Financial News* on August 8, 1932 published 37 inches of Reuters's news as compared with 22 inches from other agencies, and the *Financial Times* carried 54 inches, compared with 9.5 inches from competitors. Table 5.8 shows a breakdown of Reuters's quotations between July 19 and September 1, 1932. In the London morning papers during the same period the approximate total space Reuters's messages occupied was 16,241 inches, compared with 4,110 inches by the combined opposition, giving a ratio of 3.9 in favor of Reuters.[89]

During December 1923 and December 1933, the proportion of space occupied by Reuters's news in relation to the proportion occupied by foreign news from all sources grew from 51.8 percent to 69 percent. In 1923, the space occupied by other Reuters's news in the morning papers, including the *Daily*

[87] J. Hills, *Telecommunications and Empire* (Urbana: University of Illinois Press, 2007), p. 222.

[88] Rickatson-Hatt to Jones, March 20 1932, Jones papers, series 1, box 41; J. Owen to Jones, August 5, 1932, Jones papers, series 1, box 69, RA. Direct contact between Reuters and the London press increased more than contact between Reuters and the provincial papers: Jones to Mann, February 19, 1937, Jones papers, series 1, box 43, RA.

[89] JA to Jones, September 1, 1932, Jones papers, series 1, box 36, RA.

TABLE 5.7. *Use of Reuters's news, August 8, 1932*

	No. of messages sent out	No. of messages published
General service	56	42
Special service	7	7
Mail stories	22	15
Sports service	16	9

Source: JA to Jones, September 1, 1932, J.1.36, RA.

TABLE 5.8. *Reuters's quotations in the London papers, July 19–September 1, 1934*

	Morning papers	Evening papers
Reuters items	4,157	1,757
All other agencies	1,666	1,218
Ratio of Reuters to opposition	2.5	1.4

Source: JA to Jones, September 1, 1932, J.1.36, RA.

Mirror and *Sketch*, was 35.4 percent of the total space occupied by foreign news and 27 percent excluding the *Mirror* and *Sketch*. The *Mirror* and *Sketch* were both pictorial papers, the latter was published weekly.[90] These papers were not known for their enterprising journalism and tended to rely more heavily on Reuters than other London papers for their foreign news. In 1933, Reuters's news occupied 42.5 percent of the total foreign news space in the morning papers including the *Mirror* and the *Sketch* and 28.4 percent when these two papers were excluded.

The percentage of space taken up by Reuters's news in the evening papers as compared with the space taken up by Reuters's news in the morning papers was in the ratio 69:42.5 in 1933 if the *Mirror* and *Sketch* are included in the paper count, or 69:28.4 if not. In 1923, the ratio was 51.8:35.4, with the *Mirror* and *Sketch* included, or 51.8:27, with them excluded. The average increase of news used by the six morning papers excluding the *Mirror* and *Sketch* was only 1.4 percent. The combined average increase of news used by the three evening papers was 17.2 percent.[91] The evening paper calculation was based on final editions. Had it been possible to take into account the lunch-time editions, many mail items sent by Reuters would have been included, and the count would probably have been still more in Reuters's favor. These calculations illustrate that the evening papers published considerably more wire news than the morning papers, which is to be expected given that the morning

[90] W.E.B. Camrose, *British Newspapers and their Controllers* (London: Cassell, 1947).
[91] Carter to Jones, January 26, 1934, Jones papers, series 1, box 78, RA.

papers tended to exhibit more individual enterprise, but such data, however intriguing, may obscure more than it reveals. Changes in editorial policy over time and the nature of the market, as well as the market sector each paper occupied, render uncertain any attempt to ascribe an increased publication of Reuters's news to any perceived improvement in its quality.

THE THREAT OF THE BBC, THE COMBINATION OF CONDUITS AND CONTENT, AND THE SHIFT OF THE PRESS SUBSIDY TO RADIO

The PA's purchase of Reuters, as well as its closer cooperation with Extel, prevented the emergence of a viable direct competitor, but it was the threat of the monopoly that Parliament promised the BBC that precipitated the PA-Reuters merger after years of discussion. In 1924, the consolidation of British radio interests under the British Broadcasting Company, the predecessor to the BBC, provided the necessary incentive to prompt negotiations between Reuters and the press. Both Reuters and the newspaper publishers believed that their bargaining power against the radio manufacturing companies would increase if they were strongly united. In seeking to restrain the threat posed by broadcasting, the several news organizations relied on the policy paradigm of the Telegraph Act of 1868, and, in particular, the clear separation between content carriers and content generators that it had established. It was widely believed that the combination of telegraphy and news provision in the hands of the telegraph companies had stymied the development of the press. The Post Office, however, was de facto a common carrier. By the 1860s, its obligation to carry all letters but interfere with none was a generally accepted rule held to apply equally to telegrams. "As a matter of course," wrote Frank Ives Scudamore to John Edward Taylor of the Manchester *Guardian* in 1868, the Post Office "would not undertake to collect news, any more than it would undertake to write letters."[92] The officers of the Post Office, said Scudamore before the parliamentary select committee on the Telegraph Bill, "could not be properly qualified for such a task, which is really that of editing a newspaper at a distance."[93]

Relying on the same argument, the press had sought to establish a similarly clear separation between conduits and content with respect to the telephone. In January 1910, the National Telephone Company supplied subscribers with poll results during the general election, which caused a deputation of the press, as well as representatives of Extel, the PA, Reuters, and others, to hold a meeting with Herbert Samuel, then postmaster-general, to protest against the telephone company being allowed to collect and distribute news. George Toulmin,

---

[92] Scudamore to Taylor, May 15, 1868, PA, Ms 35356/1, GL.
[93] As quoted in Manager's memoranda, 1868, PA, Ms 35362/1, p. 259, GL.

managing director of the *Lancashire Daily Post* and Liberal MP for Bury, told Samuel that the telegraph companies had "prevented Free Trade in news," and it was for this reason that the newspapers welcomed government control, it being clearly understood that the Post Office would be a transmitter of news only and not a collector or seller of news. The principle, said Toulmin, applied equally to telephony as it did to telegraphy. Samuel was receptive to the principle, but contended that in practice there were exceptions. The Post Office, he rightly explained, supplied a variety of different types of information for public consumption, such as storm warnings to fishermen, the course of ships, maritime casualties, electrophone hearings, speeches, sermons, time signals, and so forth, and therefore the rigid interpretation by the press of the distinction between carriers and content generators was incorrect. Conversely, newspapers and agencies, such as Extel, had the right, albeit in special circumstances, to work their own telegraphic and telephonic equipment.[94]

Simultaneously, the press and the news agencies attempted to apply the principle of a clear separation between carriers and creators of content to the development of wireless telegraphy. The Post Office asserted its control over wireless spectrum under the Wireless Telegraphy Act of 1904, which was a natural extension of earlier Telegraph Acts. The same year as the passage of the Act, the Post Office completed a licensing agreement with the Marconi Company for the erection and operation of wireless telegraph stations.[95] By 1910, the Marconi Company, the organization formed by the Italian inventor Guglielmo Marconi in 1897, had formed a press agency and was offering to newspapers throughout the British Isles news of interest occurring on board the principal liners at sea in all parts of the world. Several newspapers, such as the *Daily Post* and the *Mercury*, both of Liverpool, completed arrangements with Marconi for the provision of shipping news. Although little of interest happened regularly aboard these vessels, Marconi's action caused considerable consternation among the majority of the press, which refused the service.[96] Reuters and the PA contended that Marconi was abusing its monopoly privileges over the means of communication. It is unclear, wrote Herbert de Reuter to Edmund Robbins of the PA in 1910, "whether an organisation like Marconi enjoying a State monopoly and Government protection, is entitled to compete with private undertakings."[97]

During World War I, the telegraph cables worked poorly or else were heavily congested, which gave Marconi a distinct advantage over Reuters, especially

---

[94] G. Toulmin, transcription of deputation before the postmaster general, July 7, 1910, PA, Ms 35362/1, p. 258 and M. Nathan to PA, PA, Ms 35362/1, pp. 288–93, GL.

[95] The Telegraph Act of 1869 gave to the postmaster-general control over "any apparatus for transmitting messages or other communications by means of electric signals."

[96] "Heads of Agreement Between the Postmaster General and Marconi's," 1906 (123) XCVIII.713; Marconi Press Agency circular, August 26, August 30, and September 13, 1910, PA, Ms 35362/1, pp. 271–2, 301, GL.

[97] Reuter to Robbins, September 3, 1910, PA, Ms 35362/1, p. 273, GL.

for German communiqués. As they had done with respect to the telephone company, newspaper publishers compared Marconi's Wireless Press to the news service the telegraph companies had provided before nationalization in 1868. Allowing Marconi to collect and broadcast news, said Sir Meredith Whittaker, proprietor and editor of the Scarborough *Evening News*, was "a reversal of the policy which existed prior to the state acquiring the Telegraphs."[98] In 1916, at a meeting before Joseph Pease, then postmaster-general and subsequently chairman of the British Broadcasting Company, representatives of Extel, PA, and Reuters argued along similar lines. "A telegraph company which figures as the transmitter of private despatches and caters for the public custom," said Jones of Reuters, "occupies the position of a common carrier and it has long been recognised that it is contrary to public policy to permit any such company to trade as a purveyor of news."[99] Frank Bird, chairman of the Federation of Northern Newspaper Owners, also wrote to Pease that it was a "recognised fact that a telegraph company which transmits private messages should not be permitted to trade as a purveyor of news." In 1919, Marconi agreed to cease its wireless press service, and instead proposed to act as a "common carrier" for the agencies and newspapers, as well as to distribute Reuters's news abroad. Reuters noted with satisfaction Marconi's "unequivocal acceptance of the doctrine, long since recognised by the cable companies, that the function of news providing and of news carrying cannot be performed by one and the same organization," wrote S. Carey Clements, an executive at the agency, to Henry W. Allen, Marconi joint general manager. However much the agency was gratified by this concession, it appears Marconi made it largely to stave off any further action by the Post Office to control wireless.[100] Thereafter, the Post Office, Marconi, and a third organization called Radio Communication operated wireless telegraphy but did not produce content.[101]

The Post Office did not impose the obligation of common carriage on wireless telephony. Instead, it deliberately placed a monopoly over wireless telephony in the hands of the British Broadcasting Company, a consortium of radio manufacturing companies, established in 1922. The patents covering the technology and the cost of building the necessary infrastructure, largely account for this anomaly. The erection of broadcasting towers on behalf of the government was not a profitable business, and the British Broadcasting Company undertook to build the stations only in return for the right to a monopoly over the exploitation of the market for radio sets, which promised to be far more

---

[98] Meredith Whittaker, April 5, 1916, PA, Ms 35362/9, p. 476, GL.

[99] Bird to postmaster general, April 11, 1916, PA, Ms 35362/9, p. 505; Jones, Robbins and Gennings to the postmaster-general (Pease), March 10, 1916, PA, Ms 35362/9, pp. 473–4, GL.

[100] Manager's memoranda, September 18, 1919, PA, Ms 35362/13, p. 2857; S.C. Clements to H.W. Allen, September 26, 1919, PA, Ms 35362/13, p. 2861; PA board minutes, October 21, 1919, PA, Ms 35358/20, pp. 297–8, GL.

[101] Manager's memoranda, December 7, 1926, PA, Ms 35362/18, GL.

lucrative. "The Government has imposed conditions which prevent us from selling broadcasting stations," observed the committee of company representatives charged with devising the British Broadcasting Company, "and since there can be but a limited number of such stations erected any direct profit from them is relatively unimportant." Consequently, the companies had three main targets: to create a market for the receiving sets, which was to be achieved by providing a quality broadcasting service; that only the broadcasting sets manufactured by members of the company be approved for licensing by the Post Office; and that the Post Office agree to attach the broadcasting fee to the price of the license so that a certain percentage of the license fee users paid per annum to the Post Office would go to the company.[102]

The reason for the implementation of a radio license levied on individuals possessing a receiving set, and the requirement that only those sets stamped with the "BBC" trademark could be licensed, was to protect the Company's monopoly and especially to prevent the importation of Austrian and German sets, which were significantly cheaper than the sets manufactured in Britain. According to the companies, by reason of the depreciated currencies in Austria and Germany, and the fact that the cost of labor had not risen in the same proportion as the currency had depreciated, both the Austrians and the Germans were able to produce wireless receiving sets, 80 percent of the cost of which was labor, at such a low figure that it was "impossible for any British manufacturer to compete." If foreign receiving sets were imported into Britain, then, said Godfrey Isaacs, general manager of Marconi, manufacturers, would not be able to

afford to take part in the Broadcasting stations and the daily programmes. In such an event, it is doubtful whether the Broadcasting stations could be constructed and run and without them the industry cannot be created. Were the Broadcasting stations erected and foreigners allowed to sell their receiving apparatus in this country, they would be having the benefit of the demand created by the Broadcasting stations, for which the British manufacturer alone would be paying.

Isaac proposed that the postmaster-general decline to authorize any wireless receiving apparatus not of British manufacture, but obtaining a formal embargo was problematic.[103] It was unlikely that wireless receiving apparatus could be put on the list of "scientific instruments" chargeable with duty under the Safeguarding of Industries Act. Any permanent prohibition would have required the involvement of ministers or even the cabinet. The Post Office instead suggested a limited time of prohibition.[104] In a letter dated July 12, 1922, the Post Office agreed to restrict the types of apparatus for the reception of broadcasting services and to a temporary prohibition on foreign sets.[105] Only

---

[102] Committee minutes, May 25, June 1, 1922, CO 1/1, BBC Archives (hereafter BBC).
[103] Isaacs' statement, June 8, 1922, CO 47/1, BBC.
[104] F.J. Brown to F. Gill, June 6, 1922; Committee minutes, June 21, 1922, CO 1/1, BBC.
[105] Murray to Gill, July 12, 1922, CO 38/1, BBC.

six days later, the question of protection was aired in the House of Commons, which was unsatisfied with the postmaster-general's explanations.[106]

The news agencies and associations of the country were concerned about how the British Broadcasting Company would obtain its news. Newspaper publishers were anxious that the broadcasting company, which could broadcast news lifted from the newspaper columns of London papers after publication, would reach people in outlying districts before provincial newspapers had a chance to arrive. They were also worried that news provided to the Company for broadcasting would be rebroadcasted in shops, music halls, and other locations. According to Robbins of the PA, it was necessary that the agencies should "assert their property in news, so as to prevent the idea growing up that broadcast news could be appropriated by anyone."

A formal property right did not exist in Britain, therefore the press and the agencies sought to restrict the broadcasting company to taking news only from the news agencies and ensuring that the news with which it was provided could not be rebroadcast.[107] The Post Office sent out announcements on the part of the agencies to the effect that rebroadcasting certain news, such as election results, would be a violation of copyright, and it subsequently modified broadcasting licenses to prevent rebroadcasting of any matter other than that sent out for general reception. In 1927, some dispute arose as to whether rebroadcasting constituted a "separate and distinct performance" and was therefore an infringement of copyright. This debate was analogous to that which occurred in the 1900s over whether a northern edition of a London paper, such as the *Daily Mail*, constituted a distinct publication.[108] Agreements with the Post Office and with the British Broadcasting Company, rather than litigation, effectively established informal property rights.

The resulting agreement between the British Broadcasting Company and the news agencies entitled the broadcasting company to receive a world news service of between 1,200 and 2,400 words per day at the inexpensive rate of £4,000 per annum. The subscription payment was placed on a sliding scale depending on the number of licenses sold. After deducting costs, Central News, Extel, PA, and Reuters divided equally the balance of the subscription that remained. Reuters and the PA, although they provided the majority of the content that formed the news reports, agreed to divide the subscription equally with Central News and Extel to secure a unified front against the British Broadcasting Company.[109] The

[106] *Hansard*, HC vol. 156, July 18, 1922, cc 1889–1890.
[107] Rebroadcasting refers in this instance to those broadcasts in which the principal foreign recipient would transmit the same report to secondary subscribers by its own devices. Additional note on copyright as regards news, December 13, 1938, R28/165/1, BBC; R.J. Brown memo, May 25, 1939, R28/162/1, BBC.
[108] Manager's memoranda, November 4, 1924, PA, Ms 35362/16, p. 4536, GL. Manager's memoranda, August 30, October 4, and Reith to Clements, December 1, 1927 as quoted in December 6, 1927, PA, Ms 35362/19, GL.
[109] BBC Subscriptions, November 1963, CR, box 4, RA.

TABLE 5.9. *Agreements between BBC and news agencies*

	Service	Among	Subscription (£)	To Reuters (£)
1922	World news	Agencies, BBC	4,000	1,000
1924	Service to British regional stations	Agencies, BBC	5,000	1,250
1927	World news, 5,000 words/day	Agencies, BBC	14,000	3,500
1929	Complete PA and Reuters services	Agencies, BBC	16,000	4,100
1934	Empire news	Reuters, BBC	6,000	6,000
1939	World news, BBC home service	Agencies, BBC	25,000	9,735
1939	World news, BBC overseas service	Reuters, BBC	15,000	14,000

Source: Summary of BBC agreements, RA, CR Box 4.

broadcasting company received news that broke between 6 a.m. and 11 p.m. and, to protect evening newspapers, it could only broadcast after 7 p.m. The result was that the news of the day's events was stale when aired. For additional services, such as local sports bulletins on Saturday evenings and reports for regional stations, the broadcasting company had to pay extra. According to a supplemental letter to the agreement, the British Broadcasting Company agreed to "rely exclusively on the news supplied to them by the four Agencies" and would "not themselves obtain news from other sources or establish, or assist in establishing, any organisation for collecting news."[110] This arrangement remained in effect until 1927 (see Table 5.9).[111]

Unfortunately for the radio manufacturing companies, and for the press, cheap radio sets from Austria and Germany were still imported and the monopoly granted to the British Broadcasting Company over the sale of radio sets proved unenforceable. The model on which the provision of programing was predicated consequently broke down. The failure of this arrangement resulted in the formation in 1926 of the BBC. The BBC, unlike the British Broadcasting Company, could apply the license fee to any set, therefore it was unconcerned about the sale of British-manufactured radio sets. The difficulty of imposing an embargo on alternative sets was removed, but the BBC still held a monopoly

[110] Unsigned to W. Noble, November 9, 1922 in Manager's memoranda, PA, Ms 35362/15, p. 3945, GL.

[111] For further use of the carrier/content-generator argument see the protests of the press before the Sykes committee, e.g., Minutes of 10th meeting, evidence of R. Jones, June 5, 1923, l. 1943–2125, POST 89/20, RM. In most European countries, news agencies held a monopoly over the delivery of news to their respective domestic broadcasting companies, and often the responsibility of editing the news also rested with the news agencies.

over the fees obtained from licensing the sets sold to the public. Unconcerned about profits, and assured a continuous and increasing source of revenue by its monopoly over the license fee, the BBC had every reason to increase the size and remit of its programing organization, especially to prevent the emergence of competitors. John Reith, formerly general manager of the British Broadcasting Company, and highly regarded by his corporate employers for his efforts in fighting the termination of their monopoly, had already spent considerable energy arguing that "universal control" of radio better positioned the British Broadcasting Company to serve the public.[112] Reith applied a similar logic to the monopoly of the BBC. Reith's ethos of "inform, educate and entertain" was part of an attempt to stave off further regulation. It helped to overturn the long-standing belief that a clear separation between carriers and content generators was in the best interests of the public and to replace it with a conviction that a combination of the two was the best way in which to ensure provision of public service content.[113] By contrast, the Radio Act of 1927 institutionalized a separation between the two in the United States.[114]

Although during the course of the interwar period the press gradually came to see radio as less of a threat to their circulation, the news agencies, and especially Reuters, continued to fight the growth of the BBC at every turn. Reuters was particularly concerned that the BBC's broadcasting of news in the Empire would adversely affect its business.[115] Being restricted to news from the agencies meant that the BBC was constrained in its use of live reporting, that it suffered a delay in transmission, and that it could not effectively alter the order or emphasis placed by the agencies on the news. In addition to restricting the size of the news report and the hours at which the BBC could broadcast news, in 1932 the agencies also successfully, albeit temporarily, prevented the BBC from taking the news reports of the BUP on grounds that it was an American-backed organization.[116] This position was hardly tenable given that

[112] Reith to William Joynson-Hicks, April 16, 1923, CO 47/2, Gaylor to postmaster-general, April 16, 1923, CO 58/1, Reith to postmaster-general, April 16, 1923, CO 58/1, Reith to postmaster-general (reply to report of the Sykes Committee), August 24, 1923, CO 1/7/1, BBC. A few years before, Theodore Vail of AT&T also attempted to stave off regulation by claiming that a "universal service" was critical to ensure the best telecommunications service. R.R. John, *Network Nation*, p. 345.

[113] Reith memo, March 25, 1929, R28/177/2, BBC. Others have made this point (see D.L. LeMahieu, "John Reith (1889–1971)" in S. Pedersen and P. Mandler (eds.), *After the Victorians* (London: Routledge, 1994), pp. 189–208), but most cultural historians have neglected it. It would be an exaggeration to characterize all Reith's efforts as an exercise in public relations intended to stave off regulation, but his motives deserve to be questioned. See E. Colpus, "*The Week's Good Cause*: Mass Culture and Cultures of Philanthropy at the Inter-war BBC," *Twentieth Century British History*, 22 (2011), 305–29.

[114] I am grateful to Richard John for bringing this point to my attention.

[115] See Chapter 6.

[116] PA board minutes, March 8, 1932, PA, Ms 35358/22, p. 296–7, GL; Report of the meeting of the special broadcasting committee, April 21, 1933, R28/154/3, Meeting at Reuters, December 10, 1937, R28/164/1, BBC.

Reuters took news from the AP and that American financiers backed Central News.[117] Indeed, Extel, the PA, and Reuters had previously rejected invitations to buy Central News, the continued existence of which saved the PA and Extel from accusations of monopoly.[118] But, after hearing that the BUP had made proposals to purchase Central News, which would have provided it with a ready-made London and provincial teleprinter system, a working home news organization, and two seats in House of Commons press gallery, the PA and Extel rapidly concluded agreements to take it over, which only made it more difficult for the BBC to negotiate individually with the agencies arrayed against it.[119]

In the face of these impediments, the government actively increased the remit of the BBC. In 1935, the Ullswater Committee, the third broadcasting committee of the interwar period, helped to free the BBC from its dependence on the news agencies by arguing that the best way in which to keep the BBC free from bias was to allow it access to multiple sources of news.[120] "In my view," said Clement Attlee, "it would be desirable that in course of time the B.B.C. should build up its own news service or take over the existing agencies." This course of action, Atlee believed, would better "enable the B.B.C. to give the public fair and impartial information."[121] This line of reasoning was analogous to that which Learned Hand used in *AP v. US*; namely, that it would inhibit the effective function of the marketplace for ideas, and therefore disadvantage the public, if any newspaper was denied the benefit of the AP news service.[122] Government approbation encouraged the BBC, which became increasingly frustrated with the uncompromising attitude of the news agencies, and especially with Jones of Reuters, who proved recalcitrant. By 1939, the BBC had become an integral part of the government's propaganda machine abroad, but Reuters, under Jones' leadership, refused to undertake unremunerated news services on behalf of the government or BBC.[123] Although the BBC pointed out to Reuters the "frightful" disadvantage at which it would be in competition with the Italian and German broadcast services if the agency did not permit the BBC greater leeway, Jones observed

---

[117] Two-thirds of the shares were held in the names of the Empire Trust Company, a New York financial house, and Melvin Johnson Woodworth, president of the New York News Bureau, a Wall Street financial agency. "American control of news agencies," *World Press News*, May 22, 1930, Rosewater papers, Ms 503, box 19, folder 18, AJA.

[118] For this rationale, see for example, R. Jones to A. Burchill, July 17, 1929, Jones papers, series 1, box 36, RA; Jones memo, May 15, 1931, LN505/1/9071166, RA.

[119] Manager's memoranda, November 2 and 22, 1937, PA, Ms 35362/24, pp. 155–6, 170–8, GL; R.J. Brown memo, January 13, 1939, R28/165/2, BBC.

[120] Report of broadcasting (Ullswater) committee, 1935, R28/154/3, p. 82, BBC.

[121] Report of the broadcasting (Ullswater) committee, 1935. Cmd 2599 (London: HMSO), 27, 50.

[122] See Chapter 2.

[123] Jones memo, October 18, 1938, Jones papers, series 1, box 42, RA.

that both the German and Italian news agencies were government-owned, whereas Reuters was a private, profit-making concern.[124]

A growing concern in official quarters over the influence of enemy broadcasters caused the Foreign Office to give news to the BBC in advance of Reuters. For example, in September 1939, the Foreign Office gave the BBC its reaction to Hitler's speech at Danzig before it gave it to Reuters.[125] Jones was further incensed that the BBC was advised a half-hour before Reuters of allied mine laying in Norwegian territorial waters. "By that time," complained Jones to the Censorship Bureau, "the B.B.C. had broadcast it all over the world, thereby unfairly and unnecessarily prejudicing the interests of Reuters's news service."[126] Such an uncompromising attitude hardly recommended Jones to officials at the Ministry of Information, especially after May 1940. By then, according to Sir Kenneth Lee, director of the Ministry of Information's Radio Relations and Communications Division, "the gravest possible emergency" had arisen, which necessitated "the utmost flexibility in the methods of broadcasting news to the public in this country."[127] Reuters's reluctance to cooperate, claimed A.E. Barker, editor of the BBC overseas news service, was akin "to the private manufacturer who would not be induced to adapt his business to the national defence requirements if he were not assured of the custom of the state." The principal issue, said Barker, was "whether the quality of the Reuter news service and the world coverage it obtains should continue to be restricted by a narrow commercial view."[128]

In this milieu, BBC executives were encouraged to seek some form of control over Reuters to better monitor its news supply. In 1937, A.E. Barker drafted an influential memo, which was revised and circulated internally on several occasions until 1941, in which he urged

that this may possibly be an opportunity for us to take a financial, and therefore to some extent controlling, interest in Reuters, as possibly part of a general scheme for putting Reuters on its feet again. If, for instance, Reuters was jointly owned by ourselves, the Press, and the Government, we would very largely have secured our future in regard to the supply of news.[129]

When, in the summer of 1938, Sir Horace Wilson, Chief Industrial Advisor to the government and an intimate advisor of Neville Chamberlain, visited the offices of the BBC, officials at the corporation told him that any reorganization of Reuters would require the removal of Jones.[130] Coordination of news

[124] R.J. Brown memo, July 18, 1939, R28/162/1, BBC.
[125] Jones to W. Will, September 21, 1939, Jones papers, series 1, box 46, RA.
[126] Jones to C.J. Radcliffe, April 8, 1940, Jones papers, series 1, box 46, RA.
[127] Jones to W. Will, May 28, 1940, Jones papers, series 1, box 46, RA.
[128] A.E. Barker memo on British overseas news, August 17, 1939, R28/162/1, BBC.
[129] C.(A.) to D.G., December 9, 1937, R28/164/1, BBC.
[130] R.J. Brown memo, October 28, 1938, R28/165/1; R.J. Brown memo, October 9, 1940, R24/164/2, BBC.

activities under a single organization, BBC executives believed, was "desirable not from a narrow broadcasting standpoint, but in the widest possible interests of British prestige throughout the world."[131] In March 1938, Wilson apparently approached Jones on the subject of his resignation, and even tempted him with a peerage, but Jones refused.[132]

In February 1941, relying largely on Jones' unilateral appointment of his successor as a pretext, and in connivance with the Ministry of Information, the Reuters board forced Jones to resign.[133] In April, concern over the backroom machinations of the BBC to gain a hand in Reuters, prompted the London newspapers, under the auspices of the NPA, to announce to the PA their renewed interest in owning a stake in Reuters. It also coincided with a collapse in the PA's principal sources of revenue and its switch to an inclusive service and a change in its method of pricing.[134] While negotiations were underway between the PA and NPA, the executives of the BBC pressed their case more fervently at the Ministry of Information.[135] Officials at the Ministry believed Reuters rested too heavily on its laurels. Brendan Bracken, then minister, was reportedly heard to say in Parliament that "Reuters to my mind has lost ground."[136] In September, with the consent of the government, the London and provincial press converted Reuters into a trust in which they both held an equal interest. The idea of running news organizations as trusts had become popular between the wars – *The Times*, *The Observer*, and the Manchester *Guardian* being three interwar examples – and William Haley, the PA and Reuters director that largely drafted the Reuters Trust deed, had helped to form a trust for the *Guardian*.[137] From 1944 to 1952, Haley served as director-general of the BBC. Whereas the newspaper trusts were at least partially intended to keep the publications free from bias, the Reuters Trust agreement, based on the stipulations of the government, was irrevocable for twenty-one years, after which it could not be amended or dissolved without the approval of the Lord Chief Justice, who was also to appoint an independent chairman of the trustees who had a casting but no ordinary vote. The Trust remained in place, and among politicians at least, Reuters continued to be perceived as a provider of a public service until 1984. That year, telecommunications in Britain were privatized, which is another indication of the influence government control of telecommunications

---

[131] JBC/GMG, "News for overseas service," July 20, 1939, R28/162/1, BBC.

[132] Read, "Sir Roderick Jones," p. 15.

[133] Read, "Sir Roderick Jones," pp. 20–2. Read, *Power of News*, pp. 208–14, 288–92. Unsigned, "Three active directors – Alexander Ewing, Samuel Storey and William Haley," undated, RA.

[134] Memorandum by the joint general managers, September 8, 1941, LN 954/1/013296, RA.

[135] Ogilvie to Ryan, September 5, 1941, R28/166, R.J. Brown memo, September 15, 1941, R28/166, A. Powell to K. Wood, September 30, 1941, R28/166, BBC.

[136] Cooper to Noyes, November 23, 1941, APo1.4B, series VII, box 37, folder 704.

[137] D. Read, "The Relationship of Reuters and Other News Agencies with the British Press 1858–1984: Service at Cost or Business for Profit?" in P. Catterall, et al. (eds.), *Northcliffe's Legacy: Aspects of the British Popular Press, 1896–1996* (Basingstoke: Macmillan, 2000), pp. 159–60.

had on Reuters's history. Although the PA firmly declined continued overtures from the BBC for an interest in the Trust, Christopher Chancellor, Jones' successor at Reuters, wished the broadcasting corporation to know it had a sympathetic ear at the agency. "The new Reuters," Chancellor wrote to the BBC director-general, "is not an ordinary commercial undertaking with the obligation to distribute a proportion of its profits in dividends," it would not "be actuated by any narrow conception of its interest, but will have well in mind the joint responsibilities to the public which form common ground between Reuters and the BBC."[138] Chancellor's comment, however much the cynic may perceive it to have been an exercise in reconciliation, is an indication of the extent to which monopolies regulated in the public interest had supplanted the free market for which the Victorians had hoped.

In Britain, legislation dictated how news was to be collected and distributed, and the Post Office, a strong administrative body, enforced it. The Telegraph Act of 1868, which was intended to establish a level playing field among provincial publishers, did so only briefly, if at all, and at the cost of a considerable reduction in the speed with which news was distributed. New technology, particularly the telephone, and subsequently the pressures of war, caused a collapse of the settlement of 1868 and reduced the subsidy the Post Office provided to the provincial press over the London press. Considerable concentration in the newspaper business following World War I caused the press to seek out private solutions to the problems of news collection and distribution. As in the United States in the 1880s, the use of leased lines in Britain in the 1920s caused a radical alteration in the size, content, and organization of newsgathering. The threat of the BBC, although mitigated somewhat by the long-standing and influential policy of separating the means of news production from the means of news distribution, helped to precipitate the merger of Reuters and the PA, which had been so long in the making and which led to the creation of the Reuters Trust. Newsgathering in Britain, more than in the United States, was shaped by telecommunications regulation, but by 1945, the position was similar insofar as the principal domestic newsgathering organization in both countries was in the hands of the press.

138 W.J. Moloney and C.J. Chancellor to BBC, October 29, 1943, R28/164/2, BBC.

6

Reluctant Imperialist? Reuters in the British Empire, 1851–1947

The tension between cooperation and exclusion in the supply of news was as pronounced throughout the British Empire as it was in the British Isles and in the United States. To spread costs and increase profits, Reuters, like the United Press in the United States, had an incentive to sell its news as widely as possible, but it too encountered a desire on the part of the press throughout the Empire to possess news exclusively. Colonial and commonwealth administrations regulated this relationship, typically by changes in telecommunications policy or by the allocation of intellectual property rights, and occasionally through judicial intervention and outright financial subsidy. On a daily basis, however, Reuters attempted to moderate the tension between exclusivity and cooperation among newspaper interests throughout the Empire. But, more often than not, access to Reuters's news reports was used as a bargaining chip in the internecine conflicts between warring factions of the colonial press. As a consequence, Reuters's news business was never particularly profitable. Before World War I, Reuters developed a private telegram business and associated lines of work to subsidize its newsgathering. After the war, in conjunction with the use of radio, Reuters developed a highly profitable and influential commercial news business. After 1930, the PA, which owned Reuters as a subsidiary, relied on these alternative sources of revenue, and the profits Reuters earned from its news services in the Empire, to offset the cost of international news to the newspapers of the British Isles.

From 1851 to 1941, there was no British organization that could replicate Reuters's arrangements for the collection of news around the globe, and Reuters was considered, and its managers and staff believed it to be, the news agency of the Empire. Although risky, imperial markets provided Reuters, like other British firms, with profitable conditions. Imperial governments could be relied on to provide generous subsidies, including payment for news services, as well as privileged access to sources and communications, which gave Reuters a

considerable advantage.[1] But Reuters's efforts to obtain from colonial governments favorable protection of the property rights it asserted in news, although
persistent, were blocked by the domestic press. In India, for example, Reuters's
agents at Bombay and Simla on several occasions over many years promoted
bills dealing with copyright in news telegrams, but they all failed to pass. The
principal obstacle, according to Reuters, was the disinclination of the authorities to run counter to the wishes of a large number of Indian publishers who
helped themselves without payment to information published in other journals.
Consequently, Reuters printed at Bombay, as it did for a short while in London,
a small paper called *Reuter's Indian Journal* solely for copyright purposes, in
which telegrams were inserted immediately on arrival. Pirating newspapers
were informed that news telegrams published in this journal were under copyright.[2] When colonial governments did pass acts granting a limited copyright
in telegram messages, the effects of the act often benefited a select portion of
the press more than Reuters.[3]

Britain's supremacy in international telegraphy placed Reuters at the center
of a web of cables that connected the globe, which enabled the agency to secure
privileged access to the means of news collection and distribution, but these
agreements typically restricted the initiative of both organizations as much as
the agreements between the AP and Western Union in the United States (see
Table 6.1).[4] Indeed, Sir John Pender, chairman of the Eastern and Associated
Telegraph Company, the largest owner of international telegraph cables, was
foremost a hardheaded businessman who had little sense of an imperial mission
unless it was remunerative.[5] Paul Julius Reuter, the founder of the eponymous
agency, was similarly driven, as was Roderick Jones, however much Jones may
have been an imperialist as well.[6] Mutually advantageous rebate agreements
existed at different times between Reuters and the Eastern and Associated. A

[1] T. Nicholas, "Enterprise and Management," in R. Floud and P. Johnson (eds.), *The Cambridge
Economic History of Modern Britain*, vol. 2: *Economic Maturity, 1860–1939* (Cambridge:
Cambridge University Press, 2004), p. 239; Hannah, *Rise of the Corporate Economy*, p. 117.

[2] W.L. Murray to H. Whorlow, May 30, 1916, Jones papers, series 1, box 24, RA. Reuters subsequently successfully prosecuted *The Deccan Herald* and *Daily Telegraph* of Pune for copyright
infringement. A copy of the decision may be found in AP01.2, KC, box 35, folder 12, AP.

[3] L. Bently, "Copyright and the Victorian Internet: Telegraphic Property Laws in Colonial
Australia," *Loyola of Los Angeles Law Review*, 38 (2004), 71–176, esp. 167–70 for a list of
related legislation.

[4] D.R. Headrick, *The Invisible Weapon: Telecommunications and International Politics,
1851–1945* (Oxford: Oxford University Press, 1991); J. Hills, *Struggle for Global Control of
Communication: The Formative Century* (Urbana, IL: University of Illinois Press, 2002); P.J.
Hugill, *Global Communications since 1844: Geopolitics and Technology* (London: Johns
Hopkins University Press, 1999); D.R. Winseck and R.M. Pike, *Communication and Empire:
Media, Markets, and Globalization, 1860–1930* (Durham, NC: Duke University Press, 2007).

[5] R.W.D. Boyce, "Imperial Dreams and National Realities: Britain, Canada and the Struggle for a
Pacific Telegraph Cable, 1879–1902," *The English Historical Review*, 115 (2000), 43.

[6] Read, "The Relationship of Reuters and Other News Agencies." p. 154; D. Read, "Reuters: News
Agency of the British Empire," *Contemporary Record*, 8 (1994), 195–212.

contract between the two companies was in place during the 1890s, although *The Times* of London benefited from similar arrangements. During World War I, the British government instructed the cable companies to cease duplicating rival press services on the Eastern and Pacific cables. One general service was supplied for the different parts of the Empire and a small supplementary service was allowed to various groups of newspapers.[7] Reuters's was the preferred service. Preferential treatment for Reuters continued after 1918. In 1923, the Eastern agreed to pay Reuters £30,000 per annum toward maintaining the agency's offices in Britain, Australasia, the Far East, India, and South Africa in return for a guarantee of £178,000 worth of telegram traffic. Reuters agreed to transmit its telegrams exclusively by Eastern cables and to give up its private telegram business, which competed with that of the telegraph company. Eastern made £20,000 on the deal and Reuters saved £5,000 per annum. In 1926, a similar agreement encompassed countries outside the Empire.[8]

From 1851 to 1930, Reuters was a trading company operating in news. Much of the company's early success abroad is attributable to its ability to plug in to existing networks of merchants in Europe and the Empire and to tap them for news.[9] In 1928, Reuters had seventy overseas correspondents. Of these, twenty were merchant companies, principally located in Africa and island nations, as well as in China. For coverage of Sub-Saharan Africa, Reuters relied on Smith, Mackenzie, and Company, the largest British trading company in East Africa in 1914.[10] Of the seventy agents and correspondents, only thirteen worked for local newspapers. The preponderance of "stringers," or part-time correspondents, were located in South Africa, followed by India. Elsewhere, and especially on the continent of Europe, thirty-four national news agencies exchanged their news with Reuters.[11] This rather diffuse arrangement was advantageous insofar as it assured Reuters of sufficient coverage in the event of breaking news, but kept overhead expenses low in quiet times.

[7] Hibberdine to Bradshaw, March 19,. 1895, LN522, RA; Contract, May 12, 1902, LN232/8713371, RA; Reuters board minutes, May 7, 1902, box 291, RA. C. Kaul, *Reporting the Raj: The British Press in India, c. 1880–1922* (Manchester: Manchester University Press, 2003), pp. 64–5; Reuters board minutes, March 9, 1904; Murray to Jones, August 2, 1919, Jones papers, series 1, box 33; Jones to Penman, August 20, 1915, Jones papers, series 1, box 22, RA. Reuters board minutes, October 4, 1916, RA.
[8] This agreement did more than provide Reuters with a rebate on its telegrams. It also enabled the agency gradually to exit the increasingly unprofitable private telegram business. Draft agreement between Reuters and Eastern, May 5, 1923, Jones papers, series 1, box 29; Clements to Jones, October 4, 1923, Jones to Balfour, October 5, 1923, and Clements to Jones, October 16, 1923, Jones papers, series 1, box 29; Clements to Jones, June 7, 1926, Jones papers, series 1, box 26, RA. Crandall to Bickell, February 17, 1936, Howard papers, box 117, LOC.
[9] G. Jones, *Merchants to Multinationals: British Trading Companies in the Nineteenth and Twentieth Centuries* (Oxford: Oxford University Press, 2002), pp. 226, 233; R.A. Church, *The Dynamics of Victorian Business* (London: George Allen & Unwin, 1980), pp. 237–9.
[10] Jones, *Merchants to Multinationals*, p. 56.
[11] List of agents and correspondents, February 1928, Jones papers, series 1, box 36, RA.

TABLE 6.1. *Private and government submarine telegraph cables, 1892 and 1923*

1892	Number of cables	Length (km)	Percentage of world total
British cables	508	163,619	66.3
American cables	27	38,986	15.8
French cables	74	21,859	8.9
Danish cables	82	13,201	5.3
Others	535	9,206	3.7
Total world cables	1,226	246,871	100.0
1923	**Number of cables**	**Length (km)**	**Percentage of world total**
British cables	795	297,802	50.5
American cables	147	142,621	24.2
French cables	108	64,933	11.0
Danish cables	26	15,590	2.6
Japanese cables	214	14,463	2.5
Others	2,276	53,819	9.2
Total world cables	3,566	589,228	100.0

Source: Headrick, *The Invisible Weapon*, pp. 39, 197.

Only during the interwar period did Reuters expand its overseas operations and establish a formal, albeit loose, hierarchy run from London. Reuters did not institute a system of regular overseas inspections until 1921, but instances of defalcation or misappropriation of commercial information appear infrequently in its minute books.[12] Operations in Europe and in North and South America were controlled from headquarters in London. The remainder of the planet was divided into five territories. These several regions were split among general managers stationed in different major cities, including Bombay (Mumbai), Cairo, Cape Town, Melbourne, New York, and Shanghai.[13] Each general manager controlled, subject to London, the managers, agents, and correspondents within his territory.[14] In addition to seven general managers, twenty-eight managers were stationed in different parts of the world, each in charge of a branch. The branches had charge of the regional staffs. Bureaus

---

[12] Giles to Jones, October 6, 1921, Jones papers, series 1, box 31, RA. See, for example, Reuters minute books, October 10, 1888, March 27, 1901, and June 1, 1904, RA.

[13] Shanghai's jurisdiction extended from the Straits Settlements, north and east, over China, Manchuria, Korea, Japan, the Philippines, Borneo, and the Dutch East Indies. Bombay had jurisdiction over India, Burma, Ceylon, Siam, Tibet, Afghanistan, Persia, and Mesopotamia. The Melbourne office covered Australia, New Zealand, and the Pacific Islands. New York covered the United States and South America. Cape Town covered South Africa, South West Africa, Portuguese East Africa and Rhodesia, beyond the Zambezi, and up the Great Lakes. Cairo was responsible for Egypt, Sudan, Abyssinia, Palestine, and Arabia.

[14] Memo, November 26, 1924, Jones papers, series 1, box 62; Jones, Report to board of directors, April 2, 1927, Jones papers, series 1, box 35, RA.

typically comprised a full-time correspondent, a controller, an editor of economic intelligence, and a support staff.

By 1938, the company's full-time staff numbered more than 1,000 employees, in addition to several hundred ordinary correspondents posted throughout the Empire. Reuters maintained a full-time staff of 676 resident correspondents, as well as 200 part-time local correspondents in the various centers of India and numerous other stringers throughout the world. By comparison, in 1938, *The Times*, which had the largest overseas staff of any British newspaper, maintained 129 correspondents (see Table 6.2). Most of Reuters's correspondents, but not all, were British born. The usual term for service, except in Europe, where transfers sometimes took place at more frequent intervals, was five years, but there was no hard rule, and members of the Reuters staff were expected to be prepared for transfer from one territory to another on short notice at any time. The biographies of Reuters's correspondents read more like those of Foreign Office bureaucrats than Fleet Street journalists and perhaps it is more useful to think of them as such. Indeed, Reuters correspondents did occasionally serve as envoys and government go-betweens. The ability of these correspondents to mix in the right circles at Cape Town, Shanghai, and Simla gave Reuters an advantage.[15] H.A. Gwynne, for example, Reuters's correspondent in South Africa during the Boer War, claimed to have gained privileged access to Lord Kitchener by writing a flattering piece about him, which helped to restore Kitchener's ego after a scathing piece in the *Spectator* claimed that Lord Roberts should travel to South Africa again and finish the war that Kitchener had failed to conclude.[16] "We try to combine, indeed circumstances have forced us to combine," explained Roderick Jones, "the elements of a Civil Service with the elements of a developing business enterprise."[17]

Despite the benefits Reuters derived by virtue of being at the heart of the British Empire, and despite its considerable first-mover advantages and overseas organization, the agency encountered significant local resistance.[18] Being the news agency of the British Empire meant that officialdom typically gave news to Reuters first, safe in the knowledge that using the agency would ensure the message was widely distributed. Giving Reuters the news first also protected officials against accusations of privileging one newspaper over another, but this privileged position obliged Reuters to cover the Empire even when

[15] Jones to Rear-Admiral J.H. Godfrey, June 13, 1939, Jones papers, series 1, box 46, RA; Carter to Ascoli, December 16, 1938, Jones papers, series 1, box 39. Buck to Maloney, July 3, 1930, Jones papers, series 1, box 35, RA.

[16] H.A. Gwynne to H. de Reuter, July 12, 1901, LN1/850102, RA.

[17] Jones to R. Neville, July 17, 1929, Jones papers, series 1, box 35, RA.

[18] *Contra* A. Nalbach, "'The Software of Empire': Telegraphic News Agencies and Imperial Publicity, 1865–1914," in J.F. Codell (ed.), *Imperial Co-histories: National Identities and the British and Colonial Press* (Madison, NJ: Fairleigh Dickinson University Press, 2003), pp. 68–94.

TABLE 6.2. *Position of correspondents for
Reuters and* The Times, *1938*

	Reuters	*The Times*
Africa	96	21
Americas	150	22
Antipodes	23	7
Asia	125	22
Europe	282	57

Source: The Reuter organization, January 10, 1938, RA,
Jones 1.39.

doing so was unprofitable.[19] The disparate demands of newspapers for news from around the world of concern to their local population also prevented the agency from deriving considerable economies from its global organization. Consequently, where it was feasible, Reuters found it economical to rely on cooperative and exclusive exchange agreements with local news organizations rather than develop infrastructure of its own throughout the Empire. Cooperative international agreements and a division of territory, as opposed to attempting to possess an independent global operation, were effective ways in which to gather and supply international news.

While they lasted, Reuters's subsidiaries in Holland, India, and South Africa provided more profits than services to independent overseas news associations or agencies, but local independence movements invariably obliged Reuters to sell or abandon its subsidiaries. During the nineteenth century, Reuters's subsidiary in the Netherlands was its most profitable property. This agency, established under Dutch management, became the principal domestic news agency for the Netherlands and received its foreign news from Reuters. Reuters retained a highly remunerative stake in the Nederlandsch Telegraaf Agentschap (NTA) until World War I. After the war, an independence movement among the Dutch press forced Reuters to sell its assets to a national concern (see Table 6.3).

In the Empire, Reuters did little business with Canada, it being more economical for the Canadian press to rely on the AP for its news. In Canada, the press originally obtained news from the United States via the Canadian Pacific Railway before forming the Canadian Press, an organization along the lines of the AP. According to Norman Smith and Fred Livesay, president and general manager respectively of the Canadian Press, the association "was founded in 1911 for the express purpose of forming a holding company for

---

[19] See, for example, R. Desbordes, "Representing 'Informal Empire' in the Nineteenth Century: Reuters in South America at the Time of the War of the Pacific, 1879–83," *Media History*, 14 (2008), 131.

TABLE 6.3. *Reuter's gross profits and losses in select overseas territories (in £ at constant 1913 prices)*

	1873	1878	1883	1888	1893	1898	1903	Total
Europe	3,611	6,089	5,974	5,605	4,463	7,491	6,445	39,678
Antipodes	3,772	-2,763	2,769	-5,883	-3,265	604	584	-4,182
Far East	–	821	568	426	-1,253	949	1,728	3,239
India	2,234	2,707	1,426	343	-771	1,694	3,518	11,151
South Africa	–	136	602	616	-530	532	5,105	6,461
Other	1,378	2,608	749	1,152	805	930	1,736	9,358
Total	10,995	9,598	12,088	2,259	-551	12,200	19,116	

	1908	1913	1918	1923	1928	1933	1938	Total
Europe	7,436	6,806	4,588	2,392	2,586	3,168	–	26,976
Antipodes	661	611	1,648	-413	4,223	4,201	4,580	15,511
Far East	1,721	480	-316	419	2,611	4,215	6,443	15,573
India	4,150	6,850	6,205	8,580	10,502	9,329	12,856	58,472
South Africa	314	4,971	2,633	2,819	3,043	3,205	4,474	21,459
Other	2,910	3,347	2,896	1,596	1,295	657	1,266	13,967
Total	17,192	23,065	17,654	15,393	24,260	24,775	29,619	

Note: At different points, "Europe" includes Austria, Constantinople, Belgium, France, Germany, Greece, and Holland. "Antipodes" refers to Austria, Java, and New Zealand. "Far East" includes China, Japan, and the Straits settlements. "India" includes Aden. "Other," at different points, includes Egypt and Tehran.

Source: Calculated from Reuters profit and loss statements, RA, LN 224.

TABLE 6.4. *Reuters's imperial relations, c. 1870–1940*

Dominion	Local environment	News agreement
Australia	Cooperative/partnership	Considerable local enterprise
Canada	Autonomous cooperative	News obtained from the AP
India	Reuters subsidiary	Reuters monopoly
South Africa	Partnership	Favourable differential

the Canadian rights of The Associated Press, these till then having been vested in the Canadian Pacific Railway."[20] The arrangement between the Canadian press and Reuters was subordinate to a covenant between Reuters and the AP, which embraced the Reuters news available to the Canadians. No Reuters or similar direct British service existed in Canada before World War I. Even in the late 1930s, the bulk of Canada's British and general world news reached the newspapers via New York and only a minor proportion was carried direct from London. In 1937, for the class of service for which the Cape Town and Johannesburg newspapers paid Reuters between £2,700 and £3,000 per year, publishers in Toronto paid Reuters £6,000 and extra for special and financial services. Only in 1942, at the instigation of the AP, was a more comprehensive agreement reached between Reuters and the Canadian press.[21] In the rest of the Empire, Australia, India, and South Africa provided limited returns before 1914, but after 1928 Reuters's commercial services improved the company's finances greatly (Table 6.4).

Cultural differences, mores, political events, and economic development influenced the profitability of Reuters's services overseas, but of greater impact than the barriers imposed by language and culture, was domestic infrastructure. There were profitable opportunities for development where local entrepreneurship was lacking.[22] As in Britain, Reuters encountered difficulties balancing the different requirements of small and large newspapers in Australia, India, and South Africa. As with American metropolitan dailies, city newspapers throughout the Empire preferred to pay extra for exclusive access to the news than to permit it to be widely available. Like the AP, Reuters had to appease the wealthy publishers who supplied the agency with the bulk of its revenue, but it could not ignore smaller publishers lest a rival emerge to serve them. Contending with the different needs of the provincial and London

---

[20] Digest of verbatim AP board minutes, April 16, 1924, AP01.1, series III, box 3, folder 27, p. 662, AP.

[21] Jones memo, July 17, 1937, Jones papers, series 1, box 73; W.J. Haley, report to the board, July 1, 1942, LN317 1/8818001, RA. G. Allen, "News Across the Border," p. 206–17.

[22] G. Jones, "British Trading Companies and Industrial Development," in F. Amatori et al. (eds.), *Deindustrialization and Reindustrialization in 20th Century Europe* (Milan: Franco Angeli, 1999), p. 348.

press presented similar problems. The strategy Jones employed in Britain – to invite the press to joint-ownership through a newspaper association – he first honed in South Africa, having been inspired to do so by Edmund Robbins of the PA.[23] He subsequently carried out a similar strategy in India and Australia. "The goal on each occasion," wrote Roderick Jones in 1936, "has been ownership by the newspapers themselves of their general news services, in affiliation with Reuters."[24] The several organizations created throughout the Empire were comparable to the extent that the newspapers either wholly or partly operated them, but the founders or promoters in each case molded the principle of newspaper control of news collection and distribution to local requirements and conditions. In effect, Reuters sought to establish in these locations subsidiaries tailored to local conditions and owned in conjunction with the local press. This was not a new strategy, but one that Reuters had pursued since the nineteenth century in the Netherlands and elsewhere.

FORGING PARTNERSHIP IN SOUTH AFRICA

Compared with Australasia and India, prior to the Boer War the colonies of South Africa were unprofitable for Reuters. Until the discovery of gold in 1886, there was little business to be had. Reuters made considerable profits during the Boer Wars, but by 1908 it encountered difficulties with the domestic press that led to a considerable falling off in revenue. That year, some of the company's principal clients, including the *Cape Times*, the *Cape Argus*, and the *Rand Daily Mail*, formed a syndicate and demanded exclusive access to Reuters's news and the right to resell it. Roderick Jones, who was made general manager at Cape Town in 1905, rejected the offer and instead played the provincial press off the city papers with a view to forming an association along the lines of the British PA.[25] In 1910, Jones negotiated the formation of a partnership between Reuters and the principal newspaper companies in South Africa, including the Cape Times Limited, the Argus Printing and Publishing Company, and the South African Mails Syndicate Limited, and saved the agency from a considerable shortfall. By 1914, the partnership, called the South African Press Agency (SAPA), served sixty-four papers.[26] This organization, although

---

[23] Manager's memoranda, November 2, 1915, PA, Ms 35362/9, p. 212, GL.
[24] Jones to Dunn, March 23, 1936, Jones papers, series 1, box 43, RA.
[25] D. Read, "Reuters and South Africa: 'South Africa is a Country of Monopolies'," *The South African Journal of Economic History*, 11 (1996), 106–26.
[26] The Argus Printing and Publishing Company, easily the most powerful newspaper concern in South Africa, owned the three leading evening journals in the country – *The Star* (Johannesburg), *The Cape Argus* (Cape Town) and *The Natal Advertiser* (Durban). It also held large interests in *The Diamond Fields Advertiser* (Kimberley) and *The Friend* (Bloemfontein) and controlled the two leading newspapers of Rhodesia, *The Rhodesia Herald* (Salisbury) and *The Bulawayo Chronicle* (Bulawayo). The morning newspapers of the three chief centers of population, *The Cape Times* (Cape Town), *The Rand Daily Mail* (Johannesburg) and *The Natal Mercury*

modified in 1916, remained in place until 1937. Reuters owned 60 percent of the SAPA and the newspapers owned the rest. British publishers, as opposed to Afrikaans publishers, controlled 87.4 percent of the voting power in the partnership. The SAPA covered domestic and foreign news. A supply of domestic news, if provided to the press through a Reuters affiliate, enabled the agency to consolidate its position with provincial newspapers.[27]

Through the partnership, Reuters was able to provide a news service to the provincial papers and the city dailies of South Africa. Newspapers in the partnership automatically received a share of every subscription paid to Reuters throughout South Africa as well as a share of the payment that Reuters's London office made to the partnership for the South African news cabled to London. The Reuters service cost the newspapers in the partnership a fraction of what their cable and inland services otherwise would have cost. The newspaper partners incurred no liability for partnership expenditure, which rested with Reuters, but were required only to pay subscriptions. In 1915, the *Cape Times* and the Johannesburg *Star*, both members of the SAPA, received approximately £1,300 in profits, so that the Reuters cable service, and the Reuters inland service in that year only cost them each about £200 notwithstanding that the service cost Reuters £16,000 to provide. This arrangement, and the absence of competition, enabled Reuters to give the provincial South African newspapers outside the association full services at much lower subscription prices than was otherwise possible. Consequently, it was not in the interest of the publishers who utilized the service but did not belong to the partnership to break it up.[28]

Reuters had an incentive to encourage widespread access to its news to prevent the development of active competition. In 1913, the Johannesburg *Star* blocked the Johannesburg *Evening Chronicle* from Reuters's news. The *Star*, along with other newspapers in the partnership, sold for three pence, but the *Chronicle* was priced at a penny. The *Chronicle* received an alternative service of foreign news cabled by its representative in London, therefore the efforts

(Durban), although under separate ownership, had a partnership and frequently cooperated in the use of syndicated feature material. Because of large distances and insufficient transportation, no newspaper achieved national status except perhaps *The Sunday Times*, of Johannesburg, published in association with *The Rand Daily Mail*. This restriction of the dailies to their own immediate territories, coupled with the sparse populations of the South African provinces, led to various noncompetitive agreements. K. Bickell to O.G. Villard, undated, Villard papers, Ms Am 1323, 3923, Houghton Library, Harvard University.

[27] Reuters board minutes, July 26, 1905, September 30, 1908, March 2, 1910; J.H. Henry, "Reuters in Africa," 1988, LN1/8812601, pp. 21–2; Jones to Dunn, February 25, 1918, Jones papers, series 1, box 23, RA. E. Potter, *The Press as Opposition: The Political Role of South African Newspapers* (London: Chatto and Windus, 1975), p. 106.

[28] Memo on the financial position of the partnership newspapers in relation to the Reuter South African Press Agency, February 4, 1916, Jones papers, series 1, box 22; Jones to L. Phillips, February 4, 1916, Jones papers, series 1, box 22; Jones to Phillips, February 4, 1916, Jones papers, series 1, box 22, RA.

of the *Star* to put it out of business by withholding Reuters's news reports failed.[29] This alternative service of foreign news and popular sympathy kept the *Chronicle* alive. Reuters was keen to provide the *Chronicle* with service. To the *Star* and the *Rand Daily Mail*, Reuters offered to surrender the whole of the subscription from the *Chronicle*, but they demurred. Reuters also offered to concede significant liberty to the newspapers for the development of their own correspondent services, which otherwise were strictly limited under their agreement, but the *Star* remained stubborn. In 1916, the *Chronicle* was still without the Reuters service. To appease both parties, Reuters promised a portion of the news report to partnership members exclusively, and provided the *Chronicle* with a smaller report. Reuters calculated, irrespective of the quality of the news, prearranged quantities for its general and special services. The bulk of the news was placed in the special service, which was only available to members of the partnership.[30]

Despite the episode with the *Chronicle*, the first real competition to the combine emerged in 1934 from I.W. Schlesinger, owner of the South African Broadcasting Company, who set up the Johannesburg *Sunday Express* followed by the *Daily Express* in 1937. These two new powerful newspapers threatened members of the combine and, from Reuters's perspective, necessitated a discussion about broadening the membership of the partnership. Jones understood the need to expand the partnership in a manner advantageous to newspapers within and outside it, but expansion was contrary to the interests of certain members. Jones orchestrated a reorganization that gave the partnership the appearance of being widely open, and anticipated any criticisms that it was exclusive, monopolistic, or racially (Brit versus Boer) or politically biased, but at the same time framed it to ensure the continued control of the incumbent members.[31]

By selling the partnership to the press, Jones reinforced the controlling power of the principal South African publishers while ensuring an adequate service to smaller papers throughout the country. The three newspaper partners of the

---

[29] In light of the refusal of the *Star* to serve the *Chronicle*, Australian publishers entertained the possibility of providing it with a service. The Australian papers, owing to cheaper cable rates, received their news from Reuters via South Africa and consequently received the same report as the South African press. The different facets of the imperial press had multiple ties, not all of which went via London or Reuters.

[30] Turner to Jones, March 3, 1916, Jones papers, series 1, box 22; Jones to J.S. Dunn, August 8, 1916, Jones papers, series 1, box 22; Jones to L. Phillips, February 4, 1916, Jones papers, series 1, box 22; Memo on South African press position, February 4, 1916, Jones papers, series 1, box 22; Jones to Dunn, August 9, 1916, Jones papers, series 1, box 22, RA. M. Walker, *Powers of the Press: The World's Great Newspapers* (London: Quartet Books, 1982), p. 318.

[31] Jones to Dunn, June 19, 1935, C.J. Murphy to Jones, December 10, 1937, Jones papers, series 1, box 43. Murray to Jones, August 2, 1935, Jones papers, series 1, box 38; Jones to Dunn, June 18, 1935, Jones papers, series 1, box 43. Jones memo, July 5, 1935, Jones papers, series 1, box 43. Jones to Dunn, July 26, 1935, Jones papers, series 1, box 43. Jones memo, May 18, 1937, Jones papers, series 1, box 42, RA. Walker, *Powers of the Press*, p. 318.

SAPA received as their portion of the purchase price of the existing agency a sum equivalent to the total sum that they as a group paid for their shareholding in the new association. In other words, they consolidated their position, and became the principal controllers, through the association, of the general news situation in South Africa, at little or no cost to themselves. Publishers outside of the partnership had to meet the full cost of the shares in the new association. Shares enabled smaller publications to have a direct voice in the conduct of the news services, but new members could only be admitted by an affirmative vote of three-fourths of the association. The new South African organization signed a long-term contract with Reuters. Explicitly borrowing from the model used by AP, a clause was inserted in the constitution of the new South African organization that restrained newspaper members from supplying news to anyone other than the association or Reuters until such news appeared in the newspapers of South Africa. This was "a course which I strongly supported on general principles," wrote Jones, "and also because it ensured to Reuters the exclusivity of all S.A.P.A. news outside of South Africa up to the moment of first publication [by newspapers] – an important advance upon anything we hitherto have enjoyed."[32]

Although the organization of the new association generally expanded access to the news reports, it also, in many respects, preserved the status quo. It was the large newspapers that had always controlled access to foreign news, bore responsibility for obtaining it, and shouldered the financial burden its procurement imposed. Requiring newcomers to pay an entrance fee reinforced the value existing members had created by contributing to the association over the course of twenty-eight years. In several countries in which the newspapers owned the news organization, especially in Australia, Canada, and the United States, newcomers had to submit to a heavy monetary impost as the price of their admission to membership, in addition to being subjected to the vote of the board or of the membership as a whole.[33] In this way, smaller newspapers were allowed access to the news without endangering the preexisting hierarchy among newspapers.

BETWEEN RAJ AND REVOLT: REUTERS'S OPERATIONS IN INDIA

In the 1860s, when Reuters first started business in India, it encountered less resistance from the indigenous press of the subcontinent than it had in the south of Africa, but this did not mean that the agency was hegemonic.[34] Reuters's

[32] Jones memo, March 23, 1937, Jones papers, series 1, box 42; Reuters board minutes, October 5, 1937, March 8, 1938; Jones to Davies, May 14, 1938, Jones papers, series 1, box 44, RA. Walker, *Powers of the Press*, p. 319.
[33] Jones to Nicholson, April 15, 1937, Jones papers, series 1, box 43, RA.
[34] C.A. Bayly, *Empire and Information: Intelligence Gathering and Social Communication in India, 1780–1870* (Cambridge: Cambridge University Press, 1986), pp. 338–44.

long-term success in the subcontinent depended on the ability of its managers to balance local nationalism and the provision of an imperial news service. Before his death in 1915, Herbert de Reuter foresaw the trend of nationalism in India and began making preparations for it. "Nationalism in India is something we will have to think about in future," wrote Herbert de Reuter to his Bombay manager in 1908.[35] Commercial considerations trumped imperial interests. After he took control of Reuters, Roderick Jones attempted to create in India an inclusive service, which satisfied the needs of all newspapers and removed the demand for a competitor.[36]

Reuters's great advantage in India lay in its control over the supply of domestic news. It gained control over the domestic market with the help of the Raj. Reuters first established offices in India and Ceylon in 1866 to cover the cotton markets and to serve the English-language press of the sub-continent. Subsequently, it sought to consolidate its position. In 1910, it purchased half of the Eastern News Agency (ENA), a free-standing company that was registered in London and traded in India. Everard Cotes, formerly correspondent in India for the London *Daily Mail* and founder of the Indian News Agency, owned the other half. Cotes and Reuters joined forces to compete against K.C. Roy, who, in 1899, established an Associated Press of India (API). After Roy was defeated, the ENA served as a holding company for both organizations, which continued to exist separately in name. The ENA employed mostly Indians at offices in Bombay (Mumbai), Calcutta (Kolkata), Lahore, and Madras (Chennai), as well as twenty-four, mostly English, correspondents. It served thirty-six newspapers throughout the country. Roy and two other Bengalis ran the API. In 1916, financial backing from the Raj enabled Reuters to consolidate its hold over the ENA. It quashed an independence movement led by Roy and in 1919 it acquired a majority holding. It was Jones' intention to create in India, as he had in South Africa, a cable and inland service in Reuters's hands.[37]

Contracts with the large British-owned press in India limited Reuters's hold over the vernacular press. Reuters's contracts with the British-owned newspapers, such as the *Calcutta Statesman, Hindustan Times*, the *Hindu* of Madras,

[35] As quoted in J.P. Howe to MacKenzie. September 15, 1930, AP01.2, KC, series I, box 35, folder 12, AP.

[36] There are already two fine published accounts of Reuters's operations in India, and what follows adds to these only insofar as it places the agency's operations in India within the larger context of its strategy throughout the Empire. M. Israel, *Communications and Power: Propaganda and the Press in the Indian Nationalist Struggle, 1920–1947* (Cambridge: Cambridge University Press, 1994); Kaul, *Reporting the Raj.*

[37] Reuters board minutes, March 16, 1910, Articles of association, March 11, 1910, Jones papers, series 1, box 38; Cotes to Napier, April 13, 1916, LN23/865218; Cotes to Bradshaw, July 16, 1915, Jones papers, series 1, box 38; Jones to Kingston, November 22, 1915, Jones papers, series 1, box 24; Kingston to Jones, July 10, 1915, Cotes to Bradshaw, July 23, 1915, Kingston to Bradshaw, July 24, 1915, Jones papers, series 1, box 38; Price, Waterhouse & Co. report, September 11, 1925, Jones papers, series 1, box 60; Jones to Kingston, May 7, 1917, LN23/865218, RA. Kaul, *Reporting the Raj*, p. 42.

and the *Times of India*, barred it from providing a service, even of a restricted size, to small papers that could not afford to pay the price of a full subscription. Reuters had made exclusive contracts with the British-owned papers to secure their support, but these contracts subsequently precluded greater price discrimination. Once messages were sent to India, there was little extra expense in redistributing them to the papers there, so Reuters was tempted to increase its profits by a service to smaller journals at reduced rates. The agency's contracts with the British-owned press prevented Reuters from doing so. India was a larger and wealthier market than South Africa, but in 1923 the service to twenty-three large newspapers in India yielded £17,200 (£800,000), while in South Africa the service to fifty-five newspapers produced revenues of £23,000 (£1 million). A judicious grading of prices increased South African revenue. Reuters could neither employ a similar pricing strategy in India, nor could it effectively serve the vernacular press. Publishers of vernacular newspapers objected to the considerable subsidies that Reuters received from the Indian government.[38] Subsidies from the Indian government were approximately one-third of the total revenue of the ENA.

As the political environment in India changed, the vernacular newspapers expanded rapidly and offered Reuters a more lucrative field than the English-language newspapers. Although British interests still controlled the great newspapers in India, each province had powerful Indian-run papers and a host of vernaculars. In the early 1920s, nationalists organized mass boycotts of British manufactured goods and in 1921 it was already apparent to Sir William Vincent, the Home Member of Bengal, "that India is going steadily on to self-government."[39] Reuters anticipated that the Indian-owned newspapers were likely to expand, whereas the Anglo-Indian element was likely to decline. Failure to provide a service to the numerically large but comparatively poor Indian press invited competition and pilfering of Reuters's reports, but so long as Reuters accepted subsidies from the Raj, the national press refused to take the agency's news service. If the Raj discontinued its financial support to the agency, Reuters would suffer a shortfall. During the 1920s, the India Office noticed that the frequency of stories it considered unfriendly or insensitive to government interests increased. Reuters's business interests topped the national interest. The Raj discovered that Reuters, like most British businesses during the interwar period, was unwilling to play the role that the Government of India envisaged, and ministers regretted having subsidized the agency.[40]

---

38 Dickinson to Kingston, November 28, 1918, Jones papers, series 1, box 24; Dunn to Jones, April 27, 1923, Jones papers, series 1, box 30, RA.

39 M. Misra, *Business, Race, and Politics in British India c. 1850–1960* (Oxford: Clarendon Press, 1999), pp. 137, 164–5.

40 Jones to Young, December 20, 1938, Jones papers, series 1, box 44; Kingston to Jones, July 4, 1917, LN23/865218, RA. Israel, *Communications and Power*, pp. 103–7. Compare with Misra, *Business, Race, and Politics*, pp. 60, 145, 165.

Reuters needed to serve the Indian-owned press without offending the Anglo-Indian papers or the Raj. During the early 1920s, the Free Press of India (FPI) and the British United Press began to serve the vernacular newspaper market.[41] In 1926, Jones instigated negotiations with Indian newspapers to serve the vernacular press and to expel these new services from India. Newspaper publishers that received Reuters's reports exclusively had an incentive to eliminate these alternative news providers from the Indian market. For them, rival services threatened to undermine the value of exclusive access to Reuters's news, bolster competing newspapers, and increase expenditure by obliging them to purchase the other news reports in self-defense. Some publishers, however, were reluctant to form a long-term exclusive alliance with Reuters lest they be prevented them from purchasing news services from obstinate, or successful rival news agencies. Other papers, such as the *Times of India*, believed a strengthened Reuters would eliminate such ruinous competition. The *Times of India* preferred to eliminate competing services, depend on an enlarged service supplied by Reuters, and supplement its report with material from London correspondents and this was the arrangement that Reuters and the Anglo-Indian papers pursued. London correspondents of the Anglo-Indian papers sent supplementary material to India, but the word limit of these services was pegged to the size of the Reuters report. In 1929, the publishers signatory to the agreement agreed to refuse news from Reuters's rivals.[42]

Rank and file newspapers welcomed the agreement. It kept the richer newspapers within such limits as enabled the smaller newspapers to maintain parity with regard to cable and telegraphic news. According to Jones, the agreement allowed Reuters to appear to be the friend of these newspapers and "their guardian against the outreaching and octopus tendencies of the principal newspapers."[43] In truth, it was the principal newspapers, quite as much as Reuters, that wanted to see these changes enforced. After a decline in support for British-owned publications, they found that they were financially unable to maintain a policy of exclusion. Reuters arranged with the British-owned Indian papers to serve the vernacular press at a rate which, although too high for some papers, was sufficient so that it was difficult for a rival service to be established. These modifications helped Reuters to cope with the difficult prospects of home rule. By 1937, only three Indian dailies were British owned,[44] yet

[41] For the history of FPI see Israel, *Communications and Power*, p. 127.

[42] Reuters board minutes, July 26 and August 31, 1926; Memo, May 25, 1926, Jones papers, series 1, box 57; Jones report, May 26, 1926, Jones papers, series 1, box 74, RA; H. Bailie to J. Moore, February 18, 1936, Howard papers, box 117, LOC.

[43] Jones to Moloney, June 19, 1926, Jones papers, series 1, box 57, RA.

[44] Jones to Clements, June 14, 1926, Jones papers, series 1, box 57; John to Jones, December 13, 1940, Jones papers, series 1, box 45; Reuters board minutes, October 5, 1937, RA; Crandall to Bickell, February 17, 1936, Howard papers, box 117, LOC; Jones report, July 2, 1940, Jones papers, series 1, box 46; John to Jones, December 13, 1940, Jones papers, series 1, box 45; Jones to Moloney, March 28, 1936, Jones papers, series 1, box 43, RA.

the success of Reuters's subsidiary in India remained critical to the company's overall profitability. In 1936, the revenue Reuters received in India was not far from double what it received from the British press.[45] Although by this time most of the money came from Reuters's commercial services, the news business was critical to maintaining Reuters's reputation. When British imperial rule in India ended in 1947, the API joined the Reuters Trust, which the PA and the London press had formed in 1941. The trust also included the principal Australian and New Zealand news associations despite the confrontational relationship Reuters had with the newspapers the Antipodes.[46]

A DUEL OF THREE: REUTERS AND THE AUSTRALIAN PRESS

A high level of local entrepreneurship had always prevented Reuters from exploiting the Australian market.[47] Newspaper competition in Australia was fierce before an international telegraph connection between Britain and the Antipodes was completed in 1872. During the 1850s, contests for foreign news among newspapers of Melbourne were similar to those that occurred among newspapers in New York during the 1840s. Such rivalry, as in North America, led to the formation of domestic partnerships, so that by the time an international cable reached Australia the press had grown accustomed to, and developed a relatively organized system for, the collection of international news.[48] Indeed, faced with the prospect of the arrival of the submarine cable in 1871, Lachlan Mackinnon, owner of the Melbourne *Argus*, proposed imitating the model of the New York Associated Press, "so as to ignore Reutterism [sic] altogether." Mackinnon's grand plan was to unite the Australasian, Chinese, and Indian newspapers into a single association to collect and distribute news.

An international organization along the lines Mackinnon envisaged never materialized and his fears that failure "to unite the whole of the Australian press in a common league" would allow Reuters to "conquer" were insufficient to compel the press to cooperate. Instead, two factions sent two different representatives on the same ship to London to negotiate with Reuters. Reuters awarded the Australian Associated Press, which included Mackinnon's

[45] Jones to Mann, May 23, 1937, Jones papers, series 1, box 80, RA.

[46] Jones AGM speech, July 4, 1939, LN36/868219; Jones report, July 2, 1940, Jones papers, series 1, box 46; Unsigned, Reuters in India, July 1987, LN1/868601, p. 10, RA.

[47] P. Putnis, "How the International News Agency Business Model Failed – Reuters in Australia, 1877–1895," *Media History*, 12 (2006), 1–17; T. Rantanen, "The Struggle for Control of Domestic News Markets (1)," in O. Boyd-Barrett and T. Rantanen (eds.), *The Globalization of News* (London: Sage, 1998), pp. 35–48. G. Storey, *Reuters' Century, 1851–1951* (London: Max Parish, 1951), p. 119.

[48] H. Mayer, *The Press in Australia* (Melbourne: Lansdowne, 1964), p. 14; Sydney *Morning Herald*, February 13, 1860, as quoted in K.T. Livingston, *The Wired Nation Continent: the Communication Revolution and Federating Australia* (Oxford: Oxford University Press, 1996), pp. 51–9.

Argus and the Sydney *Morning Herald*, an exclusive contract on the condition that the association admit to membership on fair terms any other paper that was willing to pay for the news. As in the United States, the rules governing membership in the Australian Associated Press practically excluded a group of newspapers led by the Melbourne *Age*, the principal rival of the *Argus*. The Australian Associated Press, much like the New York Associated Press, sold Reuters's news to subscribers in Australasia that were barred from the association. The association additionally sought to increase protection for its exclusive contractual right to Reuters's news by obtaining a limited property right in overseas telegrams. Newspapers outside the association protested that a property right would effectively grant the Australian Associated Press a "monopoly" over foreign news. The Telegraphic Messages Act (1871) sought to prevent the unauthorized republication of news within a limited time of its publication in a paper that had lawfully acquired it from outside Australia. In Victoria and South Australia the period was twenty-four hours and, in Western Australia, it was seventy-two hours.[49]

The comparatively advanced state of newspaper competition in Australia placed Reuters in a weakened negotiation position and obliged it to sign exclusive contracts against its better judgment. To prevent the emergence of rivals, it was in Reuters's interests to be inclusive, but until after World War I the Australian press prevented Reuters from increasing the share of the market it served directly. The newspaper publishers of Australia were not so much concerned about their independence from Reuters, although this was part of the initial motivation, as much as they wanted to prevent other newspapers in Australia from having access to Reuters's news.[50] Until 1877, Reuters sold its news exclusively to the Melbourne *Argus* and Sydney *Morning Herald*, although there were two other morning papers in Melbourne, the *Age* and the *Daily Telegraph*. The Sydney *Daily Telegraph*, a rival to the *Morning Herald*, was first published in 1879. To secure the right to distribute Reuters's news in the Antipodes, the *Argus* and *Morning Herald* agreed to pay a high rate of £4,000 per month, exclusive of telegraph tolls, which prohibited Reuters from serving competitors, such as the Sydney *Evening News*. The *Argus* and *Morning Herald* protected their investments by excluding certain publications, which complained about the "ring" of select publishers that controlled the news.

Conditions similar to those in Australia existed in New Zealand. In 1872, after the submarine cable connected to Auckland, a New Zealand Press Agency formed, which served as the exclusive supplier of Reuters's telegrams in New Zealand. In 1878, those newspapers excluded from the Press Agency formed a New Zealand Press Association. In New Zealand, the government controlled the domestic telegraph lines. The government granted a private wire for use

---

49 Bently, "Copyright and the Victorian Internet, pp. 83–5.

50 *Contra* P. Putnis, "Reuters in Australia: the Supply and Exchange of News, 1859–1877," *Media History*, 10 (2004), 67–88.

by the Press Association, but not the Press Agency, which demanded similar facilities. In Britain, the Post Office avoided such accusations of favoritism by not providing news organizations with leased lines at all. Both organizations in New Zealand had access to Reuters's telegrams. According to George Fenwick, head of the Press Association at the time, having two organizations in receipt of Reuters's news reports for resale to the press led to "ruinous" and "wasteful" competition. In 1879, the two organizations merged. The only way in which a newspaper could obtain Reuters's news reports thereafter was by joining the association, the rules of which were as exclusive as those of the American associations of the time. Similarly, each member of the New Zealand organization was obliged to share its breaking news with the association. The passage of the Protection of Telegrams Act, 1882, like the Australian Telegraphic Messages Act, 1871, reinforced the control the association exercised over access to foreign news in New Zealand.[51]

In Australia, rival news services soon emerged to serve the portion of the market excluded from the exclusive arrangement between Reuters and the Australian Associated Press. John Byron, a former representative of Greville's Telegram Company, which had acted as Reuters's agent in Australia and New Zealand before 1871, opened an office in London in 1877 to send news to the excluded portion of the Australian press. Reuters sought to purchase Byron's business, but he persisted.[52] Such rivalry caused Reuters to regret its exclusive agreement with the *Argus* and *Herald*, especially when the combine found it difficult to meet its high monthly payments. To better combat Byron, Reuters sought unsuccessfully to modify its contract with the *Argus* and *Herald* so that it could supply news to all Australian and New Zealand newspapers. Reuters occasionally recruited the help of the PA to block introduction to the British market of rivals similar to Byron.[53]

A reduction in the price of telegrams between Britain and Australia increased competition among the sizable Australian newspaper population. In 1887, the Eastern and Associated granted especially low telegraph rates of 2s 8d per word between Britain and Australia. This precipitated the formation of a

---

[51] G. Hannis, "The New Zealand Press Association 1880–2006: The Rise and Fall of a Cooperative Model for News-gathering," *Australian Economic History Review*, 48 (2008), 47–67. See also R. Harvey, "Bringing the News to New Zealand: The Supply and Control of Overseas News in the Nineteenth Century," *Media History*, 8 (2002), 21–34.

[52] *The Star* (Christchurch) was using Greville's, (see the issue for September 26, 1871, p. 2), as were many other papers, including the *Age*. See Putnis, "Reuters in Australia," pp. 67, 70–72; and Harvey, "Bringing the News to New Zealand," pp. 25–6.

[53] Rantanen, "The Struggle," p. 38; D. Cryle, *Disreputable Profession: Journalists and Journalism in Colonial Australia* (Rockhampton, Queensland: Central Queensland University Press, 1997), pp. 34–6. Mayer, *Press in Australia*, p. 28; Reuters board minutes, Jun 24 to July 24, 1874, October 10, 1877, January 30, 1878, RA. For an instance of Reuters requesting PA aid see Manager's memoranda, October 7, 1908, PA, Ms 35358/15, pp. 3–4, GL.

newspaper syndicate among select Australian papers, including the *Argus* and the Melbourne *Star*, which effectively limited Reuters's service to only Victoria and Queensland. The press of New Zealand joined this movement. This syndicate attempted to control access to foreign news in the Antipodes. Reuters fought against this mutinous faction in conjunction with the Melbourne *Daily Telegraph*, Melbourne *Herald*, Brisbane *Telegraph*, and several provincial papers, which had been excluded from the new association. Between 1887 and 1889, this contest caused a reduction in Reuters's revenue from Australia from £14,489 to £4,646. The rift between the Australian newspaper empires of Hugh Denison in Sydney and Keith Murdoch in Melbourne perpetuated the existing rift between the different factions of the Australian press.[54]

Reuters's paltry revenue from Australia illustrates how difficult it was for the agency to play each side of the Australian press off against the other.[55] Indeed, Roderick Jones compared Reuters's relations in Australia to the famous duel of three in Marryat's *Mr. Midshipman Easy*. The division in the Australian press grew during the interwar period and further disadvantaged Reuters. An Australian Press Association (APA) served Denison's papers and Murdoch started a United Service to meet his needs. In 1921, an agreement with the APA prohibited Reuters from supplying news to other Australian papers at a cost below that charged to the APA. Additionally, Reuters had to pay to the APA 75 percent of the revenue it earned from subscriptions in Australia.[56] In 1926, Jones attempted to unite the two Australian agencies and to bind them to Reuters, but they preempted Jones by forming an offensive and defensive alliance against him. Except for an insignificant minority, the whole press of Australia, as represented by the combine, agreed to deal with Reuters as a single body. The publishers intended that they should have access to all of Reuters's news in London. They wanted rights to pick and choose from this

---

[54] Reuters board minutes, June 27 to September 14, 1887, May 13, 1885, June 27, 1887, January 4, 1888, RA; E. Morrison, "Newspapers," in G. Davison, et al. (eds.), *The Oxford Companion to Australian History* (Oxford: Oxford University Press, 2001), p. 468; Mayer, *Press in Australia*, pp. 10–11, 29–31; Boyce, "Imperial Dreams and National Realities," p. 10; Headrick, *Invisible Weapon*, p. 35; A. Moyal, "The History of Telecommunication in Australia, 1854–1930," in N. Reingold and M. Rothenberg (eds.), *Scientific Colonialism: A Cross-Cultural Comparison* (Washington, DC: Smithsonian Institution Press, 1987), pp. 35–54; K.S. Inglis, "The Imperial Connection: Telegraphic Communication between England and Australia, 1872–1902," in A.F. Madden and W.H. Morris-Jones (eds.) *Australia and Britain: Studies in a Changing Relationship* (London: University of London, 1980) pp. 21–38; G. Blainey, *The Tyranny of Distance: How Distance Shaped Australia's History* (London: Macmillan, 1968), pp. 222–7; Harvey, "Bringing the News to New Zealand," 31; B. Griffen-Foley, "The Fairfax, Murdoch and Packer Dynasties in Twentieth-Century Australia," *Media History*, 8 (2002), 89–102.

[55] *Contra* Rantanen, "The Struggle," p. 42; "The End of the Electronic News Cartel, 1927–1934" in P. Putnis, J Wilke and C. Kaul (eds.) *International Circuits of News: Historical Development and Impacts*. Cresskill: Hampton Press, 2011.

[56] Agreement with APA, November 18, 1921, LN 247/8715611, RA. See F. Marryat, *Mr. Midshipman Easy* (Boston: Marsh, Capen, and Lyon, 1836), p. 214; Jones to Clements, July 31, 1926, Jones papers, series 1, box 57, RA.

store of news, to mingle it with their own, and then to transmit the whole as their own news reports into Australia, where it would be solely the property of the combine.[57]

Jones met these demands, in return for protection against competing news services. He stipulated that no Australian paper could be shut out of the combine and that Reuters's copyright over its telegrams was preserved. This meant abolishing the dual system of working between Reuters and sections of the Australian press, which had generated bitter competition. Jones also demanded a large price. He achieved an increase in net revenue of 50 percent, and at the end of five years this increase grew again by £1,000 per year for ten years. Under these contracts, Reuters paid the two associations £4,000 per annum for their news report from Australia. The new contract with the APA and the United Service, as opposed to previous contracts with only one organization, meant that approximately 90 percent of the Australian and New Zealand press took its news from Reuters. By reason of this long-term agreement, Australia became a greater source of revenue for Reuters, but it was gained at a loss of control over its news.[58]

To control the Australian market, Jones endeavored to convince leading publishers to admit as many newspapers to the news association as possible. In 1935, the APA and United Service amalgamated as the Australian Associated Press (AAP) and took over the two contracts that existed with Reuters. Jones helped to write the articles of association, which were drawn so that the control of the organization was assured to the two dominant groups that united in founding it.[59] A distinction was created between founding and future members. Applicants for membership had to secure a three-fourths majority vote of the members of the association. Successful candidates had to pay an entrance fee depending on time, frequency, and location of publication. The entrance fee was £10,000 for a newspaper in a district of less than 500,000 inhabitants, and £20,000 for a newspaper in a district with more than 500,000 inhabitants. The revenue from the subscriptions of nonmembers in a district went toward reducing the assessments of members in the same district. Keith Murdoch effectively controlled the organization. By shaping the nature of competition among the press, the AAP, like the partnership arranged in South Africa, and the agreement achieved in India, determined the way in which news was collected and distributed.[60]

57 Jones to Cooper, July 30, 1934, Cooper papers, Ms II, LL.
58 Jones to Holtz, August 27, 1926, Jones papers, series 1, box 57; Jones memo regarding conversation with Delamore McCay and Lloyd Dumas, May 9, 1935, Jones papers, series 1, box 42; Jones memo, October 9, 1926, Jones papers, series 1, box 57, RA. See also G.D. Seymour, "Confidential report to the general manager on New Zealand newspapers and press associations," October 1, 1934, APo1.2, KC, box 35, folder 11, AP.
59 The United Service was renamed the Australian Newspapers Cable Service.
60 Jones to Holtz, August 27, 1926, Jones papers, series 1, box 57; Jones to Nicholson, April 15, 1937, Jones papers, series 1, box 43, RA; M. Meehan, "Australian press octopus," January 30, 1946, McCormick papers, box 6, Cantigny.

Given the limited advantages Reuters derived from centralizing the collection and distribution of imperial news in London, there was much to recommend the establishment of an Empire-wide news association cooperative, so that each domestic organization would exchange its news with the others to assemble comprehensive reports. The Canadians, who depended on Reuters least, proposed to link with all the other dominions in a mutual news exchange. According to Fred Livesay, general manager of the Canadian Press, Reuters was an "anachronism" that ought to make way for a genuine cooperative Empire press association.[61] The existing system, said Livesay,

under which Reuters has a monopoly of the export of news is all wrong. Australians and Canadians can never understand each other until they can exchange news freely as between themselves without passing it through the tight discriminating mesh of London opinion as to what is good for us.[62]

But the principal South African publishers were concerned that the formation of such an organization would undermine the advantages of their beneficial arrangement with Reuters. The Australian publishers, who had at great expense developed their own system for supplying imperial news, were reluctant to diminish the value of their investment by forming an imperial agency. London publishers feared that the formation of such an organization would adversely affect their position of prominence in the Empire and injure profitable exchange arrangements they had in place with colonial papers. The PA, being intimately bound to Reuters, was also against joining an imperial news association, and without the PA on board, any Empire-wide organization would lack news from the British Isles. In 1918, Lord Beaverbrook, then at the Ministry of Information, raised the possibility of establishing a news pool in London to facilitate the wider dissemination of imperial news, but the PA, Reuters, and London press rejected the idea in favor of reducing the rates of cable transmission. Reuters was "the news agency of the British Empire," as its principal chronicler has claimed, only because the imperial press lacked sufficient incentives to cooperate.[63]

---

[61] Rickatson-Hatt to Jones, March 21, 1934, Jones papers, series 1, box 35, RA.

[62] As cited in G. Allen, "North American Triangle: Canadian Press, Associated Press, and Reuters, 1918–1939," in P. Putnis, C. Kaul, and J. Wilke (eds.), *International Circuits of News: Historical Studies* (Cresskill, NJ: Hampton Press, 2011), p. 17.

[63] Canadian empire cooperative news scheme, February 23, 1931, Jones papers, series 1, box 37; Jones memo, September 8, 1932, Jones papers, series 1, box 37; Jones memo, July 5, 1934, Jones papers, series 1, box 37; Jones to Dunn, July 13, 1934, Jones papers, series 1, box 42; Jones to Ewing, October 3, 1934, Jones papers, series 1, box 34; Unsigned, undated, 1935, Jones papers, series 1, box 41; Jones to Livesay, August 9, 1939, Jones papers, series 1, box 46, RA; Manager's memoranda, July 10, 1918, PA, Ms 35358/20, pp. 118–9, GL. D. Cryle, "The Empire Press Union and Antipodean Communications: Australian-New Zealand Involvement, 1909–50," *Media History*, 8 (2002), 49–62; S.J. Potter, *News and the British World: The Emergence of an Imperial Press System, 1876–1922* (Oxford: Clarendon Press, 2003); S.J.

THE THREAT OF IMPERIAL BROADCASTING

As the long-standing British subsidy for the domestic press shifted to radio, the BBC Empire Wireless service, inaugurated in 1932, jeopardized the tenuous hold Reuters had over the distribution of news in the colonies and dominions. By 1926, Reuters already complained of unfair competition from the British Official Wireless (BOW), the government's publicity service. In the summer of that year, local unrest in Aden prompted dissemination of the BOW service there. The BOW service threatened to kill entirely, or render unprofitable, Reuters's service at Aden. The naval or army authorities at Aden received the service, and the handling costs incurred delivering the radiograms were nominal. The official service considerably undercut Reuters, which had to pay the cost of wireless or telegraphic transmission. "Here is a case that illustrates the iniquity and monstrous injustice of this state-paid-for news service," wrote Roderick Jones, "I fear our Aden revenue is seriously threatened."[64]

The BBC Empire Wireless service, which contained the cream of Reuters's world news report, was especially damaging to the agency's exclusive overseas contracts. The imperial broadcast presented particular problems for Reuters with respect to Australia, where the agency had sold to the Australian Press Association the copyright to its news for publication in newspapers. Reuters was willing, under the pretense of imperial and public policy considerations, to assent to the broadcasting of its news by the BBC to dissuade the corporation from conducting its own newsgathering, but the Australian press objected to the agreement and demanded indemnity for breach of contract and any losses incurred by permitting the BBC to broadcast Reuters's news in Australia.[65]

Reuters's managers contended that the Empire service perpetrated the same unfair competition overseas as it did at home and that it threatened to undermine the market value of Reuters's news reports throughout the Empire. "Normally," wrote Roderick Jones to John Reith, director-general of the BBC,

we should reimburse ourselves by raising our charges to the newspapers. We have been able to do this stage by stage in the case of the overseas press. But we have been prevented from doing so in the case of the newspapers of the British Isles because in their view the increase in the market value to them of the admitted improvement in the Reuter Service has been cancelled out by the widespread B.B.C. publication in the

---

Potter, "Communication and Integration: the British Dominion Press and the British World, c. 1876–1914," *Journal of Imperial and Commonwealth History*, 31 (2003), 190–206; S.J. Potter, "Webs, Networks, and Systems: Globalization and the Mass Media in the Nineteenth- and Twentieth-Century British Empire," *Journal of British Studies*, 46 (2007), 634.

64 Jones to Clements, June 7, 1926, Jones papers, series 1, box 57, RA.
65 Jones to Reith, December 16, 1932, R28/162/1, BBC; Australian news associations and the empire broadcast. Interview with Sir John Reith, July 15, 1932, Jones papers, series 1, box 37, RA.

British Isles of Reuters' news. We are now going to be faced with exactly the same situation overseas.[66]

In fact, the real but unmentioned threat to Reuters was that potential rivals to the established combines in the dominions and colonies would use the broadcast service to the detriment of Reuters and its allied publishers. A service controlled by Reuters at all times could be reserved exclusively for its subscribers. Newspaper publishers throughout the Empire who benefitted from privileged access to Reuters's news reports were also reluctant to have them distributed throughout the world at all hours for anybody to pick up at no cost. In response to the perceived threat of broadcasting, the publishers attached to Reuters throughout the Empire pursued a strategy similar to that taken by the British press. Through the Empire Press Union, these publishers combined and sought to confine the BBC news service within certain limits.[67]

Reuters achieved some success in limiting the BBC's independent newsgathering. In 1935, Jones and the newspapers prevented the Corporation from sending its own correspondent to cover the Italian invasion of Abyssinia. "It certainly would put up the backs of the newspapers," wrote Jones to Reith, "who would resent, and in my judgment rightly resent, the introduction of this new competition into their news field." After the report of the Ullswater Committee in 1936, which argued in favor of an increased remit for the BBC, the news agencies and newspapers could no longer object to the BBC obtaining news for its own broadcasting purposes from any source on which it desired to draw. But, wrote Jones to Samuel Storey MP, founder of the Sunderland *Echo*, "that should not entitle them, a monopoly established under Royal Charter, to enter into trade competition with the existing and old-established News Agencies."[68] Jones anticipated that the service from Abyssinia would cost Reuters £4,000 per month, for which they charged the newspapers extra and agreed to provide to the BBC gratis. Jones claimed, however, that if the BBC elected to send its own correspondent to the field then Reuters would have to charge the BBC similarly.[69] In effect, the only thing that prevented the BBC from undertaking its own newsgathering was the promise of a subsidy from the press.

Efforts by Reuters to stem the tide in news broadcasting achieved only limited success. In 1936, the BBC beat Reuters's cabled reports of the death of King George by half an hour in South Africa, in the Straits Settlements, and likewise in India, which caused the newspapers of the Empire anxiety. In the case of the royal funeral, the first that was broadcast, the BBC had outside Westminster six microphones that enabled listeners to follow closely the departure of the cortege and its progress past St. James' Palace, where the BBC

---

[66] Jones to Reith, December 16, 1932, R28/162/1, BBC.
[67] Australian news association and the Empire broadcast. Meeting with sub-committee of the Empire Press Union, July 15, 1932, Jones papers, series 1, box 37, RA.
[68] RJ to Storey, December 16, 1936, Jones papers, series 1, box 43, RA.
[69] Jones on meeting with Reith, September 18, 1935, Jones papers, series 1, box 42, RA.

placed an additional three microphones. There were also two microphones in Hyde Park and sixteen at Windsor Castle together with two microphones for the special use of foreign officials. Direct channels for supplying the broadcast to countries abroad were placed at the disposal of the BBC by the postmaster-general, with the result that nearly every European country, North and South America, Japan, and several countries of North Africa simultaneously received a broadcast of the funeral service from Windsor Castle.[70] In October 1938, Jones wrote to C.G. Graves, BBC deputy director-general, explaining that Reuters's Australian clients were irked by the redistribution of a recent speech by Hitler. "Had the public necessity for maintaining rediffusion persisted much longer, we should have been faced with a major problem," wrote Jones. "I do trust that, for all our sakes, we shall not be confronted with it some day in the future."[71]

In India, vernacular papers not under contract to Reuters took material off the BBC wireless and published it in advance of the arrival of Reuters's service, which greatly annoyed the agency's allies. Reuters again drafted and proposed a news protection bill that would have granted it a limited property right in its telegrams, but it did not become law.[72] The request by the BBC to rebroadcast Hitler's Nuremberg speech in September 1939 on grounds of grave international emergency created a significant conflict for Reuters, which had to break its contracts with newspapers and news agencies abroad to permit the BBC this use of its news. "We decided that at such a critical juncture the national interest must come first," wrote Jones to Sir Keith Murdoch in Australia, "and we gave the desired permission, though only after anxious thought, bearing in mind the serious consequences to ourselves, as well as to the newspapers." "If there is anything we can do to strengthen your hands against wireless and other telegraphic or broadcasting news rivalries with which you have to contend," continued Jones, "you may confidently count upon our co-operating with you to the utmost of our ability."[73]

Reuters was gored on the horns of a dilemma: continued good relations with the Foreign Office obliged Reuters to consider the "national interest," but by authorizing rebroadcasting over the whole of the world Reuters incurred substantial risk. Jones was obliged to authorize rebroadcasting via the BBC of Reuters's news, both in English and in foreign languages, to all foreign countries, to all ships at sea, and eventually throughout the British Empire. Copyright in the overseas bulletin belonged to the BBC, but the corporation assigned to Reuters the publication rights in the bulletins for the purpose of enabling it to authorize newspapers to print parts of the bulletin and to prevent

[70] Murray to Jones, February 25, 1936, Jones papers, series 1, box 39, RA.
[71] Jones to Graves, October 20, 1938, Jones papers, series 1, box 44, RA.
[72] Jones to Desmond Young, October 10, 1938, Jones papers, series 1, box 44, RA.
[73] RJ to Sir Keith Murdoch, January 14, 1939, Jones papers, series 1, box 44, RA.

the news from being misappropriated by newspapers not privy to Reuters's reports.[74] As the war progressed, the government deemed new emergency measures necessary to keep the populace informed. These measures further contradicted Reuters's interests. Privately, Jones lamented the passing of the clubby days when John Reith was at the helm. By 1940, complained Jones, he had to contend with "an increasingly self-satisfied, not to say arrogant, spirit of the B.B.C. in all that appertains to news." "I realize more and more," wrote Jones, "how much we owed to Sir John's restraining hand," although "at the same time it must in fairness be admitted that War conditions have contributed in every direction to the advancement of B.B.C. ambitions."[75] Reith believed that the agencies were "honest" and "out to give us the best service they can," but new management was convinced that the interests of a news seller and a propaganda news broadcaster were incompatible.[76]

A STRATEGY OF DIVERSIFICATION: REUTERS, RADIO, AND THE RISE OF MARKET INTELLIGENCE

Although news was Reuters's flagship business, owing to the difficulties it encountered at home and abroad, news could not serve as its principal source of profit. In 1865, Paul Julius Reuter took his company public to raise capital for the construction of a telegraph cable between Lowestoft and the north-German island of Nordeney. Sale of the cable to the British government in 1868 generated considerable profits. Disproportionately high profits between 1873 and 1877 were attributable to a joint-purse agreement with Agence Havas, the French news agency. Profits were stable thereafter until they declined in 1885 and dropped drastically in 1888. Successive conflicts in Burma, Egypt, Russia, Servo-Bulgaria, and Sudan greatly depleted the company's working capital. The protracted civil war between the settlers of Canudos and the nascent republic of the United States of Brazil, troubles in Argentina between the government and the Union Civica, an organization of radical farmers, and the Matabele War in present-day Zimbabwe occasioned heavy expenditures. The financial crisis in 1893 exacerbated the downward trend. A fall in eastern exchanges attributable to the devaluation of Chinese, Indian, and Japanese currencies, which followed the demonetization and subsequent over-abundance of silver after 1870, compounded the large outlay necessitated by political events. Subscriptions to Reuters's news services in China, India, and the Straits Settlements were paid in silver and the company lost considerably by the decline in the value of the dollar and rupee. Losses led to modifications in arrangements for the transmission of news to China and the Straits (Table 6.5).

---

[74] Brown to Turner, November 27, 1939, R28/159, BBC.
[75] RJ to Ewing, March 27, 1940, Jones papers, series 1, box 72, RA.
[76] Reith memo, March 25, 1929, R28/177/2, BBC.

TABLE 6.5. *Reuters's average overseas gross profits, 1869–1938 (in £ at constant 1913 prices)*

	1869/73	1874/78	1879/83	1884/88	1889/93	1894/98	1899/03
Profits	5,587.4	10,772.2	9,999.2	8,050.0	2,286.0	8,846.0	15,937.6

	1904/08	1909/13	1914/18	1919/23	1924/28	1929/33	1934/38
Profits	22,516.0	21,364.8	22,831.8	15,471.6	21,033.6	24,124.3	26,303.6

Source: Calculated from profit and loss statements, LN 224, RA.

Development during the 1890s of alternative sources of revenue helped to counteract these fluctuations and improved the financial position of the company. A private telegram and a remittance business provided Reuters with a significant proportion of its gross profits between 1890 and 1920, but during World War I, several poorly placed loans crippled Reuters's bank and the remittance business withered. The custom of the private telegram department dwindled after 1900 as imperial telegram tariffs decreased. It fell off drastically during the war, but flourished briefly during the early 1920s.[77] Revenue from the British press did not compensate for these losses. More and more, circumstances in Britain obliged Reuters to subsidize its news services to the PA out of the money it obtained abroad, and particularly from its growing commercial news services. "It is impossible not to realise," said Jones to the Reuters's board of directors in 1937, "how dependent we are for our financial stability, indeed for our very existence, upon our territories abroad." In the financial year prior to Jones' report to the board, Reuters's total revenue from the newspapers of Britain was £68,400 out of a total press revenue of nearly £300,000, or out of a combined press and commercial services revenue of £473,000.[78]

After 1924, most of the revenue Reuters earned abroad came from its commercial news services, not from its services to newspapers. Although the company had always been in the commercial news business, it did not make much money from this line of work until the 1920s. Between 1869 and 1915, the return on Reuters's commercial services averaged less than 2 percent of total profits per annum.[79] Before arriving in England, Paul Julius Reuter had filled a niche by bridging interstices in the nascent European telegraph network with alternative means of communication, such as homing pigeons. By the 1850s, the rapid erection of special telegraph lines connecting the principal British exchanges and linking these exchanges directly to important banks and merchants in the City of London closed off this market to Reuters. Indeed, bankers and brokers made the greatest use of private telegraph and telephone

---

[77] Termination of private telegram service, March 22, 1915, LN/8715619, RA.
[78] Report to annual meeting of shareholders, June 17, 1937, Jones papers, series 1, box 71, RA.
[79] *Contra* O. Boyd-Barrett, "'Global' News Agencies," in Boyd-Barrett and Rantanen, *Globalization of News*, p. 24.

lines. Connections to foreign markets, however, were still tenuous.[80] Reuters focused on the European market, in which Paul Julius Reuter's personal connections gave the company an advantage, but by the 1870s, telegraph connections abroad had improved and companies obtained their own information from foreign markets. Reuters's advantage lay in its far-reaching organization and consequent ability to assemble market information from numerous locations, but telegraphic dispatch times, both in terms of collection and distribution, and the need to readdress reports to multiple locations, limited the value of this otherwise impressive organization. During the 1890s, Herbert de Reuter made attempts to develop the company's commercial services, but found it difficult to locate customers.[81] The lackluster performance of Reuters's news services, commercial and otherwise, accounts for the company's strategy of diversification, and explains why, in addition to collecting and distributing the news, the company also developed a business of private telegrams, remittances, and eventually a banking business.

Reuters's domestic alliances also restricted the early development of its commercial news business in Britain. In the PA-Reuters agreement of 1884, Reuters retained the right to supply foreign commercial information to private subscribers in the provinces but not to newspapers, newsrooms, exchanges, or public institutions. Reuters's rights in this respect were carried forward in subsequent agreements up to 1944. Additionally, a restrictive agreement with Lloyd's of London, which Reuters had entered into in 1889, curtailed the development of the agency's shipping news.[82] Until a short time after World War I, Reuters had its own provincial offices in Manchester, Liverpool, Birmingham, and Glasgow, on account of the importance of the inward and outward cotton services edited and distributed from there. These provincial offices collected and supplied commercial intelligence for private subscribers, but they dealt mainly with the supplementary private telegram and remittance business, and consequently closed when these services failed during war.

In the 1920s and 1930s, the PA's preexisting agreements with Extel for the distribution of commercial information further restricted Reuters's opportunity to maneuver in Britain. In 1920, Reuters established its Trade Service, which contained reports principally for trade periodicals and merchants and did not include raw data and financial prices. The PA was invited but chose not to participate in this enterprise. Consequently, the Trade Service was specifically

[80] R.C. Michie, *The London and New York Stock Exchanges, 1850–1914* (London: Allen & Unwin, 1987), pp. 9, 38–9; N. Ferguson, *The World's Banker: The History of the House of Rothschild* (London: Weidenfeld & Nicolson, 1998), p. 573; D. Gabel, "Private Telecommunications Networks: an Historical Perspective," in E. Noam and A. NiShuilleabhain (eds.), *Private Networks Public Objectives* (Amsterdam: Elsevier, 1996), pp. 41–2.

[81] Murray to Jones, August 12, 1922, Clements to Jones, August 15, 1922, Jones papers, series 1, box 32, RA.

[82] Memorandum agreement with Reuters, February 4, 1889, in Memorandum with regard to the agreements with Reuters and the Press Association, Lloyd's Archives, Ms 31646, GL.

excluded from the contract between Reuters and the PA in 1921 and Reuters was left free to exploit it anywhere except in daily and Sunday newspapers in Britain. The PA was to supply all its general, sports, and commercial news to Reuters, but it withheld from Reuters the commercial service it jointly created with Extel. In their 1930 agreement, the PA service to Reuters included all general, parliamentary, financial, commercial, and sporting news services "other than the PA-Extel Joint Service of sporting news and service of London Stock Exchange and market news."[83] The PA granted the "opportunity," not the "right," to Reuters to supply its overseas commercial and financial intelligence to private subscribers and exchanges as long as it did not compete, displace, or interfere with the services of the PA and Extel. The PA was to receive 10 percent of all subscriptions obtained under this concession, but the limitations imposed on Reuters meant it obtained few. This led to a modification in 1931. The PA then agreed to the inclusion in Reuters's commercial ticker service of some Reuters-collected British commercial news and occasional PA items of important home news having a bearing on commercial affairs. In return, Reuters paid the PA a rebate of £1 10s per annum per subscriber.

The PA controlled the territory outside London, therefore Reuters could neither meet requests from provincial firms for its services nor could it advertise its commercial ticker service. Small firms ate into Reuters's profits. "How long," complained W.L. Murray, Reuters's secretary, "must potential revenue be lost because of our lacking a free hand with out commercial service in the Provinces!"[84] Extel exploited Reuters's precarious position. Meanwhile, the commercial news service from the PA and Extel suffered for want of foreign news. Only in 1944 did Reuters gain the right to supply home news of market interest in London and Liverpool and to sell its Trade Service to newspapers.[85]

[83] Proposed tape service, April 15, 1919, Jones papers, series 1, box 33; Murray to Jones, November 4, 1919, Jones papers, series 1, box 33; Murray to Jones, October 14, 1929, Jones papers, series 1, box 68; Murray to Jones, January 10 and 22, 1930, Jones papers, series 1, box 68; Unsigned memo, March 6, 1930, Jones papers, series 1, box 68; Unsigned, Reuters' commercial services to the British Isles, July 28, 1933, Jones papers, series 1, box 37; Murray to Jones, September 24, 1937, Jones papers, series 1, box 69; Fleetwood-May to Jones, December 17, 1937, Jones papers, series 1, box 38; Jones to Mann, February 16, 1940, Jones papers, series 1, box 72, RA.

[84] Assistant controller to Jones, September 5, 1938, Jones papers, series 1, box 38, RA.

[85] Murray to Jones, November 12, 1919, Jones papers, series 1, box 33; Fleetwood-May to Murray, May 26, 1932, Jones papers, series 1, box 38; Fleetwood-May to Jones, October 14, 1932, Jones papers, series 1, box 38; Jones memo, May 30, 1934, Jones papers, series 1, box 37; Jones to Napier, July 16, 1934, Jones papers, series 1, box 42; Jones memo, October 16, 1935, Jones papers, series 1, box 42; Jones to Fleetwood-May, November 28, 1935, Jones papers, series 1, box 42; Murray to Jones, January 14, 1936, Jones papers, series 1, box 82; Murray to Jones, February 26, 1936, Jones papers, series 1, box 39; Fleetwood-May to Jones, March 18, 1936, Jones papers, series 1, box 39; Fleetwood-May to Jones, May 4, 1936, Jones papers, series 1, box 82; Murray to Jones, May 5, 1936, Jones papers, series 1, box 82; Jones memo, July 21, 1936, Jones papers, series 1, box 42; Jones to Bayley, July 23, 1936, Jones papers, series 1, box

After World War I, wireless telegraphy created a new market for Reuters's commercial news services abroad. Reuters exploited this opportunity to considerable gain, which laid the foundation for the company's future in the financial information sector. Owing to the favorable treatment it received from the Ministry of Information, Reuters's position in the commercial news market improved during the war, but it was wireless that enabled Reuters to succeed. Reuters could send by wireless a multi-addressed commercial service and forestall private firms that relied on the telegraph and telephone to obtain such information. Telephones, cables, and land-lines all performed essential functions, but it was only via wireless that simultaneous communication to large numbers of widely separated points, irrespective of distance, could be achieved. A wireless service displaced a considerable proportion of the telegraphic matter that bankers, brokers, and others obtained privately on their own account, and enabled them to effect such savings in their telegraph bills that they paid the substantial subscription that Reuters charged for the service.

By 1928, Roderick Jones could proudly claim that Reuters's "service of Financial and Commercial quotations and Markets intelligence generally is now, after several years of assiduous labour, easily the largest, the most widely distributed, and the most trusted in the world."[86] Between 1926 and 1930, these services nearly doubled in terms of wordage. By 1934, Reuters's revenue from the British press represented only two-thirds of the commercial service revenue from the Far East alone, and by the end of the 1930s, these services provided the revenue necessary to cover losses the company incurred in its news operations.[87] The continued expansion of these services enabled Reuters's revenue to exceed that of the AP by the late 1970s.[88]

To assemble a commercial news report with information from around the world required extensive organization. It was critical to keep the service uniform at each bureau so that subscribers could be transferred from one branch to another in India or the Far East and find the same form of service. Reuters's managers could also be changed around and issue the service without having to learn a different set of operations. The work was more labor intensive than the preparation of regular news services and required an increase in staff. In the London office a staff of more than sixty workers were engaged in this work. Large staffs were also employed at offices in Bombay, New York, and Shanghai. London served as the main distribution center from which the quotations were sent via wireless. Stock prices were transmitted two or three minutes after

---

43; Minutes of board meeting, July 28, 1936, Jones papers, series 1, box 73; Jones to Wearne, August 5, 1936, Jones papers, series 1, box 43; Fleetwood-May, Reuters' commercial services in the United Kingdom, August 14, 1957, LN 954/013299, RA.

[86] Jones AGM speech, June 5, 1928, Jones papers, series 1, box 66, RA.

[87] Lelas to Jones, October 20, 1925, Jones papers, series 1, box 36; W. Turner, Memorandum on the commercial-news side of Reuter, October 23, 1934, Jones papers, series 1, box 39; Jones, AGM speech, July 5, 1938, LN36/868218, RA.

[88] Unsigned, report, May 26, 1981, AP-Reuters red file, RA.

transactions took place in London, Liverpool, or New York. By the late 1930s, between 9 a.m. and 11 p.m. daily, 175 separate wireless broadcasts were sent from Reuters to branches and affiliations. Quotations were also telephoned and extensive services were made by cable throughout the world.[89]

Reuters kept an eye on a wide array of daily commercial figures. It monitored the Kaffir trade for subscribers in Johannesburg, provided a Liverpool cotton review, tracked payments on Chinese loan coupons, and sent Dundee flax reports to Riga. It transmitted a report on fruit to Jerusalem from the Imperial Economic Committee and notices on pineapple to Singapore. Reports from London wool auctions were sent to Amsterdam, Belgium, Johannesburg, and Marseilles. Silk statistics were sent monthly to New York from Berlin, London, and Paris, as were returns from the Board of Trade. Linen and linen waste reports were sent to Russian subscribers, and a weekly stock market report was assembled for the BBC. Aside from this wealth of data, of great interest to subscribers was the cause of fluctuations in these figures. To find an explanation required knowledge of the market, an appreciation of current developments, and discussion with those involved in the respective market. For example, prior to a routine meeting of the International Rubber Committee at which an announcement was made regarding quotas, Reuters's staff discussed the prospects and outlook with various experts and the arguments were crystalized and sent to interested subscribers. At the time of the meeting, a reporter waited on the Colonial Office for the communiqué and the office in London flashed the result everywhere. After the communiqué a "first reaction" was prepared and sent and after that as soon as possible market opinion was sought and a "reaction cable" prepared and sent (Table 6.6).[90]

Reuters's index of twenty-one staple commodity prices provided a new and important market service. Each commodity was weighted in accordance with its importance in international trade and adjustments were made to the individual prices to ensure accuracy and continuity. This was the first index of its kind in Britain, and it gained worldwide acceptance. Prior to its development, one could learn that cotton had risen fifteen points a pound, rubber had declined a farthing a pound, sugar sixpence a hundredweight, and so on for a large number of commodities. But there was no way of knowing what had been the general movement of prices, whether, and by how much, the rises in wheat and cotton were more important than the falls in rubber and sugar, and so on. Various authorities did publish index numbers, but only at weekly or monthly intervals and then not promptly. Their methods were, in some cases,

---

[89] Outward financial and commercial services, October 8, 1919; Murray to Jones, October 14, 1919, Jones papers, series 1, box 33; Murray to Jones, February 17, 1920, Jones papers, series 1, box 33; Lelas to Jones, January 3, 1928, Jones papers, series 1, box 36; Jones, note for Mr. Burgess, April 20, 1931, Jones papers, series 1, box 34, RA.

[90] Lelas, to Jones, January 3, 1928, Jones papers, series 1, box 36; Unsigned memo, April 11, 1939, Jones papers, series 1, box 45; Report of H. Jacobi, April 12, 1939, Jones papers, series 1, box 45, RA.

TABLE 6.6. *Reuters's commercial clients, 1939*

Location	No. of clients	Service
Australasia	345	Stocks and shares, cotton, wool, metals, wheat, petroleum, etc.
South Africa	176	Grain, hides and skins, wool, coffee, metals, stocks and shares, exchange rates, etc.
India, Burma, Ceylon	296	"
Singapore	56	"
Hong Kong	89	"
Palestine, Egypt	190	"
Far East	258	"

Source: Reuters's economic services, November 25, 1939, RA, J.1.45.

not up-to-date and in no case were the compilers of the index also the authorities for the individual prices they included, with the result that the latter were sometimes unrealistic. In Reuters's case, its own reporters obtained every price on the various exchanges, so that the agency was able to check immediately on any report that appeared inaccurate, and could guarantee that each price included was the genuine market quotation. The index was issued on Reuters's commercial ticker within twenty-five minutes of the close of the principal markets each day, and featured daily in the leading newspapers of England as well as being widely quoted in Japan and South Africa. Initially, because the service was not used much in the United States, the American government cabled its embassy in England requesting Reuters's information.[91]

Markets for wheat and cotton were susceptible to weather reports, which frequently caused wide fluctuations in prices. Several exchanges supplied Reuters with weather maps that showed conditions each day in the areas where the crops were grown. In the case of cotton, Reuters posted two such maps each day. To show the weather existing in the cotton belt, and also conditions in areas that might affect the cotton belt later, reports were obtained from a large number of stations in a wide area – practically the whole of the continental United States as well as the West Indies and other areas, and reports from ships in those areas. This information was mapped and posted in Liverpool within about an hour-and-a-half of the actual taking of the observation in the various interior points in the United States.

The effects of the commercial and financial services were most pronounced in countries where market information was scarce and prices fluctuated, such as China. In Hong Kong, Reuters had benefited from the Telegraph Messages Ordinance of 1894, which, like the other acts throughout the Empire, provided

---

[91] Unsigned, notes on statistical department work supplied by Mr. Gampell, undated, Jones papers, series 1, box 39, RA.

a limited copyright in telegrams. In effect, the Ordinance granted Reuters a property right in news for thirty-six hours. Although this protection served the agency's purposes for many years, with the advent of Reuters's commercial service in Hong Kong, and wireless telegraphy and wireless telephony, Reuters found that unauthorized persons retransmitted portions of its news by wireless and telegraphy to nonsubscribers in Canton and other places outside of the colony immediately after publication in Hong Kong.[92]

Reuters eliminated smaller niche information services provided by local markets, exchanges, and chambers of commerce throughout the world. In India, Reuters conquered competition from chambers of commerce at Bombay, Cawnpore (Kanpore), and Calcutta as well as the Government Sugar Bureau at Pusa and the Cotton Information Bureau, which served a number of bucket shops. Stock exchanges throughout the world, although initially unwilling to permit Reuters to have access to their ticker tape machines for fear that access would undermine the control and utility of the exchange, gradually were obliged to grant Reuters entry.[93] By providing frequent and reliable information, Reuters's commercial service appears to have increased knowledge among businesspeople about foreign markets and decreased market imperfections. In 1934, urgent dispatches traveled from New York to London in thirty-five seconds, from New York to Bombay in sixty seconds, from Shanghai to Bombay via London in two to four minutes, and from London to Berlin and the main Continental centers in twenty seconds. Through Reuters, private traders in Asian cotton markets knew the official figures of the American cotton crops one and a half minutes after they were announced in Washington. The financial centers of Europe and Asia first learned the Bank of England rate a few seconds after it was announced. Bank of England officials, in other parts of the headquarters building also first learned the rate through Reuters's ticker service. Exchanges in Alexandria, Kolkata, Hong Kong, Shanghai, Singapore, and Tokyo, among others, knew the New York-London opening and closing cross-rates a few minutes after their issue in London and New York. These times were significantly faster than reception times achieved via telegraph. Increased speed in transmission reduced variable reception times and made consumption of information between recipients more equal in time.[94]

---

[92] W. Turner to Reuters general manager, New York, December 11, 1924, APo.2A, box 14, folder 2, AP.

[93] Lelas to Jones, October 20, 1925; Fleetwood-May memo, February 16, 1926, Jones papers, series 1, box 36, RA; Fleetwood-May to Jones, March 30, 1931, Jones papers, series 1, box 36, RA; Fleetwood-May to Jones, August 13, 1931, Jones papers, series 1, box 36, RA; Jones to Dunn, November 8, 1934, Jones papers, series 1, box 42, RA.

[94] Fleetwood-May, Reuters' commercial services, October 3, 1934, Jones papers, series 1, box 39, RA; G. Bakker, "Trading facts: Arrow's Fundamental Paradox and the Emergence of Global News Networks, 1750–1900," *Working Papers on the Nature of Evidence: How Well do Facts Travel?* (June 2007), pp. 16–9. September 13, 2008 (www.lse.ac.uk).

Anecdotally, Reuters's services provided a high standard of accuracy that facilitated transactions. Oil importers signed contracts to accept deliveries at "Reuters' current quotation," and the same quotations were accepted as a final authority in courts of law both in England and abroad. The BBC announced that a Reuters message regarding the South African gold mine tax had reversed a decline in the market.[95] Through these commercial services, Reuters finally found a stable way in which to subsidize its newsgathering business, just when the international field was becoming less cooperative and more competitive.

Reuters, the so-called news agency of the British Empire, found conducting its imperial mission problematic. The principal source of difficulty lay in finding an appropriate balance between cooperation and exclusivity. Beginning in South Africa, Reuters sought to achieve a suitable balance by forming partnerships with the imperial press. Ownership of the apparatus of news provision by the press increased transparency overseas just as it did in the British Isles and in the United States. It also enabled the press in conjunction with Reuters to exercise greater control over access to the news throughout the Empire. But Reuters's troubled position in the Empire restricted its profitability. Matters became worse for Reuters when British policy makers began to favor the BBC over the press. Consequently Reuters had to rely increasingly on alternative sources of revenue to cross-subsidize the supply of news. As with the PA and telegraphy, the Post Office granted Reuters preferential access to broadcasting facilities, which enabled the news agency to establish a profitable business of market intelligence that underwrote the supply of foreign news to the newspapers of the British Isles. As the next chapter shows, Reuters's partnerships with the imperial press and its move toward the supply of commercial information also helped it to contend with increased global competition.

[95] Jones, notes for Mr. Burgess, April 20, 1931, Jones papers, series 1, box 34; Unsigned, May 5, 1925, LN960 1/013632; Murray to Jones, May 25, 1933, Jones papers, series 1, box 69; Fleetwood-May to Jones, June 2, 1933, Jones papers, series 1, box 78, RA.

7

Cartel or Free Trade: Supplying the World's News, 1856–1947

In 1942, Kent Cooper, general manager of the AP, wrote *Barriers Down*, a book in which he told of his "great crusade" against the "most powerful international monopoly of the nineteenth century": the European news agencies. In the book, Cooper developed his thesis that through exclusive cooperative agreements, these agencies had placed restrictions on the "freedom of international news exchange," contributed to the causes of World War II, and that there could be no "permanent peace" unless this freedom was guaranteed.[1] Yet these agreements were at the center of the antitrust suit brought against the AP. In fact, Cooper's book was partly intended to exculpate the AP from the suit. The eminent First-Amendment scholar Zechariah Chafee found it "inconceivable" that "men like Kent Cooper who put the barriers down in Europe think the barriers to the free flow of news should be kept high at home."[2] Managers at the UP, Reuters, and even the AP regarded the book's narrative as misleading. In fact, in 1942, the same year the book was published, Cooper and Reuters concluded another cooperative contract. Agreements along these lines continued in various forms until at least 1967.

Cooper's bias and hypocrisy are insufficient reasons to ignore his central thesis. Cooper's idea that breaking down "the dams holding up the free exchange of news" would contribute to peace was a byproduct of, and integral to, the metaphor of the marketplace for ideas. Such logic was also a continuation, albeit in another form, of the rationalist illusion according to which

[1] K. Cooper, *Barriers Down; The Story of the News Agency Epoch* (Port Washington, NY: Kennikat Press, 1942), pp. 7–9. For a more concise statement of the same thesis see, K. Cooper, "Newspaper Statesmanship for Peace," in F.L. Mott (ed.), *Journalism in Wartime* (Washington, DC: American Council on Public Affairs, 1943), pp. 214–16.

[2] Chafee, "How the Associated Press can Uphold Liberty of the Press," undated (c. 1943), AP01.4B, series IX, box 52, folder 882, AP.

news, if freely and competitively traded, is said to increase knowledge. In fact, cooperation was an effective means to subsidize the collection and supply of international news. However, as in the United States, the British Isles, and the British Empire, the world's leading news agencies had to search continually for a balance between exclusivity and cooperation that fit with changing economic, political, and technological conditions.

From the 1850s until the 1930s, the principal news agencies of Europe exchanged news exclusively. These arrangements constituted a cartel, albeit particularly suited to the unusual needs of the newsgathering business.³ Scholars familiar with the history of cartels will recognize that the agreements among the news agencies and associations were unusual in several respects. The news agency cartel lasted in one form or another for more than 100 years, which is longer than most cartels. It is also atypical that the news agency cartel formed during the nineteenth century, in a time of "high globalization" when few cartels existed, and encountered difficulties in the interwar period, when globalization was at a low ebb and cartels proliferated.⁴ Despite its unusual features and operation, the news agency cartel, like all other cartel agreements, was designed to bring competition under control and enhance the long-term profits of its members. Although advantageous to members and disadvantageous to nonmembers, it also facilitated the distribution of news.

³ These agreements are now widely referred to as a cartel, but the word was not widely used at the time. Neither Victor Rosewater, publisher of the Omaha *Bee*, nor Karl Bickel, UP president from 1923 to 1935, made mention of the word in their books about the history of newsgathering, nor did Webb Miller, correspondent for the UP, or Oliver Gramling, head of the AP membership department, whose official history of the AP was published in 1940. K. Bickel, *News Empires: The Newspaper and the Radio* (Philadelphia: J.B. Lippincott Co., 1930); W. Miller, *I Found no Peace* (Garden City, NY: Garden City Publishing, 1938); Gramling, *AP*. Roderick Jones did not use the word in his biography, and Graham Storey had no place for it in his history of Reuters. Cooper used the word in "Freedom of information," *Life*, 17 (November 13, 1944), pp. 55–60 and UNESCO used it once in a 1953 report. Cooper made liberal use of the word in his next book, *The Right to Know*, and Joe Alex Morris, once foreign editor of the UP, deployed it in his history of that agency. R. Jones, *A Life in Reuters* (London: Hodder and Stoughton, 1951); G. Storey, *Reuters' Century*; UNESCO, *News Agencies, Their Structure and Operation* (Paris: UNESCO, 1953); K. Cooper, *The Right to Know: An Exposition of the Evils of News Suppression and Propaganda* (New York: Farrar, Straus and Cudahy, 1956); Morris, *Deadline Every Minute*. Starting with O. Boyd-Barrett, *The International News Agencies* (London: Constable, 1980), most academics have described the relationship as a cartel. See J. Fenby, *The International News Services* (New York: Schocken Books, 1986); R.A. Schwarzlose, *Nation's Newsbrokers*; Boyd-Barrett and Rantanen (eds.), *Globalization of News*; Nalbach, "'The Software of Empire'"; S.J. Potter, *Newspapers and Empire in Ireland and Britain* (Dublin: Four Courts, 2004); Winseck and Pike, *Communication and Empire*. A notable exception is Read, *Power of News*.
⁴ Cartels can come in many forms. See J. Fear, "Cartels," in G. Jones and J. Zeitlin (eds.), *The Oxford Handbook of Business History* (Oxford: Oxford University Press, 2008), pp. 268–92.

FORGING INTERNATIONAL COOPERATION

In the 1850s, during the heyday of free trade, the British, French, and German news agencies – Reuters, Havas, and Wolff – agreed to cooperate. The New York Associated Press participated in these agreements by 1865, and the AP inherited the contracts in 1893. Paul Julius Reuter, Charles Havas, and Bernard Wolff, the founders of the three eponymous agencies, all of whom knew each other before Reuter set up shop in London in 1851, agreed to avoid competition with each other, divide markets, enter into exclusive contracts, and refuse to exchange or sell their news to rival organizations. Personal connections contributed to the success of these agencies in much the same way as they did for the great banks of nineteenth-century Europe.[5] In their formal agreement of 1859, the oldest that survives in the archives but apparently their second since 1856, Havas, Reuter, and Wolff agreed "mutually to assist one another in the extension and the development of the telegraphic services, in such a way as to prevent attempts at competition and to increase the services according to the needs of the public, of the press and the development of the telegraphic lines."[6] Reuter, Havas, and Wolff believed, just as much as the members of the PA and the AP who came later, that by combining their efforts they could better serve the public and themselves.

The reasons for cooperating in the assembly of international news reports were the same as those behind the establishment of cooperative arrangements for the collection of domestic news. The great expense, uncertainty, and other difficulties surrounding international newsgathering in the 1850s made the rationale for cooperation even stronger. Some form of exchange among the agencies promised to reduce the costs of collection, control competition, increase the quantity of news available for distribution, and build up each agency into an effective partner. For each agency to employ correspondents in every European city was unnecessary if their task was to copy the news from the local papers and wire it to the central office. It was cheaper to rely on the agents of a local organization to obtain the information, even more so if the agent was a trustworthy friend. In their early contracts, the agencies agreed to send telegrams abroad exclusively through the allied agencies, and each news agency was required to gather news from its respective territory. For good business reasons as much as diplomacy, the agencies apportioned territory according to geographic propinquity and the sphere of political influence of each agency's home country. The news collected by the different agencies was transmitted from one to the next and there was no central pool where it was assembled. Exchange did not stifle individual enterprise insofar as agen-

---

[5] Ferguson, *World's Banker*, pp. 43, 82–3.

[6] Agreement, July 18, 1859, Jones papers, series 1, box 72, RA. D. Basse claims to have found an agreement from 1856. D. Basse, *Wolff's Telegraphisches Bureau 1849 bis 1933: Agenturpublizistik zwischen Politik und Wirtschaft* (Munich: K.G. Saur, 1991), p. 26; Read, *Power of News*, p. 55.

cies party to the agreements were permitted to collect news in regions in which their partners had exclusive rights of sale.

In the 1860s, it became apparent that contractual agreements for the division of territory, although advantageous, were insufficiently cooperative. Territories were left unexploited and there remained substantial room for opportunistic behavior. Consequently, the agencies discussed merging to form a pan-European organization. Whereas the existence in the United States by the end of the nineteenth century of an integrated market allowed for a combination of the numerous regional American news associations into a nationwide organization, there was no comparable European-wide market, and national political agendas repeatedly sabotaged efforts to merge the agencies of Britain, France, and Germany. In the 1860s, Reuters attempted to expand on the Continent and subsequently sought to merge with Havas and Wolff. Reuters's investment in a telegraph cable between Lowestoft and Nordeney was an integral part of this strategy, and the reason for taking the company public in 1865. When he laid before the company board his plans for a cable to Nordeney, Paul Julius Reuter explained that construction was the first step toward the development of "a very extensive business on the Continent of Europe."[7] Gerson Bleichröder, the famous Prussian banker who owned a majority stake in Wolff, was friendly with Paul Julius Reuter and on several occasions the two met in German spa towns to discuss the possibility of "die Fusion." The plan was to form a holding company, the International Telegraph Company, in which each agency had an equal stake. In this way, each agency would retain its political independence, but still benefit from joint working. Management at Wolff was keen to make a deal, but – for reasons of national security – Bismarck intervened and frustrated these plans.[8] Reuter also attempted unsuccessfully to buy out Stefani, the Italian agency, and Ritzau, the Danish agency.[9]

Legal and political complications also prevented a complete merger between Reuters and Havas. In 1870, the two agencies entered into a joint-purse agreement. An agency in Brussels was jointly exploited and an office was established at Constantinople. On completion of direct telegraphic communication between Europe and South America during the summer of 1874, Reuters and Havas founded a joint-service in Bahia (Salvador), Buenos Aires, Montevideo, and Pernambuco, with a head office in Rio de Janeiro, but opportunistic behavior and inadequate communication between the parties prevented effective joint operation. Account details from Havas frequently arrived late and prevented Reuters from conducting its own bookkeeping. The two agencies

---

[7] Reuters board minutes, September 28, 1865, LN 288 1/883502, RA.
[8] Wentzel to Reuter, January 1, 1875, Meeting of the advisory board, February 6, 1875, and Reuter to Bleichröder, December 29, 1874, Bleichröder papers, box XXIII (A), folder 3; Reuter to Bleichröder, January 21, 1875, Bleichröder papers, box XXXIII (A), folder 66, Baker Library, Harvard; F.R. Stern, *Gold and Iron: Bismarck, Bleichröder and the Building of the German Empire* (London: Allen and Unwin, 1977), p. 264.
[9] Read, *Power of News*, p. 55.

disagreed over the way in which profits should be apportioned. Havas and Reuters repeatedly attempted to charge each other with excessive expenses. Distrust became acute. To bolster its own prestige, Reuters conveniently forgot to include Havas' byline in its report to Holland, Hamburg, Greece, and the Far East.[10] The two organizations sought to establish a complete merger to eradicate these problems, but the intervention of the French government prevented it. European firms of the time often expanded abroad in collaboration with other firms, but continental politicians considered news to be so intimately bound up in national security that they imposed limitations on the boundaries of commercial globalization to protect against external influence.[11] Although commercial considerations had little if any bearing on these political decisions, the effect of government intervention was to perpetuate contractual relations when the agencies wanted to merge. The continuance of contractual relations maintained, albeit unintentionally, the appearance of continued rivalry.

In 1876, the agencies returned to a contractual arrangement and a clear division of territory. Although the terms of their agreements subsequently changed in accordance with shifts in the balance of power and alterations in the boundaries of empires, they remained largely the same until World War I. Reuters took the British Empire. Havas occupied the Iberian Peninsula, Latin America, and the Maghreb. Wolff controlled parts of Eastern Europe and Scandinavia. Reuters and Havas initially split North America between them. Territories outside traditional spheres of influence were either shared or allocated. With lesser agencies, in countries such as Austria, Italy, and Spain, Reuters, Havas, and Wolff signed exclusive agreements in terms similar to those that Reuters formed with the news associations and agencies in the colonies and dominions of the British Empire.

Reuters, Havas, and Wolff, on the one hand, and the agencies in other European countries, on the other hand, benefitted from these agreements in a manner similar to the way in which membership agreements in American news associations simultaneously helped the organization and its members. Reuters, Havas, and Wolff gained an exclusive source of news from a particular region and the Austrian, Italian, Spanish, and other agencies became, by virtue of the exclusive report they received from Reuters, Havas, and Wolff, the dominant agencies in their respective countries. Entrenching the position of lesser foreign agencies transformed them into partners of a status acceptable to the triumvirate of Reuters, Havas, and Wolff while also reinforcing their dominant position. The smaller agencies party to these agreements,

---

[10] Reuters board minutes, February 21 and May 1, 1872, April 30, 1873, February 17, and December 8, 1875, box 288; Havas to Griffiths, April 25, May 3, November 22, 1873; Griffiths to Havas, May 5 and 15, 1873; Griffiths to Engländer, April 9, 1873, LN 1/890503. Reuters board minutes, April 2, 187; Havas to Griffiths, December 3, 1873, RA LN 1/890503.

[11] G. Jones, *The Evolution of International Business: An Introduction* (London: Routledge, 1996), p. 33; H. James, *The End of Globalization: Lessons from the Great Depression* (London: Harvard University Press, 2001), pp. 13–21.

such as the Korrespondenzbureau of Austria and Stefani of Italy, obtained international news reports at a fraction of the price they cost to produce, although secondary agencies typically paid the larger agencies a differential in addition to sharing their news reports, much like smaller papers in the AP granted larger papers certain concessions, such as voting rights. Smaller agencies were like smaller newspapers. By virtue of their membership in the AP, newspapers obtained a larger quantity of news than it was possible for them to obtain independently. Likewise, had the agreements among the agencies not existed, the secondary agencies would not have been able to obtain such a large amount of news.

An exclusive cooperative agreement with Reuters, Havas, and Wolff was a source of advantage for these lesser national news agencies. An exclusive agreement with the principal news agencies of Europe was a key to success in the early contests between rival American news organizations. Reuters first completed an exclusive agreement with the NYAP, which helped that organization grow into the dominant provider of foreign news in the United States. In 1866, the NYAP refused to pay the differential of £3,000 ($44,000 in today's prices) demanded by Reuters to receive the agency's report at the same time as the London papers. The New York publishers offered Reuters a mutual exchange, but the London newspapers, given that New York was five hours behind London, obtained the news from the published evening papers, which were as accessible to the Reuters agent in New York as to anyone else, and then cabled the news independently in time for their morning editions the following day. Consequently, the NYAP decided to forego its deal with Reuters on the belief that no other American organization could pay the high cost required to transmit Reuters's news reports across the Atlantic. If no party took Reuters's telegrams in the United States, the representatives of the NYAP in London could clip Reuters's news from the London newspapers in the morning and, owing to the difference in time, still have them in New York before the deadline for the day's paper. Instead, Daniel H. Craig, who eventually ran the NYAP, agreed to pay Reuters the requested sum. Craig planned to resell the news to the Western Associated Press. This unwelcome prospect caused the New York papers to scramble for a new agreement with Reuters.[12]

Access to Reuters's news reports was also a decisive factor in the American news agency battle of the 1890s. In the British Empire, Herbert de Reuter sought to prevent competition against Reuters by selling his news to as many newspapers as possible despite the desires of newspaper publishers to receive it exclusively. In the American market, he originally proposed an agreement with the AP and the UPA, but Victor Lawson of the AP, much like Lachlan

---

[12] "Reuters's Telegrams," Chicago *Tribune*, December 12, 1866; Halstead to Marble, February 15, 1867, Manton Marble papers, vol. 14, LOC; Various agreements, April 20, 1867, LN288/883501, RA.

Mackinnon of the Melbourne *Argus*, demanded an exclusive contract. Melville Stone successfully traveled to London to negotiate terms.[13] When recruiting members to the AP, Victor Lawson made much of this connection. "Its exclusive contract with the well-known Reuter Agency in London, together with the allied agencies of Havas in Paris, and Wolff in Berlin," wrote Lawson to Frank McLaughlan of the Philadelphia *Times* in November 1893, "give it an absolute advantage over all possible competitors."[14] As was the case throughout the British Empire, foreign news arrived in the United States via channels other than Reuters. But just as American newspaper publishers had an incentive to patronize Western Union exclusively, so did news association managers have encouragement to give all their support to Reuters.[15] Patronizing Reuters alone avoided wasteful expenditure on rival but largely similar news reports, which reduced the AP's expenditure on the collection of foreign news. An exclusive relationship also gave the Americans some influence over the composition of Reuters's news reports.[16]

Exclusive agreements were occasionally susceptible to abuse, but newspaper editors could always decline to publish news agency reports. A term in the early treaties permitted the agencies to disseminate government propaganda via their partners. For the German Foreign Ministry, access to the news agencies of Europe through Wolff was a means to disseminate favorable news abroad, but newspaper editors could and did refuse to publish these messages.[17] In the 1890s, American publishers complained that Reuters's service

[13] W.H. Smith to Neef, February 8, 1893, W.H. Smith papers, box 13, folder 32, OHS; Neef to Smith, February 21, 1893, LN522/9012054, RA; Lawson memo, undated and Lawson to Knapp, March 17, 1893, Lawson papers, box 2, folder 5, pp. 238, 260, Newberry Library (NL). Lawson believed in the importance of foreign correspondence and went to great lengths to develop foreign coverage in his papers. J. Cole and J.M. Hamilton, "A Natural History of Foreign Correspondence: A Study of the Chicago *Daily News*, 1900–1921," *Journalism and Mass Communication Quarterly*, 84 (2007), 151–66.

[14] Lawson to McLaughlan, November 1, 1893, Lawson papers, box 113, folder 730, NL.

[15] W.H. Smith to W.P. Nixon, July 13, 1891 and Neef to W.H. Smith, July 29, 1891, W.H. Smith papers, box 5, folder 1, OHS.

[16] W.B. Somerville to W.H. Smith, August 12, 1876, Delevan Smith papers, box 1, folder 2, Indiana Historical Society (HIS); J. McLean to Somerville, August 18, 1876, W.H. Smith papers, box 5, folder 1, OHS; M.E. Stone to W.H. Smith, December 5, 1882, M.E. Stone papers, box 4, folder 412, NL; Reid to W.H. Smith, undated, W.H. Smith papers, box 3, folder 7, OHS; W. Neef to W.H. Smith, undated, W.H. Smith papers, box 5, folder 2, OHS. See, for example, the row over Dunlap's and Dalziell's. Dunlap's Cable News Co., prospectus, 1891, IHS, Delevan Smith papers, box 13, folder 8; Unsigned, undated (1891) re Dalziell's, Delevan Smith papers, box 13, folder 13, IHS; Neef to W.H. Smith, January 5, 1891, W.H. Smith papers, box 4, folder 6, OHS; W.H. Smith to C. Dana, February 6, 1891, W.H. Smith papers, box 4, folder 6, OHS.

[17] These telegrams were sent under the code name "tractatus." A. Nalbach, "The Ring Combination: Information, Power, and the World News Agency Cartel, 1856–1914" (unpublished PhD thesis, University of Chicago, 1999). See also, M. Blondheim, "'Public Sentiment is Everything': The Union's Public Communications Strategy and the Bogus Proclamation of 1864," *Journal of*

was "hampered with officialism."[18] A strong domestic press held the agencies in line. An inexpensive global news report from a well-established news agency helped to diminish the costs the press incurred, which freed up revenue for further independent newspaper enterprise, and so reinforced the strength of the press.

There were rivals to the cartel, but high start-up costs dissuaded new entrants. In an internal company memorandum of 1889, Lloyd's calculated that if it undertook to pay correspondents "to compete with Reuters the expense must be very serious since we know that although Reuters has receipts of about £80,000 a year, the expenses are so large for cost of telegrams and payment of correspondents that the dividend has latterly been exceedingly small and this year will probably be nothing."[19] When rivals did emerge, such as Dalziel's agency, which briefly vexed Reuters and the PA and was connected to Dunlap's, the agency that sought an injunction against the New York Associated Press in the 1890s, their appearance only led to greater cooperation among the agencies, as the invention of the PA-Reuters special service demonstrates.[20]

Cooperation also expanded the market in which national news agencies and associations could dispose of their reports, which helped to fund the gathering and supply of news to domestic newspapers. This was most clearly the case in Britain where Reuters's foreign operations subsidized the supply of news to the PA's members. Disagreements between agencies over expansion were infrequent and were invariably resolved. In 1900, after the Spanish-American War, the AP requested the right to serve Cuba, the Philippines, and Porto Rico, which had hitherto been the exclusive domain of Havas. Reuters facilitated this agreement, despite the misgivings of the French agency, by agreeing that it and Wolff would pay Havas an annuity for relinquishing the territory. In 1911–1912, the AP secured the right to serve newspapers in Argentina, Brazil, and Chile with North American news. This territory had also belonged exclusively to Havas.[21] No one asked the newspapers in these countries from where they preferred to receive their news, but if the history of Reuters's operations in the British Empire is representative, the position of the agencies in foreign countries was usually challenged.

American History, 89 (2002), 880; M. Blondheim, "'Slender Bridges' of Misunderstanding: the Social Legacy of Transatlantic Cable Communication," in N. Finzsch and U. Lehmkuhl, *Atlantic Communications: The Media in American and German History from the Seventeenth to the Twentieth Century* (Oxford: Berg, 2004), pp. 162–5.

[18] W. Neef to W.H. Smith, March 26, 1892, W.H. Smith papers, box 5, folder 2, OHS.

[19] "Memorandum with regard to the agreements with Reuters and the Press Association," February 4, 1889, Lloyd's papers, Ms 31646, GL.

[20] See Chapter 3. See also W. Neef to W.H. Smith, January 5, 1891 and W.H. Smith to C. Dana, February 6, 1891, W.H. Smith papers, Mss 2, box 4, folder 6, OHS.

[21] Contract, November 5, 1902, LN291/883508, RA; *AP Annual Report* (1911–1912), 3–4.

COMPETITION AND COOPERATION: THE THREAT OF THE UP

World War I, and especially the distribution of propaganda in neutral countries (see Table 7.1), produced rancorous feelings among the news agencies of Europe and disrupted established relations, but cooperation resumed after Versailles.[22] Before the war, one instrument – a tripartite arrangement among Reuters, Havas, and Wolff (besides two pro forma arrangements with the Austrian and Italian news agencies) – governed Reuters's relations in Europe. After the war, Reuters had sixteen agreements with the new countries of Europe, including in the Netherlands, where it had hitherto maintained a subsidiary.[23] Contracts among Reuters, Havas, and Wolff persisted, although the German agency was confined to domestic operations and it was obliged to pay Reuters and Havas a hefty differential akin to reparations.[24] Havas and Reuters jointly exploited what remained of the former Ottoman Empire as well as Switzerland, which before the war was territory of Havas and Wolff. In keeping with general British trade policy of the 1920s, and predicated on hopes of a "return to normalcy," Reuters instigated among the new news agencies of Europe a movement to form a group of Allied Agencies, or *Agences Alliées* as it was known, which consisted of approximately thirty different organizations. These agencies held annual conferences to discuss issues affecting the international trade in news, such as copyright law, technological advancements in wireless broadcasting, telecommunications tariffs, and trade policy.[25] The AP was a member of this alliance until the late 1920s.

Despite continued cooperation during the interwar period among the news agencies of Europe, the UP, insofar as it competed with the AP, threatened cooperation between the AP and its European allies. The UP, which was unrestrained by agreements with the agencies, began selling its news abroad, first in South America, where it went in 1918 compelled by reasons of state. After the war, the oil boom in Argentina caused a growth in American involvement in South America and President Woodrow Wilson took an interest in South

[22] See, for example, Maloney to Jones, August 18, 1917, Jones papers, series 1, box 25, RA.
[23] Clements to Jones, December 30, 1919, Jones papers, series 1, box 31; Ministry of Information to Jones, August 17, 1918, LN784/973616; Memo, "Societa Granaria Italiana," September 2, 1919, Jones papers, series 1, box 33; Agencies allied to Reuters, November 17, 1924, Jones papers, series 1, box 28, RA.
[24] Murray to Jones, November 17, 1919, Jones papers, series 1, box 33; Jones memo, November 23, 1919 and Jones memo, December 19, 1919, Jones papers, series 1, box 30; Agreement, December 20, 1919, LN246/8715518; Murray to Jones, May 6, 1920, Jones papers, series 1, box 33, RA.
[25] Rapport du Comité Permanent aux Agences Alliées, October 14, 1929, Cooper papers, Ms I, LL; Bureau Central des Agences Alliées, October 13, 1930, AP01.2, KC, box 35, folder 13, AP; Sixième assemblée ordinaire des Agences Alliées, June 20, 1938, Jones papers, series 1, box 38, RA.

TABLE 7.1. *Use of Reuters's propaganda services abroad,*
1917–1918

Country	Number of newspapers publishing Reuters's propaganda service
Argentina and Uruguay	30
Denmark	52
France	56
Greece	23
Italy	92
Japan	188
Norway	153
Portugal	19
Romania	78
Spain	42
Sweden	120
Switzerland	128

Source: J.1.26, RA.

American affairs.[26] When Roy Howard, the general manager of the UP, traveled to South America in 1918, a paper in Rio called him "President Wilson's mule skinner."[27] The UP received plaudits and support from the American government and public for its efforts.[28] The UP next threatened the allied agencies in China and Japan.[29] In Asia, as in South America, American foreign policy encouraged the UP to enter the market. The Nine Power Pact of 1922, the culmination of American Open Door policy in the Far East, opened the way for American entry into Japan. Conversely, the decline of Anglo-Japanese relations adversely affected Reuters's position.[30] These events caused the AP to seek

[26] "President Wilson and Latin America," *The American Journal of International Law*, 7 (1913), 331; D. Rock, "Argentina from the First World War to the Revolution of 1930," in L. Bethell (ed.), *The Cambridge History of Latin America*, vol. 5: *c. 1870 to 1930* (Cambridge: Cambridge University Press, 1986), pp. 443–4.

[27] A person who drives mules – the idea being that Howard went on behalf of Wilson to beat the South American press into line. R.W. Howard to J.I. Miller, November 27, 1928, Howard papers, UIB.

[28] Morgan to State Department, June 3, 1918; Howard to Mrs. Frank Zuber, June 13, 1918; Howard to W.W. Hawkins, September 6, 1918; W.G. Harding to Howard, July 14, 1922; Howard to Harding, July 18, 1922, Howard papers, UIB. "N.Y. to be News Clearing House of the World," *Editor & Publisher*, 49 (November 11, 1926).

[29] The extent of this threat must have been limited. In 1933, Reuters far surpassed the UP in terms of total number of inches daily published in the English-language Shanghai papers. MRM to Cooper, July 25, 1933, Cooper papers, box 41, folder 11, AP.

[30] I. Hata, "Continental Expansion, 1905–1941," trans. A.D. Coox, in J.W. Hall et al., *The Cambridge History of Japan*, vol. 6: *The Twentieth Century* (Cambridge: Cambridge University

greater freedom from the European agencies, but the UP did not, contrary to the claims of some historians, break up the international cartel in 1934.[31]

The agreements between the European agencies and the AP were sufficiently flexible to permit the AP to counter the UP while continuing to cooperate. Greater competition from the UP initially caused Reuters and the AP to cooperate more closely. During World War I, the AP, like the UP, was under political pressure to enter the South American market.[32] Havas was against the AP entering the South American market, but allowed it, albeit only after intervention from the U.S. State Department, in much the same way as it had allowed an expansion of AP territory before the war. By 1920, the AP had forty-one members in South America, the UP had been largely ousted, and President Wilson wrote the association to express his "great satisfaction" with the new relations between the AP and the South American press.[33] Likewise in Asia, Reuters and the AP worked together to counteract the UP, although Japan had historically been Reuters's exclusive domain.

Although cooperation between Reuters and the AP continued, it did change, and for this Kent Cooper was largely responsible. The problem with closer cooperation for the AP was not increased competition from the UP, it was the decision in the intellectual property case of *INS*, combined with the limitations of the association's charter, which restricted the AP's freedom of action abroad. As explained in Chapter 2, the AP sought a property right in news to prevent rivals, namely the UP, from taking news. Contrary to what commentators and scholars have always believed, the AP was not out to protect the news reports that the association generated. Instead, the AP brought the suit to prevent pilfering of the news its members gathered and published in their papers, and over which the AP claimed exclusive rights. If the UP was not legally barred from copying the news of AP members, then owing to the difference in time between the east and west coasts of the United States, agents of the UP could take the news from member newspapers published in New York and replicate the news reports of the AP in time for use by its clients in California. Unlike the AP, Havas, Reuters, Wolff, and the other European agencies did not have arrangements with newspapers in their countries for the exchange of news

Press, 1988), p. 283; I. Nish, *Alliance in Decline: a Study in Anglo-Japanese Relations, 1908–1923* (London: Athlone Press, 1972).

[31] For the first iteration of this thesis, see T. Rantanen, "Mr. Howard goes to South America. The United Press Associations and Foreign Expansion," *Roy W. Howard Monographs in Journalism and Mass Communication Research*, 2 (1992).

[32] Digest of verbatim board minutes, December 10, 1913 and October 4, 1917, AP01.1, series III, box 3, folder 26, pp. 263–4, 352–4, AP; Draft board minutes, November 3, 1926, Jones papers, series 2, box 3, RA.

[33] H. Bailey to Howard, July 19, 1933, LOC, Howard papers, box 82, UIB; Memo, January 1 and 2, 1919, LN23/865213, RA; F.R. Martin to Jones, June 26, 1922, Cooper papers, Ms I, LL; *AP Annual Report* (1918–1919), p. 151; *AP Annual Report* (1919–1920), p. 4.

before publication. The correspondents of the European agencies, when they did not write their own stories, took them from published papers and wired them to headquarters. These various reports were then assembled and shared with the AP. The AP's correspondents abroad also copied from published newspapers. This meant that the special advantages of the AP organization were not, and could not be, replicated abroad.

Following the decision of the United States Supreme Court in *INS*, the AP was convinced its correspondents could no longer copy from published papers at home and abroad. The UP continued to do so, and it therefore consistently scooped the AP. "The decision of the Supreme Court of the United States in the proprietary news case had not only great advantage for us, but it had some disadvantage," said Melville Stone to the AP board of directors in 1919. "It necessarily put an end to our pirating news from the London papers." In a survey Stone made of the news the AP collected in England, only five out of thirty-five items came from Reuters and most of the rest came from the London papers. Although Stone acknowledged that there was no law in England that prohibited the AP from pilfering news from the English papers, he believed that the prospect of violating American law was sufficient reason to stop the practice. The AP solicited the permission of the London papers to take their news after publication, but only one allowed it. The AP was "bound by the theory of property in news," wrote Frank Noyes, president of the AP, to Roderick Jones, general manager of Reuters. "We are not free to take from the London papers, with or without credit, any matter without a distinct permission so to do." But the AP's rivals did "not feel morally and legally bound as we do" and were therefore "placed at a distinct advantage." All over Europe it was the same. Although unforeseen by members of the AP, the pursuit of a property right in news increased the cost of creating an international news report as opposed to reducing it.[34]

By 1918, the difference in time between London and New York, which the NYAP had attempted to work to its advantage in 1866, injured the AP in the same way as the time difference between New York and California, except the time difference was greater and so was the disadvantage. Going from west to east, the difference in time made having the AP news indispensable to Reuters's service from the United States. Taking news from published New York morning papers could not make editions of the London morning papers, but having access in New York to the AP report permitted Reuters to send its report in time for the deadline. The AP had contractual relations with 1,200 daily newspapers of the United States, providing that each one of them furnished to the AP exclusively the news of their immediate vicinage, and consequently, when news was received in New York it went to Reuters

---

[34] Compare with W.M. Landes and R.A. Posner, "An Economic Analysis of Copyright Law," *The Journal of Legal Studies*, 18 (1989), 326.

instantly, even before it reached many of the members.[35] A story provided to Reuters as late as 8 p.m. or 9 p.m. Eastern Standard Time could appear in the London papers the next morning. Such news, and such a period of availability, Reuters only could obtain through direct access to the AP report. If it did not have access to the AP report, Reuters would have missed London morning editions with American night news. Indeed, the AP put Reuters twenty-four hours ahead of any British or European rival without similar facilities. Additionally, the AP had exclusive access to news from most major American newspapers before publication, which usually put it ahead of the UP and INS. The AP suffered as much on westbound news as Reuters gained on eastbound news. The difference in time favored the practice of pilfering published news in Europe and sending it westbound to the United States. The advantage to be had from using published news in westbound cable matter meant that agencies and individuals working in opposition to the AP could use the London papers as well as Reuters's matter from tickers and still have the news to editors in New York in time for publication. The AP, however, could no longer engage in this practice.

The problem might not have been so serious for the AP had the news agencies of Europe been quicker assembling and dispatching their reports, but World War I exposed the American agencies to the comparatively poor facilities in place on the Continent for the collection of news. During the war, the AP encountered considerable difficulty reporting from France, received little constructive help from Havas, and its correspondents lamented their lack of closer connections with the domestic press.[36] Arrangements in Britain were also comparatively less advanced and slower than in the United States.[37] The UP, in addition to continuing to copy from published newspapers, also undertook to make exclusive agreements directly with foreign newspapers, which made the situation worse for the AP. The AP, owing to noncompete clauses in its contracts with the European agencies, could not make similar arrangements insofar as it entailed an exchange of news. If it had simply been a matter of the AP obtaining greater revenue for its news reports, a new agreement might have been reached between the European news agencies and the AP; but the AP, being a membership corporation, was prohibited from selling news. At root, the problem with cooperation arose from a national property rights regime and a corresponding mode of organization geared toward protecting exclusivity. The actions of the UP exacerbated this complication. To remedy it, the AP had to have a free hand to exchange news with newspapers abroad.

---

[35] Digest of verbatim board minutes, October 1, 1919, AP01.1, series III, box 3, folder 26, pp. 411–15, AP; Jones memo, August 5, 1919, Jones papers, series 2, box 3, RA; Stone to Jones, August 21, 1919, AP02A, box 9, folder 12, AP; Jones memo, October 9, 1920, Noyes to Jones, October 18, 1920, Cooper to Jones, October 26, 1923, Jones papers, series 2, box 3, RA.

[36] C.E. Kloeber to Stone, December 1, 1915, AP, Noyes correspondence, box 2; K. Cooper to Stone, September 1, 1919, Cooper papers, Ms II, folder 2, LL.

[37] See Chapters 3 and 4.

Privately, Cooper acknowledged that he might have come to an arrangement with European newspapers for the exchange of news before publication and still have maintained cooperation with the agencies, but he wanted to reinforce the AP's control over news before publication. Rather than simply exchange directly with the European press, Cooper intended to export the AP model abroad to create sister organizations throughout the world that the AP could lead and with which it could form close alliances. "We ought to collect that news over there as we do it here," said Cooper to the AP board in 1919. "Somebody is going to do it some time and I would like to be the first." Cooper pursued a modification of the status quo not to supplant cooperation with free trade or competition, but to replace it with a tighter, more integrated form of cooperation akin to the international merger his predecessors had imagined in the 1860s.

If the AP could exchange news abroad at cost and before publication, there would be little opportunity for commercial agencies to compete. Members of the AP board liked the idea, but were unwilling to precipitate a rupture in relations with the European agencies. Melville Stone supported forming a "world alliance of co-operative organizations" and he raised the question of forming a cooperative news agency with newspaper publishers in France, England, and Italy, but none of them were willing to take up the burden. "They admired it when I outlined it," said Stone, but that was all. Until some form of cooperative alliance could be created, Stone was committed to cooperating with the European agencies for fear of the increased expense independence entailed. Frank Noyes, president of the AP, hoped for a European property right akin to that gained through *INS* that would prevent the UP from pilfering news.

Cooper believed that an international property right in news, akin to that created by the United States Supreme Court, would prevent the UP from taking news from published European newspapers and afford the AP greater protection. To this end, Cooper lobbied the Conference of Press Experts of the League of Nations to affirm "its acceptance of the principle of the property right in news." Cooper spoke on the resolution. Jones of Reuters and the representative of Havas seconded it. Lord Riddell, publisher of the *News of the World* among other publications, was quick to point out that the Americans had not ratified the Berne Convention regarding copyright, that the alleged American property right in news of which Cooper spoke was of a nebulous character, and that the press of Britain emphatically disagreed with the resolution. "There is a tendency at the present time on the part of America to formulate policies for the benefit of a benighted Europe," Riddell reportedly said in 1927, and "then to walk home and say: 'We have put Europe right but at the same time we are not going to be put right ourselves; let Europe mind their own business.'"[38]

---

[38] Digest of verbatim board minutes, April 19 and October 1 and 4, 1919, AP01.1, series III, box 3, folder 26, pp. 401–3, 411–15, 423, AP; H. Wood to R. Howard, June 8, 1927, Howard

The Conference resolved that questions of property rights should be decided by national governments, but it did affirm

the principle that newspapers, news agencies, and other news organisations are entitled to the fruits of their labour, enterprise and financial expenditure upon the production of news reports, but holds that this principle shall not be so interpreted as to result in the creation or the encouragement of any monopoly in news.

News could only be published provided it "reached the person who publishes it by regular and unobjectionable means, and not by an act of unfair trade." Unpublished news, or news in the course of transmission or publication, the Conference granted full protection and suggested that it should be illegal for any unauthorized person to receive for publication or to use it in any way.[39]

TOWARD AN AP OF APS

Whether or not a property right was forthcoming, Cooper remained committed to the idealistic goal of an international league of news associations, which he likened to the League of Nations. In a memo written in the spring of 1920, Cooper explained how he envisioned such an international cooperative organization might work. The members would represent the best press association effort within their respective home territories and there would be an international committee of executives that would meet to administer the joint efforts and affairs of the alliance.[40] In 1922, Cooper again raised the matter with his board. "So far as the agencies are concerned," said Cooper,

they have no news from their clients in Europe unless they take it from the published newspapers, and, to that extent, their method of operation is entirely different from ours. We could take it from the published newspapers there, but so can the United Press, so can our competitors, and the day will arrive – I anticipate this and I hope for it – if it can be done with the agencies agreeing, all right, it must be done, – that we must exchange news with some form of a newspaper organization.

Despite Jones' plan to sell Reuters to the British press, Cooper remained convinced that the newspapers of France and England would "have to adopt the same principles of news exchange that we have in this country." The AP had to have the news before publication. Without it, complained Cooper, "we cannot today, because of their methods of operation, obtain any exclusive story from the Havas agency. It is in the street over there at the same time that Havas gives

---

papers, box 18, LOC; Cooper, *Barriers down*, pp. 159–62. The Berne Conference of June 11, 1924 passed a resolution to protect property in news. See J.F.B. Livesay, "Report of the special committee on property right in news," November 23, 1925, AP02A.3, box 14, folder 2, AP.

39   "Declaration and Resolutions Adopted by the Conference of Press Experts," in *League of Nations Official Journal* (Geneva: League of Nations, 1927), 10 (XLVI), pp. 1155–8.

40   Cooper memo, May 17, 1920, Cooper papers, Ms II, folder 2, LL.

it to us and is available to the United Press."[41] In *Barriers Down*, Cooper would tell his readers of his "crusade" against the European news agencies, but in exporting the model of the AP abroad he was more a missionary.

Only in Canada had the AP successfully exported its model of organization. In 1910, the inability of the Canadian Pacific Railway to protect the AP report, which was being telegraphed back into the United States by rival press associations, caused the AP to terminate the contract it had with the railway and to instigate the formation of an association of the Canadian papers. The Canadian Press, an association modeled along the lines of the AP, was, as its president and general manager acknowledged, merely a license holder for the AP news.[42] In return for this license, wrote E.F. Mack, publisher of the Montreal *Gazette* and a founding member of the Canadian Press, the AP was "given a monopoly in the United States of the news controlled by us."[43] To permit the AP access to South America, contracts with Havas, although they continued to bar the AP from exchanging news with any proprietary organization, left it at liberty to make agreements with cooperative organizations along the lines of AP. The AP brought the South American newspapers into membership to deal with this difficulty. As Cooper observed, part of the reason for the AP entering South America was to "acquaint them with the Associated Press ideals."[44] In April 1923, the AP board passed a resolution to increase the size of its news report from the Far East and to that end to seek to establish an AP-like organization in China among the English and vernacular press for the exchange of news. Political dislocation hindered these initiatives, but Japan showed more promising signs for development.[45]

In 1919, the AP began instigating for the formation of a Japanese associated press, but in 1923, Kokusai, the Japanese agency, renewed its exclusive agreements with Reuters.[46] Negotiating this contract, in light of the Great Kanto Earthquake and Japan's poor financial condition, was particularly difficult for Jones of Reuters. Despite the hardships it faced, the Japanese agency, like the country, wanted greater say in international news agency relations. Yukichi Iwanaga, head of Kokusai, requested the right to distribute Reuters's

[41] Jones memo, April 28, 1922, Jones papers, series 2, box 3, RA; Digest of verbatim board minutes, October 5, 1922, AP01.1, series III, box 3, folder 27, p. 596, AP.

[42] See Chapter 5.

[43] M. Stone to C. Taylor, April 13, 1910 and E.F. Mack to Stone, October 27, 1910, AP01.2, series 1, AP. See Chapter 5.

[44] *AP Annual Report* (1918–1919), pp. 5–8; Digest of verbatim board minutes, April 17, 1924, AP01.1, series III, box 3, folder 27, p. 668, AP.

[45] Digest of verbatim board minutes, April 17, 1923, AP01.1, series III, box 3, folder 27, p. 614, AP. On American-British-Chinese trade relations see C.B. Davis, "Limits of Effacement: Britain and the problem of American Cooperation and Competition in China, 1915–1917," *Pacific Historical Review*, 48 (1979), 47–63.

[46] On the history of the Japanese news agencies, see T. Akami, *Japan's News Propaganda and Reuters' News Empire in Northeast Asia, 1870–1934* (Dordorecht: Republic of Letters, 2012) and S. Iwanaga, *Story of Japanese News Agencies* (Tokyo: Shinbun Tsushin Chosa-kai, 1980).

news report under the Kokusai byline, as the AP, Havas, and Wolff did in their respective countries, as well as the right to contract directly with the AP. Jones agreed to the former but was unwilling to assent to the latter. He did, however, consent to carry a larger service of news from the AP into the Far East, albeit under Reuters's byline. For these concessions, and to stave off greater calls from the Japanese for independence, Jones tied Kokusai down with a long-term debenture and a heavy subscription fee of £6,000.[47]

Being bound to take his news from Reuters, Iwanaga was anxious that Dempo, his rival, ought not to have access to the American news of the UP. Historically, news only traveled to Japan overland by telegraph from Europe. This limited method of communication made an exclusive arrangement with Reuters advantageous and unproblematic, but the advent of wireless threatened to undermine it. Wireless had adverse effects on similar arrangements all over the world as Reuters had already experienced throughout the British Isles. If wireless news reports could be sent from the United States to Japan, Dempo could use them, but Kokusai, being bound to Reuters, could not. The cost of wireless transmission from San Francisco to Japan was significantly cheaper than the ordinary cable service from London, but Iwanaga was compelled to lobby the Japanese government to disallow it. "It will be a matter of sincere regret to us if, through this economical channel the United Press effects a competition against you which it might be hard for you to overcome," wrote Cooper to Iwanaga. In the autumn of 1925, Radio Corporation of America reached an agreement with UP to send 1,000 words daily to Japan, but on account of Iwanaga's lobbying the Japanese Department of Communications refused to allow it. According to Iwanaga, a governmental decree that set the charge for newspaper delivery at ¥1 kept Japanese newspapers small. This decree, argued Iwanaga spuriously, limited the number of pages newspapers could afford to publish and an influx of foreign news by wireless would threaten the perilous finances of Japanese newspapers. Further, argued Iwanaga, if there was to be an influx of foreign news there needed to be an association of Japanese newspapers, such as Kokusai, to gather it in common.[48]

An associated press promised to liberate Japanese publishers from the heavy price Reuters demanded, and Iwanaga pursued it with zeal that matched Cooper's. For Cooper and Iwanaga, the idea of news associations cooperating around the globe was more than good business, it mirrored the "general association of nations" that was the centerpiece of President Wilson's Fourteen Points for Peace of 1918, and which led to the signing of the Covenant of the

[47] Murray to Jones, July 23, 1919, Jones papers, series 1, box 33; AP board resolutions, December 15, 1921, Cooper papers, Ms I, LL; Agreement, December 19, 1923, LN242/8714753; Jones report, May 9, 1924, Jones papers, series 1, box 56; Jones to Noyes, July 9, 1924, Jones papers, series 1, box 24; Price, Waterhouse & Co. report, September 11, 1925, Jones papers, series 1, box 60, RA.

[48] Culbertson to Cooper, September 1, Cooper to Iwanaga September 4, Iwanaga to Cooper, September 28, Iwanaga to Cooper, December 28, 1925, Cooper papers, Ms I, LL.

League of Nations in 1919. Before the war, Colonel Edward M. House listened sympathetically to Cooper's grand plans. House, Wilson's chief deputy at Versailles and his foreign policy adviser, helped to outline the Fourteen Points, draft the Versailles Treaty, and compose the Covenant of the League of Nations. Cooper and House were reunited at the Paris Peace Conference. Cooper then attempted again to impress on House the importance of breaking down the "obstacles" that confronted the AP in the "free exchange of news" as well as placing a clause in the Versailles Treaty respecting the freedom of the press and "freedom of international news exchange."[49] At the Conference, the United States advocated open communications for all nations under international control and it denounced British control of submarine telegraphy through the possession of exclusive shoreline landing rights in much the same rhetoric that Cooper used, but that was all.[50]

Cooper had more luck converting Iwanaga to the cause. Iwanaga and Cooper believed that their ideas for a new arrangement among the worlds' news agencies were as different from those of the old agencies as Wilson's "New Diplomacy" was from the "Old Diplomacy" of Europe.[51] In an undated memo entitled "A tentative draft for the Covenant of the Proposed League of the News Agencies," Iwanaga explained the vision he and Cooper shared. "The days of secret diplomacy and secret treaties have gone," wrote Iwanaga, "why then should contracts between agencies, which are very similar to international treaties in their eventual effects upon the interests of the public, alone still adhere to the obsolete idea of secret commercial transactions?" Instead, Iwanaga encouraged his imagined signatories to "agree to this Covenant of the League of the News Agencies of the World" so as "to facilitate the means of the exchange of news" and "to promote thereby a better understanding among nations by mutual co-operative services." This "League of News Agencies of the World" was to be an "AP of APs."[52] Commercial interests and American Wilsonian idealism went hand in hand in Japan as they did in Europe.[53]

Nippon Shimbun Rengo, the name of the new Japanese association that formed in the spring of 1926, was purposefully a direct translation of "associated press," and similar in organization to the AP.[54] Iwanaga proposed the

[49] Cooper, *Barriers down*, pp. 89–90.
[50] R. Pike and D. Winseck, "The Politics of Global Media Reform, 1907–23," *Media, Culture & Society*, 26 (2004), 660; G. Atcheson, Jr., "The Cable Situation in the Pacific Ocean, with Special Reference to the Far East," *Annals of the American Academy of Political and Social Science*, 122 (1925), 70–7.
[51] But see N. Kawamura, "Wilsonian Idealism and Japanese Claims at the Paris Peace Conference," *Pacific Historical Review*, 66 (1997), 503–26.
[52] Y. Iwanaga, "A Tentative Draft for the Covenant of the Proposed League of the News Agencies," undated, AP02A, box 9, folder 11, AP.
[53] See V. de Grazia, *Irresistible Empire: America's Advance Through Twentieth-Century Europe* (London: Belknap Press, 2005).
[54] Eubank to Cooper, March 31, Cooper to Noyes, May 17, 1926, Cooper papers, Ms I, LL.

association to the leading newspapers of Osaka and Tokyo. There were eight major newspapers in Japan, the joint circulation of which constituted nearly 75 percent of the total newspaper circulation of the country, which made coordination among them fairly easy. Iwanaga started with the eight leading papers only, although the door was kept open for any paper to come in later on "reasonable terms." Given the way these things went in other countries and at the AP, it is likely that the terms were reasonably restrictive. Of the eight papers invited, six had exclusive access to Reuters's news.[55] The news service was sold to nonmembers, including foreign papers in Japan. Although Iwanaga attempted to arrange an association along the lines of the AP, local conditions demanded modifications. Like Reuters, the organization had to be arranged so as not to encroach on existing domestic newsgathering efforts. "You will easily understand how difficult it is to organize an associated press in Japan exactly similar to yours," wrote Iwanaga to Cooper in March 1926 when he was engaged in drafting a constitution for the new organization. "The *Asahi* alone has nearly 2,000 local correspondents all over the country, who are also acting as salesmen and advertising agents, and who would lose their jobs if deprived of their work as correspondents." There was a clause requiring members to furnish their local news to the association, but only for distribution abroad. "It is perhaps due to the narrow extent of territory in Japan," explained Iwanaga, "that each big paper is able to have its own powerful news-gathering system, with which even the strongest domestic agency is unable to compete."[56] The AP was to have first and exclusive access to the news of this new association.[57]

While Cooper was busy planning with Iwanaga, he still believed that cooperation with the European agencies was advantageous. "My idea," wrote Cooper to Noyes while arrangements for the Japanese association were being finalized, "has not changed since I made my first study of it in 1919." It ought to be the case, wrote Cooper,

that any allied agency could make its service contract with any allied agency that it might choose, all of the allied agencies first to be signatory to a general contract that would designate home territories and unlimited activities therein and, where a country had no organized agency to enter the alliance, that country be open territory.[58]

In October 1926, the AP, Havas, Reuters, and Wolff completed a new contract. The differential that the AP had always paid to the European agencies ceased and the AP was granted rights throughout the western hemisphere. It was permitted to serve the Nippon Shimbun Rengo, but if the Japanese association opted for the AP over Reuters, then the AP was to pay Reuters an

55 V. Eubank to Cooper, June 18, 1926, Cooper papers, Ms I, LL.
56 Iwanaga to Cooper, March 9, 1926, Cooper papers, Ms I, LL.
57 Iwanaga to Cooper, May 13, 1926, Cooper papers, Ms I, LL.
58 Cooper to Noyes, May 19, 1926, Cooper papers, Ms I, LL.

indemnity. Any news that the AP sent to Japan was available to Reuters gratis for distribution throughout Asia. The AP was permitted to furnish its news reports to any newspaper in Britain that took Reuters's provided that the newspaper supplied its news to the AP and that the AP paid Reuters a fee. If, for instance, Reuters found that the AP was making a direct service to *The Times* of London, Reuters could offer the *Daily Mail* or even *The Times* the AP service it received, which would have forestalled, and probably supplanted, the AP report sent from New York. In addition, the consent of the PA was required before the AP could distribute its news to any paper in the British Isles outside London.[59] The contracts excluded other news agencies and associations.[60] According to Roderick Jones, these adjustments were made on "the frank readiness more closely to cooperate with each other." Closer cooperation, wrote Jones to Cooper, adopting the latter's lofty language, would not only enable the agencies to serve the press better, but also would contribute "something to the cause of international peace and to the well-being of mankind."[61] Cooper wrote in reply that he had "no thought" of breaking with Reuters.[62]

After Jones had sold Reuters to the PA, Cooper raised with him the prospect of a "European Associated Press." The idea, explained Cooper to Jones, would be that news that they each collected from their own sources in Europe would become the nucleus of a European Associated Press report. The European Associated Press would handle with the AP's advice and consent the business arrangements with the newspapers, and make the delivery. The AP would obtain 50 percent of the net receipts. "Jones is quite enthusiastic about this idea of mine," noted Cooper in an aide-mémoire. For Jones, the plan was an assurance of new revenue, and a means to displace the UP in Europe.[63] "All of this is on the assumption that we should not turn aside from our determination to go along with the agencies," wrote Cooper. "It is the only solution I can think of that puts us in the position of not competing with the European agencies, and it gives us opportunity to work indirectly with the newspapers in the matter of obtaining direct access to their news."[64] Meanwhile, Cooper confided to Iwanaga his "wish" that "cooperation as it has developed in America, Canada and Japan had reached equal development in the other great countries of the world," but, wrote Cooper, "frankly, I do not see much hope of some of the European countries coming to what we call the idealistic basis in this respect. But we can hope!"[65]

[59] Clements to Jones, October 7, 1926, Jones papers, series 2, box 3, RA.
[60] Agreement, October 7, 1926, Jones papers, series 2, box 2, RA.
[61] Jones to Cooper, October 6, 1926, Jones papers, series 2, box 3, RA.
[62] Cooper to Noyes, September 10, 1926, AP02A, box 10, folder 4, AP.
[63] Jones memo, May 13, 1927, LN80/874208, RA; Jones report, June 25, 1927, Jones papers, series 2, box 3, RA.
[64] July–October, 1927, Cooper papers, Ms I, LL.
[65] Cooper to Iwanaga, December 12, 1927, Cooper papers, series I, box 35, folder 7, AP.

Cooper sought to modify existing relations to create a new international alliance with the world's great news agencies, but Roy Howard of the UP berated him and the AP for maintaining the old system. "These agencies, almost without exception the propaganda distributors of their respective governments," wrote Howard of the European group in a circular to the editors of the UP, "are today one of the most pernicious influences blocking international amity," and it was from these agencies that the AP received its news. "To break away from some of the news swill-barrels from which they have been feeding, would require great additional expenditures and would be a tax on the energies of the A.P.'s antiquated and somewhat rheumatic European staff."[66] Much of this hyperbole was an exercise in publicity. Howard knew that not all of the agencies were tainted by government propaganda.[67] But just as much as Cooper relied on the rhetoric of Wilsonian liberalism to effect a change in the status quo, Howard counted on it to mock Cooper for failing to break sufficiently with the past. Cooper's idealism, and lack of progress, in the face of Howard's fiery rhetoric, although the rationale for both may have had similar origins, was one manifestation of the dichotomy that precipitated a more general shift in the United States away from Wilsonian liberalism toward isolationism.

COOPERATIVE COMPETITION

The real turning point away from close cooperation between the AP and the European agencies and toward cooperative competition came with the stock market crash of 1929, but the reason behind it was a mixture of Cooper's pursuit of a journalistic League of Nations and isolationism. The leading members of the AP board – Robert McCormick in particular – were convinced by neither Cooper's idealism nor Wilson's liberalism. The board was to Cooper as the American Senate was to Wilson. "If you dub it a 'New League of Nations,'" wrote Cooper to Noyes, who was receptive to the grand plan, "every member of the Board will be frightened away from it."[68] The stock market crash coincided with a noticeable shift in thinking at the AP away from Europe, just as it did at the American Federal Reserve. At their April board meeting in 1929, months before the crash, Adolph Ochs, publisher of the New York *Times*, and Robert McCormick, publisher of the Chicago *Tribune*, called for an end of relations with Reuters. Ochs claimed that Reuters's service was propagandistic and that the AP could put an end to the circulation of propaganda by terminating its alliances. "I do not know any larger contribution we could make to the peace of the world than to have a freer circulation of the news," said Ochs, "free from the influences of the governments." McCormick, who was fiercely anti-British

---

[66] Howard to all editors, June 20, 1927, Howard papers, UIB.
[67] E. Keen to Howard, May 12, 1927, Howard papers, box 18, LOC.
[68] Cooper to Noyes, July 30, 1926, AP02A, box 10, folder 4, AP.

and a dyed-in-the-wool isolationist, was convinced not only of Reuters's bias, but also the AP's supremacy.[69] According to McCormick,

the wealth of American newspapers is probably three quarters of the wealth of all of the newspapers in the world, or more. So it would be very easy for us to just dominate the news field of the world. We print much more news than all the other newspapers of the world, and I would be very glad to see the Associated Press step out and dominate the news service of the world.[70]

Although Cooper professed a desire to maintain a connection with Reuters if possible, "Roy Howard," said Cooper, was "willing to sign an agreement with me that if we will break with Reuters he will not take them on."[71] Despite the outward appearance of rivalry, Howard of the UP and Cooper of the AP formed a defensive alliance against Reuters that was known as the Ritz-Carlton agreement after the location in which it was concluded. Cooper made a similar pact with Iwanaga.[72]

Also at the AP board meeting of April 1929, Cooper proposed forming an Associated Press of Great Britain as a subsidiary through which the AP could contract directly with the press. The European agencies hindered the AP's expansion and provided inadequate news coverage while the AP corporate "structure [did] not lend itself to the activity of news dissemination abroad," said Cooper when explaining the plan. The AP needed to set up companies in Europe, argued Cooper, that were free to sell to any newspaper or news agency the news the AP collected, so long as such news would not be retransmitted by the recipients anywhere without the consent of the company that forwarded it. The plan, explained Cooper subsequently, was to "incorporate the present activities of The Associated Press abroad." Eventually, "each such company might be transformed into a mutual cooperative organization like The Associated Press."[73] In this regard, Cooper reported approvingly to the AP board the efforts of the Canadian Press to create an imperial cooperative organization along the lines of the AP, but whether he instigated the movement among the Canadians is unclear.[74] In 1931, the AP incorporated the Associated Press of Great Britain. From Jones' vantage, it appeared that the AP, by seeking to establish and exchange news with news associations on a non-commercial basis, threatened to undermine Reuters's business all over the world.

---

[69] L.G. Svendsgard, "McCormick, Robert Rutherford," *American National Biography Online* (February 2008).

[70] Minutes of AP meeting, April 17, 1929, Robert McCormick papers, box 9, Cantigny.

[71] Digest of verbatim board minutes, April 16–18 and 23, 1929, AP01.1, series III, box 3, folder 28, pp. 1021–2, AP.

[72] Cooper memo, December 18, 1929, Cooper papers, Ms I, LL.

[73] Cooper to Noyes, September 10, 1930, series I, box 23, folder 9, AP.

[74] Digest of verbatim board minutes, September 30, 1930, AP01.1, series III, box 3, folder 28, p. 1086, AP.

Although Jones and Cooper believed cooperation was useful, their aims were contradictory: Jones sought to sell his news abroad; Cooper wanted to exchange his. Jones attempted to placate the AP by granting it greater freedom of movement. He proposed that the allied agencies en masse could deny service to newspapers and news agencies that contracted with their rivals, but the AP had considered a similar strategy in the United States to prevent its members from taking the UP service and was advised by counsel that doing so would be in restraint of trade. The AP therefore feared that similar action abroad would incur the disapproval of the American Department of Justice.[75] Again, domestic law affected the AP's method of operation abroad. Exclusive foreign distributor agreements, such as those between the AP and Reuters, although not subject to the strict proscriptions of the Clayton Act, could be prosecuted under Section 1 of the Sherman Act. In 1914, however, the American Attorney General Thomas Watt Gregory considered the legality of the AP's agreements with Havas, Reuters, and Wolff and found nothing illegal about them. Although there was no attempt to test the legality of such agreements in the field of foreign trade before 1950, according to one legal scholar writing in 1953, the possibility was like the "sword of Damocles to foreign traders, particularly American manufacturers with large, well-developed foreign markets."[76] Apparently, the threat could be felt equally in the service sector.

Failing a rapprochement with Cooper, Jones appealed to the UP, claimed a special affinity with like-minded commercial news agencies, and sought a connection in case of a rupture with the AP. Roy Howard and Karl Bickel of the UP gave Jones reason to hope that such an alliance might be in the offing, but Jones never knew of the Ritz-Carlton agreement, the secret separate peace that already existed between Howard and Cooper.[77] Although the AP continued to press for greater independence, it had "no thought or desire," wrote Noyes to Jones, to "supplant or injuriously affect the relations of the agencies with their members or clients." Cooper agreed. "There is not in my opinion," wrote Cooper to the AP manager in London, "the slightest possibility of our breaking away from Reuters in our time." Bernard Rickatson-Hatt's reforms at Reuters's London headquarters had begun to bear fruit and the AP was favorably impressed with Reuters's news reports.[78] "Let me repeat my cordial

[75] Jones to Clements, October 25, 1923, Jones papers, series 1, box 56, RA; Cooper to Jones, October 9, 1930, Cooper papers, series I, box 36, folder 6, AP; Digest of verbatim board minutes, January 14, 1931, AP01.1, series III, box 3, folder 29, p. 1093, AP.

[76] W.N. Keyes, "Exclusive Foreign Distributor Agreements. Are they Illegal?," *California Law Review*, 41 (1953), 439–53.

[77] C.S.S. to Cooper, March 23, 1931, Cooper papers, Ms I, LL; Howard to Bickel, May 12,1931, Howard papers, UIB. Jones told the UP that Reuters was still a profit-making concern and at the same time told the AP that it was cooperative. See Jones to Cooper, March 4, 1931, Cooper papers, Ms I, LL.

[78] See Chapter 4.

satisfaction of the increasing solidarity of our relationships," wrote Cooper to Jones in January 1933.[79]

In May 1933, when Cooper departed New York for Vancouver en route to Japan to solidify relations with Iwanaga before the termination of Rengo's contract with Reuters, he found much to his dismay that Roy Howard had followed him. Cooper "was frostier than a traffic judge's smile" wrote Howard to Karl Bickel. "I'm not exactly sure why I am going, but I'm on my way, enjoying the tranquility of mind which nothing but my Hoosier confrere's disgruntled state could have raised so successfully."[80] Cooper was "consternated," he wrote, to learn that Howard was going to Japan, and, as Howard put it, "wherever you force me to go, besides." This was the second time that Howard had followed Cooper abroad. In the summer of 1918, Howard had tailed Cooper around South America.[81] Howard's notes of the journey across the United States and to Japan are revealing of Cooper's relationship with Reuters and with the AP board. "Cooper spoke very contemptuously of Jones and the latter's swankiness," wrote Howard. "It was very obvious to me, as it has been when I have talked with Jones, that there is no love lost between these two." Apparently, "Kent" also said "very frankly that Noyes absolutely dominates and runs the AP." Cooper regarded "Noyes as a dodo." He thought that the continued attitude of Noyes and Adolph Ochs – that the AP could put the UP out of business when it wanted – was misguided, but Cooper could do nothing about it for fear of "clashing head on into Noyes."

Noyes and Ochs were responsible for Cooper's appointment as AP general manager in 1925. When Melville Stone retired in 1921, he had kept Cooper out of the position and forced in Frederick Roy Martin, who had worked with Stone at the AP since 1912. Noyes and Ochs forced the resignation of Martin and put Cooper in against Stone's protest. Even after Cooper was elected, Stone moved back into his big office and Cooper was forced to take a small, obscure one. Stone made life miserable for Cooper for a year until, tiring of the experience of being back on the job, Stone withdrew, became reconciled to Cooper's appointment, and "mellowed considerably toward him in his last years." Stone died in 1929. Howard's notes of the trip also illustrate the close relationship he and Cooper had, which was behind their defensive pact against Reuters. Howard was certain that Cooper was amenable to "some sort of decent live-and-let-live working basis with the UP which would maintain an aggressive attitude on the part of both organizations, especially as regards news coverage, but which would eliminate the constant drive to beat down rates." Indeed,

[79] Noyes to Jones, March 31, 1931, series I, box 36, folder 14; Jones memo, May 13, 1931, series I, box 36, folder 12; Cooper to D. McKenzie, November 18, 1931, series I, box 36, folder 12; McKenzie to Cooper, December 22, 1932, series I, box 36, folder 15; Jones to Cooper, January 12, 1933, series I, box 36, folder 16; Cooper to Jones, January 21, 1933, series I, box 36, folder 16, AP.
[80] Howard to Bickel, May 5, 1933, Howard papers, UIB.
[81] Cooper to Noyes, May 6, 1933, Cooper papers, Ms I, LL.

Cooper proposed that the AP and UP partner to negotiate prices for telegraphic equipment from AT&T.[82]

When Cooper arrived in Japan in June 1933, he signed a new agreement with Iwanaga on the basis of a mutual exchange without any additional charge. This made it next to impossible for Reuters to extract a subscription. Iwanaga was deeply committed ideologically to a relationship with the AP, but, ideals aside, an exchange agreement with the AP promised to free Rengo of the heavy price Reuters's demanded for its news report. In June 1929, Iwanaga had signed a new contract with Reuters that allowed Rengo to receive news from the AP, but he remained dissatisfied. He sought a "fundamental revision of the old contract" according to the principles he and Cooper had laid out in the "Covenant of the League of News Agencies of the World," but he had to pay Jones £6,000 per annum.[83] In a long letter to Jones in which he explained his proposal for an agreement with Iwanaga, Cooper estimated that the consequent loss to Reuters's revenue would be $12,000. "In the magnitude of Reuters's income throughout the world," wrote Cooper, it "must be a negligible amount."[84] The comment could only have been calculated to irritate Jones, who had labored tirelessly to extract this sum from Iwanaga in the first place. Four days after writing to Jones, Cooper instructed staff at the AP to prepare a full service for Japan if relations with Reuters ceased.[85]

Cooper presented his agreement with Iwanaga as a fait accompli. Jones believed that this threat could only be countered with bold action or else Reuters would be forced into a position of accepting Cooper's proposed contract. After receiving Cooper's letter, Jones reported to his board his conviction that Cooper was deliberately intriguing against Reuters in the Far East and requested authorization to terminate Reuters's existing contract with a view to formulating a new understanding with AP. Barring a new satisfactory agreement with the AP, Jones declared that Reuters had to be prepared to look for other alliances or to go ahead alone. He explained to his PA directors that a break would inevitably bring the AP into England, but the board unanimously agreed to leave the matter entirely in Jones' hands, and a resolution to this effect was adopted. Ignorant of the Ritz-Carlton agreement between Cooper and Howard, Jones believed that the UP would willingly sign a contract with Reuters if a rupture with the AP ensued.[86] Jones was not eager to contract

[82] Howard to Bickel, May 11, 1933, Howard papers, box 82, LOC. See also T. Rantanen, "After Five O'clock Friends," *Roy W. Howard Monographs in Journalism and Mass Communication Research*, 4 (1998), 1–35.

[83] Iwanaga to Cooper, November 5, W. Turner to Iwanaga, November 7, Iwanaga to Turner, November 27, Iwanaga to Cooper, December 26, 1928, Iwanaga to Cooper, July 16, 1929, Cooper papers, Ms I, LL.

[84] Cooper to Jones, June 11, 1933, Cooper papers, Ms I, LL.

[85] J.S. Elliott to Noyes, June 16, 1933, Cooper papers, Ms I, LL.

[86] Bickel to Howard, June 28, 1933; Bickel to Vaughn, August 3, 1933; Bickel to Vaughn, August 15, 1933; Bickel to Howard, September 15, 1933, Howard papers, box 82, LOC; Jones memos,

with the UP, but he anticipated that the prospect of an agreement between the two agencies would be enough of a threat to induce the AP to continue relations along lines advantageous to Reuters.[87] In July 1933, Cooper arrived in London from Japan to negotiate with Jones the relationship between the AP and Rengo. Although Cooper professed to be apologetic and repeatedly attempted to assure Jones how important it was to him and to the AP board to continue satisfactory relations with Reuters, Jones found him insincere. Cooper claimed that he had gone into Japan for the benefit of Reuters and the AP with a hope of saving Rengo from financial ruin, but Jones was reluctant to believe this claim of good intentions, and felt particularly put on by the fact that AP had undersold Reuters. In November, Jones denounced Reuters's alliance with the AP.[88]

The split between Reuters and the AP rearranged the pattern of alliances, but did not eliminate them. The prospect of competition was too harrowing and the benefits of cooperation were too significant, although more so for Reuters than for the AP.[89] The PA, although it deplored a break with the AP, was unwilling to forsake Reuters, and Jones was sent to New York to ask Cooper for a new agreement.[90] Cooper exploited his position of power to gain an advantage over Reuters, which he later admitted was unfair, but by November 1934 at least the appearance of pleasant relations had returned. "The Associated Press can look to us with confidence not only for co-operation wherever it can be given but for real friendship and abundant goodwill," wrote Jones to Cooper.[91] By the terms of their new contract, the news of North America was valued the same as the news of the British Isles and the news that Reuters collected throughout the world. Each agency could now serve a newspaper that already received news through an allied agency, but could not serve it to a paper not connected to an allied agency. In theory, the news agencies could now sell their services to anyone anywhere and without consulting the other agencies. All deals for press association contracts were to be nonexclusive. In practice, Reuters, Havas, and Deutsches Nachrichtenbüro, the Nazi agency that replaced Wolff, renewed their contracts and pledged their allegiance to an alliance against American

---

November 7, 1933, Jones papers, series 1, box 37; Notes of phone conversation between Jones and Bickel, January 15, 1934, Jones papers, series 2, box 2, RA; Cooper to Noyes, January 30 and 31, 1934, Cooper papers, Ms I, LL; Bickel to Keen, February 8, 1934, Bickel to Howard, February 9, 1934, Howard papers, box 94, LOC.

[87] Jones to board, June 20, 1933, Jones papers, series 1, box 38, RA.

[88] Cooper to Noyes, July 30, 1933; Treaty between AP and Rengo, May 27, 1933; Cooper to Elliott, Jun 5, 1933, Cooper papers, Ms I, LL. Jones memo, "Reuters' relationship with the Associated Press," July 27, 1933 Jones papers, series 1, box 37; B. Rickatson-Hatt to Jones, March 31, 1934, Jones papers, series 1, box 35, RA.

[89] Reuters suffered not having access to the AP report. A.B. Maloney to Jones, April 21, 1934, Jones papers, series 1, box 35, RA.

[90] Cooper to Noyes, January 24, 1934, O. Mejer to Cooper, January 31, 1934, Cooper papers, Ms I, LL.

[91] Jones to Cooper, November 16, 1934, Jones, series 1, box 42, RA.

competition. Foreign newspapers and news agencies resented attempts by the AP to make "the world safe for American news."[92] Reuters served the INS, but only after Cooper agreed. He allowed Reuters to provide the service, but provided that it did not duplicate or improve on the service that the AP received from Reuters.

The AP continued to take the news service of the European triumvirate, which allowed Reuters to hold its allies in line and nullified the force of Cooper's attack on the Reuters-Havas organization. Only via Reuters and Havas could the allied agencies in Europe continue to distribute their news through the AP in the United States.[93] The new relationship between the AP and Reuters, was on "a basis of greater freedom vis-à-vis the other than either hitherto has enjoyed," wrote Jones to Cooper, "but I am confident that neither of us in the exercise of that freedom wishes to cut across the interests of the other."[94] In 1936, Roy Howard instructed Hugh Baillie, UP president from 1935 to 1955, to make a "working agreement" with Reuters in Asia that would allow each agency "to specialize on certain lines which the other would agree not to invade, and would enable them to just about double or treble they returns they are now getting."[95] In Japan, the AP service supplanted Reuters'. By 1937, less than 5 percent of foreign news distributed by the Japanese news agency derived from Reuters's sources. The bulk of Rengo's European news, including British news published in Japan under a London dateline, came from American sources through the AP and the UP.[96]

In 1939, the AP began making its news report available directly to the press of the United Kingdom through the Associated Press of Great Britain, which had incorporated in 1931. By April that year, more than 150 English newspapers outside London and three London papers took the AP service. By contrast, the British United Press served sixty-two.[97] Arthur Hays Sulzberger, publisher of the New York *Times* and a member of the AP board, acknowledged privately that the AP board had "determined to promote the idea of a free flow of news," but that "since we were unable to go out to make propaganda for this cause, we decided to do it through the extension of the AP facilities throughout the world." Unfortunately, conceded Sulzberger, Cooper had pursued his mission

---

92 C. Chancellor to Jones, May 10, 1945, Jones papers, series 2, box 4, RA.
93 W.J. Haley, report to the board, July 1, 1942, LN317 1/8818001; Jones to Mejer, March 9, Mejer to Jones, March 12, Jones memo, March 21, 1934, Jones papers, series 1, box 38; Contract, March 15, 1934, LN228/8712438, RA; Bickel to Keen, February 14, 1934, Howard papers, box 94, LOC; Jones to Cooper and reply, July 31, 1934, Jones papers, series 1, box 42, RA.
94 Jones to Cooper, June 22, 1934, Cooper papers, Ms II, LL.
95 Howard to H. Baillie, March 31, 1936, Howard papers, folder 117, LOC. Reuters and the UP made an agreement in 1939. "Arrangement between Reuters and the United Press," June 15, 1939, LN954/1/013298, RA.
96 Jones memo (copy), January 9, 1937, Jones papers, series 1, box 73, RA.
97 Digest of verbatim board minutes, April 24, 1939, AP01.1, series III, box 3, folder 29, p. 1142, AP; J.H. Furay to Baillie, June 16, 1939, Howard papers, folder 155, LOC.

with excessive zeal. "If anyone were to talk about the AP's virtues now, wrote Sulzberger in 1945, "he would be laughed at. They regard our organization rather cynically and they think we have blown our horn entirely too loud."[98] Lloyd Stratton, Cooper's successor, pursued a similar policy of establishing news exchange agreements with foreign newspapers but he did so without Cooper's ideological priggishness. For Stratton, news exchange was openly a means for ensuring mutual protection. "The greater the number of news sources, the broader and more thorough its news protection," wrote Stratton to his manager in Berlin. "The Associated Press wants the availability of its news for exchange with all other AP newspapers," wrote Stratton, but "the exception, of course, is that news furnished by one newspaper in a city is not delivered to a competitor or another newspaper in the same city."[99] The same ideas of cooperation and exclusivity that had historically informed the AP's domestic news arrangements continued to be the basis for its contracts abroad even after the United States Supreme Court's antitrust decision in 1945.

The contract signed between Cooper and Jones in 1934 injured the long-standing cooperation between the AP and Reuters, but in 1942, when *Barriers Down* was published, Cooper and W.J. Haley, Reuters's representative, signed an entirely new contract and pledged their agencies to each other as "blood brothers" in an "unreserved alliance all over the world in the matter of protective coverage against all comers." The basis covering their relationship was "compete and co-operate." Agreements along these lines continued in various forms until at least 1967, at which point Reuters's interests lay sufficiently in the commercial news arena that it no longer found its alliance with the AP useful. After 1943, Reuters principally sold its service in the United States through newspapers such as the New York *Times* and the Chicago *Tribune*, the publishers of which, nearly twenty years earlier, had helped to bring about a break with Reuters. These papers now had exclusive rights to the Reuters service. The contract with the Chicago *Tribune* restricted Reuters's general news service to the area west of the Mississippi River. For these large papers, which could afford to pay for a second report in addition to the AP, Reuters's news became a source of exclusive advantage. Smaller papers, which previously had access to Reuters's reports through the AP, were now excluded.[100]

"International intercourse," wrote Cooper in *Barriers Down*, "would rise to heights of perfection with the barriers down as to news exchange," yet the book was an exercise in propaganda.[101] The AP owned the copyright to it and Cooper had written it at the express urging of the board. "My own opinion," wrote Robert McCormick to Cooper when the book was published, "is that

[98] A.H. Sulzberger to McLean, July 23, 1945, AP01.4B, series VII, box 36, folder 683, AP.
[99] Stratton to Gallagher, February 19, 1947, AP01.4B, series IV, box 20, folder 277, AP.
[100] W.J. Haley, July 1, 1942, LN317 1/8818001; General order regarding United States, July 13, 1967, LN801/1/974582, RA.
[101] Cooper, *Barriers Down*, p. 320.

it should come out just two or three days before the [United States Supreme Court] trial opens. Then there will be a barrage of literary reviews all thru the trial and the book will get a tremendous advertising." The book was also more than mere publicity. Cooper, who started working for the AP in 1910, had devoted his life to the "cooperative principle" of newsgathering. Howard and Jones retired wealthy men, but Cooper had little else to show for his chosen path aside from the moral high ground, and even this was denied him. "All Kent was ever interested in was freedom – for him – of the rights of expansion against his colleagues in the international news distribution business," observed Karl Bickel, a UP executive. The comments of Hugh Bailie, another UP executive, regarding *Barriers Down* were more insightful:

All this adds up, of course, to Kent's campaign to deify himself as a combination of Abe Lincoln-Christopher Columbus of the press association scene. As Lincoln he emancipated us all from the thralldom of the foreign agencies; as Columbus he discovered new worlds in press association practice.[102]

Perhaps Cooper had little more to cling to than his own "crusade" after the AP was found in violation of American antitrust legislation. He kept at it during the war and after. In 1944, he appealed to Secretary of State Cordell Hull to promote "world news freedom."[103] Simultaneously, however, he contributed to the perpetuation of cooperation. Seen this way, Cooper's crusade is further evidence that free trade in the supply of news was always a fiction. Cooperation substituted for market competition. The agreements among the agencies facilitated the exchange of news and decreased the cost agencies incurred to assemble news reports. In turn, the expenses of individual newspaper publishers were reduced, their own newsgathering could increase, and access to international news improved.

Although cooperation was advantageous, a cartel was always the second best alternative to horizontal integration. Gerson Bleichröder and Paul Julius Reuters's idea of "die Fusion" was blocked for reasons of state. The joint-purse agreement between Reuters and Havas suffered for want of communication, and, as shown in the preceding chapter, the Canadians' hope for a British imperial news association floundered for want of coordination. Cooper and Iwanaga's idea for an "AP of APs" proved as idealistic and doomed as the League of Nations on which it was modeled. Attempts to export to other countries the AP's model of exclusive access to newspaper content before publication, however advantageous it may have been for the supply of news, encountered considerable local resistance. Instead, entangling alliances, although occasionally debilitating, remained the norm. Domestic political economy played a

---

[102] R. McCormick to Cooper, November 12, 1942, McCormick papers, box 6, Cantigny; K.A. Bickel to Baillie, December 22, 1942, Howard papers, box 186; Howard to W. Miller, December 24, 1942, Howard papers, box 187; Baillie to Bickel, December 28, 1942, Howard papers, box 186, LOC.

[103] Cooper to members, September 27, 1944, AP01.4B, series IX, box 58, folder 947, AP.

significant, if unintended, role in determining the extent of international cooperation. Concerns about national security precluded the formation of a nineteenth-century European-wide news organization. The decision of the Supreme Court in *INS v. AP*, which helped the AP to protect its method of organization, limited the association's actions abroad. The fear of antitrust regulation encouraged the AP to modify its relations with its foreign partners. By precluding outright merger or greater horizontal integration the state did not encourage competition so much as it perpetuated cartelization.

8

Conclusion

Between 1848 and 1947, institutional arrangements protected the supply of news. In the United States, weak regulation of telegraphy, permissive state laws, and favorable court decisions facilitated the maintenance of an exclusive form of news association that privileged those newspapers fortunate enough to be among its members. Although the AP's exclusive organization encouraged the emergence of rivals, competition was always contrived. When the UP threatened the AP, the latter became more inclusive. To increase the number of newspapers that benefited from the fruits of cooperation, *AP v. US* prohibited the association from excluding newspapers from membership based on concerns about newspaper competition. After the Supreme Court forced open the AP in 1945, as the Illinois Supreme Court had done in 1900, the AP resembled a public utility. In this respect, it was similar to the British PA, which from the time of its establishment in 1868 was required by the Post Office to provide its news reports to all paying provincial newspapers.

In Britain, the Telegraph Act of 1868, and continued attempts to maintain the market structure it engendered, provided considerable protection for the provincial press until World War I. The operation of telegraphy in Britain enabled members of the PA to benefit from the comparative wealth of the London press and from the revenues of Extel and Reuters. First telephony and then the onset of war in 1914 contributed to undermining the mid-Victorian settlement brought about by the Telegraph Act. After the war, it broke down entirely. Protection for the supply of news continued but shifted from the press to radio. By 1930, the PA had largely ceased to rely on the public system of telegraphy the Post Office provided, and instead developed a private network of leased lines.

The diminution and then disappearance of the postal subsidy for the press, combined with considerable concentration in the newspaper business, contributed to a period of post-war "rationalization" in the newspaper and newsgathering markets. Greater collusion and closer cooperation among the principal British news agencies and associations, as well as the legacy of the Telegraph Acts, imposed on the British Broadcasting Company an obligation to take news from existing news agencies and associations, but only temporarily. In broadcasting, profits derived not from distinct content generators, as with telegraphy, but from listeners. It made sense that broadcasters should offset the price of erecting broadcasting infrastructure by producing programming, even if this meant upsetting the traditional separation between content generation and distribution. After 1926, when the monopoly over broadcasting passed to the BBC, the modus vivendi with the news agencies and associations deteriorated. As the subsidy for the press passed to radio, the newspaper business became more concentrated, which helped to bridge the historic rift between the London and provincial press. This process, coupled with government pressure, led to the creation of the Reuters Trust. Following World War II, two regulated monopolies – the Reuters Trust, owned by the press, and the BBC – towered over the media landscape in Britain.

Throughout the colonies and dominions of the British Empire, newspapers also cooperated, often to the detriment of Reuters, the so-called imperial news agency. Newspapers throughout the British Empire also benefited from limited copyrights in news, which strengthened their bargaining position against Reuters. Initially, Reuters benefited from privileged access to international submarine cables, but still it frequently found imperial markets inhospitable. The key to solving Reuters's difficulties throughout the Empire lay in striking an appropriate balance between cooperation and exclusion. The most effective way in which to achieve this balance was to form combinations with the imperial press. Reuters only developed this strategy during the interwar period. Before that, Reuters substituted the lackluster profits it derived from selling news by embarking on various alternative lines of business. By the time Reuters brought the majority of the imperial press into partnership, it had become a subsidiary of the PA and the profits the agency made overseas subsidized the supply of news to the provincial press of the British Isles. Privileged access to wireless telegraphy in Britain enabled Reuters to develop highly remunerative services of commercial news, which helped increasingly to offset the cost of the agency's unremunerative news business.

Domestic institutional arrangements affected the extent to which news agencies and associations cooperated abroad. American competition policy, intellectual property rights, and regulation influenced the international strategy of the AP. Reuters's position in the British Isles, which was a direct outcome of the nationalization of telegraphy in 1868, also influenced the manner in which the agency behaved overseas. At various times during the nineteenth century, governments intervened to prevent mergers among the several major news organizations of Britain, Germany, and France, but doing so only perpetuated cartelization. The considerable benefits that closer cooperation

promised kept the idea of an international news organization alive. In addition
to the coordination problems inherent in establishing any global cooperative
endeavor, isolationism, nationalism, self-interest, and the onset of World War
II all prohibited the realization of Iwanaga and Cooper's dream of an international League of News Agencies, yet cooperation continued in another form.

It is apparent that cooperation for the supply of news was most successful
when content generators were in control. This is why Reuters found that the
only way in which to resolve the longstanding difficulties that confronted its
news business was to sell out to the press or bring it into partnership. Since
the 1930s, Reuters has made its profits from supplying financial information
and related services. In hindsight, it makes sense that content generators, such
as newspaper publishers, would be more willing to pay for an assembled news
report when they could exercise control over the way in which it was distributed, but this model did not always prevail. In the United States, the small group
of publishers who constituted the NYAP exercised control over the distribution of news throughout the country, in large part because of their geographic
position, but also because of their close connection with American telegraph
companies. Before the nationalization of telegraphy in Britain in 1868, a cartel
of telegraph companies also supplied news reports to the provincial press. As a
consequence, Reuters, a joint-stock company owned principally by shareholders unconnected to newspaper publishing, supplied foreign and imperial news
to the British Isles until 1925.

Private contracts among newspapers for the exclusive exchange of news
before publication were the most effective way in which to generate a de facto
property right in news. Before publication, the news was customarily regarded
as private property. Once the news was published, it was free for all to appropriate. Establishing the contractual relations necessary to achieve exclusive
exchange before publication required considerable coordination. The history
of the AP and its predecessors demonstrates that the prospect of a de facto
property right in news, and a corresponding ability to exclude others, was sufficiently enticing to facilitate the level of commitment and coordination necessary for cooperation. Exclusive exchange before publication was more readily
achieved when the newspaper publishers that supplied the news owned the
clearinghouse. It did not have to be this way, but newspaper ownership enabled
publishers to allocate different rights to different members depending on their
relative contribution to the common pool of news, control which newspapers
had access to the news reports, and bar competitors. The extent to which the
courts upheld the contractual relationships necessary to maintain the exclusive
exchange of news before publication determined the strength of the de facto
property right that members of the AP held over the news reports generated by
the association.

It was not necessarily the case that the supply of news benefited from a
clear separation between the organizations that distributed it and those that
produced it. As with common carriers generally, it has been an established

principle for centuries that distributors of news ought not to censor the content
they carry. Rarely in the past did distributors undertake to write or censor the
news, but, nevertheless, networks have never been neutral.[1] Every means of
telecommunication since the Post Office has favored the distribution of certain
types of information over the circulation of other types. In both Britain and the
United States, the Post Office privileged newspapers over other forms of mail.
Whether newspapers published in the cities or in the provinces received the
majority of this subsidy depended on the way in which the post office priced
its services.[2]

Telegraphy and broadcasting were not neutral either. Collusion between
Western Union and the NYAP privileged the newspapers of that organization
over those excluded from it. The leasing of telegraph lines to news associations, which Western Union undertook extensively in the 1880s, gave news
associations greater control over the means of news distribution. By improving
the ability of the AP to exchange news exclusively before publication, leased
lines reinforced the common property right members of the association held in
the news report. Leased lines also generated significant economies because the
price of distributing news was determined by the hour instead of by the word.
This encouraged an increase in the speed with which news was collected and in
the quantity of news that was distributed.

In Britain, after the nationalization of telegraphy, the postal subsidy for the
press continued, but it favored the provincial over the London press. By contrast, telephony in Britain, which was initially privately owned and largely
unregulated, favored the London press and wealthy publishers in the provinces. For this reason, telephony helped to bring about the end of the settlement established by nationalization. The granting of leased lines by the Post
Office to the provincial British press in many ways marked the end of the
long-standing postal subsidy for the press and the beginning of the subsidy for
broadcasting. The formation of the British Broadcasting Company brought
conduits and content even closer. Although the press self-servingly complained
that this violated the traditional separation between conduits and content, it
was the culmination of a trend toward a closer connection between the two. In
the United States, there was no clear separation either. Newspaper publishers
started radio stations in droves. The AP's initial reluctance to admit broadcasting companies to membership proved untenable. Invariably, parties excluded
from preferential access to particular telecommunications networks screamed
unfair competition or restraint on trade, but neutrality was never achieved.
Instead, preferences simply shifted.

The state in Britain and the United States not only played an important role
in news markets generally, it facilitated the creation of mechanisms required

[1] *Contra* T. Wu, "Network Neutrality, Broadband Discrimination," *Journal On Telecommunications and High Technology Law*, 2 (2003), p. 142.
[2] John, *Spreading the News*, p. 39.

to render access to news exclusive. In the United States, loose regulation of telegraphy allowed the formation of exclusive news associations along the lines of the AP. The corporation laws of New York protected the private contracts necessary for the exchange of news before publication. Then, in 1918, in the landmark case of *INS*, the United States Supreme Court granted the AP a quasi-property right against its competitors over the news of its members even after publication. This decision further reinforced the viability of the AP's method of exchanging news exclusively before publication. In Britain, the Post Office encouraged the formation of a monopolistic provincial news association. Granting the PA privileged use of telegraphy enabled the association to leverage the comparative wealth of the London press to fund the supply of news to its provincial members. Preferential treatment from the Post Office also placed the PA in a strong position against Reuters, the principal supplier of foreign news to the British Isles. Throughout the British Empire, the press benefited from de jure but limited copyrights in news.

Competition was always contrived. By controlling its membership, the AP explicitly promoted the establishment of the UP as a viable rival to counter accusations of monopoly. The antitrust case in 1945, inasmuch as it had any significant impact on the newsgathering market, probably increased the strength of the AP. In any event, the AP, UP, and INS were not competitors. The so-called Ritz Carlton Pact that Cooper and Howard signed against Reuters is a prime example of the way in which competition was more a guise than reality. In Britain, collusive relationships were pervasive. The PA and Reuters cooperated closely until the agency became a subsidiary of the association. During the nineteenth century, Central News and Extel were occasional rivals to the PA, like the UP was to the AP, but they were partners by the interwar period. Internationally, cooperation and cartelization was the norm. Indeed, disparate firms existed more because of the barriers to merger erected by culture and the costs of coordination than because of competition.

A freely competitive marketplace for ideas was always a fiction, but a steadfast belief in the educational and democratic value of news provided the ideological rationale for encouraging the establishment of different institutional arrangements that protected its supply. The so-called rationalist illusion – the transubstantiation by which Georgians and Victorians magically converted the printed word into the stuff of education and class conditioning – accounts in part for the postal subsidy to the press in Colonial America and Britain. It accounts as well for the perpetuation of that subsidy after the nationalization of telegraphy in Britain in 1868. In the United States, in part because of a right enshrined in the First Amendment, private restraints and public censorship were two sides of the same coin. The representatives of the press made extensive use the First Amendment to stave off regulation, but it was also the rationale behind judicial intervention. Certainly it was at the forefront of the mind of Judge Augustus Hand when he wrote his opinion in *INS v. AP*. Likewise, it was an important consideration for Judge Learned Hand and Justice Felix

Frankfurter when *AP v. US* came before them. In Britain, there was a clearer separation in rhetoric between business practice and considerations of press freedom, yet a belief in the democratic function of the press was still influential in political economy. However much economics and technology mattered, convictions about the importance of a free press, although predicated on idealistic theories of communication, shaped the supply of news.

Bibliography

List of Archives

American Jewish Archives, Cincinnati, OH
   Ochs, A. papers
   Rosewater, V. papers
Associated Press Corporate Archives, New York, NY
Bancroft Library, Berkeley University, Berkeley, CA
   Hearst, W.R. papers
   Neylan, J.F. papers
BBC Written Archives Centre, Caversham
British Telecom Archives, London
Cantigny Park, Robert McCormick Archives, Wheaton, IL
E.H. Butler Library, Buffalo State College, Buffalo, NY
   Butler, E.H. papers
Harvard University, Cambridge, MA
   Bleichröder, G. papers (Baker Library)
   Frankfurter, F. papers (Law School Library)
   New England Associated Press papers (Baker Library)
   Villard, O.G. papers (Houghton Library)
Indiana Historical Society, Indianapolis, IN
   Smith, D. papers
   Smith, W.H. papers
Library of Congress, Washington, DC
   Ackerman, C. papers
   Bennett, J.G. papers
   Clapper, R. papers
   Greeley, H. papers
   Howard, R.W. papers
   Marble, M. papers
   Pulitzer, J. papers
   Pulitzer, J. Jr. papers

Lilly Library, Indiana University, Bloomington, IN
  Cooper, K. papers
London Metropolitan Archives, London
  Exchange Telegraph Co. papers
  Press Association papers
National Archives, Washington, DC
National Archives, Public Record Office, Kew Gardens
New York Historical Society, New York, NY
  Lefferts, M. papers
New York Public Library, New York, NY
  Bennett, J.G. papers
  Bryan-Godwin papers
  Dana, C. papers
  Field, C. papers
  Ford, G.L. papers
  George, H. papers
  Greeley, H. papers
  Jones, G. papers
  Mail and Express papers
  McElway, S.C., papers
  Ochs, A. papers
  Raymond, H.J. papers
Newberry Library, Chicago
  Field Enterprises papers
  Lawson, V. papers
  Stone, M.E. papers
Ohio Historical Society, Columbus, OH
  Smith, W.H. papers
Post Office Archives, London
Reuters Archive, London
Roy W. Howard Archives, Indiana University, Bloomington, IN
Western Union archives, Smithsonian Institute, Washington, DC

Newspapers

Nineteenth-Century British Library Newspapers (online)
Nineteenth-Century U.S. Newspapers (online)
The Fourth Estate
The New York Times
The Times Digital Archive

Unpublished Materials

Beauchamp, C. "The Telephone Patents: Intellectual Property, Business, and the Law in the United States and Britain, 1876–1900," (PhD thesis, University of Cambridge, 2007).
Nalbach, A. "The Ring Combination: Information, Power, and the World News Agency Cartel, 1856–1914," (unpublished PhD thesis, University of Chicago, 1999).

Select Articles and Books

Adams, E.E. "Collusion and Price Fixing in the American Newspaper Industry: Market Preservation Trends, 1890–1910," *Journalism and Mass Communication Quarterly*, 79 (2002), 416–26.

Akami, T. *Japan's News Propaganda and Reuters' News Empire in Northeast Asia, 1870–1934*. Dordorecht: Republic of Letters, 2012.

Albion, R.G. *The Rise of New York Port*. London: Charles Scribner's Sons, 1939.

Alchian, A.A. and Woodward, S. "The Firm Is Dead; Long Live the Firm: A Review of Oliver Williamson's *The Economic Institutions of Capitalism*," *Journal of Economic Literature*, 26 (1988), 65–79.

Allen, G. "News Across the Border: Associated Press in Canada, 1894–1917," *Journalism History*, 31 (2006), 206–17.

  "New Media, Old Media, and Competition: Canadian Press and the Emergence of Radio News, 1922–1941," in G. Allen and D.J. Robinson (eds.), *Communicating in Canada's Past: Essays in Media History*. Toronto: University of Toronto Press, 2009, 47–77.

  "North American Triangle: Canadian Press, Associated Press, and Reuters, 1918–1939," in P. Putnis, C. Kaul, and J. Wilke (eds.), *International Communication and Global News Networks: Historical Perspectives*. Cresskill, NJ: Hampton Press, 2011, 189–216.

Aspinall, A. *Lord Brougham and the Whig Party*. London: Longmans, 1928.

Asquith, I. "The Structure, Ownership and Control of the Press, 1780–1855," in G. Boyce, J. Curran, and P. Wingate (eds.), *Newspaper History from the Seventeenth Century to the Present Day*. London: Constable, 1978, 98–116.

Atcheson, Jr., G. "The Cable Situation in the Pacific Ocean, with Special Reference to the Far East," *Annals of the American Academy of Political and Social Science*, 122 (1925), 70–7.

Baehr Jr., H.W. *The* New York *Tribune since the Civil War*. New York: Dodd, Mead & Company, 1936.

Bagdikian, B.H. *Media Monopoly*. Boston: Beacon Press, 2000.

Baird, D.G. "Common Law Intellectual Property and the Legacy of International News Service v. Associated Press," *University of Chicago Law Review*, 50 (1983), 411–29.

  "Property, Natural Monopoly, and the Uneasy Legacy of *INS v. AP*," *University Chicago Law & Economics, Olin Working Paper* no. 246. (2008).

Bakker, G. "Trading Facts: Arrow's Fundamental Paradox and the Emergence of Global News Networks, 1750–1900," *Working Papers on the Nature of Evidence: How Well do Facts Travel?* (2007).

Baldasty, G.J. *The Commercialization of News in the Nineteenth Century*. Madison: University of Wisconsin Press, 1992.

  E.W. Scripps and the Business of Newspapers. Urbana: University of Illinois Press, 1999.

  "The Economics of Working-Class Journalism, the E.W. Scripps Newspaper Chain, 1878–1908," *Journalism History*, 25 (1999), 3–12.

Balganesh, S. "'Hot News': The Enduring Myth of Property in News," *Columbia Law Review*, 111 (2011), 419–95.

Baillie, H. *High Tension: The Recollections of Hugh Baillie*. London: Werner Laurie, 1960.

Baker, C.E., *Media, Markets, and Democracy*. Cambridge: Cambridge University Press, 2004.

Barton, R.N. "New Media: the Birth of Telegraphic News in Britain," *Media History*, 16 (2010), 379–406.

Basse, D. *Wolff's Telegraphisches Bureau, 1849 bis 1933*. Munich: K.G. Saur, 1991.

Bayly, C.A. *Empire and Information: Intelligence Gathering and Social Communication in India, 1780–1870*. Cambridge: Cambridge University Press, 1986.

Beckert, S. *The Monied Metropolis: New York City and the Consolidation of the American Bourgeoisie, 1850–1896*. Cambridge: Cambridge University Press, 2001.

Belknap, G.N. "Oregon Sentinel Extras – 1858–1864," *Pacific Northwest Quarterly*, 70 (1979), 178–80.

Bekken, J. "'The Most Vindictive and Most Vengeful Power': Labor Confronts the Chicago Newspaper Trust," *Journalism History*, 18 (1992), 11–17.

Bensel, R.F. *The Political Economy of American Industrialization, 1877–1900*. Cambridge: Cambridge University Press, 2000.

Bentley, L. "The Electric Telegraph and the Struggle over Copyright in News in Australia, Great Britain and India," in B. Sherman and L. Wiseman (eds.), *Copyright and the Challenge of the New*. Alphen an den Rijn: Kluwer, 2012, 43–76.

Bently, L. "Copyright and the Victorian Internet: Telegraphic Property Laws in Colonial Australia," *Loyola of Los Angeles Law Review*, 38 (2004), 71–176.

Bickel, K. *News Empires: The Newspaper and the Radio*. Philadelphia: J.B. Lippincott Co., 1930.

Blainey, G. *The Tyranny of Distance: How Distance Shaped Australia's History*. London: Macmillan, 1968.

Blanchard, M.A. "The Associated Press Antitrust Suit: A Philosophical Clash over Ownership of First Amendment Rights," *The Business History Review*, 61 (1987), 43–85.

Blondheim, M. *News Over the Wires: the Telegraph and the Flow of Public Information in America, 1844–1897*. London: Harvard University Press, 1994.

"'Public Sentiment is Everything': The Union's Public Communications Strategy and the Bogus Proclamation of 1864," *Journal of American History*, 89 (2002), 869–99.

"'Slender Bridges' of Misunderstanding: The Social Legacy of Transatlantic Cable Communication," in N. Finzsch and U. Lehmkuhl (eds.), *Atlantic Communications: The Media in American and German History from the Seventeenth to the Twentieth Century*. Oxford: Berg, 2004, 153–69.

Blundell, J.W. *Telegraph Companies Considered as Investments; with Remarks on the Superior Advantages of Submarine Cables*. London: Effingham Wilson, 1869.

Bouckaert, B. "What Is Property?" *Harvard Journal of Law & Public Policy*, 13 (1990), 775–817.

Boyce, R.W.D. "Imperial Dreams and National Realities: Britain, Canada and the Struggle for a Pacific Telegraph Cable, 1879–1902," *The English Historical Review*, 115 (2000), 39–70.

Boyd-Barrett, O. *The International News Agencies*. London: Constable, 1980.

"'Global' News Agencies," in O. Boyd-Barrett and T. Rantanen (eds.), *The Globalization of News*. London: Sage, 1998, 19–34.

Brinkley, A. *The End of Reform: New Deal Liberalism in Recession and War.* New York: Alfred A. Knopf, 1995.

Broadberry, S. *Market Services and the Productivity Race, 1850–2000.* Cambridge: Cambridge University Press, 2006.

Broadberry, S.N. and Ghosal, S. "From the Counting House to the Modern Office: Explaining Anglo-American Productivity Differences in Services, 1870–1990," *The Journal of Economic History*, 62 (2002), 967–98.

Brooker-Gross, S.R. "News Wire Services in the Nineteenth-Century United States," *Journal of Historical Geography*, 7 (1981), 167–79.

Brown, L. *Victorian News and Newspapers.* Oxford: Clarendon Press, 1985.

Brown, R.D. *Knowledge Is Power: The Diffusion of Information in Early America, 1700–1865.* Oxford: Oxford University Press, 1989.

Bruchey, S. *The Roots of American Economic Growth, 1607–1861.* New York: Harper & Row, 1965.

Bruton, P.W. "United States v. Associated Press," *University of Pennsylvania Law Review*, 92 (1943), 209–10.

Burdick, C.K. "The Origin of the Peculiar Duties of Public Service Companies. Part II," *Columbia Law Review*, 11 (1911), 514–31.

Campbell, L.R. and Wolseley, R.E. (eds.). *Newsmen at Work: Reporting and Writing the News.* New York: Houghton Mifflin Co., 1949.

Campbell-Kelly, M. "Data Processing and Technological Change: The Post Office Savings Bank, 1861–1930," *Technology and Culture*, 39 (1998), 1–32.

Camrose, W.E.B. *British Newspapers and Their Controllers.* London: Cassell, 1947.

Carter, J.D. "Before the Telegraph: The News Service of the *San Francisco Bulletin*, 1855–1861," *Pacific Historical Review*, 11 (1942), 301–17.

Catledge, T. *My Life and The Times.* New York: Harper & Row, 1971.

Chadwick, E. "On the Economy of Telegraphy as Part of a Public System of Postal Communication," *Royal Society of Arts*, 15 (1867), 222–30.

"Results of Different Principles of Legislations and Administration in Europe; of Competition for the Field, as Compared with Competition within the Field, of Service," *Journal of the Statistical Society of London*, 22 (1859), 381–420.

Chandler, Jr., A. "The Growth of the Transnational Industrial Firm in the United States and the United Kingdom: A Comparative Analysis," *The Economic History Review*, 33 (1980), 396–410.

The Visible Hand: The Managerial Revolution in American Business. London: Harvard University Press, 1977.

Scale and Scope: The Dynamics of Industrial Capitalism. Cambridge, MA: Belknap Press, 1990.

Charnley, M.V. *News by Radio.* New York: Macmillan Co., 1948.

Church, R.A. *The Dynamics of Victorian Business.* London: George Allen & Unwin, 1980.

Coase, R. "The Federal Communications Commission," *The Journal of Law and Economics*, 2 (1959), 1–40.

"The British Post Office and the Messenger Companies," *The Journal of Law and Economics*, 4 (1961), 12–65.

"Rowland Hill and the Penny Post," *Economica*, 6 (1939), 423–35.

"The Market for Goods and the Market for Ideas," *The American Economic Review*, 64 (1974), 384–91.

Cole, J. and Hamilton, J.M. "A Natural History of Foreign Correspondence: A Study of the Chicago *Daily News*, 1900–1921," *Journalism and Mass Communication Quarterly*, 84 (2007), 151–66.

Collins, H.M. *From Pigeon Post to Wireless*. London: Hodder and Stoughton, 1925.

Colpus, E. "*The Week's Good Cause*: Mass Culture and Cultures of Philanthropy at the Inter-war BBC," *Twentieth Century British History*, 22 (2011), 305–29.

Cook, F.H. "The Application of the Commerce Clause to the Intangible," *University of Pennsylvania Law Review*, 58 (1910), 411–25.

Cooper, K. *Barriers Down: The Story of the News Agency Epoch*. Port Washington, NY: Kennikat Press, 1942.

"Newspaper Statesmanship for Peace," in F.L. Mott (ed.), *Journalism in Wartime*. Washington, DC: American Council on Public Affairs, 1943, 214–16.

"Freedom of information," *Life*, 17 (1944), 55–60.

The Right to Know: An Exposition of the Evils of News Suppression and Propaganda. New York: Farrar, Straus and Cudahy, 1956.

Kent Cooper and the Associated Press: An Autobiography. New York: Random House, 1959.

Crouthamel, J.L. "The Newspaper Revolution in New York, 1830–1860," *New York History*, 45 (1964), 91–113.

Bennett's New York Herald and the Rise of the Popular Press. Syracuse, NY: Syracuse University Press, 1989.

Cronon, W. *Nature's Metropolis: Chicago and the Great West*. London: Norton, 1991.

Cryle, D. *Disreputable Profession: Journalists and Journalism in Colonial Australia*. Rockhampton, Queensland: Central Queensland University Press, 1997.

"The Empire Press Union and Antipodean Communications: Australian-New Zealand Involvement, 1909–50," *Media History*, 8 (2002), 49–62.

Curl, D.W. *Murat Halstead and the Cincinnati Commercial*. Boca Raton: University Press of Florida, 1980.

Curran, J. and Seaton, J. *Power without Responsibility: The Press and Broadcasting in Britain*. London: Routledge, 1997.

Curran, K.J. "Exclusive Dealing and Public Policy," *The Journal of Marketing*, 15 (1950), 133–44.

Daunton, M. *Royal Mail: The Post Office since 1840*. London: Athlone Press, 1985.

Dennis, C.H. *Victor Lawson: His Time and His Work*. Chicago: The University of Chicago Press, 1935.

Desbordes, R. "Representing 'Informal Empire' in the Nineteenth Century: Reuters in South America at the Time of the War of the Pacific, 1879–83," *Media History*, 14 (2008), 121–39.

Diehl, C.S. *The Staff Correspondent*. San Antonio, TX: Clegg, 1931.

Dobbin, F. "The Social Construction of the Great Depression: Industrial Policy during the 1930s in the United States, Britain, and France," *Theory and Society*, 22 (1993), 1–56.

Forging Industrial Policy: The United States, Britain, and France in the Railway Age. Cambridge: Cambridge University Press, 1997.

DuBoff, R.B. "The Telegraph in Nineteenth-Century America: Technology and Monopoly," *Comparative Studies in Society and History*, 26 (1984), 571–86.

Ekelund Jr., R.B. and Price III, E.O. "Sir Edwin Chadwick on Competition and the Social Control of Industry: Railroads," *History of Political Economy*, 11 (1979), 213–39.

Ellis, H. "Paradoxes of the Associated Press Decision: A Reply," *The University of Chicago Law Review*, 13 (1946), 471–6.

Ellis, K. *The Post Office in the Eighteenth Century: A Study in Administrative History*. London: Oxford University Press, 1958.

Emery, M., Emery, E., and N.L. Roberts. *The Press and America: An Interpretive History of the Mass Media*, 9th ed. Boston: Allyn & Bacon, 2000.

Epstein, R.A. "International News Service v. Associated Press: Custom and Law as Sources of Property Rights in News," *Virginia Law Review*, 78 (1992), 85–128.

Fear, J. "Cartels," in G. Jones and J. Zeitlin (eds.), *The Oxford Handbook of Business History*. Oxford: Oxford University Press, 2008, 268–92.

Fenby, J. *The International News Services*. New York: Schocken Books, 1986.

Ferguson, N. *The World's Banker: The History of the House of Rothschild*. London: Weidenfeld & Nicolson, 1998.

Field, A.J. "Communications," in R. Such and S.B. Carter (eds.), *Historical Statistics of the United States, Vol. 4: Economic Sectors*. Cambridge: Cambridge University Press, 2006, 977–98.

Foreman-Peck, J. "Competition, Co-operation, and Nationalisation in the Nineteenth-century Telegraph System," *Business History*, 31 (1989), 81–99.

Foreman-Peck, J. and R. Millward, *Public and Private Ownership of British Industry, 1820–1990*. Oxford: Clarendon Press, 1994.

Freyer, T.A. *Regulating Big Business: Antitrust in Great Britain and America, 1880–1990*. Cambridge: Cambridge University Press, 1994.

"Business Law and American Economic History," in S.L. Engerman and R.E. Gallman (eds.), *The Cambridge Economic History of the United States, Vol. 2: The Long Nineteenth Century*. Cambridge: Cambridge University Press, 2000, 435–82.

Fuller, W.E. "The Populists and the Post Office," *Agricultural History*, 65 (1991), 1–16.

Gabel, D. "Private Telecommunications Networks: an Historical Perspective," in E. Noam and A. NiShuilleabhain (eds.), *Private Networks Public Objectives*. Amsterdam: Elsevier, 1996, 35–49.

Gabler, E. *The American Telegrapher: A Social History, 1860–1900*. London: Rutgers University Press, 1988.

Galambos, L. "The Triumph of Oligopoly," in D. Schaefer and T.J. Weiss (eds.), *American Economic Development in Historical Perspective*. Stanford, CA: Stanford University Press, 1994, 244–53.

Gramling, O. *AP: The Story of News*. Port Washington, NY: Kennikat Press, 1969.

Gray, K. "Property in Thin Air," *Cambridge Law Journal*, 50 (1991), 252–307.

de Grazia, V. *Irresistible Empire: America's Advance through Twentieth-Century Europe*. Cambridge, MA: Belknap Press, 2005.

Greenwood, J. *Newspapers and the Post Office, 1635–1834*. Reigate: Postal History Society, 1971.

Griffen-Foley, B. "The Fairfax, Murdoch and Packer Dynasties in Twentieth-Century Australia," *Media History*, 8 (2002), 89–102.

Hallock, W.H. *Life of Gerard Hallock: Editor of the New York Journal of Commerce*. New York: Oakley, Mason & Co., 1869.

Hamilton, M.W. *The Country Printer: New York State, 1785–1830.* New York: Columbia University Press, 1936.

Hannah, L. "Managerial Innovation and the Rise of the Large-Scale Company in Interwar Britain," *The Economic History Review,* 27 (1974a), 252–70.

"Mergers in British Manufacturing Industry, 1880–1918," *Oxford Economic Papers,* 26 (1974b), 1–20.

"Mergers, Cartels and Concentration: Legal Factors in the U.S. and European Experience," in N. Horn and J. Kocka (eds.), *Recht und Entwicklung der Großunternehmen im 19. und frühen 20. Jahrhundert.* Göttingen: Vandenhoeck & Ruprecht, 1979, 306–16.

The Rise of the Corporate Economy, 2nd ed. London: Methuen, 1983.

"A Failed Experiment: the State Ownership of Industry," in R. Floud and P. Johnson (eds.), *The Cambridge Economic History of Modern Britain, Vol. 3: Structural Change and Growth, 1939–2000.* Cambridge: Cambridge University Press, 2004, 81–111.

Hannis, G. "The New Zealand Press Association 1880–2006: The Rise and Fall of a Cooperative Model for News-Gathering," *Australian Economic History Review,* 48 (2008), 47–67.

Harlow, A.F. *Old Wires and New Waves: The History of the Telegraph, Telephone, and Wireless.* London: D. Appleton-Century Co., 1936.

Harvey, R. "Bringing the News to New Zealand: The Supply and Control of Overseas News in the Nineteenth Century," *Media History,* 8 (2002), 21–34.

He, J. *Die Nachrichtenagenturen in Deutschland: Geschichte und Gegenwart.* Frankfurt: Peter Lang, 1996.

Headrick, D.R. *The Invisible Weapon: Telecommunications and International Politics, 1851–1945.* Oxford: Oxford University Press, 1991.

Headrick, D.R. and Griset, P. "Submarine Telegraph Cables: Business and Politics, 1838–1939," *The Business History Review,* 75 (2001), 543–78.

Hemmeon, J.C. *The History of the British Post Office.* Cambridge, MA: Harvard University Press, 1912.

Herd, H. *The March of Journalism: The Story of the British Press from 1622 to the Present Day.* London: Allen & Unwin, 1952.

Hill, R. *Post Office Reform: Its Importance and Practicability,* 3rd ed. London: Charles Knight & Co., 1837.

Hills, J. *Struggle for Global Control of Communication: The Formative Century.* Urbana: University of Illinois Press, 2002.

Telecommunications and Empire. Urbana: University of Illinois Press, 2007.

Hilton, B. *A Mad, Bad, and Dangerous People? England, 1783–1846.* Oxford: Clarendon Press, 2006.

Hochfelder, D. "A Comparison of the Postal Telegraph Movement in Great Britain and the United States, 1866–1900," *Enterprise & Society,* 1 (2000), 739–61.

Hovenkamp, H. *Enterprise and American Law, 1836–1937.* London: Harvard University Press, 1991.

Hudson, F. *Journalism in the United States, from 1690 to 1872.* New York: Harper & Brothers, 1873, reprinted London: Routledge, 2000.

Hugill, P.J. *Global Communications since 1844: Geopolitics and Technology.* London: Johns Hopkins University Press, 1999.

Huntzicker, W. *The Popular Press, 1833–1865.* Westport, CT: Greenwood Press, 1999.

Hyde, F.E. *Cunard and the North Atlantic, 1840–1973: A History of Shipping and Financial Management*. London: The Macmillan Company, 1975.

Inglis, K.S. "The Imperial Connection: Telegraphic Communication between England and Australia, 1872–1902," in A.F. Madden and W.H. Morris-Jones (eds.) *Australia and Britain: Studies in a Changing Relationship*. London: University of London, 1980, 21–38.

Innis, H. "Technology and Public Opinion in the United States," *The Canadian Journal of Economics and Political Science*, 17 (1951), 1–24.

Israel, M. *Communications and Power: Propaganda and the Press in the Indian Nationalist Struggle, 1920–1947*. Cambridge: Cambridge University Press, 1994.

Iwanaga, S. *Story of Japanese News Agencies*. Tokyo: Shinbun Tsushin Chosa-kai, 1980.

James, H. *The End of Globalization: Lessons from the Great Depression*. London: Harvard University Press, 2001.

Jevons, W.S. *Methods of Social Reform*. London: Macmillan, 1883.

John, R.R. *Spreading the News: The American Postal System from Franklin to Morse*. Cambridge, MA: Harvard University Press 1995.

"Elaborations, Revisions, Dissents: Alfred D. Chandler Jr.'s, 'The Visible Hand' after Twenty Years," *The Business History Review*, 71 (1997), 151–200.

Network Nation: Inventing American Telecommunications. Cambridge, MA: Belknap Press, 2010a.

"The Political Economy of Postal Reform in the Victorian Age," *Smithsonian Contributions to History and Technology*, 55 (2010b), 3–12.

Jones, G. *The Evolution of International Business: An Introduction*. London: Routledge, 1996.

"British Trading Companies and Industrial Development," in F. Amatori, A. Colli and N. Crepas (eds.), *Deindustrialization and Reindustrialization in 20th Century Europe*. Milan: Franco Angeli, 1999, 354–71.

Merchants to Multinationals: British Trading Companies in the Nineteenth and Twentieth Centuries. Oxford: Oxford University Press, 2002.

Jones, G.G. "The British Government and the Oil Companies 1912–1924: The Search for an Oil Policy," *The Historical Journal*, 20 (1977), 647–72.

Jones, R. *A Life in Reuters*. London: Hodder and Stoughton, 1951.

Kaldor, N. and Silverman, R. *A Statistical Analysis of Advertising Expenditure and the Revenue of the Press*. Cambridge: Cambridge University Press, 1948.

Karjala, D.S. "The Board of Directors in English and American Companies through 1920," in N. Horn and J. Kocka (eds.), *Recht und Entwicklung der Großunternehmen im 19. und frühen 20. Jahrhundert*. Göttingen: Vandenhoeck & Ruprecht, 1979, 204–26.

Kaul, C. "Popular Press and Empire: Northcliffe, India and the Daily Mail," in P. Catterall, C. Seymour-Ure, and A. Smith (eds.), *Northcliffe's Legacy: Aspects of the British Popular Press, 1896–1996*. Basingstoke: Macmillan, 2000, 45–70.

Reporting the Raj: The British Press in India, c. 1880–1922. Manchester: Manchester University Press, 2003.

Kawamura, N. "Wilsonian Idealism and Japanese Claims at the Paris Peace Conference," *Pacific Historical Review*, 66 (1997), 503–26.

Keller, M. "Regulation of Larger Enterprise: The United States Experience in Comparative Perspective," in A. Chandler and H. Daems (eds.), *Managerial Hierarchies:*

Comparative Perspectives on the Rise of the Modern Industrial Enterprise. London: Harvard University Press, 1980, 161–81.

"The Pluralist State: American Economic Regulation in Comparative Perspective," in T. McGraw (ed.), *Regulation in Perspective: Historical Essays.* London: Harvard University Press, 1981, 56–94.

Kennedy, P.M. "Imperial Cable Communications and Strategy, 1870–1914," *The English Historical Review*, 86 (1971), 728–52.

Keyes, W.N. "Exclusive Foreign Distributor Agreements. Are They Illegal?" *California Law Review*, 41 (1953), 439–53.

Kielbowicz, R. "News Gathering by Mail in the Age of the Telegraph: Adapting to a New Technology," *Technology and Culture*, 28 (1987), 26–41.

News in the Mail: The Press, Post Office and Public Information, 1700–1860s. New York: Greenwood, 1989.

Kieve, J.L. *The Electric Telegraph.* Newton Abbot: David & Charles, 1973.

Klein, M. *Unfinished Business: The Railroad in American Life.* Hanover, NH: University Press of New England, 1994.

The Life and Legend of Jay Gould. Baltimore: Johns Hopkins University Press, 1997.

Knight, O. *I Protest: Selected Disquisitions of E. W. Scripps.* Madison: University of Wisconsin Press, 1966.

Knights, P.R. "The Press Association War of 1866–1867," *Journalism Monographs*, 6 (1967), 1–57.

Lamoreaux, N. *The Great Merger Movement in American Business, 1895–1904.* Cambridge: Cambridge University Press, 1985.

Landes, W.M. and Posner, R.A. "An Economic Analysis of Copyright Law," *The Journal of Legal Studies*, 18 (1989), 325–63.

Lawrenson, J. and Barber, L. *The Price of Truth: The Story of Reuters Millions.* Edinburgh: Mainstream Publishing, 1985.

Lee, A.J. "The Management of a Victorian Local Newspaper: the Manchester *City News*, 1864–1900," *Business History*, 15 (1973), 131–48.

The Origins of the Popular Press in England: 1855–1914. London: Croom Helm, 1976.

"The Structure, Ownership and Control of the Press, 1855–1914," in G. Boyce, J. Curran, and P. Wingate (eds.), *Newspaper History from the Seventeenth Century to the Present Day.* London: Constable, 1978, 117–29.

Lee, A.M. "Recent Developments in the Daily Newspaper Industry," *The Public Opinion Quarterly*, 2 (1938), 126–33.

The Daily Newspaper in America: The Evolution of a Social Instrument. New York: The Macmillan Company, 1973.

Lee, J.M. *History of American Journalism.* New York: Houghton Mifflin Co., 1923.

LeMahieu, D.L. "John Reith (1889–1971)," in S. Pedersen and P. Mandler (eds.), *After the Victorians.* London: Routledge, 1994, 189–206.

Lewin, J.H. "The Associated Press Decision: an Extension of the Sherman Act," *The University of Chicago Law Review*, 13 (1946), 247–65.

Livingston, K.T. *The Wired Nation Continent: The Communication Revolution and Federating Australia.* Oxford: Oxford University Press, 1996.

Lurie, J. *The Chicago Board of Trade, 1859–1905.* Urbana: University of Illinois Press, 1979.

Mayer, H. *The Press in Australia*. Melbourne: Lansdowne, 1964.

McCabe, C. *Damned Old Crank: a Self-Portrait of E. W. Scripps*. New York: Harper, 1951.

McCormick, M. *Terre Haute: Queen City of the Wabash*. Charleston, SC: Arcadia Publishing, 2005.

McCraw, T.K. "Regulation in America: a Review Article," *The Business History Review*, 49 (1975), 159–83.

"Rethinking the Trust Question," in T.K. McCraw and M. Keller (eds.), *Regulation in Perspective: Historical Essays*. London: Harvard University Press, 1981, 1–55.

McEwen, J.M. *The Riddell Diaries 1908–1923*. London: Athlone Press, 1986.

McKibbin, R. *Ideologies of Class: Social Relations in Britain, 1880–1950*. Oxford: Clarendon Press, 1990.

McRae, M.A. *Forty Years in Newspaperdom: The Autobiography of a Newspaper Man*. New York: Brentano's, 1925.

Meinig, D.W. *The Shaping of America: A Geographical Perspective on 500 years of History*. London: Yale University Press, 1998.

Mercer, H. *Constructing a Competitive Order: The Hidden History of British Antitrust Policies*. Cambridge: Cambridge University Press, 1995.

Michie, R.C. *The London and New York Stock Exchanges, 1850–1914*. London: Allen & Unwin, 1987.

Miller, W. *I Found no Peace*. Garden City, NY: Garden City Publishing, 1938.

Millward, R. *Private and Public Enterprise in Europe: Energy, Telecommunications and Transport, 1830–1990*. Cambridge: Cambridge University Press, 2005.

Misra, M. *Business, Race, and Politics in British India c. 1850–1960*. Oxford: Clarendon Press, 1999.

Moncrieff, C. *Living on a Deadline: A History of the Press Association*. London: Virgin, 2001.

Morris, J.A. *Deadline Every Minute: The Story of the United Press*. Garden City, NY: Doubleday, 1957.

Morrison, E. "Newspapers," in G. Davison, J. Hirst, and S. Macintyre (eds.), *The Oxford Companion to Australian History*. Oxford: Oxford University Press, 2001, 470–72.

Mott, F.L. *American Journalism: A History of Newspapers in the United States through 260 Years, 1690 to 1950*. New York: Macmillan, 1947.

The News in America. Cambridge, MA: Harvard University Press, 1952.

Moyal, A. "The History of Telecommunication in Australia, 1854–1930," in N. Reingold and M. Rothenberg (eds.), *Scientific Colonialism: A Cross-Cultural Comparison*. Washington, DC: Smithsonian Institution Press, 1987, 23–41.

Murdock, G. and Golding, P. "The Structure, Ownership and Control of the Press, 1914–76," in G. Boyce, J. Curran, and P. Wingate (eds.), *Newspaper History from the Seventeenth Century to the Present Day*. London: Constable, 1978, 130–48.

Nalbach, A. "'Poisoned at the Source'? Telegraphic News Services and Big Business in the Nineteenth Century," *The Business History Review*, 77 (2003a), 577–610.

"'The Software of Empire': Telegraphic News Agencies and Imperial Publicity, 1865–1914," in J.F. Codell (ed.), *Imperial Co-histories: National Identities and the British and Colonial Press*. Madison, NJ: Fairleigh Dickinson University Press, 2003b, 68–94.

Newspaper Society. *The Newspaper Society, 1836–1936; a Centenary Retrospect*. Birmingham: Silk & Terry, Ltd., 1936.

Nicholas, T. "Enterprise and Management," in R. Floud and P. Johnson (eds.), *The Cambridge Economic History of Modern Britain, Vol. 2: Economic Maturity, 1860–1939.* Cambridge: Cambridge University Press, 2004, 227–52.

Nixon, R.B. "Trends in U.S. Newspaper Ownership: Concentration with Competition," *International Communication Gazette*, 14 (1968), 181–93.

Noam, E. "The Tragedy of the Common Network: Theory for the Formation and Breakdown of Public Telecommunications," in E. Noam and A. NiShuilleabhain (eds.), *Private Networks Public Objectives.* Amsterdam: North Holland, 1996, 51–64.

N.W.H. "Recent Legislative Proposals to Classify Newspapers and Magazines as Public Utilities and to Regulate them Accordingly," *Virginia Law Review*, 17 (1931), 705–9.

Ostrom, E. *Governing the Commons: The Evolution of Institutions for Collective Action.* Cambridge: Cambridge University Press, 1990.

Palmer, M. *Des Petits Journaux aux Grandes Agences: Naissance du Journalisme Moderne, 1863–1914.* Paris: Aubier, 1983.

Peritz, R.J.R. *Competition Policy in America, 1888–1992.* Oxford: Oxford University Press, 1996.

Perkin, H. "Individualism Versus Collectivism in Nineteenth Century Britain: a False Antithesis," *The Journal of British Studies*, 17 (1977), 105–18.

Perry, C.R. "Frank Ives Scudamore and the Post Office Telegraphs," *Albion*, 12 (1980), 305–67.

  The Victorian Post Office: the Growth of a Bureaucracy. Woodbridge: Boydell Press, 1992.

Pike R. and Winseck, D. "The Politics of Global Media Reform, 1907–23," *Media, Culture & Society*, 26 (2004), 350–67.

Pilgrim, T.A. "Newspapers as Natural Monopolies: Some Historical Considerations," *Journalism History* 18 (1992), 3–10.

Political and Economic Planning (PEP). *The State of the Press*, No. 58. London: PEP, 1935.

Political and Economic Planning. *Report of the British Press.* London: PEP, 1938.

Pollard, S. *The Development of the British Economy 1914–1990*, 4th ed. London: Edward Arnold, 1992.

Porter, R. *English Society in the Eighteenth Century.* London: Penguin, 1990.

  Enlightenment: Britain and the Creation of the Modern World. London: Allen Lane, 2000.

Potter, E. *The Press as Opposition: The Political Role of South African Newspapers.* London: Chatto and Windus, 1975.

Potter, S.J. "Communication and Integration: the British Dominion Press and the British World, c. 1876–1914," *Journal of Imperial and Commonwealth History*, 31 (2003), 190–206.

  News and the British World: The Emergence of an Imperial Press System, 1876–1922. Oxford: Clarendon Press, 2003.

  Newspapers and Empire in Ireland and Britain. Dublin: Four Courts, 2004.

  "Webs, Networks, and Systems: Globalization and the Mass Media in the Nineteenth- and Twentieth-Century British Empire," *Journal of British Studies*, 46 (2007), 621–46.

Putnis, P. "Reuters in Australia: the Supply and Exchange of News, 1859–1877," *Media History*, 10 (2004), 67–88.

"How the International News Agency Business Model Failed – Reuters in Australia, 1877–1895," *Media History*, 12 (2006), 1–17.

"Share 999. British government control of Reuters during World War I," *Media History*, 14 (2008), 141–65.

"Reuters and the British Government – Re-visited," *Media History*, 16 (2010), 295–9.

Rantanen, T. "Mr. Howard goes to South America. The United Press Associations and Foreign Expansion," *Roy W. Howard Monographs in Journalism and Mass Communication Research*, 2 (1992).

"The Globalization of Electronic News in the 19th Century," *Media, Culture & Society*, 19 (1997), 605–20.

"The Struggle for Control of Domestic News Markets (1)," in O. Boyd-Barrett and T. Rantanen (eds.), *The Globalization of News*. London: Sage, 1998a, 35–48.

"After Five O'clock Friends," *Roy W. Howard Monographs in Journalism and Mass Communication Research*, 4 (1998b), 1–35.

"Foreign Dependence and Domestic Monopoly: the European news Cartel and U.S. Associated Presses, 1861–1932," *Media History*, 12 (2006), 19–35.

"The End of the Electronic News Cartel, 1927–1934," in P. Putnis, J. Wilke, and C. Kaul (eds.), *International Communication and Global News Networks: Historical Perspectives*. Cresskill: Hampton Press, 2011, 167–88.

Read, D. "Sir Roderick Jones and Reuters: Rise and Fall of a News Emperor," in D. Fraser (ed.), *Cities, Class and Communication: Essays in Honour of Asa Briggs*. London: Harvester Wheatsheaf, 1990, 175–99.

"Reuters: News Agency of the British Empire," *Contemporary Record*, 8 (1994), 195–212.

"Truth in News: Reuters and the Manchester *Guardian*, 1858–1964," *Northern History*, 31 (1995), 281–97.

"Reuters and South Africa: 'South Africa Is a Country of Monopolies'," *The South African Journal of Economic History*, 11 (1996), 106–26.

The Power of News: The History of Reuters, 2nd ed. Oxford: Oxford University Press, 1999.

"The Relationship of Reuters and Other News Agencies with the British Press 1858–1984: Service at Cost or Business for Profit?" in P. Catterall, C. Seymour-Ure, and A. Smith (eds.), *Northcliffe's Legacy: Aspects of the British Popular Press, 1896–1996*. Basingstoke: Macmillan, 2000, 149–68.

Regan, J.W. "The Inception of the Associated Press: The Pony Express That in 1849 Forwarded European News from Halifax to Digby, to Be Conveyed by Vessel to St. John, and Thence Telegraphed to New York," *Transactions of the Nova Scotia Historical Society*, 19 (1912).

Rens, J. *The Invisible Empire: A History of the Telecommunications Industry in Canada*. London: McGill-Queen's University Press, 2001.

Roberts, K. "Antitrust Problems in the Newspaper Industry," *Harvard Law Review*, 82 (1968), 319–66.

Robinson, H. *The British Post Office: A History*. Princeton, NJ: Princeton University Press, 1949.

Britain's Post Office. Oxford: Oxford University Press, 1953.

Rosewater, V. *History of Cooperative News-Gathering in the United States*. London: D. Appleton and Co., 1930.

Schmanske, S. "News as a Public Good: Cooperative Ownership, Price Commitments, and the Success of the Associated Press," *The Business History Review*, 60 (1986), 55–80.

Schudson, M. *Discovering the News: A Social History of American Newspapers*. New York: Basic Books, 1978.

"Toward a Troubleshooting Manual for Journalism History," *Journalism & Mass Communication Quarterly*, 74 (1997), 463–76.

Schwarzlose, R.A. "Harbor News Association: The Formal Origin of the AP," *Journalism Quarterly*, 45 (1968), 253–60.

"The Nation's First Wire Service: Evidence Supporting a Footnote," *Journalism Quarterly*, 57 (1980), 555–62.

The Nation's Newsbrokers, vol. 1–2. Evanston, IL: Northwestern University Press, 1989.

Scott, G. *Reporter Anonymous: The Story of the Press Association*. London: Hutchinson, 1968.

Scott, J.M. *Extel 100: The Centenary History of the Exchange Telegraph Company*. London: Benn, 1972.

Sherover, M. *Fakes in American Journalism*, 3rd ed. Brooklyn, NY: Buffalo Publishing Co., 1916.

Silberstein-Loeb, J. "The structure of the News Market in Britain, 1870–1914," *Business History Review*, 83 (2009), 759–88.

"Foreign Office control of Reuters during the First World War," *Media History*, 16 (2010), 281–93.

"Exclusivity and Cooperation in the supply of News: The Example of the associated press, 1893–1945," *Journal of Policy History*, 24 (2012), 466–98.

Sinclair, U. *The Brass Check: A Study of American Journalism*. Pasadena, CA, 1920.

Sklar, M. *The Corporate Reconstruction of American Capitalism, 1890–1916: The Market, the Law and Politics*. Cambridge: Cambridge University Press, 1988.

Skowronek, S. *Building a New American State: The Expansion of National Administrative Capacity, 1877–1920*. Cambridge: Cambridge University Press, 1982.

Sola Pool, I de, *Technologies without Boundaries*, ed. E. Noam. London: Harvard University Press, 1990.

Stamm, M. *Sound Business: Newspapers, Radio, and the Politics of New Media*. Philadelphia: University of Pennsylvania Press, 2011.

Starr, P. *The Creation of the Media: Political Origins of Modern Communications*. New York: Basic Books, 2004.

Stern, F.R. *Gold and Iron: Bismarck, Bleichröder and the Building of the German Empire*. London: Allen and Unwin, 1977.

Stevens, J.D. and Garcia, H.D. *Communication History*. Beverly Hills, CA: Sage Publications, 1980.

Stone, C. *Dana and the Sun*. New York: Dodd, Mead & Co., 1938.

Stone, M.E. *Fifty Years a Journalist*. London: Heinemann, 1922.

Storey, G. *Reuters' Century, 1851–1951*. London: Max Parish, 1951.

Swindler, W.F. "The AP Anti-trust Case in Historical Perspective," *Journalism Quarterly*, 23 (1946), 40–57.

Tarbell, I. *The Nationalizing of Business, 1878–1898*. New York: Macmillan, 1936.

Tegg, W. *Post and Telegraphs, Past and Present: With an Account of the Telephone and Phonograph*. London: William Tegg & Co., 1878.

Thompson, E.P. *The Making of the English Working Class*. Harmondsworth: Penguin, 1968.

Trimble, V. *The Astonishing Mr. Scripps: The Turbulent Life of America's Penny Press Lord*. Ames: Iowa State Press, 1992.

UNESCO. *News Agencies, Their Structure and Operation*. Paris: UNESCO, 1953.

Vietor, R.H.K. *Contrived Competition: Regulation and Deregulation in America*. Cambridge, MA: Harvard University Press, 1994.

"Government Regulation of Business," in S.L. Engerman and R.E. Gallman (eds.), *The Cambridge Economic History of the United States, Vol. 3: The Twentieth Century*. Cambridge: Cambridge University Press, 2000, 969–1012.

Villard, O.G. *Some Newspapers and Newspaper-Men*. New York: Alfred M. Knopf, 1923.

Wadsworth, A.P. *Newspaper Circulations, 1800–1954*. Manchester: Norbury, Lockwood, & Co., 1955.

Walker, M. *Powers of the Press: The World's Great Newspapers*. London: Quartet Books, 1982.

Walsten, S. "Returning to Victorian Competition, Ownership, and Regulation: an Empirical study of European Telecommunications at the Turn of the Twentieth Century," *The Journal of Economic History*, 65 (2005), 693–722.

Westley, B. "How a Narrow Application of 'Hot News' Misappropriation Can Help Save Journalism," *American University Law Review*, 60 (2011), 691–730.

Wilson, C. *First with the News: The History of W.H. Smith, 1792–1972*. London: Cape, 1985.

Winseck, D.R. and Pike, R.M. *Communication and Empire: Media, Markets, and Globalization, 1860–1930*. Durham, NC: Duke University Press, 2007.

Woods O. and Bishop, J. *The Story of The Times*. London: Michael Joseph, 1985.

Wu, T. "Network Neutrality, Broadband Discrimination," *Journal On Telecommunications and High Technology Law*, 2 (2003), 141–79.

Yates, J. *Control through Communication: The Rise of System in American Management*. Baltimore: Johns Hopkins University Press, 1989.

Index